SpringBoard®

Level 4

English Textual Power™

CollegeBoard
inspiring minds™

THE COLLEGE BOARD
inspiring minds™

About the College Board

The College Board is a mission-driven not-for-profit organization that connects students to college success and opportunity. Founded in 1900, the College Board was created to expand access to higher education. Today, the membership association is made up of more than 5,900 of the nation's leading educational institutions and is dedicated to promoting excellence and equity in education. Each year, the College Board helps more than seven million students prepare for a successful transition to college through programs and services in college readiness and college success — including the SAT® and the Advanced Placement Program®. The organization also serves the education community through research and advocacy on behalf of students, educators and schools.

For further information, visit www.collegeboard.com.

ISBN: 0-87447-915-0
ISBN: 978-0-87447-915-7

3 4 5 6 7 8   13 14
Printed in the United States of America

Acknowledgments

The College Board gratefully acknowledges the outstanding work of the classroom teachers and writers who have been integral to the development of this revised program. The end product is testimony to their expertise, understanding of student learning needs, and dedication to rigorous but accessible language arts education.

Susie Challancin
English Teacher
Bellevue School District 405
Bellevue, Washington

Paul De Maret
English Teacher
Poudre School District
Fort Collins, Colorado

Suzie Doss
District English/ Language Arts
    Coordinator
Hobbs Municipal Schools
Hobbs, New Mexico

John Golden
English Teacher
Grant High School
Portland, Oregon

Nancy Gray
English Teacher
West Shore Junior/Senior High School
Melbourne, Florida

Ellen Greig
English Teacher, Consultant
Charlotte, North Carolina

Karen Hanson
Exceptional Student Teacher
Volusia Public Schools
DeLand, Florida

Cheryl Harris
English Teacher Consultant
Bedford, Texas

Susie Lowry
English Teacher
Volusia Public Schools
DeLand, Florida

Julie Manley
Middle School Language Arts
    Tech-Curriculum Coach and
    Humanities Teacher
Bellevue School District 405
Bellevue, Washington

Joely Negedly
Secondary Reading and
    Language Arts Specialists
Volusia Public Schools
DeLand, Florida

JoEllen Victoreen
Instructional Specialist,
    SpringBoard
San Jose, California

Douglas Waugh
Administrative Coach,
    SpringBoard
Bellevue, Washington

Nina Wooldridge
Instructional Specialist,
    SpringBoard
Los Angeles, California

Advisors, Reviewers, Special Feature Writers

The following teachers and writers provided invaluable assistance in creating special features and reviewing manuscript. We gratefully acknowledge their contributions to this revised edition.

Gary Cowan
English/Language Arts Coordinator
Metro Nashville Public Schools
Nashville, Tennessee

Nicki Junkins
Administrative Coach,
    SpringBoard
DeLand, Florida

Jeanneine Jones
Professor, Departments of Middle,
    Secondary, and K-12 Education
University of North Carolina
Charlotte, North Carolina

William McBride
Emeritus Professor of English
Colorado State University
Fort Collins, Colorado

Daniel Millet
English Teacher
Weld county School District
    Re-8
Fort Lupton, Colorado

Melanie Sangalli
English Teacher
Irving Public Schools
Irving, Texas

Special Acknowledgments

The College Board wishes especially to acknowledge the writers of the original *Pacesetter* program. Much of their work continues in use today. The result of their efforts was a program that helped both teachers and students succeed. With its roots in Pacesetter, the current program had an excellent foundation on which to build.

Willie Mae Crews
Educator
Birmingham, Alabama

R. Steven Green, Ed.D.
Educator
Kansas City, Missouri

Ellen Greenblatt
University High School
San Francisco, California

Alice Kawazoe
Educational Consultant, California Academic
   Partnership Program
San Carlos, California

Jenny Oren Krugman
Vice President, Southern Region
College Board
Miami, Florida

William McBride, Ph.D.
Emeritus Professor of English
Colorado State University
Fort Collins, Colorado

Robert Scholes, Ph.D.
Research Professor, Brown University
Providence, Rhode Island

In addition, we wish to acknowledge the educators and writers whose work on prior editions helped to continue the *Pacesetter* excellence and to establish the high expectations for which the College Board's SpringBoard program is known.

Lance Balla
Bellevue, Washington

Bryant Crisp
Charlotte, North Carolina

Nancy Elrod
Atlanta, Georgia

Ann Foster
Melbourne, Florida

Ana Gandara
Edinburg, Texas

Alex Gordin
Portland, Oregon

Kenyatta Graves
Washington, DC

Don Keagy
Poultney, Vermont

Don Kirk
Poultney, Vermont

Dana Mebane
Baltimore, Maryland

Bob Messinger
Providence, Rhode Island

Debi Miller
Miami, Florida

Melanie Ross Mitchell
Atlanta, Georgia

Lisa Rehm
DeLand, Florida

Penny Riffe
Palm Bay, Florida

Rick Robb
Clarksville, Maryland

Sue Rodriguez
Miami, Florida

Research and Planning Advisors

We also wish to thank the members of our SpringBoard Advisory Council, the SpringBoard Language Arts Trainers, and the many educators who gave generously of their time and their ideas as we conducted research for the program. Their suggestions and reactions to ideas helped immeasurably as we planned the revisions. We gratefully acknowledge the teachers and administrators in the following districts:

Broward County Public Schools
Fort Lauderdale, Florida

Cherry Creek School District
Cherry Creek, Colorado

Chicago Public Schools
Chicago, Illinois

DeKalb County School System
DeKalb County, Georgia

Duval County Public Schools
Jacksonville, Florida

Guilford County Schools
Greensboro, North Carolina

Hillsborough County Public Schools
Tampa, Florida

Hobbs Municipal Schools
Hobbs, New Mexico

Indianapolis Public Schools
Indianapolis, Indiana

Miami-Dade County Public Schools
Miami, Florida

Metropolitan Nashville Public Schools
Nashville, Tennessee

The City School District of New Rochelle
New Rochelle, New York

Orange County Public Schools
Orlando, Florida

School District of Palm Beach County
Palm Beach, Florida

Peninsula School District
Gig Harbor, Washington

Pinellas County Schools
Largo, Florida

San Antonio Independent School District
San Antonio, Texas

Spokane Public Schools
Spokane, Washington

Volusia County Schools
DeLand, Florida

Editorial Leadership

The College Board gratefully acknowledges the expertise, time, and commitment of the language arts editorial manager.

Betty Barnett
Educational Publishing Consultant

Level 4 Contents

To the Student viii

Instructional Units

Welcome to the SpringBoard program. We hope you will discover how SpringBoard can help you achieve high academic standards, reach your learning goals, and prepare for success in your study of literature and language arts. The program has been created with you in mind: the content you need to learn, the tools to help you learn, and the critical-thinking skills that help you build confidence in your own knowledge and skills.

The College Board publishes the SpringBoard program as a complete language arts curriculum that prepares you for Advanced Placement and college-level study. SpringBoard maps out what successful students should know and be able to do at each grade level to develop the language, reading, writing, and communication skills needed for success. College Board also publishes the SAT and Advanced Placement exams—exams that you are likely to encounter in your high school years.

Connection to Advanced Placement

The College Board's Advanced Placement program provides the opportunity to complete college-level courses while in high school. In addition to receiving college credits, participation in AP courses helps you develop the skills and knowledge that add to your confidence and ease the transition from high school to college.

The SpringBoard program assists you in preparing for AP-level courses in several ways:

▶ Exposing you to the same types of tasks as on the AP Language and Literature exams; for example, close reading of fiction and nonfiction texts, responding to writing prompts, writing under timed conditions, and writing for multiple purposes (persuasion, argumentation, literary analysis, and synthesis).

▶ Introducing you to AP strategies, such as TP-CASTT and SOAPSTone, that help you analyze literary and other texts, giving you the tools you need to independently analyze any text.

▶ Preparing you for higher-order skills and behaviors required for college-level work through ongoing practice in key skills such as generating and organizing ideas, analysis of different types of texts, synthesis and explanation of concepts, and original writing in a variety of modes.

What Is the Foundation for SpringBoard?

The foundation of SpringBoard is the College Board Standards for College Success, which set out the knowledge and critical-thinking skills you should acquire to succeed in high school and in future college-level work.

The English Language Arts College Board Standards are divided into five categories: reading, writing, speaking, listening, and media literacy.

Your success as a **reader** depends on many factors, including your interest and motivation to read, the amount of time you spend reading, understanding the purpose for reading, knowledge about a topic, and knowledge about how to read different kinds of text.

Your success as a **writer** depends on learning many words and how to use those words effectively to communicate a story or information for others to read and understand. Successful writers determine their purpose for writing, such as to explore, inform, express an opinion, persuade, entertain, or to share an experience or emotion. As they write, they also consider their audiences and choose the language that will help them communicate with that audience. Writing is a process that involves several steps, and you will have many opportunities in this program to learn the process and to improve your own writing.

Your success as a **speaker** is based on how well you communicate orally. What is your message, what words will best communicate it, how do you prepare, or rehearse, for a speech? Good speakers also consider the audience and what they know about a specific topic. They can then deliver a message that uses a shared understanding, or develops one based on common knowledge, with their listeners.

Being a good **listener** is the other part of effective communication. Communication includes the speaker, listener, message, feedback, and noise (the conditions surrounding the communication). You'll have opportunities throughout the program to practice both your speaking and listening skills.

Finally, being **media literate** means that you can interpret, analyze, and evaluate the messages you receive daily from various types of media. Being media literate also means that you can use the information you gain to express or support a point of view and influence others.

As you complete the activities in this text, you will develop your skills and knowledge in all of these areas.

How Is SpringBoard Unique?

SpringBoard is unique because it provides instruction with hands-on participation that involves you and your classmates in daily discussions and analysis of what you're reading and learning. The book is organized into multiple activities that invite participation by providing adequate space for taking notes and writing your own thoughts and analyses about texts you're reading or questions you're answering. Among the key features that make SpringBoard a unique learning experience are:

▶ Activities that thoroughly develop topics, leading to deep understanding of the concepts and enabling you to apply learning in multiple situations.

▶ Extensive opportunities to explore a variety of texts—both fiction and nonfiction—that introduce you to many different ways of thinking, writing, and communicating.

▶ Questions that help you examine writing from the perspective of a reader and a writer and the techniques that good writers use to communicate their messages effectively.

▶ Built-in class discussions and collaborative work that help you explore and express your own ideas while integrating the ideas of others into your base of knowledge.

▶ Integrated performance-based assessments that give you practice in showing what you know and can do, not just repeating what you've read.

▶ Assessments that help you decipher tasks and plan how to accomplish those tasks in timed situations like those for standardized tests.

Strategies for Learning

As you complete the activities in this text, you will work on many reading, writing, and oral presentation assignments. You will often work in groups and pairs. To help you do your best, you and your teacher will use a variety of reading, writing, and collaborative learning strategies.

Reading strategies give you specific tools to help you improve your skills in reading and making meaning from text. These strategies will help you improve your ability to analyze text by developing skills in using context clues, finding meaning for unfamiliar words, or organizing your responses to what you read. As you learn to use different reading strategies, it's important to think about which ones work best for you and why.

Writing strategies help you focus on your purpose for writing and the message you want to communicate to your readers. Using writing strategies will help you analyze your own writing for specific purposes and identify how to improve that writing using better word choices or punctuating differently or using sentence structure in different ways.

You and your classmates will use *collaborative strategies* to explore concepts and answer text-related questions as you work in pairs or in groups to discuss the work you're doing and to learn from each other.

Performance Portfolio

You will learn to use language in both written and spoken forms in this course. You are encouraged to keep your work in a Working Folder from which you can choose examples to show where you started and how you are growing in your skills and knowledge during the year. Presenting your best work in a Portfolio not only helps you evaluate your own work and improvement, but also helps you explore your unique style and analyze how your work can best represent you.

Presenting your portfolio provides direction as you revisit, revise, and reflect on your work throughout the year. Your teacher will guide you as you include items in your portfolio that illustrate a wide range of work, including examples of reading, writing, oral literacy, and collaborative activities. As you progress through the course, you will have opportunities to revisit prior work, revise it based on new learning, and reflect on the learning strategies and activities that help you be successful. The portfolio:

- ▶ Gives you a specific place to feature your work and a way to share it with others.
- ▶ Provides an organized, focused way to view your progress throughout the year.
- ▶ Allows you to reflect on the new skills and strategies you are learning.
- ▶ Enables you to measure your growth as a reader, writer, speaker, and performer.
- ▶ Encourages you to revise pieces of work to incorporate new skills.

As you move through each unit, your teacher will instruct you to include certain items in your portfolio. Strong portfolios will include a variety of work from each unit, such as first drafts, final drafts, quickwrites, notes, reading logs, audio and video examples, and graphics that represent a wide variety of genre, forms, and media created for a variety of purposes.

We hope you enjoy using the SpringBoard program. It will give you many opportunities to explore your own and others' ideas about becoming effective readers, writers, and communicators.

How to Use This Book

English Textual Power, Level 4, introduces you to the theme of "coming of age." This year marks an important transition to your high school years. This year you will explore multiple "voices" from writers describing coming-of-age experiences. You will also learn about style in both print and nonprint texts, along with poetic voices and dramatic performance. You'll conclude the year by analyzing how writers communicate voice through social, cultural, geographical, and historical context.

Preview the Unit

Essential Questions pose questions to help you think about the "big ideas" and make connections between what you learn and how you apply that learning.

Unit Overview sets the stage by:

▶ Providing a bridge from what you know to what you'll be learning in the unit.

▶ Outlining the big ideas in the unit and how the book's theme is connected from unit to unit.

Unit Contents give a snapshot of the unit activities and identify the texts and genres you'll explore in the unit.

▶ **Goals**—skills and knowledge you'll learn in the unit.

▶ **Academic Vocabulary**—key terms to use in the unit and to help you gain the vocabulary needed for AP courses and college.

Unit 2

Defining Style

Essential Questions

? How do authors and directors use specific techniques to achieve a desired effect?

? What are the essential features of an effective style analysis?

Unit Overview

Through the ages, stories have been passed from generation to generation. Then, sometime between 1830 and 1835, Edgar Allan Poe began to write structured stories for various magazines. His structure provided a format that characterizes the genre today. Poe felt that a story should be short enough to be read in one sitting and that it should contain a single line of action with a limited number of characters, building to a climactic moment and then quickly reaching resolution. Poe's influence can also be felt in modern cinema through the unique style of film director Tim Burton. This unit will uncover the connection between Poe and Burton along with the commonalities between written [...] This unit also introduces [...] visual media affect or [...] reactions. By studying [...] film as a separate and [...] rious study along with [...] prose.

85

Unit 2
Defining Style
Contents

ACADEMIC VOCABULARY

Point of View
Commentary
Cinematic Techniques
Style
Effect

Preparing for Learning

Learning Focus connects what you already know with what you'll learn in the unit and why it's important.

▶ Highlights key terms.

▶ Connects learning from unit to unit.

▶ Introduces concepts for the unit.

Previewing the Unit helps you identify the expectations for knowledge and skills you'll need to learn in the unit by asking you to read and respond to:

▶ **Essential Questions**

▶ **Unit Overview–Learning Focus**

▶ **Embedded Assessment and Scoring Guide**

Starting with the End in Mind

Graphic organizer helps you:

▶ Map out the skills and knowledge you'll need for the Embedded Assessments.

▶ Read the assignment and the Scoring Guide (see page xvi) and outline what you'll need to do.

▶ Identify skills and knowledge to be assessed.

Learning Focus:

What Is Your Style?

Whether it is the clothes you wear, how you walk and talk, or the way you decorate your room, you have your own unique style. How you choose to present yourself in a variety of situations reflects your individual style. This concept of style is similar in literary works.

Style in a written text can be investigated from a number of vantage points. It may be seen, for instance, in the way in which an author's diction, imagery, and rhetorical devices create a particular effect.

But what about film? In past units, you have viewed film much like a narrative, with plot, characters, conflicts, etc. Now, you will expand your view of film by approaching this visual medium through the lens of the director as author. Thus, you will begin to see the explicit connections between an author's choices of literary techniques and a director's choices of cinematic techniques. You can see some of these comparisons below.

▶ Tone/Mood   may be represented by   Lighting and Sound

142 Spring

Previewing the Unit

ACTIVITY
2.1

SUGGESTED LEARNING STRATEGIES: Close Reading, KWL, Marking the Text, Skimming/Scanning, Summarizing/Paraphrasing, Think-Pair-Share

Essential Questions

1. How do authors and directors use specific techniques to achieve a desired effect?

2. What are the essential features of an effective style analysis?

Unit Overview and **Learning Focus**

Predict what you think this unit is about. Use the words or phrases that stood out to you when you read the Unit Overview and the Learning Focus.

Embedded Assessment 1

What knowledge must you have (what do you need to know) to succeed on Embedded Assessment 1? What skills must you have (what must you be able to do)?

Unit 2 • Defining Style 89

Conduct research on a poet

Revise and edit essay

Analyze poetry for tone and diction

Analyzing and Presenting a Poet

Develop and sustain an assertion throughout the essay

Identify, interpret, and critique an author's style

Write a style analysis essay

Generate a thesis and provide textual support

Unit Activities and Learning Strategies

Literary and Other Texts

from classic to contemporary introduce you to a variety of writers, stories, themes, and perspectives to help you interact with all types of writing.

▶ **About the Author** provides author's background and insights about the text.

▶ **Texts** include examples from a variety of genres, including poetry, film, autobiography, essay, print and online articles, folk tales, myths, fables, memoir, short stories, novel excerpts, interviews, informational text, and drama.

My Notes provides space for you to interact with the text by

▶ Jotting down your thoughts and ideas as you read.

▶ Using the space to analyze text.

▶ Writing notes about literary elements in texts.

Suggested Learning Strategies

▶ Clearly listed at the top of the page.

▶ Suggest strategies that are most appropriate for the activity.

▶ Over the course of the year, you'll learn which strategies work best for you.

▶ You'll find these strategies consistent with those used in AP courses.

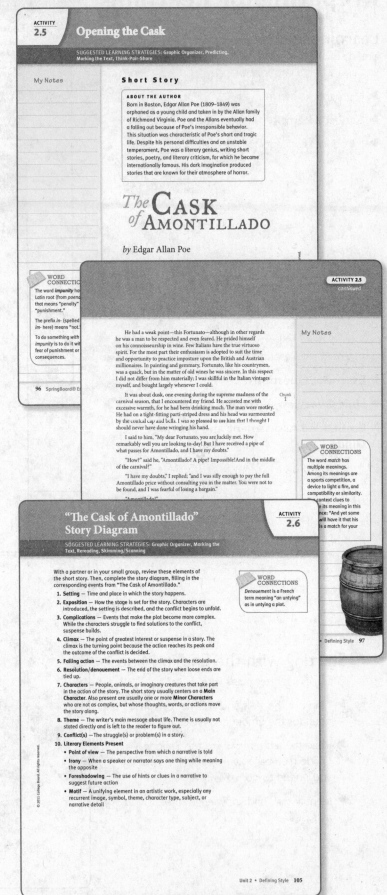

Integrated Language Skills

Vocabulary and Word Study

▶ **Academic Vocabulary** highlights key words you'll need to know for the unit and to expand your vocabulary for AP and college.

▶ **Literary Terms** define key words as you encounter them in your reading and analysis of text.

▶ **Word Connections** help you use context clues from Latin and other roots, understand analogies, and identify words with multiple meanings.

Grammar & Usage

▶ Offers tips about points of grammar and how to avoid common errors.

▶ Shows how writers use various grammatical constructions to clarify their text and to convey meaning for readers.

▶ Helps both speakers <u>and</u> writers use grammar to make their text or message more effective.

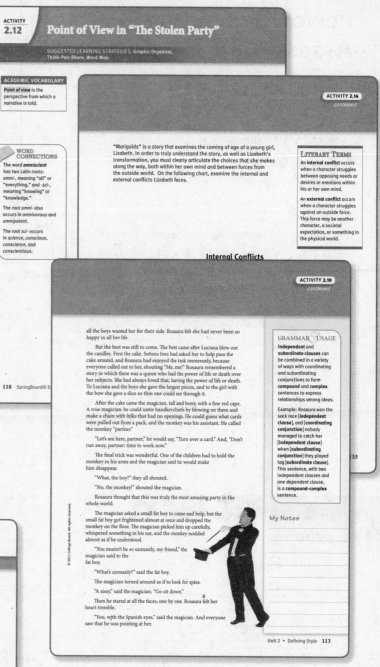

Writing

▶ **Writing Process** is defined and practiced through opportunities to draft, revise, edit, and prepare publishable writing.

▶ **Writing Prompts & Timed Writings** provide practice in identifying specific writing tasks and writing under timed conditions.

▶ **Portfolios** are encouraged to collect your writing throughout the year to show your progress.

Performance-Based Assessment

▶ **Embedded Assessments** provide opportunities to demonstrate your knowledge and your skills in applying that knowledge in a variety of assessments.

▶ **Scoring Guide** walks you through the expectations for performance.

- Descriptions under Exemplary, Proficient, and Emerging describe the level of work required and set the expectations for what you need to know and do <u>before</u> you start the Embedded Assessment.

- Using the descriptions for Exemplary, Proficient, and Emerging, you decide what you'll do and take responsibility for your performance.

Writing a Style Analysis Essay

SUGGESTED LEARNING STRATEGIES: Graphic Organizer, Prewriting, Marking The Draft, Outlining, Sharing and Responding, Self Editing

Assignment

Your assignment is to write an essay analyzing the cinematic style of director Tim Burton. Your essay will focus on the ways in which the director uses stylistic techniques across films to achieve a desired effect.

Steps

Prewriting

1. Review the graphic organizers and double-entry journals you have completed throughout the unit, and consider the multiple examples of Tim Burton's stylistic choices. Make a list of the stylistic elements you can incorporate into your essay. Narrow your list to include only three or four stylistic techniques for which you have clear examples.

2. Create a thesis statement in which you identify the stylistic techniques you will discuss. Then, use a prewriting strategy (e.g., mapping, webbing, or outlining) to develop the details and examples you can include to support each topic. You might consider talking to your Writing Group to refine your thinking about the examples you can include for each stylistic element.

Drafting

3. Draft your essay. Consult your mapping plan and outline. Use ample

181

Writing a Style Analysis Essay

SCORING GUIDE

Scoring Criteria	Exemplary	Proficient	Emerging
Ideas	The writer insightfully identifies and analyzes Burton's stylistic techniques employing textual support from multiple films. The analysis displays an in-depth understanding of how Burton achieves his intended effect on the audience.	The writer clearly identifies and describes Burton's stylistic techniques using support from more than one film. The analysis displays a clear understanding of how Burton achieves his intended effect on the audience.	The writer demonstrates a limited understanding of Burton's stylistic techniques; support is insufficient or inaccurate. The analysis displays a misunderstanding of how Burton achieves the intended effect on the audience and/or may be replaced with plot summary.
Organization	The essay is multi-paragraphed and logically organized to enhance the reader's understanding. It includes an innovative introduction with an insightful lead or hook and strong thesis, coherent body paragraphs, and a perceptive conclusion. Effective transitions exist throughout and add to the essay's coherence.	The essay is multi-paragraphed and organized. It includes an introduction with a lead or hook and clear thesis, detailed body paragraphs, and a conclusion. Transitions create coherence.	Organization is attempted, but key components are lacking. It may include an introduction with an unfocused thesis, undeveloped body paragraphs, and/or inadequate conclusion. Transitions, if attempted, do little to create coherence.
Use of Language	Diction is appropriate for an academic audience. The essay demonstrates a sophisticated use of terminology to knowledgeably discuss film.	Diction is mostly appropriate for an academic essay. The essay demonstrates a basic use of terminology to discuss film.	Diction is informal or inappropriate for an academic essay. The essay may demonstrate limited or inaccurate use of terminology to discuss film.
Conventions	Writing is virtually error-free.	Writing is generally error-free.	Writing contains errors that distract from meaning.

Reflection

An important aspect of growing as a learner is to reflect on where you have been, what you have accomplished, what helped you to learn, and how you will apply your new knowledge in the future. Use the following questions to guide your thinking and to identify evidence of your learning. Use separate notebook paper.

Thinking about Concepts

1. Using specific examples from this unit, respond to the Essential Questions:
   - How do authors and directors use specific techniques to achieve a desired effect?
   - What are the essential features of an effective style analysis?

2. Consider the new academic vocabulary from this unit (**Point of View, Style, Cinematic Techniques, Effect, Commentary**) as well as academic vocabulary from previous units, and select 3-4 terms of which your understanding has grown. For each term, answer the following questions:
   - What was your understanding of the term before you completed this unit?
   - How has your understanding of the term evolved throughout this unit?
   - How will you apply your understanding in the future?

Thinking about Connections

3. Review the activities and products (artifacts) you created. Choose those that most reflect your growth or increase in understanding.

4. For each artifact that you choose, record, respond to, and reflect on your thinking and understanding, using the following questions as a guide:
   a. What skill/knowledge does this artifact reflect, and how did you learn this skill/knowledge?
   b. How did your understanding of the power of language expand through your engagement with this artifact?
   c. How will you apply this skill or knowledge in the future?

5. Create this reflection as Portfolio pages—one for each artifact you choose. Use the model in the box for your headings and commentary on questions.

> **Thinking About Thinking**
> Portfolio Entry
>
> Concept:
>
> Description of Artifact:
>
> Commentary on Questions:

Unit Reflection helps you to take ownership of your learning by stopping at regular points to think about:

▶ What you've learned.

▶ What strategies and tools helped you learn.

▶ What you still need to work on in the future.

Coming of Age

Essential Questions

 What does it mean to "come of age"?

 How are rhetorical appeals used to influence an audience?

Unit Overview

Ninth grade marks many important transitions. Whether through physical changes (changing schools, moving to a new area, growing older) or emotional changes (new friends or new teachers), each student comes of age. This unit introduces the theme of "coming of age" and explores how each of us shapes our unique voice though our experiences and our exposure to the strong voices around us. You will interview others and produce a narrative of your experiences in this important transition. This unit also explores the ways that we are influenced through advertising techniques and rhetorical appeals in media. By studying an independent novel as well as the likes and dislikes of your classmates, you will begin to understand the complex relationship between an author's purpose, the intended audience, and the ways in which the author appeals to your needs and desires. Your "coming of age" will not only be marked by physical and emotional changes, but also by a heightened understanding of voice, appeals, and persuasive techniques.

Contents

Goals

▶ To understand the concept of coming of age

▶ To identify diction, syntax, and tone and the way they work together to convey an author's or speaker's voice

▶ To incorporate voice effectively in your own writing

▶ To analyze and use rhetorical appeals to influence an audience

ACADEMIC VOCABULARY

Voice

Advertising Techniques

Rhetorical Appeals

3

Learning Focus:

Let's Hear It for Voice!

Have you ever read something that made you say, "Wow! That was great!"? Have you ever felt as though a writer's words were providing a glimpse of the speaker's or character's personality? How often does this happen? When you read an essay, for example, can you sometimes tell a great deal about the writer, and other times find yourself unable to identify any characteristics of the writer at all? When you read descriptive writing, why do some descriptions sound authentic, while others sound phony? Chances are, the writing that speaks to you contains a characteristic known as **voice**. In this unit you will explore the concept of voice and its effect on personal writing. You will learn that **diction**, **tone**, and **imagery** work together to convey voice effectively.

While you are learning to express your own voice, you will also be reading essays, poems, and even a novel that have **narrators** with strong and engaging personal voices. As you are identifying voice in your reading and applying it to your writing, you will also have an opportunity to capture the voice of another when you conduct an interview and write about the interview experience. You will study these elements while you explore the idea of "**coming of age**." You will make connections between coming-of-age texts and your own experiences as a ninth-grade student. By the end of the first half of Unit 1, you will have multiple opportunities to read deeply, write convincingly, and communicate effectively. Each of the skills you refine in these activities will enhance your abilities and prepare you for the academic challenges that await in the rest of your year.

Independent Reading: In this unit, you will read a variety of texts by writers describing their memories of growing up. For independent reading, choose a genre and a writer whose coming-of-age experiences appeal to you.

Previewing the Unit

Essential Questions

1. What does it mean to "come of age"?

2. How are rhetorical appeals used to influence an audience?

Unit Overview and Learning Focus

Predict what you think this unit is about. Use the words or phrases that stood out to you when you read the Unit Overview and the Learning Focus.

Embedded Assessment 1

What knowledge must you have (what do you need to know) to succeed on Embedded Assessment 1? What skills must you have (what must you be able to do)?

Coming of Age: Let Me Count the Ways!

"Coming of Age"

What I think this phrase might mean:

Take a few minutes to think about the ages when people traditionally receive certain privileges and responsibilities. Plot the ages on the arrow, and label the privileges and responsibilities. Place the labels for privileges above the line and the labels for responsibilities below the line.

Privileges

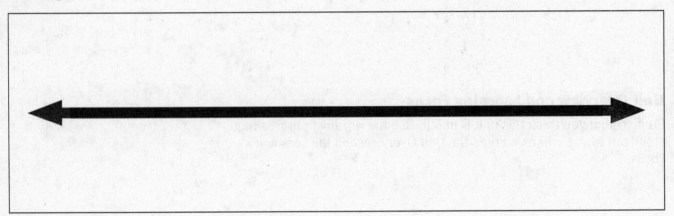

Responsibilities

After your brainstorming and class discussion, reconsider your ideas about the meaning of "coming of age." Write your revised definition below.

Coming of age means:

What's in a Name?

If several different people were asked to describe pizza, you might expect to get a variety of responses. Even though the subject would be the same, the descriptions might be quite different because each used a different voice. In pairs, read the following pizza descriptions and see what you can infer about the speakers. Then, examine each speaker's diction, syntax, and imagery, and identify choices that create four distinctive voices.

- **Diction** – Word choice intended to convey a certain effect
- **Syntax** – The arrangement of words and the order of grammatical elements in a sentence
- **Imagery** – The words or phrases a writer uses to represent persons, objects, actions, feelings, and ideas descriptively by appealing to the senses

Speaker 1: Eating pizza is rather like embarking on a transcontinental excursion. You embark on the journey without being quite certain of what you will encounter. A well-made pizza contains the aromatic essence of fresh basil, oregano, and garlic that beckon invitingly. Once you bite into a perfectly sliced piece of pizza, your taste buds awaken and celebrate. When properly prepared, pizza is an extraordinary culinary creation.

Speaker 2: It's yummy. I like it when the cheese is really gooey. My mom makes it for dinner on the weekends. When it's too hot, I have to wait for it to cool. Mom says if I don't wait I will burn my tongue. I like the way pizza smells. When I smell pizza cooking it always makes me want to eat it right up!

Speaker 3: As long as not one speck of gross disgusting animal flesh comes anywhere near my pizza, I can eat it. I prefer pizza with mushrooms, tomatoes, and spinach. Goat cheese is especially nice too. A thin whole-wheat crust topped with imported cheese and organic vegetables makes a satisfying meal.

Speaker 4: Pizza is, like, one of the basic food groups, right? I mean, dude, who doesn't eat pizza? Me and my friends order it like every day. We usually get pepperoni, and it's great when they are, like, covering the whole top! Dude, hot steamy pizza dripping with cheese and loaded with pepperoni is awesome.

ACADEMIC VOCABULARY

Voice is a writer's (or speaker's) distinctive use of language.

WORD CONNECTIONS

The word *syntax* contains the Greek prefix *syn-*, which means "together," and the root *-tax-*, meaning "arrangement" or "order."

The prefix *syn-* is found in words like *synthesis*, *synonym*, and *synchronize*. The root *-tax-* occurs in *taxonomy* and *taxidermy*.

What's in a Name?

LITERARY TERMS

Tone is a writer's or speaker's attitude toward the subject. Tone is conveyed through the writer's choice of words and detail.

Fill in the organizer with details about diction, syntax, and imagery that you notice about each speaker's description of pizza. Then, make inferences about each speaker and that speaker's **tone** or attitude toward pizza.

Pizza Descriptions

Speaker	Diction (What word choices does the speaker make? Formal or informal?)	Syntax (Are the sentences short, long, simple, complex?)	Imagery (What words and phrases are used to describe sensory details?)	Tone (What can you conclude about the speaker's attitude toward the subject?)	Inferences About the Speaker (What might you infer about the speaker's age, status, preferences?)
1					
2					
3					
4					

"My Name"

from The House on Mango Street

by Sandra Cisneros

ABOUT THE AUTHOR

Sandra Cisneros grew up in Chicago and now lives in San Antonio, Texas. Her novel *The House on Mango Street* reveals the life of a young girl growing up in the Latino section of Chicago. In talking about her writing, Cisneros says she creates stories from things that have touched her deeply: "...in real life a story doesn't have shape, and it's the writer that gives it a beginning, a middle, and an end."

My Notes

1   In English my name means hope. In Spanish it means too many letters. It means sadness, it means waiting. It is like the number nine. A muddy color. It is the Mexican records my father plays on Sunday mornings when he is shaving, songs like sobbing.

2   It was my great-grandmother's name and now it is mine. She was a horse woman too, born like me in the Chinese year of the horse — which is supposed to be bad luck if you're born female — but I think this is a Chinese lie because the Chinese, like the Mexicans, don't like their women strong.

3   My great-grandmother. I would've liked to have known her, a wild horse of a woman, so wild she wouldn't marry. Until my great-grandfather threw a sack over her head and carried her off. Just like that, as if she were a fancy chandelier. That's the way he did it.

4   And the story goes she never forgave him. She looked out the window her whole life, the way so many women sit their sadness on an elbow. I wonder if she made the best with what she got or was she sorry because she couldn't be all the things she wanted to be. Esperanza. I have inherited her name, but I don't want to inherit her place by the window.

5   At school they say my name funny as if the syllables were made out of tin and hurt the roof of your mouth. But in Spanish my name is made out of a softer something, like silver, not quite as thick as sister's name — Magdalena — which is uglier than mine. Magdalena who at least can come home and become Nenny. But I am always Esperanza.

6   I would like to baptize myself under a new name, a name more like the real me, the one nobody sees. Esperanza as Lisandra or Maritza or Zeze the X. Yes. Something like Zeze the X will do.

My Notes

Personal Narrative

"Why Couldn't I Have Been Named *Ashley*?"

by Imma Achilike

NAAMAN FOREST HIGH SCHOOL

GARLAND, TEXAS

1   "Ashley!" exclaimed Mrs. Renfro, and simultaneously three heads whipped around at attention towards the perturbed[1] teacher. At the same time, all three Ashleys proudly replied, "Yes, ma'am?"

2   When I was a fourth grader, I remember sitting in class that day just before the bell rang for dismissal. I remember thinking of all the names in the world, how I could have possibly been stuck with such an alien one. I thought about all the popular kids in the class. I figured that I wasn't popular because of my weird name. I put some things together in my mind and came up with a plausible[2] equation: COOL NAME = POPULARITY. The dismissal bell rang. As I mechanically walked out to catch my ride, I thought to myself, "Why couldn't I have been named Ashley?"

3   I was born, on July 7th, 1986, at Parkland Hospital of Dallas, Texas. I was the first American-born Nigerian in both of my parents' families. I was my parents' first joy, and in their joy, they gave me the name that would haunt me for the rest of my life, Immaculeta Uzoma Achilike.

4   The first time I actually became aware of my name was on the first day of first grade. I went to school loaded with all my school supplies and excited to see all of my old kindergarten friends. I couldn't wait to see who my new teacher was. As I walked into the classroom, all my friends pushed up to me, cooing my name: "Imma, Imma I missed you so much." The teacher walked in with the attendance sheet. She told everyone to quiet down so she could call roll. Before she started, she said something I thought would have never applied to me. She said, "Before I call roll, I apologize if I mispronounce anyone's name" with a very apologetic look on her face. She looked down at the attendance sheet, paused for a minute, and then looked up with an extremely puzzled look on her face. I remember thinking that there was probably some weird name before mine; although, my name was always the first name to be called

---

> **GRAMMAR & USAGE**
>
> A **compound-complex sentence** is one that has two or more independent clauses and one or more subordinate clauses.
>
> Example: I was my parents' first joy, and in their joy, they gave me the name that would haunt me for the rest of my life, Immaculeta Uzoma Achilike.

---

[1] **perturbed:** troubled or disturbed
[2] **plausible:** credible or believable

in kindergarten. Suddenly, my palms started sweating and then she began to hopelessly stutter my name, "Im-Immaculet Arch-liki, I mean, Achei...." Here, I interrupted. My ears burned with embarrassment and droplets of perspiration formed on my nose. "Did I say it right?" she said with the same apologetic look on her face. Before I responded, the laughs that the other kids in class had been holding back suddenly exploded, like a volatile[3] vial of [nitro]glycerin, into peals of laughter. One kid thought it was so funny his chubby face started turning red and I could see a tear gradually making its way down his face. I found myself wishing I could sink into the ground and never come back. I hated being the laughing stock.

5   I never really recovered from the shock of that day. From that day forward, the first day of school was always my most feared day. I didn't know what to do; all I could do was to tell my teachers, "I go by Imma."

6   I felt so alone when all the other girls in my class had sparkly, pink pencils with their names printed on them. You know, the ones they sell in the stores along with name-embossed[4] sharpeners, rulers and pencil pouches. Every year I searched through and rummaged around that rack at the store, but I could never find a pencil with my name on it.

7   The summer of my seventh-grade year, my family and I took a vacation to our "home" in Nigeria, where my parents were born. My cousin and I were playing cards, talking girl talk, and relating our most embarrassing moments. Each tried to see whose story could top whose. I told one story of how I wet the bed at a sleepover, and she told me how she had farted in class during a test. That was a hoot. Then, I told her the story of how I was laughed at because of my weird name. I thought it was pretty funny, but she didn't laugh. She had the most serious look on her face, then she asked me, "Immaculeta Uzoma Achilike, do you know what your name means?" I shook my head at her and that's when she started laughing. I thought she was making fun of me, and as I started to leave she said: "Immaculeta means 'purity', 'Uzoma' means 'the good road' and...." Having heard her words, I stopped walking away and turned around in amazement. What does Achilike mean?" I asked. After a long pause she calmly said, "Achilike means 'to rule without force.'" I was astonished and pleased. I never knew what my name meant.

8   My name is Immaculeta Uzoma Achilike. I am the daughter of first-generation Nigerian immigrants. I am the daughter of hardworking and brave parents. My name means "to rule without force." My grandfather was a wealthy man of generous character. When I say my name in Nigeria, people know me as the granddaughter of a wealthy man of generous character. They know me by my name. There my name is not embossed on any pencil or vanity plate. It is etched in the minds of the people.

My name is Immaculeta Uzoma Achilike.

---

[3] **volatile:** unstable, explosive
[4] **embossed:** raised above the surface

What's in a Name?

Observations from Published Texts

Text	Diction (What word choices does the speaker make? For example, how does the author describe youth? Formal or informal?)	Syntax (Are the sentences short, long, simple, complex?)	Imagery (What words and phrases are used to describe sensory details?)	Tone (What can you conclude about the speaker's attitude toward the subject?)	Inferences About the Speaker (What might you infer about the speaker's age, status, preferences?)
"My Name"					
"Why Couldn't I Have Been Named Ashley?"					

You will interview another student in your class and then introduce that person to the rest of the class.

1. The first information you need is your partner's name:

_____.

2. Write four questions that you could ask to learn important information about your partner.

-

-

-

-

3. When you interview someone, it is important to ask open-ended questions. Open-ended questions or statements cannot be answered with a simple "yes" or "no." They give your interviewee an opportunity to provide insight and explanation. In the question pairs below, circle the open-ended question or statement.

a. Explain some of the best parts of playing soccer.

Do you like playing soccer?

b. As the youngest child in your family, do you think you get your own way?

What are the advantages and disadvantages of being the youngest child in your family?

4. Revise each of the following to be an open-ended question.

Is it fun to be in the band?

Revision:

How many kids are in your family?

Revision:

5. Look back at the four questions you wrote. Make sure they are open-ended questions or statements. If they are not, revise them as you write them on the next page.

I'd Like to Introduce...

6. Write your four interview questions or statements in the Question boxes below. Leave the Answer boxes empty for now.

Question 1:	Question 2:
Answer:	Answer:
Question 3:	Question 4:
Answer:	Answer:

7. Now interview your partner. While your partner is answering, take notes in the Answer boxes on your chart. Try to write down some parts of the answer exactly, using quotation marks to show you are quoting your partner word for word.

Introductions

8. Prepare to introduce your partner to the class. Look back over your interview notes and highlight the parts that seem to be the most important, such as tone of voice, purpose, target audience, circumstances. You will want to include this information in your introduction.

The hardest part of any presentation can be the beginning. Here are some ways you might begin your introduction (your partner's name goes in the blank):

- I would like to introduce _____.

- I would like you all to meet _____.

- This is my new friend _____.

Write the opening of your introduction:

9. The other challenging part of any presentation is the closing. Sometimes people do not know how to end the introduction, so they say "That's it." Don't end your introduction that way! You cannot possibly have said all there is to say about your partner in this brief introduction. You want to end your introduction on a strong note that encourages the rest of your class to get to know your partner.

You might end your introduction like this:

- I enjoyed getting to talk to _____ because _____.

- _____ is an interesting person and I'm glad I got the chance to meet my partner because _____.

Write the ending of your introduction:

10. Now write your introduction on a separate sheet of paper. Use the opener you already wrote, include the information from your notes that you highlighted, and then finish with the closing you wrote. Be sure your introduction shows respect for your partner.

When you introduce your partner, you may use your written introduction, but try not to rely on it the whole time. Avoid hiding behind your paper!

GRAMMAR & USAGE

A **direct quotation** represents a person's exact words. These words are enclosed in quotation marks.

Example: Then she asked me, "Immaculeta Uzoma Achilike, do you know what your name means?"

An **indirect quotation** restates the general meaning of what a person said. Quotation marks are not used with indirect quotations.

Example: She asked whether I knew what my name means.

Introduction to Learning Logs and Word Walls

In this course, you will use many learning strategies to increase your ability to read, understand, create, and present texts. To help keep track of the strategies that work best for you, you will keep a Learning Log. Use the template below as a model; record information about the new strategies you encounter on a separate sheet of paper.

Strategies Learning Log

Name of strategy	
Purpose of strategy	
How I used the strategy	
How the strategy helped	
When I might use this strategy again	

Introducing Independent Reading

To help you select a novel to read on your own, think about the following questions:

- What do you know about the author?
- Does the title grab your attention? What does it mean?
- What information does the book jacket provide about the author, the story, or reviews by others who have read the novel?
- Are the visuals appealing (the cover, the layout of the book, the type size, illustrations)?
- After reading the first few paragraphs, do you find the beginning of the novel interesting?

As you read the novel you choose, stay focused on the story. Avoid letting your mind takes its own journey somewhere else. One way that good readers stay focused on a book is by responding to key events or situations. A double-entry journal is one strategy for responding to a text and even questioning what you are reading. In your journal, you can relate your own experiences to those of the characters in the novel, share your opinions about what is happening in the novel, and trace the development of the **protagonist**.

Use the format below as a model for your journal. In the left column, copy or summarize passages that catch your attention, including the page number. In the right column, write your own thoughts about the passage.

If you are having trouble thinking of what to write, you might try using these stems:

- I really like / dislike this part because …
- I wonder why…
- The diction / imagery creates a tone of…
- This quote shows the narrator / character's voice by…
- I predict that…
- I think the character should…
- This reminds me of the time when I …

WORD CONNECTIONS

The word **protagonist** has a form of the Greek prefix *proto-*, which means "first," and the Greek root *-agon-*, which means "contest" or "struggle."

The prefix *proto-* is also found in these words: *prototype*, *protozoa*, and *protocol*.

The root *-agon-* is also found in *agony*.

LITERARY TERMS

A **protagonist** is the main character who initiates actions that move the plot along.

Textual Evidence (The book says...)	Analysis/Question/Opinion (I say...)

Defining Moments

LITERARY TERMS

A **simile** is a comparison of two different things or ideas, using the words *like* or *as*. It is a stated comparison in which the author says one thing is *like* another.

Hyperbole is deliberate, extravagant, and often outrageous exaggeration. It may be used for either serious or comic effect.

"Coming of age" usually occurs over a period of time, but there are often key incidents that individuals can point to as significant milestones in their coming-of-age experience. Follow your teacher's directions for reading the three texts that follow, and use the organizer below to track your observations about how the authors portray youthful voices. After completing the chart, follow your teacher's directions to complete a visual representation based on one of the texts.

In addition to guiding you to trace the elements identified in your graphic organizer, your teacher will also refer to two literary terms: **similes** and **hyperbole**.

Text	Diction	Syntax	Imagery	Tone	Inferences About the Speaker Based on Voice
"Eleven"					
"Oranges"					
Excerpt from *Speak*					

Writing Prompt: Write a brief analysis of one author's use of diction, syntax, and/or imagery to achieve the effect of a youthful voice.

ELEVEN

by Sandra Cisneros

My Notes

1   What they don't understand about birthdays and what they never tell you is that when you're eleven, you're also ten, and nine, and eight, and seven, and six, and five, and four, and three, and two, and one. And when you wake up on your eleventh birthday you expect to feel eleven, but you don't. You open your eyes and everything's just like yesterday, only it's today. And you don't feel eleven at all. You feel like you're still ten. And you are — underneath the year that makes you eleven.

2   Like some days you might say something stupid, and that's the part of you that's still ten. Or maybe some days you might need to sit on your mama's lap because you're scared, and that's the part of you that's five. And maybe one day when you're all grown up maybe you will need to cry like if you're three, and that's okay. That's what I tell Mama when she's sad and needs to cry. Maybe she's feeling three.

3   Because the way you grow old is kind of like an onion or like the rings inside a tree trunk or like my little wooden dolls that fit one inside the other, each year inside the next one. That's how being eleven years old is.

4   You don't feel eleven. Not right away. It takes a few days, weeks even, sometimes even months before you say Eleven when they ask you. And you don't feel smart eleven, not until you're almost twelve. That's the way it is.

5   Only today I wish I didn't have only eleven years rattling inside me like pennies in a tin Band-Aid box. Today I wish I was one hundred and two instead of eleven because if I was one hundred and two I'd have known what to say when Mrs. Price put the red sweater on my desk. I would've known how to tell her it wasn't mine instead of just sitting there with that look on my face and nothing coming out of my mouth.

6   "Whose is this?" Mrs. Price says, and she holds the red sweater up in the air for all the class to see. "Whose? It's been sitting in the coatroom for a month."

7   "Not mine," says everybody. "Not me."

8   "It has to belong to somebody," Mrs. Price keeps saying, but nobody can remember. It's an ugly sweater with red plastic buttons and a collar and sleeves all stretched out like you could use it for a jump rope. It's maybe a thousand years old and even if it belonged to me I wouldn't say so.

My Notes

9   Maybe because I'm skinny, maybe because she doesn't like me, that stupid Sylvia Saldívar says, "I think it belongs to Rachel." An ugly sweater like that, all raggedy and old, but Mrs. Price believes her. Mrs. Price takes the sweater and puts it right on my desk, but when I open my mouth nothing comes out.

10   "That's not, I don't, you're not . . . Not mine," I finally say in a little voice that was maybe me when I was four.

11   "Of course it's yours," Mrs. Price says. "I remember you wearing it once." Because she's older and the teacher, she's right and I'm not.

12   Not mine, not mine, not mine, but Mrs. Price is already turning to page thirty-two, and math problem number four. I don't know why but all of a sudden I'm feeling sick inside, like the part of me that's three wants to come out of my eyes, only I squeeze them shut tight and bite down on my teeth real hard and try to remember today I am eleven, eleven. Mama is making a cake for me for tonight, and when Papa comes home everybody will sing Happy birthday, happy birthday to you.

13   But when the sick feeling goes away and I open my eyes, the red sweater's still sitting there like a big red mountain. I move the red sweater to the corner of my desk with my ruler. I move my pencil and books and eraser as far from it as possible. I even move my chair a little to the right. Not mine, not mine, not mine.

14   In my head I'm thinking how long till lunchtime, how long till I can take the red sweater and throw it over the schoolyard fence, or leave it hanging on a parking meter, or bunch it up into a little ball and toss it in the alley. Except when math period ends, Mrs. Price says loud and in front of everybody, "Now, Rachel, that's enough," because she sees I've shoved the red sweater to the tippy-tip corner of my desk and it's hanging all over the edge like a waterfall, but I don't care.

15   "Rachel," Mrs. Price says. She says it like she's getting mad. "You put that sweater on right now and no more nonsense."

16   "But it's not —"

17   "Now!" Mrs. Price says.

18   This is when I wish I wasn't eleven, because all the years inside of me — ten, nine, eight, seven, six, five, four, three, two, and one — are pushing at the back of my eyes when I put one arm through one sleeve of the sweater that smells like cottage cheese, and then the other arm through the other and stand there with my arms apart like if the sweater hurts me and it does, all itchy and full of germs that aren't even mine.

GRAMMAR & USAGE

Syntax refers to the arrangement of words and the order of grammatical elements in a sentence—that is, the way the writer puts words together to make meaningful elements, such as phrases and clauses.

Notice the syntax in the last sentence in paragraph 19 (beginning with "My face all hot...").

That's when everything I've been holding in since this morning, since when Mrs. Price put the sweater on my desk, finally lets go, and all of a sudden I'm crying in front of everybody. I wish I was invisible but I'm not. I'm eleven and it's my birthday today and I'm crying like I'm three in front of everybody. I put my head down on the desk and bury my face in my stupid clown-sweater arms. My face all hot and spit coming out of my mouth because I can't stop the little animal noises from coming out of me, until there aren't any more tears left in my eyes, and it's just my body shaking like when you have the hiccups, and my whole head hurts like when you drink milk too fast.

19

But the worst part is right before the bell rings for lunch. That stupid Phyllis Lopez, who is even dumber than Sylvia Saldívar, says she remembers the red sweater is hers! I take it off right away and give it to her, only Mrs. Price pretends like everything's okay.

20

Today I'm eleven. There's a cake Mama's making for tonight, and when Papa comes home from work we'll eat it. There'll be candles and presents, and everybody will sing Happy birthday, happy birthday to you, Rachel, only it's too late.

21

I'm eleven today. I'm eleven, ten, nine, eight, seven, six, five, four, three, two, and one, but I wish I was one hundred and two. I wish I was anything but eleven, because I want today to be far away already, far away like a runaway balloon, like a tiny o in the sky, so tiny-tiny you have to close your eyes to see it.

22

My Notes

Poetry

ABOUT THE AUTHOR

Of Mexican-American heritage, Gary Soto grew up in Fresno, California. In high school, he discovered a love of reading and knew he wanted to be a writer. He started writing while in college. He has written poems, short stories, and novels, which capture the vivid details of everyday life and which have won numerous awards and prizes.

ORANGES

by Gary Soto

The first time I walked
With a girl, I was twelve,
Cold, and weighted down
With two oranges in my jacket.
5   December. Frost cracking
Beneath my steps, my breath
Before me, then gone,
As I walked toward
Her house, the one whose
10   Porch light burned yellow
Night and day, in any weather.
A dog barked at me, until
She came out pulling
At her gloves, face bright
15   With rouge. I smiled,
Touched her shoulder, and led
Her down the street, across
A used car lot and a line
Of newly planted trees,

Until we were breathing   20
Before a drugstore. We
Entered, the tiny bell
Bringing a saleslady
Down a narrow aisle of goods.
I turned to the candies   25
Tiered like bleachers,
And asked what she wanted —
Light in her eyes, a smile
Starting at the corners
Of her mouth. I fingered   30
A nickel in my pocket,
And when she lifted a chocolate
That cost a dime,
I didn't say anything.
I took the nickel from   35
My pocket, then an orange,
And set them quietly on
The counter. When I looked up,
The lady's eyes met mine,
And held them, knowing   40
Very well what it was all
About.

Outside,
A few cars hissing past,
Fog hanging like old   45
Coats between the trees.
I took my girl's hand
In mine for two blocks,
Then released it to let
Her unwrap the chocolate.   50
I peeled my orange
That was so bright against
The gray of December
That, from some distance,
Someone might have thought   55
I was making a fire in my hands.

My Notes

My Notes

Novel Excerpt

ABOUT THE AUTHOR

Born in 1961, Laurie Halse Anderson always loved reading and writing. Even as a child, she made up stories and wrote for fun. As an adult, she did freelance reporting until she began publishing her work. Her novel *Speak*, which won numerous awards and was a best seller, was made into a movie. In 2009, she won the Margaret A. Edwards Award for *Catalyst, Fever 1793*, and *Speak*. She continues to write historical fiction, like *Chains*, and young adult novels, like *Wintergirls*. She says she is inspired by her readers, who write to her with comments or come to her readings.

SPOTLIGHT

from Speak
by Laurie Halse Anderson

I find my locker after social studies. The lock sticks a little, but I open it. I dive into the stream of fourth-period lunch students and swim down the hall to the cafeteria.

I know enough not to bring lunch on the first day of high school. There is no way of telling what the acceptable fashion will be. Brown bags—humble testament to suburbia, or terminal geek gear? Insulated lunch bags—hip way to save the planet, or sign of an overinvolved mother? Buying is the only solution. And it gives me time to scan the cafeteria for a friendly face or an inconspicuous corner.

The hot lunch is turkey with reconstituted dried mashed potatoes and gravy, a damp green vegetable, and a cookie. I'm not sure how to order anything else, so I just slide my tray along and let the lunch drones fill it. This eight-foot senior in front of me somehow gets three cheeseburgers, French fries, and two Ho-Hos without saying a word. Some sort of Morse code with his eyes, maybe. Must study this further. I follow the Basketball Pole into the cafeteria.

I see a few friends—people I used to think were my friends—but they look away. Think fast, think fast. There's that new girl, Heather, reading by the window. I could sit across from her. Or I could crawl behind a trash can. Or maybe I could dump my lunch straight into the trash and keep moving right on out the door.

The Basketball Pole waves to a table of friends. Or course. The basketball team. They all swear at him—a bizarre greeting practiced by athletic boys with zits. He smiles and throws a Ho-Ho. I try to scoot around him.

Thwap! A lump of potatoes and gravy hits me square in the center of my chest. All conversation stops as the entire lunchroom gawks, my face burning into their retinas. I will be forever known as "that girl who got nailed by potatoes the first day." The Basketball Pole apologizes and says something else, but four hundred people explode in laughter and I can't read lips. I ditch my tray and bolt for the door.

I motor so fast out of the lunchroom the track coach would draft me for varsity if he were around. But no, Mr. Neck has cafeteria duty. And Mr. Neck has no use for girls who can run the one hundred in under ten seconds, unless they're willing to do it while holding on to a football.

Mr. Neck: "We meet again."

Me:

Would he listen to "I need to go home and change," or "Did you see what that bozo did"? Not a chance. I keep my mouth shut.

Mr. Neck: "Where do you think you're going?"

Me:

It is easier not to say anything. Shut your trap, button your lip, can it. All that crap you hear on TV about communication and expressing feelings is a lie. Nobody really wants to hear what you have to say.

Mr. Neck makes a note in his book. "I knew you were trouble the first time I saw you. I've taught here for twenty-four years and I can tell what's going on in a kid's head just by looking in their eyes. No more warnings. You just earned a demerit for wandering the halls without a pass."

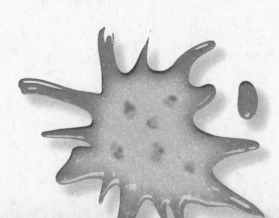

Getting Cut: Coming of Age the Hard Way

What does the title "Cut" make you think about? What do you predict this text will be about?

As you read, or read along with, the vignettes in "Cut," take notes on the graphic organizer below.

Vignette	Name	Profession	Describe Incident	How He Felt Then	Effect of Incident in Future
1					
2					
3					
4					
5					

CUT

by Bob Greene

> **ABOUT THE AUTHOR**
> Born in 1947, Bob Greene is best known for the column he wrote for the *Chicago Tribune* for many years. Referring to the breadth of Greene's topics, one writer said, "Water covers two-thirds of the earth, and Bob Greene covers the rest." Greene has written two biographies of basketball player Michael Jordan as well as the novel *All Summer Long*; his columns have also been collected into several books. The following piece tells a lot about Greene and a significant moment in his own "coming of age."

WORD CONNECTIONS

Several words in this text have been glossed to aid understanding. To **gloss** a word is to add an explanation that is not in the original text (see the footnotes on the next pages). The word *gloss* has multiple meanings depending on how it is used; for example, something shiny may have a high gloss, or someone wishing to hide something may gloss over the facts.

My Notes

1

I remember vividly the last time I cried. I was twelve years old, in the seventh grade, and I had tried out for the junior high school basketball team. I walked into the gymnasium; there was a piece of paper tacked to the bulletin board.

It was a cut list. The seventh-grade coach had put it up on the board. The boys whose names were on the list were still on the team; they were welcome to keep coming to practices. The boys whose names were not on the list had been cut; their presence was no longer desired. My name was not on the list.

I had not known the cut was coming that day. I stood and I stared at the list. The coach had not composed it with a great deal of subtlety; the names of the very best athletes were at the top of the sheet of paper, and the other members of the squad were listed in what appeared to be a descending order of talent. I kept looking at the bottom of the list, hoping against hope that my name would miraculously appear there if I looked hard enough.

I held myself together as I walked out of the gym and out of the school, but when I got home I began to sob. I couldn't stop. For the first time in my life, I had been told officially that I wasn't good enough. Athletics meant everything to boys that age; if you were on the team, even as a substitute, it put you in the desirable group. If you weren't on the team, you might as well not be alive.

I had tried desperately in practice, but the coach never seemed to notice. It didn't matter how hard I was willing to work; he didn't want me there. I knew that when I went to school the next morning I would have to face the boys who had not been cut — the boys whose names were on the list, who were still on the team, who had been judged worthy while I had been judged unworthy.

Getting Cut: Coming of Age the Hard Way

My Notes

As you read, diffuse the text by using the My Notes space to identify the phrases or context clues that help you understand the meanings of glossed words.

GRAMMAR & USAGE

Writers use the subjunctive form of the verb to express a doubt, a wish, a possibility, or a situation contrary to fact. Bob Greene uses the subjunctive in the phrase *as if I were* to express a situation contrary to fact:

"All these years later, I remember it as if I were still standing right there in the gym."

All these years later, I remember it as if I were still standing right there in the gym. And a curious thing has happened: in traveling around the country, I have found that an inordinately[1] large proportion of successful men share the same memory — the memory of being cut from a sports team as a boy.

I don't know how the mind works in matters like this; I don't know what went on in my head following that day when I was cut. But I know that my ambition has been enormous ever since then: I know that for all my life since that day, I have done more work than I had to be doing, taken more assignments than I had to be taking, put in more hours than I had to be spending. I don't know if all of that came from a determination never to allow myself to be cut again — but I know it's there. And apparently it's there in a lot of other men, too.

2

Bob Graham, thirty-six, is a partner with the Jenner & Block law firm in Chicago. "When I was sixteen, baseball was my whole life," he said. "I had gone to a relatively small high school, and I had been on the team. But then my family moved, and I was going to a much bigger high school. All during the winter months I told everyone that I was a ballplayer. When spring came, of course I went out for the team.

"The cut list went up. I did not make the team. Reading that cut list is one of the clearest things I have in my memory. I wanted not to believe it, but there it was.

"I went home and told my father about it. He suggested that maybe I should talk to the coach. So I did. I pleaded to be put back on the team. He said there was nothing he could do; he said he didn't have enough room.

"I know for a fact that it altered[2] my perception of myself. My view of myself was knocked down; my self-esteem was lowered. I felt so embarrassed; my whole life up to that point had revolved around sports, and particularly around playing baseball. That was the group I wanted to be in — the guys on the baseball team. And I was told that I wasn't good enough to be one of them.

"I know now that it changed me. I found out, even though I couldn't articulate[3] it at the time, that there would be times in my life when certain people would be in a position to say 'You're not good enough' to me. I did not want that to happen ever again.

---

[1] **inordinately**: not within reasonable limits; much too great
[2] **altered**: changed; made different
[3] **articulate**: put into words clearly and easily

"It seems obvious to me now that being cut was what started me in determining that my success would always be based on my own abilities, and not on someone else's perceptions. Since then I've always been something of an overachiever; when I came to the law firm I was very aggressive in trying to run my own cases right away, to be the lead lawyer in the cases with which I was involved. I made partner at thirty-one; I never wanted to be left behind.

"Looking back, maybe it shouldn't have been that important. It was only baseball. You pass that by. Here I am. That coach is probably still there, still a high school baseball coach, still cutting boys off the baseball team every year. I wonder how many hundreds of boys he's cut in his life?"

3

Maurice McGrath is senior vice-president of Genstar Mortgage Corporation, a mortgage banking firm in Glendale, California. "I'm forty-seven years old, and I was fourteen when it happened to me, and I still feel something when I think about it," he said.

"I was in the eighth grade. I went to St. Philip's School of Pasadena. I went out for the baseball team, and one day at practice the coach came over to me. He was an Occidental College student who had been hired as the eighth-grade coach.

"He said, 'You're no good.' Those were his words. I asked him why he was saying that. He said, 'You can't hit the ball. I don't want you here.' I didn't know what to do, so I went over and sat off to the side, watching the others practice. The coach said I should leave the practice field. He said that I wasn't on the team, and that I didn't belong there anymore.

"I was outwardly stoic[4] about it. I didn't want anyone to see how I felt. I didn't want to show that it hurt. But oh, did it hurt. All my friends played baseball after school every day. My best friend was the pitcher of the team. After I got whittled down by the coach, I would hear the other boys talking in class about what they were going to do at practice after school. I knew that I'd just have to go home.

"I guess you make your mind up never to allow yourself to be hurt like that again. In some way I must have been saying to myself, 'I'll play the game better.' Not the sports game, but anything I tried. I must have been saying, 'if I have to, I'll sit on the bench, but I'll be part of the team.'

"I try to make my own kids believe that, too. I try to tell them that they should show that they're a little bit better than the rest. I tell them to think of themselves as better. Who cares what anyone else thinks? You know, I can almost hear that coach saying the words. 'You're no good.'"

---

[4] **stoic:** indifferent; remaining calm and self-controlled in the face of difficulty

My Notes

4

Author Malcolm MacPherson (*The Blood of His Servants*), forty, lives in New York. "It happened to me in the ninth grade, at the Yalesville School in Yalesville, Connecticut," he said. "Both of my parents had just been killed in a car crash, and as you can imagine, it was a very difficult time in my life. I went out for the baseball team, and I did pretty well in practice.

"But in the first game I clutched. I was playing second base; the batter hit a popup, and I moved back to catch it. I can see it now. I felt dizzy as I looked up at the ball. It was like I was moving in slow motion, but the ball was going at regular speed. I couldn't get out of the way of my own feet. The ball dropped to the ground. I didn't catch it.

"The next day at practice, the coach read off the lineup. I wasn't on it. I was off the squad.

"I remember what I did: I walked. It was a cold spring afternoon, and the ground was wet, and I just walked. I was living with an aunt and uncle, and I didn't want to go home. I just wanted to walk forever.

"It drove my opinion of myself right into a tunnel. Right into a cave. And when I came out of that cave, something inside of me wanted to make sure in one manner or another that I would never again be told I wasn't good enough.

"I will confess that my ambition, to this day, is out of control. It's like a fire. I think the fire would have pretty much stayed in control if I hadn't been cut from the team. But that got it going. You don't slice ambition two ways; it's either there or it isn't. Those of us who went through something like that always know that we have to catch the ball. We'd rather die than have the ball fall at our feet.

"Once that fire is started in us, it never gets extinguished,[5] until we die or have heart attacks or something. Sometimes I wonder about the home-run hitters; the guys who never even had to worry about being cut. They may have gotten the applause and the attention back then, but I wonder if they ever got the fire. I doubt it. I think maybe you have to get kicked in the teeth to get the fire started.

"You can tell the effect of something like that by examining the trail you've left in your life, and tracing it backward. It's almost like being a junkie with a need for success. You get attention and applause and you like it, but you never quite trust it. Because you know that back then you were good enough if only they would have given you a chance. You don't trust what you achieve, because you're afraid that someone will take it away from you. You know that it can happen; it already did.

"So you try to show people how good you are. Maybe you don't go out and become Dan Rather; maybe you just end up owning the Pontiac

---

[5] **extinguished:** put out; ended

dealership in your town. But it's your dealership, and you're the top man, and every day you're showing people that you're good enough."

5

Dan Rather, fifty-two, is anchor of the "CBS Evening News." "When I was thirteen, I had rheumatic fever," he said. "I became extremely skinny and extremely weak, but I still went out for the seventh-grade baseball team at Alexander Hamilton Junior High School in Houston.

"The school was small enough that there was no cut as such; you were supposed to figure out that you weren't good enough, and quit. Game after game I sat at the end of the bench, hoping that maybe this was the time I would get in. The coach never even looked at me; I might as well have been invisible.

"I told my mother about it. Her advice was not to quit. So I went to practice every day, and I tried to do well so that the coach would be impressed. He never even knew I was there. At home in my room I would fantasize that there was a big game, and the three guys in front of me would all get hurt, and the coach would turn to me and put me in, and I would make the winning hit. But then there'd be another game, and the late innings would come, and if we were way ahead I'd keep hoping that this was the game when the coach would put me in. He never did.

"When you're that age, you're looking for someone to tell you you're okay. Your sense of self-esteem is just being formed. And what that experience that baseball season did was make me think that perhaps I wasn't okay.

"In the last game of the season something terrible happened. It was the last of the ninth inning, there were two outs, and there were two strikes on the batter. And the coach turned to me and told me to go out to right field.

"It was a totally humiliating thing for him to do. For him to put me in for one pitch, the last pitch of the season, in front of all the other guys on the team. I stood out there for that one pitch, and I just wanted to sink into the ground and disappear. Looking back on it, it was an extremely unkind thing for him to have done. That was nearly forty years ago, and I don't know why the memory should be so vivid now; I've never known if the coach was purposely making fun of me — and if he was, why a grown man would do that to a thirteen-year-old boy.

"I'm not a psychologist. I don't know if a man can point to one event in his life and say that that's the thing that made him the way he is. But when you're that age, and you're searching for your own identity, and all you want is to be told that you're all right... I wish I understood it better, but I know the feeling is still there."

My Notes

WORD CONNECTIONS

An analogy is a comparison of the relationship between two groups of words. One way to analyze an analogy is to look at a relationship that describes a function. For example, eye : see :: ear : hear. Choose an appropriate word to complete the following analogies.

a. architect : building :: coach : _____.

b. _____ : artwork :: lawyer : case.

Writing Prompt: Write a paragraph explaining how the voice of one of the speakers helps to shape the reader's response.

Dan Rather had a tothing story but it also made me angry. Dan is very smart, he isn't picking his coach for his problem/success. When he was young he had rheumatic fever, rendering him skinny and weak. He still tried out for baseball. The way he speaks of his humiliation really makes you sad and angry.

Most of the text included in the vignettes is presented as direct quotations from the men being interviewed. In order to capture the insights of each of the men, Bob Greene, the author, most likely had to ask them a series of questions. What questions might he have asked them? What additional questions or follow-up questions might you want to ask each of these men? Use the subjunctive form to write questions that would elicit responses about each interviewee's doubts, wishes, or possibilities relating the experience of being cut from a team.

- Questions Bob Greene may have asked:

- Follow-up questions you would like to ask: What was your motivation for this?

Strategies Learning Log

Name of strategy:

Purpose of strategy:

How strategy was used:

How strategy helped you make meaning from the text, create a text, or orally present a text:

When you would use this strategy again:

Strategies Learning Log

Name of strategy:

Purpose of strategy:

How strategy was used:

How strategy helped you make meaning from the text, create a text, or orally present a text:

When you would use this strategy again:

Two Versions of One Memory

LITERARY TERMS

Prose is ordinary written or spoken language, using sentences and paragraphs, without deliberate or regular meter or rhyme; not poetry, drama, or song.

You will read two texts about the same incident by the same author. One version is in **prose** and the other is in poetry. As you listen to both read aloud, visualize the incident and take notes on the graphic organizers below. Think about which version paints the most vivid picture for you.

Prose Version: "Always Running"

Diction	Imagery	Syntax	Inferences About the Speaker Based on Voice

Poetry Version: "'Race' Politics"

Diction	Imagery	Syntax	Inferences About the Speaker Based on Voice

Discussion

Which version do you think is more powerful? Which is easier to visualize and understand? What components of coming of age are present in the two texts?

ALWAYS RUNNING

by Luis J. Rodriguez

ABOUT THE AUTHOR
Award-winning author Luis Rodriguez was born near the
US-Mexican border. He is a leading Chicano writer and
is best known for his memoir of gang life in Los Angeles,
Always Running. Rodriguez left the gang life in his late
teens and has since worked in many jobs, from bus
driver to newspaper reporter and community activist. He
has developed many outreach programs to assist teens
throughout the country. He continues to write both poetry
and narrative works and is a co-organizer of the Chicago
Poetry Festival.

My Notes

One day, my mother asked Rano and me to go to the grocery store. We
decided to go across the railroad tracks into South Gate. In those days, South
Gate was an Anglo neighborhood, filled with the families of workers from the
auto plant and other nearby industry. Like Lynnwood or Huntington Park, it
was forbidden territory for the people of Watts.

My brother insisted we go. I don't know what possessed him, but then I
never did. It was useless to argue; he'd force me anyway. He was nine then,
I was six. So without ceremony, we started over the tracks, climbing over
discarded[1] market carts and tore-up sofas, across Alameda Street, into South
Gate: all-white, all-American.

We entered the first small corner grocery store we found. Everything
was cool at first. We bought some bread, milk, soup cans and candy. We
each walked out with a bag filled with food. We barely got a few feet, though,
when five teenagers on bikes approached. We tried not to pay any attention
and proceeded to our side of the tracks. But the youths pulled up in front of
us. While two of them stood nearby on their bikes, three of them jumped off
theirs and walked over to us.

"What do we got here?" one of the boys said. "Spics to order — maybe
with some beans?"

He pushed me to the ground; the groceries splattered onto the asphalt. I
felt melted gum and chips of broken beer bottle on my lips and cheek. Then
somebody picked me up and held me while the two others seized my brother,
tossed his groceries out, and pounded on him. They punched him in the face,
in the stomach, then his face again, cutting his lip, causing him to vomit.

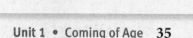

---

[1] **discarded:** thrown away as useless

My Notes

I remember the shrill[2], maddening laughter of one of the kids on a bike, this laughing like a raven's wail, a harsh wind's shriek, a laugh that I would hear in countless beatings thereafter. I watched the others take turns on my brother, this terror of a brother, and he doubled over, had blood and spew on his shirt, and tears down his face. I wanted to do something, but they held me and I just looked on, as every strike against Rano opened me up inside.

They finally let my brother go and he slid to the ground, like a rotten banana squeezed out of its peeling. They threw us back over the tracks. In the sunset I could see the Watts Towers, shimmers of 70,000 pieces of broken bottles, sea shells, ceramic and metal on spiraling points puncturing the heavens, which reflected back the rays of a falling sun. My brother and I then picked ourselves up, saw the teenagers take off, still laughing, still talking about those stupid greasers who dared to cross over to South Gate.

Up until then my brother had never shown any emotion to me other than disdain. He had never asked me anything, unless it was a demand, an expectation, an obligation[3] to be his throwaway boy-doll. But for this once he looked at me, tears welled in his eyes, blood streamed from several cuts — lips and cheeks swollen.

"Swear — you got to swear — you'll never tell anybody how I cried," he said.

I suppose I did promise. It was his one last thing to hold onto, his rep as someone who could take a belt whipping, who could take a beating in the neighborhood and still go back risking more — it was this pathetic plea from the pavement I remember. I must have promised.

---

[2] **shrill:** high-pitched and sharp
[3] **obligation:** a duty

"RACE" POLITICS

by Luis J. Rodriguez

My brother and I
— shopping for *la jefita* —
decided to get the "good food"
over on the other side
of the tracks.   5

We dared each other.
Laughed a little.
Thought about it.
Said, what's the big deal.
Thought about that.   10
Decided we were men,
not boys.
Decided we should go wherever
we damn wanted to.

Oh, my brother — now he was bad.   15
Tough dude. Afraid of nothing.
I was afraid of him.

So there we go,
climbing over
the iron and wood ties,   20
over discarded sofas
    and bent-up market carts,
over a weed-and-dirt road,
into a place called South Gate
— all white. All American.   25

We entered the forbidden
narrow line of hate,
imposed,
transposed,
supposed,   30
a line of power/powerlessness
full of meaning,
meaning nothing —
those lines that crisscross
the abdomen of this land,   35
that strangle you
in your days, in your nights.
When you dream.

My Notes

GRAMMAR & USAGE

Rodriguez uses "each other" when he speaks of himself and his brother in line 6.

Each other and *one another* are **reciprocal pronouns.** When you write, use *each other* to refer to two people and *one another* to refer to three or more.

My Notes

There we were, two Mexicans,
40   six and nine — from Watts no less.
Oh, this was plenty reason
to hate us.

Plenty reason to run up behind us.
Five teenagers on bikes.
45   Plenty reason to knock
the groceries out from our arms —
a splattering heap of soup
cans, bread and candy.

Plenty reason to hold me down
50   on the hot asphalt; melted gum,
and chips of broken
beer bottle on my lips
and cheek.
Plenty reason to get my brother
55   by the throat, taking turns
punching him in the face,
cutting his lower lip,
punching, him vomiting.
Punching until swollen and dark blue
60   he slid from their grasp
like a rotten banana from its peeling.

When they had enough, they threw us back,
dirty and lacerated;
back to Watts, its towers shiny
65   across the orange-red sky.

My brother then forced me
to promise not to tell anybody
how he cried.
He forced me to swear to God,
70   to Jesus Christ, to our long-dead
Indian Grandmother —
keepers of our meddling souls.

Imagine that the speaker has changed to Rano, the older brother.
Write a piece in Rano's voice describing the same incident from his
perspective and using sensory images.

How does the speaker influence the telling of the incident?

Two Versions of One Memory

Now choose the voice of one of the characters and practice answering interview questions. With your partner, **role play** how the interview might sound. First, one of you can ask questions while the other answers in the voice of one of the characters. The interviewee should try to maintain the voice of the character by keeping word choice, language, and culture in mind. Once all questions have been asked and answered, switch roles. Now the interviewee will answer in the voice of the other character.

Here are some possible questions to help you get started. Ask additional open-ended follow-up questions. Remember that good interview questions are open-ended — they cannot be answered with a simple "yes" or "no."

Q: Can you tell me what happened today outside the grocery store?

A:

Q: Who would you say is mostly to blame for the incident and why?

A:

Q: Can you think of a way this incident could possibly end up having a positive outcome?

A:

Q: If you could give any advice to the parties involved, what would it be and why?

A:

Q: If you could go back and change the incident, what would you do differently and why?

A:

Q: What did you learn from this incident?

A:

Conversations with Characters

SUGGESTED LEARNING STRATEGIES: Close Reading, Double-Entry Journal, Marking the Text, Sharing and Responding, Think Aloud, Visualization

In class, you have been reading texts that depict an incident that causes the character to grow or mature. "First Love" is another text that addresses the "coming of age" theme. As you read "First Love", notice how the **diction, syntax,** and **imagery** portray the events from the character's **point of view**.

1. Write a list of the key events in "First Love."

> **LITERARY TERMS**
> **Point of view** refers to the perspective from which a narrative is told.

2. Why is this considered a coming-of-age story?

3. What if you had the opportunity to interview the narrator? Write five open-ended questions you would ask as well as possible responses in the voice of the narrator. Complete the organizer to help focus your thoughts.

How would you describe the voice of the character?	What kind of language does the character tend to use?	What kinds of things does the character usually talk about?

Questions to ask the narrator:

4. Now, consider the novel you have been reading independently and review your double-entry journal. On separate paper, write a list of the key events, explain why your novel can be considered a coming-of-age novel, and complete a mock interview of the narrator.

My Notes

Chunk 1

Personal Narrative

> **ABOUT THE AUTHOR**
> Judith Ortiz Cofer was born in Puerto Rico, but she grew up in New Jersey. Her family often spent time in Puerto Rico, and she became comfortable with both cultures. Much of her writing addresses the immigrant experience for Puerto Ricans, especially cultural conflicts and the coming-of-age experience for young Puerto Rican Americans.

First Love

from Silent Dancing
by Judith Ortiz Cofer

1   I fell in love, or my hormones awakened from their long slumber in my body, and suddenly the goal of my days was focused on one thing: to catch a glimpse of my secret love. And it had to remain secret, because I had, of course, in the great tradition of tragic romance, chosen to love a boy who was totally out of my reach. He was not Puerto Rican; he was Italian and rich. He was also an older man. He was a senior at the high school when I came in as a freshman. I first saw him in the hall, leaning casually on a wall that was the border line between girlside and boyside for underclassmen. He looked extraordinarily like a young Marlon Brando—down to the ironic little smile. The total of what I knew about the boy who starred in every one of my awkward fantasies was this: that he was the nephew of the man who owned the supermarket on my block; that he often had parties at his parents' beautiful home in the suburbs which I would hear about; that his family had money (which came to our school in many ways)—and this fact made my knees weak: and that he worked at the store near my apartment building on weekends and in the summer.

2   My mother could not understand why I became so eager to be the one sent out on her endless errands. I pounced on every opportunity from Friday to late Saturday afternoon to go after eggs, cigarettes, milk (I tried to drink as much of it as possible, although I hated the stuff)—the staple items that she would order from the "American" store.

Week after week I wandered up and down the aisles, taking furtive glances at the stock room in the back, breathlessly hoping to see my prince. Not that I had a plan. I felt like a pilgrim waiting for a glimpse of Mecca. I did not expect him to notice me. It was sweet agony.

One day I did see him. Dressed in a white outfit like a surgeon; white pants and shirt, white cap, and (gross sigh, but not to my love-glazed eyes) blood-smeared butcher's apron. He was helping to drag a side of beef into the freezer storage area of the store. I must have stood there like an idiot, because I remember that he did see me, he even spoke to me! I could have died. I think he said, "Excuse me," and smiled vaguely in my direction.

After that, I willed occasions to go to the supermarket. I watched my mother's cigarettes empty ever so slowly. I wanted her to smoke them fast. I drank milk and forced it on my brother (although a second glass for him had to be bought with my share of Fig Newton cookies which we both liked, but were restricted to one row each). I gave my cookies up for love, and watched my mother smoke her L&M's with so little enthusiasm that I thought (God, no!) that she might be cutting down on her smoking or maybe even giving up the habit. At this crucial time!

I thought I had kept my lonely romance a secret. Often I cried hot tears on my pillow for the things that kept us apart. In my mind there was no doubt that he would never notice me (and that is why I felt free to stare at him—I was invisible). He could not see me because I was a skinny Puerto Rican girl, a freshman who did not belong to any group he associated with.

At the end of the year I found out that I had not been invisible. I learned one little lesson about human nature—adulation (flattery) leaves a scent, one that we are all equipped to recognize, and no matter how insignificant the source, we seek it.

In June the nuns at our school would always arrange for some cultural extravaganza.[1] In my freshman year it was a Roman banquet. We had been studying Greek drama (as a prelude to church history—it was at a fast clip that we galloped through Sophocles and Euripides toward the early Christian martyrs), and our young, energetic Sister Agnes was in the mood for a spectacle. She ordered the entire student body (it was a small group of under 300 students) to have our mothers make us togas out of sheets. She handed out a pattern on mimeo pages fresh out of the machine. I remember the intense smell of the alcohol on the sheets of paper, and how almost everyone in the auditorium brought theirs to their noses and inhaled deeply—mimeographed handouts were the school-day buzz that the new Xerox generation of kids is missing out on. Then, as the last couple of weeks of school dragged on, the city of Paterson becoming a

3

4

5

6

7

8

[1] **extravaganza**: an elaborate and fantastic show

My Notes

_____

_____

_____

_____

_____

_____

_____

GRAMMAR & USAGE

For variety and emphasis, Ortiz Cofer uses different types of sentences.

A **periodic sentence** is one that makes sense fully only when the reader reaches the end of the sentence, that is, when the main clause comes last. A periodic sentence emphasizes the idea in the main clause by making the reader wait for it.

Example: Then, as the last couple of weeks of school dragged on, the city of Paterson becoming a concrete oven, and us wilting in our uncomfortable uniforms, we labored like frantic Roman slaves to build a splendid banquet hall in our small auditorium.

© 2011 College Board. All rights reserved.

My Notes

concrete oven, and us wilting in our uncomfortable uniforms, we labored like frantic Roman slaves to build a splendid banquet hall in our small auditorium. Sister Agnes wanted a raised dais where the host and hostess would be regally enthroned.

9   She had already chosen our Senator and Lady from among our ranks. The Lady was to be a beautiful new student named Sophia, a recent Polish immigrant, whose English was still practically unintelligible, but whose features, classically perfect without a trace of makeup, enthralled[2] us. Everyone talked about her gold hair cascading past her waist, and her voice which could carry a note right up to heaven in choir. The nuns wanted her for God. They kept saying she had a vocation. We just looked at her in awe, and the boys seemed afraid of her. She just smiled and did as she was told. I don't know what she thought of it all. The main privilege of beauty is that others will do almost everything for you, including thinking.

10   Her partner was to be our best basketball player, a tall, red-haired senior whose family sent its many offspring to our school. Together, Sophia and her senator looked like the best combination of immigrant genes our community could produce. It did not occur to me to ask then whether anything but their physical beauty qualified them for the starring roles in our production. I had the highest average in the church history class, but I was given the part of one of many "Roman Citizens." I was to sit in front of the plastic fruit and recite a greeting in Latin along with the rest of the school when our hosts came into the hall and took their places on the throne.

11   On the night of our banquet, my father escorted me in my toga to the door of our school. I felt foolish in my awkwardly draped sheet (blouse and skirt required underneath). My mother had no great skill as a seamstress. The best she could do was hem a skirt or a pair of pants. That night I would have traded her for a peasant woman with a golden needle. I saw other Roman ladies emerging from their parents' cars looking authentic in sheets of material that folded over their bodies like the garments on a statue by Michelangelo. How did they do it? How was it that I always got it just slightly wrong, and worse, I believed that other people were just too polite to mention it. "The poor little Puerto Rican girl," I could hear them thinking. But in reality, I must have been my worst critic, self-conscious as I was.

12   Soon, we were all sitting at our circle of tables joined together around the dais. Sophia glittered like a golden statue. Her smile was beatific: a perfect, silent Roman lady. Her "senator" looked uncomfortable, glancing around at his buddies, perhaps waiting for the ridicule that he would surely get in the locker room later. The nuns in their black habits stood in the background watching us. What were they supposed to be, the Fates?

---

[2] **enthralled**: captivated or fascinated

Nubian slaves? The dancing girls did their modest little dance to tinny music from their finger cymbals, then the speeches were made. Then the grape vine "wine" was raised in a toast to the Roman Empire we all knew would fall within the week—before finals anyway.

All during the program I had been in a state of controlled hysteria.[3] My secret love sat across the room from me looking supremely bored. I watched his every move, taking him in gluttonously. I relished the shadow of his eyelashes on his ruddy cheeks, his pouty lips smirking sarcastically at the ridiculous sight of our little play. Once he slumped down on his chair, and our sergeant-at-arms nun came over and tapped him sharply on the shoulder. He drew himself up slowly, with disdain.[4] I loved his rebellious spirit. I believed myself still invisible to him in my "nothing" status as I looked upon my beloved. But towards the end of the evening, as we stood chanting our farewells in Latin, he looked straight across the room and into my eyes! How did I survive the killing power of those dark pupils? I trembled in a new way. I was not cold—I was burning! Yet I shook from the inside out, feeling light-headed, dizzy.

The room began to empty and I headed for the girls' lavatory. I wanted to relish the miracle in silence. I did not think for a minute that anything more would follow. I was satisfied with the enormous favor of a look from my beloved. I took my time, knowing that my father would be waiting outside for me, impatient, perhaps glowing in the dark in his phosphorescent white Navy uniform. The others would ride home. I would walk home with my father, both of us in costume. I wanted as few witnesses as possible. When I could no longer hear the crowds in the hallway, I emerged from the bathroom, still under the spell of those mesmerizing[5] eyes.

The lights had been turned off in the hallway and all I could see was the lighted stairwell, at the bottom of which a nun would be stationed. My father would be waiting just outside. I nearly screamed when I felt someone grab me by the waist. But my mouth was quickly covered by someone else's mouth. I was being kissed. My first kiss and I could not even tell who it was. I pulled away to see that face not two inches away from mine. It was he. He smiled down at me. Did I have a silly expression on my face? My glasses felt crooked on my nose. I was unable to move or to speak. More gently, he lifted up my chin and touched his lips to mine. This time I did not forget to enjoy it. Then, like the phantom lover that he was, he walked away into the darkened corridor and disappeared.

I don't know how long I stood there. My body was changing right there in the hallway of a Catholic school. My cells were tuning up like musicians in an orchestra, and my heart was a chorus. It was an opera I was composing, and I wanted to stand very still and just listen. But, of

13

14

15

16

---

[3] **hysteria:** uncontrollable emotion or fear
[4] **disdain:** a feeling of scorn
[5] **mesmerizing:** hypnotizing

GRAMMAR & USAGE

A **cumulative sentence** is one that makes complete sense if brought to close before its actual ending.

Example: Her "senator" looked uncomfortable, glancing around at his buddies, perhaps waiting for the ridicule that he would surely get in the locker room later.

My Notes

My Notes

course, I heard my father's voice talking to the nun. I was in trouble if he had to ask about me. I hurried down the stairs making up a story on the way about feeling sick. That would explain my flushed face and it would buy me a little privacy when I got home.

17   The next day Father announced at the breakfast table that he was leaving on a six month tour of Europe with the Navy in a few weeks and, that at the end of the school year my mother, my brother, and I would be sent to Puerto Rico to stay for half a year at Mama's (my mother's mother) house. I was devastated. This was the usual routine for us. We had always gone to Mama's to stay when Father was away for long periods. But this year it was different for me. I was in love, and . . . my heart knocked against my bony chest at this thought . . . he loved me too? I broke into sobs and left the table.

18   In the next week I discovered the inexorable[6] truth about parents. They can actually carry on with their plans right through tears, threats, and the awful spectacle of a teenager's broken heart. My father left me to my mother who impassively packed while I explained over and over that I was at a crucial time in my studies and that if I left my entire life would be ruined. All she would say is, "You are an intelligent girl, you'll catch up." Her head was filled with visions of casa and family reunions, long gossip sessions with her mama and sisters. What did she care that I was losing my one chance at true love?

19   In the meantime I tried desperately to see him. I thought he would look for me too. But the few times I saw him in the hallway, he was always rushing away. It would be long weeks of confusion and pain before I realized that the kiss was nothing but a little trophy for his ego. He had no interest in me other than as his adorer. He was flattered by my silent worship of him, and he had bestowed a kiss on me to please himself, and to fan the flames. I learned a lesson about the battle of the sexes then that I have never forgotten: the object is not always to win, but most times simply to keep your opponent (synonymous at times with "the loved one") guessing.

20   But this is too cynical a view to sustain in the face that overwhelming rush of emotion that is first love. And in thinking back about my own experience with it, I can be objective only to the point where I recall how sweet the anguish was, how caught up in the moment I felt, and how every nerve in my body was involved in this salute to life. Later, much later, after what seemed like an eternity of dragging the weight of unrequited love around with me, I learned to make myself visible and to relish the little battles required to win the greatest prize of all. And much later, I read and understood Camus' statement about the subject that concerns both adolescent and philosopher alike: if love were easy, life would be too simple.

---

[6] **inexorable:** unyielding; not to be persuaded

GRAMMAR & USAGE

The final sentence is a **balanced sentence.** A sentence is balanced when ideas of similar weight are expressed in similar grammatical structures or lengths.

Creating a Playlist for a Novel

SUGGESTED LEARNING STRATEGIES: Double-Entry Journal, Brainstorming

As your class discusses playlists, respond to the following questions and instructions:

1. Based on your class discussion, what are some of the different types of playlists you or your classmates have on your MP3 players?

2. Consider the texts you have read in this unit. What type of music might the main characters include in a playlist? Keep in mind that music is a sensory experience that often inspires the same kinds of emotions that the words on a page can inspire. Think about the narrator from *Speak*, for example. Would her playlist include rock songs, slow songs, instrumental music, or even angry music? Why? Now, focus on one of the texts you've read, and create a possible playlist for the main character. Write your ideas and explanation below.

Name of Text:

Possible Playlist:

Explanation:

3. Now, look back at your double-entry journal and character interview for the novel you are reading. Create a playlist for the main character. Then write a short piece summarizing an interview with the character in which the character explains the reasons these songs are included in his or her playlist. Use language from the book that is typical of the character's voice.

Viewing an Interview

Pretending to interview a character is easier than interviewing a real person. In a mock interview, you are in complete control. In a real interview, you never know what your interviewee will say. You may have carefully planned questions only to find that the interviewee wants to talk about something different altogether. Although you do want to keep some sense of focus in an interview, sometimes the best thing to do is to follow the lead of your interviewee. That's why it is important to ask good follow-up questions.

Follow-up questions do exactly what the name implies: They follow up on something the interviewee has said. For example:

Q: What was the best thing that happened to you in high school?

A: I guess that would be when my boyfriend broke up with me at the prom.

Follow-up Q: That doesn't sound like a very good thing. Why was it the best thing that happened to you?

You might not have anticipated the answer to that question, but pursuing that topic could lead to some interesting information about your interviewee. That's why you need to be flexible about your planned questions and allow for follow-up questions. Here are a few ways you could follow up on an answer:

- Why do you think that?
- That sounds interesting. Could you tell me more about it?
- What happened next?
- How has that influenced your life?

1. Practice writing follow-up questions to these questions and answers:

   Q: What kind of friends did you hang out with in high school?

   A: Mostly jocks, like me.

   Follow-up Q:

   Q: What is your worst memory from high school?

   A: A kid I knew was badly injured in a car accident.

   Follow-up Q:

2. Make up your own question and answer using the subjunctive form to ask an interviewee about doubts or wishes the person may have had. Include a good follow-up question.

   Q:

   A:

   Follow-up Q:

3. Your teacher will show you a video recording of an interview. As you watch, take notes below, writing down all the questions asked, and summarizing the answers given.

Interviewer:	Interviewee:
Questions:	**Answers:**

What seems to be the focus of this interview?

4. Now that you have watched the interview, go back to your notes and identify the kinds of questions:

- In one color, highlight the first question and any questions that start a new line of questioning.

- In a second color, highlight the follow-up questions.

- In a third color, write any follow-up questions you think the interviewer could have asked but didn't.

5. Choose one of the questions you think the interviewer could have asked but didn't. Why do you think the interviewer didn't ask this (or a similar) question?

6. Circle the number that best describes your evaluation of this interview.

1 = I learned a lot about the person being interviewed.

2 = I learned some things about the person being interviewed, but I wanted to learn more.

3 = I did not learn very much about the person being interviewed.

Why did you choose the rating you did?

7. Write a reflection on the importance of asking follow-up questions.

Reading an Interview Narrative

You have seen interviews written in the Q and A format, but many interview narratives are not presented in this way. As you read "Bethany Only Looking Ahead," consider the ways in which the writer describes Bethany, captures her voice, considers a significant incident in her life, and conveys the significance to the reader.

After reading and discussing the interview narrative with a partner or group, answer the questions below.

Name of Interviewee:	Name of Interviewer:

What seems to be the focus of this interview?

Describe the voice of the interviewee.

What does the writer do that makes the voice of the interviewee clear?

Most interview narratives present both **direct** and **indirect quotations**.

- **Direct quotations** are *word-for-word* quotations. Direct quotations should be written inside quotation marks. Here are some examples:

  "Have another slice of pie," my mother said.

  "No thank you," I replied. "I can't eat another bite."

- **Indirect quotations** *summarize* and are not written inside quotation marks. For example:

  My mother offered me another slice of pie.

  I told her that I could not eat another bite.

Use one color to highlight the direct quotations in "Bethany Only Looking Ahead." Then use a different color to highlight the indirect quotations.

My Notes

Article

BETHANY
only looking ahead

by Jan TenBruggencate

KILAUEA, Kaua'i — Three weeks after a "gray blur" bit off her left arm, Bethany Hamilton is putting her life back together.

The stitches covering the wound caused by the 14-foot tiger shark were to come out yesterday afternoon, and she was eager for her doctor's permission to get back in the water. Bethany is still listed among the top-ranked women surfers, and she insists that she'll be back on the waves soon.

The 13-year-old Princeville girl woke up at 5 a.m. on Halloween morning, eager to surf the reef at Tunnels because the waves had been good nearby the night before. She had cereal for breakfast before her mother drove her to the beach. Her dad was going into the hospital for knee surgery.

Bethany paddled out with her best friend, Alana Blanchard, and Alana's brother, Byron, and father, Holt.

They surfed for about a half-hour and she caught maybe 10 waves before she took a rest, lying on her surfboard parallel to shore, her right hand holding the board, her left dangling in the water.

"We never saw it, or anything, before it bit. It shook me. It lasted about three seconds long. All I saw was, like, a gray blur.

"It let go and I just looked at the red blood in the water."

Holt Blanchard and his son pushed Bethany onto a small wave, then they dragged her in the water, one or the other of them paddling while she held on to their board or their shorts with her remaining hand. When they got into an area shallow enough to stand, the elder Blanchard wrapped his rashguard around her arm. As they reached shore, he used a surfboard leash as a tourniquet.

Until that moment, Bethany had been conscious.

"I was talking. I was praying. I don't know the exact words. I just asked for help," she said.

She passed out as she came ashore, but came to again quickly.

"I woke up and they had a lot of towels on me. I was thinking that the ambulance should hurry up," she said.

She recalls details uncannily, like firefighters asking about the kind of cars her parents drove, like her asking ambulance attendants where they were during the 30-mile ride to the hospital.

And she remembers her mother, trying to keep up with the ambulance to follow her daughter to the hospital and being pulled over by a police officer for speeding. Ambulance attendants radioed the police to explain the situation and her mother was free to go.

At Wilcox Memorial Hospital, Tom Hamilton was hauled out of the operating room to make room for his daughter. He already had been sedated for his scheduled knee operation, and was not able to see Bethany before she underwent surgery.

He got the knee surgery later, and yesterday afternoon, he and Bethany were to have their respective stitches out at the same time.

Within hours of the shark's bite, her story became an international sensation. The family was barraged by media and well-wishers. Friends who saw that they were too fragile to handle the stress stepped up and began trying to manage the situation.

Part-time Kaua'i resident Roy Hofstetter, a Los Angeles entertainment agent, was asked to help handle the media. He is making arrangements for Bethany to be paid for many of her appearances to help secure her future. Although the family has medical insurance, there will be additional uncovered medical costs, including the development of artificial limbs that will have to be replaced as Bethany grows.

Bethany seems to handle the turmoil with aplomb. She credits church and kin for her personal strength and resilience.

"Strong faith and strong family helps me, does it for me," said Bethany, whose family attends North Shore Christian Church.

She seems hesitant to go further, but it's just that she's said it all so many times before. She looks at her dad.

"I wish we had recorded my answers, so we could just play them back," she said.

To some extent, she has been insulated, spending most of her time since the injury with family and a few close girlfriends, including best friend Alana, and that feels normal. Yet, undeniably, life is different.

"Everything's changed. If you just think about it, there's all these people saying, 'How are you feeling?' I just wish I could say, 'I'm fine. You don't have to ask.' But then, I guess I'd ask, too."

GRAMMAR & USAGE

Commas help clarify meaning. When a phrase or a clause is not essential (**nonrestrictive**) to the meaning of a sentence, set it off with commas. However, if it is essential (**restrictive**), do not use commas. Look at these nonrestrictive phrases:

Appositive phrase: Part-time Kaua'i resident Roy Hofstetter, **a Los Angeles entertainment agent,** was asked....

Participial phrase: ...there will be additional uncovered medical costs, **including the development of artificial limbs,**....

The commas indicate that the information in these phrases is additional but not necessary. In your writing, use commas to make clear the distinction between restrictive and nonrestrictive phrases.

My Notes

She looks fine. Surfer's blond hair frames lively eyes and a ready smile. A gold and diamond pendant around her neck is in the shape of a surfboard with a bite taken out of it — looking much like her board did after the attack. It was a gift from a friend who prefers to remain anonymous, she said.

Bethany's right hand is fidgety during the interview, toying with a lacquered chopstick that she uses to arrange her hair. At her left shoulder is a mound of flesh where an arm used to be, a semicircle of scar tissue closing the wound. Bethany appears comfortable with herself, and makes no attempt to shield the injury from view.

This slim, strong teenager doesn't appear to dwell too much on the loss of her arm. It's done, and she said she's ready to move on.

"Consciously or unconsciously, she's doing a lot of stuff on her own," Tom Hamilton said.

"I saw her sitting on the floor, cutting oranges and tangerines, using her feet to hold them."

Bethany is hoping to salvage her semester at school, but it will take hard work. She has been recovering for three weeks, and a couple of weeks of Mainland visits are scheduled in December for national media appearances. The family is talking to her teachers at her online charter school, the Myron B. Thompson Academy, and they're working on bringing her up to speed.

Once she and her dad get their doctor's approval to return to the water, Tom Hamilton said, "we'll probably do some workouts together in the local pool."

When they're ready, it's on to the surf — something they haven't been able to do together for several months because of Tom's bad knee.

"We look forward to surfing together," Tom Hamilton said.

Bethany has a specific goal when she paddles back into the ocean.

"When I first go surfing, I want to make sure I catch the first wave myself. Then, they can help me," she said.

Strategies Learning Log

Name of strategy:

Purpose of strategy:

How strategy was used:

How strategy helped you make meaning from the text, create a text, or orally present a text:

When you would use this strategy again:

Strategies Learning Log

Name of strategy:

Purpose of strategy:

How strategy was used:

How strategy helped you make meaning from the text, create a text, or orally present a text:

When you would use this strategy again:

Interviewing Together

Your teacher will arrange for your class to interview someone. Your focus for the interview is to find out about an incident that happened while this person was in high school so that you can write about it.

1. Begin by filling in the first two columns of the KWL chart:

Interviewee's name:

K What I Know	W What I Want to Know	L What I Learned

2. Based on what you already know, either from your own knowledge of the person or from what your teacher tells you, make a list of questions that you think might get and keep the interview flowing.

   •

   •

   •

   Your class will work together to choose the best starting question.

3. During the group interview, take notes on your own paper. Include the questions asked and the interviewee's answers. You will work with a partner. One of you should capture quotes verbatim, while the other summarizes important information from the answers. Remember, the most important information usually comes from follow-up questions, so ask good follow-up questions.

   At the end of the interview, be sure to thank the interviewee. Being interviewed by a group of teenagers is not easy.

4. Now that the interview is complete, go back to your KWL chart and fill in the L column, explaining what you learned during the interview. You may need to write this on your own paper.

5. Look over the notes that you took during the interview.

   • In one color, highlight the questions that begin a new topic or direction in the questioning.

   • In a second color, highlight the questions that follow up on a previous answer.

   • In a third color, write any follow-up questions that you might have asked, but you either did not have the chance or you did not think of them until later.

   Now look at the L column of your KWL chart. How much of what you learned came from follow-up questions?

6. Circle the number that describes your evaluation of the interview:

   1 = I learned a lot about the person being interviewed.

   2 = I learned some things about the person being interviewed, but I wanted to learn more.

   3 = I did not learn very much about the person being interviewed.

Writing Prompt: Using your notes, write a narrative of the interview on another sheet of paper. Try to capture the voice and personality of the interviewee as you retell his or her coming-of-age experience. Following the model of "Bethany Only Looking Ahead," you can convey the personality of the interviewee by these methods:

   • describing how the interviewee is speaking, acting, and looking

   • describing the setting of the interview

   • conveying the significance of the events discussed

   • including both direct and indirect quotations.

Planning an Interview

For Embedded Assessment 1, you will conduct an interview and write a narrative in which you present that interview. You have probably noticed that conducting an interview takes a good deal of planning. You need to begin thinking about the interview you will conduct.

The focus of your interview will be to find out about a person's overall experience during high school, and to present at least one important incident during that time that influenced the interviewee's coming of age.

Step One

Make a list of people you might be able to interview. Include only people with whom you could have a face-to-face meeting before the assignment is due.

Name of Person I Might Be Able to Interview	Why I Would Like to Interview This Person About His or Her Experience in High School

Step Two

Contact the people on your list to schedule your interview with one of them. Let them know why you are conducting the interview and that some portions of it may be shared with your classmates.

Step Three

Write the details of your appointment:

- I have arranged to interview:

- Date the interview is scheduled:

- Time:

- Place:

Step Four

Brainstorm a list of questions and possible follow-up questions you might ask during the interview. Keep in mind the focus of your interview as you think of potential questions.

1.

2.

3.

4.

5.

6.

Remember, you probably will not ask all of these questions. Once your conversation begins to flow, you will ask follow-up questions. It is important, though, to walk into your interview with a list of questions to start the interview and to keep it going.

Presenting an Interview Narrative

SUGGESTED LEARNING STRATEGIES: **Drafting, Peer Editing**

Assignment

Your assignment is to interview a person who has attended high school and to write an interview narrative that effectively portrays the voice and experience of the interviewee.

Steps

Interview

1. You have already arranged a time and place to meet with the person whom you will interview, and you have already created a list of questions you might ask. Before you begin the interview, thank the person for giving you the opportunity to interview him or her. If you want to tape the interview, ask for permission before you begin.

2. Start your interview with one of your questions regarding the person's experience in high school. Then try to let the interview flow like a conversation as much as possible. Remember that asking good follow-up questions is more effective than asking all the questions on your list.

3. Try to get the person to describe at least one incident from his or her high school experience that influenced his or her coming of age. When you feel that you have adequate information, you can begin to draw the interview to a close.

4. As you conduct the interview, remember to take descriptive notes as well as recording the conversation (if you have obtained permission from the interviewee).

Prewriting

5. As soon as possible after the interview, read over your notes and add anything that you can remember. Fill in gaps in your description of the person and the way he or she seemed to feel during the interview. It is important to do this as close to the interview as possible so that it is still fresh in your memory.

Drafting

6. Write a draft of your report.

   - In your introduction, include a description of the person you have interviewed.

   - In your body paragraphs, tell about the person's overall experience in high school. Be sure to describe in detail at least one incident from the person's high school days. Try to use vivid imagery, careful diction, and a mix of direct and indirect quotations to convey a sense of the interviewee's voice in your narrative.

   - In your conclusion, you may want to predict how you can use what you learned from the interview as you experience high school yourself.

Revising and Editing for Publication

7. Share your draft with a partner. Consult the Scoring Guide to revise for the following:

   • Vivid descriptions of the incident and interviewee

   • Clear use of direct and indirect quotes to convey the interviewee's voice

   • Sentence variety that incorporates various sentence structures such as balanced, periodic, and cumulative sentences (Grammar & Usage, pages 43, 45, 46) as well as the subjunctive verb form to express doubt or possibility as appropriate (Grammar & Usage, page 28).

   • Proper punctuation and capitalization of quotations

8. Use your available resources (e.g., spell check, dictionaries, grammar references) to edit for conventions and prepare your narrative for publication. If you are writing your narrative by hand, remember to use legible handwriting.

TECHNOLOGY TIP If you have access to word processing software, use its spell-check and grammar-check features. Be aware, though, that the spell-check program may not recognize proper nouns. The grammar-check feature will often highlight sentences with passive verbs. Look carefully at the suggestions offered, and determine how best to revise your writing to present a document ready for publication.

Presenting an Interview Narrative

SCORING GUIDE

Scoring Criteria	Exemplary	Proficient	Emerging
Ideas	The narrative insightfully describes at least one incident from the person's high school experience which influenced his or her coming of age with careful attention to detail. The writer vividly uses examples from the three descriptive categories.	The narrative describes an incident from the person's high school experience clearly and effectively. The writer mentions examples from the three descriptive categories.	An incident may not be described in detail and little to no attention is paid to the descriptive categories.
Organization	The narrative is multi-paragraphed and organized in a way that enhances the reader's understanding.	The narrative is multi-paragraphed and organized in a logical fashion.	The narrative may not be multi-paragraphed and/or organized in a logical fashion.
Use of Language	Vivid imagery, careful diction, and effective use of direct and indirect quotes convey a strong sense of the interviewee's voice.	Clear imagery, diction, and use of quotations convey a sense of the interviewee's voice.	The voice of the interviewee is not clear. Imagery, diction, and use of quotations are inappropriate or missing.
Conventions	Writing is virtually error-free. The writer uses proper punctuation and capitalization to smoothly embed quotations from the interview into text.	Though some errors may appear, they do not seriously impede readability. The writer properly punctuates and capitalizes quotations in the text.	Frequent errors in standard writing conventions interfere with the meaning. Quotations from the interview are not properly incorporated into the text.
Evidence of Writing Process	The writing demonstrates thoughtful planning, significant revision, and careful editing in preparing a publishable draft.	The writing demonstrates planning, revision, and editing in preparing a publishable draft.	The writing lacks evidence of planning, revision, and/or editing. The draft is not ready for publication.
Additional Criteria			

Comments: _____

_____

Learning Focus:

How Can You Appeal to Readers?

Consider a typical week in your life. How many decisions do you think you make that are affected by advertisers' attempts to persuade you? What areas of your life are most influenced by advertising? Now, think about your reading habits and the reading habits of your peers. Is it possible to use the power of advertising to influence teenagers' reading choices? The next activities give you an opportunity to find out.

You have already studied **voice**, **coming of age**, and interviewing, and you have completed or almost completed reading a coming-of-age novel. Now, you will continue your interviewing skills by interviewing peers about their reading preferences. Then, you'll review **advertising techniques** that you encountered in earlier grades. In addition to advertising techniques, you'll learn about the **rhetorical appeals** of **ethos**, **pathos**, and **logos** and the way they work together with **advertising techniques** to persuade an audience. Finally, you will put all of these pieces together as you work with a group to create an advertising campaign for your novel. Can you use advertising techniques and rhetorical appeals to persuade your peers to read your book? Here's your chance to discover just how persuasive you can be.

Teens and Books: What Are the Influences?

1. Think about the kinds of things you read outside of class. List the titles of some of the books or other texts you've read recently.

2. Based on your list and your class discussion, create a list of questions you can use to interview some of your peers who are not in this class about the kinds of books and other texts they read. Be sure your questions are open-ended, and be sure to ask them about their preferences as well as what influences their reading choices.

   List of interview questions:

3. After conducting your interviews, compare your findings with those of the members of your group. Synthesize your findings and create a chart or graph that displays your results for the rest of your classmates.

4. Read the following article about marketing books to teens. Take notes on the types of advertising formats that advertisers consider effective for teen audiences. While you are reading, make text-to-self connections, and take notes in the margin on whether or not you agree with the points made in the article.

5. Finally, synthesize information from the peer interviews, group discussions, facts from the article, and your own notes to write a response to the following prompt:

   Judith Rosen's article states that teens said their "ideal" activity is reading a book. For the majority of teens, do you think reading a book is their ideal activity? Explain why you agree or disagree, and cite specific examples to support your position.

AS IF!
Marketing to Older Teens

by Judith Rosen

U.S. teens controlled an estimated $169 billion in disposable income last year—or $91 per week per teen—according to a study by Teenage Research Unlimited. But publishers trying to grab a share of that cash face stiff challenges. "Teens are very savvy and they have a cynical radar. Marketers have to get around that with marketing that doesn't seem like marketing," says Boston College sociology professor Juliet Schor, author of *Born to Buy: The Commercialized Culture and the New Consumerism* (Scribner).

Still, there's reason to think teens could be enticed to buy a lot more books, says Hollywood-based youth culture expert Sharon Lee, co-president and co-founder of market research firm Look-Look Inc. The firm did a recent study in which teens cited writing as one of their main creative outlets. They also said their "ideal" activity is reading a book, followed by exercising and shopping. That's the "ideal." In reality, according to the study, teens are much more likely to spend their free time surfing the Internet, watching TV and listening to music. "I look at as a huge opportunity," Lee says. "The desire to read, the desire to write, the desire to engage with words is there."

Seeking to translate that desire into sales, publishers are using a variety of strategies, ranging from the tech-heavy to traditional-with-a-twist—all tailored to reach those wary but free-spending 14-to-19-year-old consumers.

Cell Phones

Hoping that teens who walk around with cell phones pressed to their ears could be persuaded to sit down with their noses in a book, HarperCollins is running a text-messaging promotion starting next week for Meg Cabot, of Princess Diaries fame. Teen readers can get news on the mobile about the release of her new novel, *Ready or Not: An All-American Girl Novel* (July), and about her monthly online chats. There's also a cell phone screensaver promoting Cabot's books, as well as a ring tone with her voice.

Harper is not the first to try a dial-up campaign. In January Random House used text messaging to promote the paperback edition of the third book in Ann Brashares's Sisterhood of the Traveling Pants series, *Girls in Pants* (Delacorte, Jan.). "The biggest shift in marketing is how important online marketing has become," says Random House Children's Books v-p of marketing Daisy Kline. "We think of driving traffic to our site as hanging onto a reader a little bit longer and having an opportunity of introducing a reader

Teens and Books: What Are the Influences?

© 2011 College Board. All rights reserved.

My Notes

to another author." Random credits the cell phone promotion, coupled with advance movie trailers for the film, with sending traffic to the Sisterhood Web site soaring 400% higher in the first quarter of the year than during the previous three months.

Playing the Net

After years of experimenting, publishers and authors have become more sophisticated about using the Internet to reach readers. "A few years ago, it was all about developing a presence," says Kira Glass, associate director of Internet marketing for Harcourt. "Now you are budgeting for advertising on the Internet and keyword searches."

For authors, the Web provides a way to connect directly with fans. When asked what prompted her to market her books via her LaurenMyracle.com Web site, the author responded with a question of her own, "Am I marketing? I'd never want to be an Amway salesman for my own books. My job is to tell the best stories I can and to let people know that writers are just people." Myracle plans to IM (instant message) with her teen fans this fall to promote *ttfn* (Ta-ta for Now) (Abrams).

Thirty thousand teens have signed up to receive information on Cabot's books through HarperCollins's Author Tracker e-mail program. In addition, Cabot receives as many as 200 e-mails a day when one of her books is first released, and young people avidly read her blog. "I was very resistant at first to keep a blog," says Cabot. "I thought it would take too much time from my 'real' writing. After I found out how much it increased traffic to my site, I was like 'Um, okay.'" Cabot even started her own online book club—with 8,500 members—and many selections are her own titles.

Phyllis Reynolds Naylor, author of the Alice McKinley series, posts e-mails from young people who look to her as an Ann Landers for teens. "E-mails come to the Web site, and I read them every day," says Naylor, 72, who spends about an hour a day answering teen queries. "They tell me that they feel they can ask me anything. They're terrified of doctors and pelvic exams. They say, 'Even though I love my mother I'm too embarrassed to ask...'"

Giving CDs a Spin

CDs are hardly cutting-edge technology, but publishers are still finding new ways to use them to reach teen consumers. This spring Harper produced 60,000 CD samplers, with 10 authors reading selections from upcoming titles. The CDs, which were tucked inside booklets about the Harper list, were mailed to book and audio buyers and to consumers who ordered from the Alloy catalogue. Harper is also starting to introduce bonus CDs packaged with books. For example, bestselling novelist Louise Rennison's May release, *Then He Ate My Boy Entrancers*, contains a "tell-all" CD on which Rennison answers fan questions.

Where the Teens Are

Offline, marketers are following this simple rule: take your message to where the teens are. Tara Lewis, v-p, global marketing for Disney Global Children's Books has seen a jump in sales from viral marketing, such as providing tee-shirts, stickers and posters to Ned Vizzini to promote the hardcover edition of his book *Be More Chill* (Miramax/Hyperion, paperback Sept.) at rock concerts. This fall, she's working on finding a way to ensure that Bat Mitzvah attendees who use the Ladies Room find postcards for Fiona Rosenbloom's *You Are SO Not Invited to My Bat Mitzvah!* (Hyperion, Sept.).

Last spring Abrams staffers distributed copies of two April releases from its year-old Amulet paperback YA line, Lauren Myracle's *ttyl* (Talk to You Later) and William Sleator's *The Boy Who Couldn't Die*, to teens gathered outside MTV's Total Request Live in Times Square. That's not to say that tried-and-true book promotions don't work. Amulet's Jason Wells believes that the 700 book displays for two of Myracle's titles helped push *ttyl* onto bestseller lists.

Scholastic reaches out to young people via marketing partnerships with teen catalogue companies like dELiA*s and Alloy, as well as through clothing and jewelry stores. "If you have the right property you can get into new accounts like Urban Outfitters or Hot Topic," says Scholastic's Jennifer Pasanen, who has placed Jim Benton's *It's Happy Bunny* books in both. Red Wheel/Weiser/Conari has also found a teen audience at those stores for its humorous, edgy books originally conceived for adults. President Michael Kerber attributes 30% of the sales for Voltaire's *What Is Goth?* (Weiser) to Hot Topic and Urban Outfitters, which have taken strong positions on this fall's follow-up, *Paint It Black: A Guide to Gothic Homemaking* (Weiser, Oct.).

Bookstore Events

It's true—teen turnout for bookstore events tends to be so sparse that many retailers don't even bother. But don't count bookstores out as a way to reach teens, who will come out for the right event. Brazos Bookstore in Houston brought Laura Mechling and former Houstonian Laura Moser in for a reading and sold 350 copies of their book, *The Rise and Fall of a 10th-Grade Social Climber* (Houghton/Graphia, May). "I learned early on that when there's a good book by a local author with supportive parents, the usual expectations don't apply," says owner Karl Kilian. In this case Moser's parents, former owners of the now-defunct children's bookstore Stop, Look and Learn, which was located a few blocks from Brazos, supplied their own personal mailing list.

Barring those kinds of connections, group readings show promise. "It's always hard to get an audience," says Barnes & Noble children's buyer Joe Monti, who used to do book readings with three or four authors. This spring he discovered that by increasing the number of writers to 11 he could attract a bigger crowd. "The more the merrier," says Monti. "It gives the reading more the feeling of a party."

My Notes

WORD CONNECTIONS

Some analogies describe the function of one word in relation to the other. For example, clock : time describes the function of the clock to give the time. Complete these analogies using their functions as the basis of the relationship.

a. thermometer : temperature :: hammer : _____

b. eye : _____ :: tongue : taste

WORD CONNECTIONS

Ad hominem is a term describing an attack on a person's character rather than the argument the person makes. It is an appeal to emotions rather than the logical facts of an argument.

My Notes

Elements of an Argument

Read the elements of an argument. Then read the response below to Judith Rosen's article, and identify the elements of an argument the writer uses.

- The **hook,** which is an opening that grabs the reader's attention and establishes a connection between the reader and the writer.

- The **claim,** which is a clear and straightforward statement of the writer's belief and what is being argued.

- **Concessions** and **refutations,** which are restatements of arguments made by the other side (concessions) and the writer's arguments against those opposing viewpoints (refutations) and why the writer's arguments are more valid.

- **Support,** which is the reasoning behind the argument. Support can include evidence as well as logical and emotional appeals (logos and pathos). It may also anticipate objections and provide reasoning to overcome those objections.

- **Summary/Call to action,** which is a closing statement with a final plea for action.

Student Example

I just read a 600-page book in a day and a half. I couldn't put it down. It had everything a girl could want: romance, friendship, adventure, and fun characters. Unfortunately, it's the only novel I've read all year. Reading just isn't my top priority, and most of my friends would agree.

After reading this article, I asked ten of my friends what their "ideal" activity would be, and not one person answered "reading." Most of my friends would rather go shopping or hang out with friends. My smartest friend, who has a 4.0, said, "I read at least an hour each night for school. Why would I choose to read more than that?" I figure if I spent the entire day as an accountant, I would not want to go home and do math problems! Plus, I have no time. Between soccer, band practice, and my friends, I could watch a movie for two hours or read a book for two weeks! I'm sure the person who says that the book is definitely better than the movie is not a teenager who has no time to read.

I can also hear my Mom telling me that someday I will wish I had read more books. Perhaps she is right, but I don't want that now. What I want now is three extra hours in every day because I have homecoming to help plan and homework to do. So until another "can't miss" book comes out, my to-do list will not include reading a novel.

Revising: Now look at the response you wrote to the writing prompt on page 64. Work with a partner to identify the elements of an argument in your responses. Revise your pieces to incorporate them.

Examining Ads and Reviewing Appeals

Part 1: Look over the advertisements provided by your teacher, and respond to the following questions:

1. What are some of the first things that you notice? Do you see anything funny, clever, creative?

2. Where is your eye drawn first?

3. Would you buy this product based on this ad? Why or why not?

Part 2: Examine one specific advertisement closely, and answer the following questions:

1. Read the ad's *slogan* carefully. Does it relate to the product at all or is it promoting a lifestyle that can come from this product?

2. Find the *product* itself in the advertisement. Is it there at all? How prominently is it featured? Is the product actually being used?

3. Read the *copy* (the text) of the ad. What is it discussing? Is it relevant to the product? Pay attention to the diction. What do you notice?

Examining Ads and Reviewing Appeals

GRAMMAR & USAGE

In examining the ads, note the ways the writers have used language to influence consumer response (**fragments, repetition, rhetorical questions**, for example).

4. Locate the corporate *logo*, slogan, or other designation that lets you know what company sells this product. How prominently is it featured? Why?

5. Try to determine the *plot* of the scene depicted in the ad. Who are the characters, what are they doing, and what is probably going to happen next?

ACADEMIC VOCABULARY

Advertising techniques are the words and images an advertiser uses to hook a reader, viewer, or listener and persuade that person to buy the product or service.

6. Identify the *audience* for this ad. How do you know this?

7. What is the *representation* of males, females, and/or cultural or age groups? What evidence leads you to this conclusion?

8. Look at the ad's *layout* and design. Is the placement of lines, actor's gestures, colors, or other attributes meant to force your eye to look at certain parts of the ad? Why?

9. Are claims made in the ad fact or opinion? Are the claims substantiated or unsubstantiated?

Writing Prompt: Write a paragraph identifying the target audience, the appeals the ad uses to reach this audience, and whether you think the ad was effective in persuading the audience of its message.

Part 3: Advertisers use many techniques to try to get you to purchase their products. Review the descriptions of various **advertising techniques** below: In the spaces after each technique, name an ad you have seen recently that might use that technique.

Bandwagon: Advertisers make it seem as if everyone is buying this product, so you better buy it too: "*The best car of the year is here…. All your friends and neighbors are driving one….*" This technique makes you feel left out if you are not buying the product.

Avant-garde: This technique is almost the reverse of bandwagon: It makes the product seem so new and so cool that you will be the first on the block to have it. Only super-cool people like you will even know about this product.

Testimonials: Advertisers use celebrities or just regular people to endorse the product. Pay close attention; sometimes the celebrity doesn't even actually say that he or she uses the product.

Facts and Figures: Statistics, percentages, and numbers are used to convince you that this product is better or more effective than another product. Be aware of what the numbers are actually saying. What does "30 percent more effective than the leading brand" really mean?

Transfer: This is a rather complicated technique for persuasion. To recognize it, you really need to pay attention to the background of the ad or to the story of the commercial. This technique gets you to associate the good feelings shown in the ad with the product itself. Then the good feelings transfer to you when you buy the product. A commercial that shows a group of people having a lot of fun while drinking a certain brand of soft drink wants you to believe that you will be a part of fun groups if you buy that brand of soft drink too.

ACTIVITY 1.17
Examining Ads and Reviewing Appeals

With your group, create an ad using two or more advertising techniques. Then, as you look at your classmates' advertisements, jot down where you see some of the advertising techniques. Keep in mind that you might not see all of them, and you may see others that were not described on the previous page. List both substantiated and unsubstantiated claims.

Bandwagon	Avant-garde
Testimonials	**Facts and Figures**
Transfer	**Other Techniques**

Based only on your examination of the advertising techniques used, who do you suppose is the audience for one of the ads? How do you know this?

How would you expect the advertising techniques to change if the audience were to change? Explain.

Using Rhetoric and Persuading an Audience

SUGGESTED LEARNING STRATEGIES: Close Reading, Drafting, Graphic Organizer, Word Map

Rhetoric

Rhetoric is the use of words to persuade, either in writing or speech. Aristotle defined rhetoric as "the ability, in each particular case, to see the available means of persuasion." He described three main types of rhetoric: *pathos, ethos,* and *logos.* Authors and speakers use these rhetorical appeals in their arguments based on their intended audience as well as on the nature of the argument itself. You might have used these appeals in persuasive writing pieces you created. Advertisers, too, make use of these appeals in their attempts to persuade an audience.

Pathos

Pathos, or emotional appeals, attempt to persuade the reader or listener by appealing to the senses and emotions. Political ads that show politicians kissing babies or shaking hands with the elderly often appeal to the emotions. Also, these appeals usually include statements with vivid sensory details, which awaken the senses and perhaps manipulate the emotions of the audience.

Ethos

Ethos are ethical appeals that attempt to persuade the reader or listener by focusing on the qualifications or the character of the speaker. The speaker's credibility is paramount in an ethical appeal. Ethical appeals focus on the speaker even more than on the situation. Examples of ethical appeals in advertising are expert or celebrity endorsements of products. Other examples of ethical appeals are a teen's argument that he or she should be allowed to do something because he or she has never been in trouble, or because his or her friend is a perfect citizen, and so on.

Logos

Logos, or logical appeals, attempt to persuade readers or listeners by leading them down the road of logic and causing them to come to their own conclusions. Logical appeals state the facts and show how the facts are interrelated. *If/then* statements are examples of logical appeals. Sometimes, the *if/then* can be inferred; for example, if a book jacket indicates the book spent 26 weeks at the top of a bestseller list, a potential reader might infer that since many people read the book it must be a book worth buying. Logical appeals are often used in courtroom situations as well.

ACADEMIC VOCABULARY

Rhetorical appeals are emotional, ethical, and logical appeals used to try to persuade an audience to agree with the writer or speaker.

WORD CONNECTIONS

The word *pathos* includes the Greek root *-path-*, which comes from the Greek word meaning "suffering." This root also occurs these English words: *pathetic, sympathy, apathy, empathy, pathology,* and *telepathy.*

LITERARY TERMS

Pathos is a rhetorical appeal to the reader's or listener's senses or emotions.

Ethos is a rhetorical appeal that focuses on the character or qualifications of the speaker.

Logos is a rhetorical appeal to reason or logic.

Using Rhetoric and Persuading an Audience

As you look back at the sample ads, list examples you find of each of the rhetorical appeals listed.

Ethos

Pathos

Logos

One of the most important elements of an advertisement is its need to reach its target audience; if it does not, it has failed. The goal of a media-literate person is to be able to identify that intended audience.

Audience Profile: Look closely at an advertisement. Answer the following questions to determine the audience for the ad.

1. What is the product that is being advertised? _____

2. In general, this product is mainly used by male / female / either.

3. The average age of people who use this product is probably _____

4. The apparent age of the people in the ad (if they are present) is _____

5. The gender of those in the ad (if they are present) is male / female / both.

6. Identify the setting of this ad (outdoors, office, classroom, etc.).

   _____

7. Briefly describe the action in the ad.

   _____

8. Describe people you know who do the actions you identified.

   _____

9. Read the written part of the ad. Rate the diction as easy / medium / difficult / complex.

10. What is the racial or cultural group shown in this ad? _____

Write a statement about the audience for this advertisement. Analyze the relevance, quality, and credibility of the persuasive rhetoric for this audience.

Imagine that this ad was created for a different audience. Describe the new audience. What would be different about this ad? What would remain the same? Why?

Using Rhetoric and Persuading an Audience

Continue your close examination of a sample ad. Consider how effectively it uses advertising techniques and rhetorical appeals to reach the target audience you identify. Take notes on the organizer. Then write a paragraph in which you analyze the effectiveness of the advertisement. Include a thesis statement that states the product name and the techniques or appeals the advertiser uses to influence the audience. Support your thesis statement with specific examples from the ad. Be sure to mention the target audience and your analysis of the overall effectiveness of the advertisement.

Product: _____

Use of Advertising Appeals	Use of Rhetoric
Target Audience	**Effectiveness**

Sampling Ads and Planning a Campaign

SUGGESTED LEARNING STRATEGIES: **Brainstorming**

An advertising campaign involves more than a single type of ad. Think about the qualities, strengths, and weaknesses of each the following types of ads. Jot down a few notes about those qualities, and describe the most likely audience for each type of ad.

PRINT ADVERTISEMENTS

- **Magazine ads:**

- **Newspaper ads:**

- **Posters:**

- **Billboards:**

- **Book Displays:**

- **Book Jackets:**

COMMERCIALS

- **Television commercials:**

- **Film or video trailer:**

- **Radio commercials:**

Sampling Ads and Planning a Campaign

INTERVIEWS

- **Television interviews:**

- **Radio interviews:**

- **Podcasts:**

Begin brainstorming how you might persuade your classmates to read the book you read independently. If you want teens to read it, where would you place your ad? On a website? In a podcast? What is it about your book that would appeal to other people and cause them to agree to read it?

Think about what elements of your book you could advertise, who might be interested in reading it, what media channel would be most effective to reach those potential readers, and how you might incorporate advertising techniques and rhetorical appeals. For example, you might market your book to student athletes by creating a poster that would appear in a locker room, and you might also market your book to teachers by creating a book display for the media center or teacher's lounge.

You do not need to make final decisions at this time. Rather, begin jotting down ideas on your own so that you and your group will have a starting point when you begin the Embedded Assessment. Use the Brainstorming chart on the next page.

Brainstorming Chart

Features of the book to include in an ad campaign:	
Interests of target audience:	
Effective channels to reach this audience:	
Advertising techniques to incorporate:	
Rhetorical appeals to incorporate:	
Imagery to include:	
Overall diction appropriate for the audience:	

Creating an Ad Campaign for a Novel

SUGGESTED LEARNING STRATEGIES: **Drafting, Sharing and Responding, Discussion Groups**

Assignment

Your assignment is to work with a group to create an advertising campaign for your independent reading novel. Your campaign must include two of the three media genres (a dramatized commercial, an interview with an author, a print advertisement) that you have examined in this unit. Your target audience is your classmates. As support for your advertising campaign, write an argument using the five elements of argumentation that you are using to persuade your classmates to read the book. Your project will also include a written analysis of the persuasive techniques and advertising claims that you use and how they appeal to your target audience.

Steps

Prewriting

1. Meet with the group who will be working on the project together. Review the questions in Activity 1.18 to develop a profile of your target audience.

2. Brainstorm a list of features of your book that would appeal to this target audience, such as themes, relevance to their own lives, good dialogue, interesting characters, timely subject matter, etc.

3. Review your work from Activities 1.16–1.19. Decide on two of the three products you have worked on in this unit (dramatization of a commercial, interview with an author, or printed advertisement), which you think would most appeal to your audience.

Drafting

4. Create rough drafts of your advertisements and your persuasive text. Be sure to incorporate a variety of advertising techniques and rhetorical appeals in your ads as well as the five elements of argumentation. Decide how to share the responsibilities of ad creation among the members of your group. One group member might work on the ad design, another member might write the script for the commercial, etc.

Revising

5. With your group, meet with another group in your class and compare your ads. Try to identify the audiences and appeals the other group is using, and provide feedback on how effective their ads are at this point. Consider the following three questions from the peer evaluation form your classmates will use to evaluate your formal presentation:

   - What information have the writers included about the book that appeals to me as a prospective reader?

   - What advertising techniques have they used to motivate me to buy the book?

   - How have they used rhetorical appeals to persuade me to read the book?

6. Listen as the other group provides similar feedback for your group. Try to incorporate their comments and suggestions as well as any other ideas that come from your group. Examine your ads closely to see how effectively you are incorporating advertising elements to persuade others to read your book. Consult the Scoring Guide to guide your revision.

Editing for Publication

Complete your final versions of your ads. Check to be sure the appearance, design, text, and language conventions are appropriate for your finished product. Make changes as needed. If it is a performance ad, allow rehearsal time.

Presentation

7. Present your finished ads either to small groups or to the whole class, depending on your teacher's directions.

Reflective Analysis

8. Write an essay evaluating your advertising campaign. Include the features of the book you are marketing, the persuasive techniques and rhetorical devices that you use, and quotes from your peer evaluators supporting your assessment of your presentation's effectiveness.

↗**TECHNOLOGY TIP** Consider using a graphics program or slide presentation software to create and present your advertising campaign. You may want to incorporate photos of the book you are marketing, as well as interesting graphic elements that support your campaign.

Peer Evaluation Feedback Form

Presenters' names:

Book being sold:

What information has the group included about the book that appeals to me as a prospective reader?

What advertising techniques have they used to motivate me to buy the book?

How have they used rhetorical appeals to persuade me to read the book?

SCORING GUIDE

Scoring Criteria	Exemplary	Proficient	Emerging
Advertising Campaign	The campaign thoughtfully devises multiple ads that are marked with a clear and consistent purpose to appeal to at least two different audiences.	The campaign ads are crafted with a clear purpose and an attempt to target at least two different audiences.	The purpose and focus of the campaign ads are not always clear. The ads do not capture their intended audience or there is no variety of audience.
Advertising Elements	The campaign shows a skillful use of advertising appeals and rhetorical appeals that work together effectively to entice the audience to read the book.	The campaign shows use of advertising appeals and rhetorical appeals that persuade the audience to read the book.	The campaign does not show the use the advertising appeals and rhetorical appeals. The campaign fails to persuade the audience.
Reflective Text	The reflection insightfully analyzes the features of the book, the persuasive techniques used to reach the intended audiences, and the overall strengths and weaknesses of the campaign.	The reflection analyzes the features of the book, the persuasive techniques used to reach the intended audiences, and some strengths and weaknesses of the campaign.	The reflection includes minimal analysis of the features of the book and persuasive techniques used. It may not identify the intended audiences or address the campaign's strengths or weaknesses.
Conventions	The campaign presents polished ads. Either no errors appear, or they are so slight that they do not interfere with the meaning.	The campaign ads demonstrate control of standard writing conventions. Though some errors may appear, they do not seriously impede readability.	The campaign ads contain frequent errors in standard writing conventions that seriously interfere with the meaning of the texts.
Evidence of Collaboration	The project demonstrates extensive evidence of successful planning and collaboration.	The project shows evidence of adequate planning and collaboration.	Inadequate planning and collaboration are evident.
Additional Criteria			

Reflection

An important aspect of growing as a learner is to reflect on where you have been, what you have accomplished, what helped you to learn, and how you will apply your new knowledge in the future. Use the following questions to guide your thinking and to identify evidence of your learning. Use separate notebook paper.

Thinking about Concepts

1. Using specific examples from this unit, respond to the Essential Questions:

   - What does it mean to "come of age"?

   - How are rhetorical appeals used to influence an audience?

2. Consider the new academic vocabulary from this unit (**Voice, Advertising Techniques, Rhetorical Appeals**), and select 2-3 terms of which your understanding has grown. For each term, answer the following questions:

   - What was your understanding of the term before you completed this unit?

   - How has your understanding of the term evolved throughout the unit?

   - How will you apply your understanding in the future?

Thinking about Connections

3. Review the activities and products (artifacts) you created. Choose those that most reflect your growth or increase in understanding.

4. For each artifact that you choose, record, respond to, and reflect on your thinking and understanding, using the following questions as a guide:

   a. What skill/knowledge does this artifact reflect, and how did you learn this skill/knowledge?

   b. How did your understanding of the power of language expand through your engagement with this artifact?

   c. How will you apply this skill or knowledge in the future?

5. Create this reflection as Portfolio pages—one for each artifact you choose. Use the model in the box for your headings and commentary on questions.

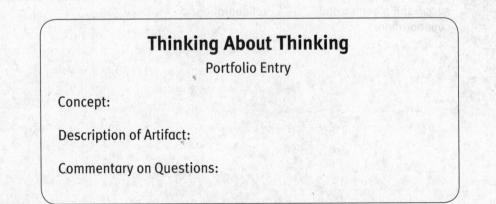

Thinking About Thinking

Portfolio Entry

Concept:

Description of Artifact:

Commentary on Questions:

Defining
Style

Essential Questions

 How do authors and directors use specific techniques to achieve a desired effect?

 What are the essential features of an effective style analysis?

Unit Overview

Through the ages, stories have been passed from generation to generation. Then, sometime between 1830 and 1835, Edgar Allan Poe began to write structured stories for various magazines. His structure provided a format that characterizes the genre today. Poe felt that a story should be short enough to be read in one sitting and that it should contain a single line of action with a limited number of characters, building to a climactic moment and then quickly reaching resolution. Poe's influence can also be felt in modern cinema through the unique style of film director Tim Burton. This unit will uncover the connection between Poe and Burton along with the commonalities between written texts and visual texts. This unit also introduces the ways that directors of visual media affect or manipulate the audience's reactions. By studying film, you will come to see film as a separate and unique genre, worthy of serious study along with drama, poetry, fiction, and prose.

Contents

Goals

▶ To identify important cinematic techniques and analyze their effects

▶ To transform a text into a new genre

▶ To identify specific elements of an author's style

▶ To develop an awareness of reading strategies to enhance comprehension

▶ To analyze the elements of fiction–setting, plot, character, theme–and the steps in plot development–exposition, complications, climax, falling action, resolution (denouement)

ACADEMIC VOCABULARY

Point of View

Commentary

Cinematic Techniques

Style

Effect

Texts not included in these materials.

Learning Focus:

Making the Text Come to Life

Have you ever watched a movie and concluded that it wasn't as good as the book? Conversely, have you ever read a book and assumed the role of a director by creating visual images of the story in your head? This unit is your opportunity to see both sides of the book/movie coin. Now that you have explored the thematic concept "coming of age," it is time to continue your investigation of that theme in two different, but complementary, genres: short story and film.

You will begin this unit by exploring essential elements of a short story. However, you will do more than just identify important plot points and narrative structure; you will develop your understanding of how authors present themes, ideas, and images through literary and stylistic elements. Some of the elements you will analyze are point of view, imagery, motif, foreshadowing, and irony.

The exciting part, however, is that you will transform these elements of written text into something visual. Cinematic techniques such as framing, movement, lighting, and sound will be the tools at your disposal to create a storyboard. You will make your directorial debut by creating a storyboard for one of the stories you have read. The goal for your storyboard is to appeal to your intended audience, and to create the effect you want.

Independent Reading: In this unit, you will read short stories and film that are examples of Gothic Literature. For independent reading, look for books or short stories that contain elements of mystery or fantasy.

Previewing the Unit

SUGGESTED LEARNING STRATEGIES: Close Reading, KWL, Marking the Text, Skimming/Scanning, Summarizing/Paraphrasing, Think-Pair-Share

Essential Questions

1. How do authors and directors use specific techniques to achieve a desired effect?

2. What are the essential features of an effective style analysis?

Unit Overview and Learning Focus

Predict what you think this unit is about. Use the words or phrases that stood out to you when you read the Unit Overview and the Learning Focus.

Embedded Assessment 1

What knowledge must you have (what do you need to know) to succeed on Embedded Assessment 1? What skills must you have (what must you be able to do)?

An Eye for an Eye

Read and interpret the following quotations. Do you agree or disagree
with them? Fill in the following chart. Then, complete the writing
assignment about revenge.

Revenge Quotations

Quotation	Interpretation of Quote	Agree/ Disagree	Reason for Agreement/ or Disagreement
"An eye for an eye only ends up making the whole world blind." — Mahatma Gandhi			
"Don't get mad, get even." — Robert F. Kennedy			
"She got even in a way that was almost cruel. She forgave them." — Ralph McGill (about Eleanor Roosevelt)			
"Success is the sweetest revenge." — Vanessa Williams			
"Revenge is often like biting a dog because the dog bit you." — Austin O'Malley			

Reflect: To which of these quotes might you want to respond? Why? Which quotes have striking *imagery*, and how does that imagery affect your response?

Writing Prompt: Draft a response in which you express your feelings about revenge. Include a personal reflection about a time when you had a choice about taking revenge or when you were the recipient of someone's vengeful attitude or action. Consider using one of the quotations in your essay, crediting the author of the quote.

Poetry

> **ABOUT THE AUTHOR**
> William Blake (1757–1827) was an artist as well as a poet. Born in London, he was apprenticed to an engraver when he was young. Blake claimed to have mystical visions, which he expressed in his poems and engravings. He engraved both the texts and illustrations for his poems. "A Poison Tree" is from his collection called *Songs of Experience*, which reflect his complex view of a world that includes good and evil, innocence and experience.

A Poison Tree

by William Blake

I was angry with my friend:
I told my wrath, my wrath[1] did end.
I was angry with my foe:
I told it not, my wrath did grow.

5   And I watered it in fears,
Night and morning with my tears;
And I sunned it with smiles,
And with soft deceitful wiles.[2]

And it grew both day and night,
10 Till it bore an apple bright.
And my foe beheld it shine.
And he knew that it was mine,

And into my garden stole
When the night had veiled the pole;
15 In the morning glad I see
My foe outstretched beneath the tree.

---

[1] **wrath**: Fierce anger; vengeance caused by anger
[2] **wiles**: tricky or clever behavior

Strategies Learning Log

Name of strategy:

Purpose of strategy:

How strategy was used:

How strategy helped you make meaning from the text, create a text, or orally present a text:

When you would use this strategy again:

Strategies Learning Log

Name of strategy:

Purpose of strategy:

How strategy was used:

How strategy helped you make meaning from the text, create a text, or orally present a text:

When you would use this strategy again:

Catacombs and Carnival

The words below are from the story "The Cask of Amontillado." To familiarize yourself with the vocabulary in the story, divide the words below into four categories. Be sure to give each category a heading.

Amontillado	cask	vaults
connoisseurship	nitre	vintages
crypt	pipe	palazzo
parti-striped dress	De Grave	puncheons
catacombs	motley	roquelaire
conical cap	Medoc	

Word Category Chart

Catacombs and Carnival

Centuries ago, in Italy, the early Christians buried their dead in *catacombs*, which are long, winding underground tunnels. Later, wealthy families built private catacombs beneath their *palazzos*, or palatial homes. These dark and cool chambers, or *vaults*, contained *nitre*, a crystalized salt growth. In order to find their way in their underground tunnels, the owners would light torches or *flambeaux*.

These *crypts* were suitable not only for burial but also for storage of fine *vintage* wines such as *Amontillado, DeGrave,* and *Medoc*. A wine expert, or *connoisseur*, would store wine carefully in these underground vaults. Wine was stored in casks or *puncheons*, which held 72 to 100 gallons, or in *pipes*, which contained 126 gallons (also known as two hogsheads).

Poe's story takes place in the catacombs during Carnival, a celebration that still takes place in many countries. The day before Ash Wednesday is celebrated as a holiday with carnivals, masquerade balls, and parades of costumed merrymakers. During Carnival, people celebrate by disguising themselves as fools, wearing *parti-striped dress* or *motley*, and capes, known as *roquelaires*. Women would celebrate wearing *conical caps*. Carnival is also called Mardi Gras, or Fat Tuesday, because of the feasting that takes place the day before Ash Wednesday. Starting on Ash Wednesday, which is the beginning of Lent, some Christians fast and do penance for their sins.

Word Study: After reading the first paragraph with your teacher, continue using the diffusing strategy by noting unfamiliar words in the space below. Then use context clues, dictionaries, and thesauruses to write definitions.

> ### WORD CONNECTIONS
>
> *Mardi Gras* is a French term meaning "fat Tuesday." Mardi Gras is celebrated in many countries, including the United States, and it is a day of fun and eating before fasting for Lent.

Opening the Cask

My Notes

Short Story

ABOUT THE AUTHOR

Born in Boston, Edgar Allan Poe (1809–1849) was orphaned as a young child and taken in by the Allan family of Richmond Virginia. Poe and the Allans eventually had a falling out because of Poe's irresponsible behavior. This situation was characteristic of Poe's short and tragic life. Despite his personal difficulties and an unstable temperament, Poe was a literary genius, writing short stories, poetry, and literary criticism, for which he became internationally famous. His dark imagination produced stories that are known for their atmosphere of horror.

The CASK *of* AMONTILLADO

by Edgar Allan Poe

The thousand injuries of Fortunato, I had borne as I best could, but when he ventured upon insult, I vowed revenge. You, who so well know the nature of my soul, will not suppose, however, that I gave utterance to a threat. At *length* I would be avenged; this was a point definitively settled—but the very definitiveness with which it was resolved precluded the idea of risk. I must not only punish, but punish with impunity. A wrong is unredressed when retribution overtakes its redresser. It is equally unredressed when the avenger fails to make himself felt as such to him who has done the wrong.

It must be understood that neither by word nor deed had I given Fortunato cause to doubt my good will. I continued as was my wont, to smile in his face, and he did not perceive that my smile *now* was at the thought of his immolation.

WORD CONNECTIONS

The word *impunity* has a Latin root (from *poena*) that means "penalty" or "punishment."

The prefix *in-* (spelled *im-* here) means "not."

To do something *with impunity* is to do it without fear of punishment or consequences.

He had a weak point—this Fortunato—although in other regards he was a man to be respected and even feared. He prided himself on his connoisseurship in wine. Few Italians have the true virtuoso spirit. For the most part their enthusiasm is adopted to suit the time and opportunity to practice imposture upon the British and Austrian millionaires. In painting and gemmary, Fortunato, like his countrymen, was a quack, but in the matter of old wines he was sincere. In this respect I did not differ from him materially; I was skillful in the Italian vintages myself, and bought largely whenever I could.

It was about dusk, one evening during the supreme madness of the carnival season, that I encountered my friend. He accosted me with excessive warmth, for he had been drinking much. The man wore motley. He had on a tight-fitting parti-striped dress and his head was surmounted by the conical cap and bells. I was so pleased to see him that I thought I should never have done wringing his hand.

Chunk 1

I said to him, "My dear Fortunato, you are luckily met. How remarkably well you are looking to-day! But I have received a pipe of what passes for Amontillado, and I have my doubts."

"How?" said he, "Amontillado? A pipe? Impossible!And in the middle of the carnival?"

"I have my doubts," I replied; "and I was silly enough to pay the full Amontillado price without consulting you in the matter. You were not to be found, and I was fearful of losing a bargain."

"Amontillado!"

"I have my doubts."

"Amontillado!"

"And I must satisfy them."

"Amontillado!"

"As you are engaged, I am on my way to Luchesi. If any one has a critical turn, it is he. He will tell me — "

"Luchesi cannot tell Amontillado from sherry."

"And yet some fools will have it that his taste is a match for your own."

"Come, let us go."

"Whither?"

"To your vaults."

My Notes

WORD CONNECTIONS

The word *match* has multiple meanings. Among its meanings are a sports competition, a device to light a fire, and compatibility or similarity. Use context clues to decide its meaning in this sentence: "And yet some fools will have it that his taste is a match for your own."

My Notes

"My friend, no; I will not impose upon your good nature. I perceive you have an engagement. Luchesi — "

"I have no engagement; come."

"My friend, no. It is not the engagement, but the severe cold with which I perceive you are afflicted. The vaults are insufferably damp. They are encrusted with nitre."

"Let us go, nevertheless. The cold is merely nothing. Amontillado! You have been imposed upon; and as for Luchesi, he cannot distinguish sherry from Amontillado."

Thus speaking, Fortunato possessed himself of my arm. Putting on a mask of black silk and drawing a *roquelaire* closely about my person, I suffered him to hurry me to my palazzo.

Chunk 2

There were no attendants at home; they had absconded to make merry in honour of the time. I had told them that I should not return until the morning and had given them explicit orders not to stir from the house. These orders were sufficient, I well knew, to insure their immediate disappearance, one and all, as soon as my back was turned.

I took from their sconces two flambeaux, and giving one to Fortunato, bowed him through several suites of rooms to the archway that led into the vaults. I passed down a long and winding staircase, requesting him to be cautious as he followed. We came at length to the foot of the descent, and stood together on the damp ground of the catacombs of the Montresors.

The gait of my friend was unsteady, and the bells upon his cap jingled as he strode.

"The pipe," said he.

"It is farther on," said I; "but observe the white webwork which gleams from these cavern walls."

He turned towards me and looked into my eyes with two filmy orbs that distilled the rheum of intoxication.

"Nitre?" he asked, at length.

"Nitre," I replied. "How long have you had that cough?"

"Ugh! ugh! ugh! — ugh! ugh! ugh! — ugh! ugh! ugh! — ugh! ugh! ugh!"

My poor friend found it impossible to reply for many minutes.

"It is nothing," he said, at last.

"Come," I said, with decision, "we will go back; your health is precious. You are rich, respected, admired, beloved; you are happy as once I was. You are a man to be missed. For me it is no matter. We will go back; you will be ill, and I cannot be responsible. Besides, there is Luchesi — "

"Enough," he said; "the cough is a mere nothing; it will not kill me. I shall not die of a cough."

"True — true," I replied; "and, indeed, I had no intention of alarming you unnecessarily—but you should use all proper caution. A draught of this Medoc will defend us from the damps." Here I knocked off the neck of a bottle which I drew from a long row of its fellows that lay upon the mould.

"Drink," I said, presenting him the wine.

He raised it to his lips with a leer. He paused and nodded to me familiarly, while his bells jingled.

"I drink," he said, "to the buried that repose around us."

"And I to your long life."

He again took my arm and we proceeded.

"These vaults," he said, "are extensive."

"The Montresors," I replied, "were a great and numerous family."

"I forget your arms."

"A huge human foot d'or, in a field azure; the foot crushes a serpent rampant whose fangs are imbedded in the heel."

"And the motto?"

"Nemo me impune lacessit."[1]

"Good!" he said.

The wine sparkled in his eyes and the bells jingled. My own fancy grew warm with the Medoc. We had passed through walls of piled bones, with casks and puncheons intermingling, into the inmost recesses of the catacombs. I paused again, and this time I made bold to seize Fortunato by an arm above the elbow.

Chunk
3

---

[1] *Nemo me impune lacessit:* No one attacks me with impunity.

My Notes

Opening the Cask

My Notes

"The nitre!" I said: "see, it increases. It hangs like moss upon the vaults. We are below the river's bed. The drops of moisture trickle among the bones. Come, we will go back ere it is too late. Your cough—"

"It is nothing," he said; "let us go on. But first, another draught of the Medoc."

I broke and reached him a flagon of De Grave. He emptied it at a breath. His eyes flashed with a fierce light. He laughed and threw the bottle upwards with a gesticulation I did not understand.

I looked at him in surprise. He repeated the movement—a grotesque one.

"You do not comprehend?" he said.

"Not I," I replied.

"Then you are not of the brotherhood."

"How?"

"You are not of the masons."

"Yes, yes," I said, "yes! Yes."

"You? Impossible! A mason?"

"A mason," I replied.

"A sign," he said.

"It is this," I answered, producing from beneath the folds of my *roquelaire* a trowel.

"You jest," he exclaimed, recoiling a few paces. "But let us proceed to the Amontillado."

"Be it so," I said, replacing the tool beneath the cloak, and again offering him my arm. He leaned upon it heavily. We continued our route in search of the Amontillado. We passed through a range of low arches, descended, passed on, and descending again, arrived at a deep crypt, in which the foulness of the air caused our flambeaux rather to glow than flame.

WORD CONNECTIONS

Crypt derives from a Greek word, *krypte*, which means "hidden" or "secret." This root is also found in the English words *cryptic* and *cryptogram*.

At the most remote end of the crypt there appeared another less spacious. Its walls had been lined with human remains piled to the vault overhead, in the fashion of the great catacombs of Paris. Three sides of this interior crypt were still ornamented in this manner. From the fourth the bones had been thrown down, and lay promiscuously upon the earth, forming at one point a mound of some size. Within the wall thus exposed by the displacing of the bones, we perceived a still interior recess, in depth about four feet, in width three, in height six or seven. It seemed to have been constructed for no special use in itself, but formed merely the interval between two of the colossal supports of the roof of the catacombs, and was backed by one of their circumscribing walls of solid granite.

Chunk 4

It was in vain that Fortunato, uplifting his dull torch, endeavoured to pry into the depths of the recess. Its termination the feeble light did not enable us to see.

"Proceed," I said; "herein is the Amontillado. As for Luchesi –"

"He is an ignoramus," interrupted my friend, as he stepped unsteadily forward, while I followed immediately at his heels. In an instant he had reached the extremity of the niche, and finding his progress arrested by the rock, stood stupidly bewildered. A moment more and I had fettered him to the granite. In its surface were two iron staples, distant from each other about two feet, horizontally. From one of these depended a short chain, from the other a padlock. Throwing the links about his waist, it was but the work of a few seconds to secure it. He was too much astounded to resist. Withdrawing the key I stepped back from the recess.

"Pass your hand," I said, "over the wall; you cannot help feeling the nitre. Indeed it is *very* damp. Once more let me *implore* you to return. No? Then I must positively leave you. But I must first render you all the little attentions in my power."

"The Amontillado!" ejaculated my friend, not yet recovered from his astonishment.

"True," I replied; "the Amontillado."

As I said these words I busied myself among the pile of bones of which I have before spoken. Throwing them aside, I soon uncovered a quantity of building stone and mortar. With these materials and with the aid of my trowel, I began vigorously to wall up the entrance of the niche.

Chunk 5

I had scarcely laid the first tier of my masonry when I discovered that the intoxication of Fortunato had in a great measure worn off. The earliest indication I had of this was a low moaning cry from the depth of the recess. It was *not* the cry of a drunken man. There was then a long and obstinate silence. I laid the second tier, and the third, and the fourth; and then I heard the furious vibrations of the chain. The noise

After reading the fourth chunk of the story, predict what Montresor intends to do. Support your prediction with clues from the story.

GRAMMAR & USAGE

A **verbal** is a form of a verb that is used as some other part of speech—a noun, an adjective, or an adverb.

A **participle** is a verbal that functions as an adjective.

> Example: **Throwing** them aside, I soon uncovered a quantity of stone and mortar. [*throwing* modifies *I*]

A **gerund** is a verbal that ends in *-ing* and functions as a noun.

> Example: When at last the **clanking** subsided, I resumed....

An **infinitive** is a verb form that can be used as a noun, an adjective, or an adverb. The word *to* usually appears in front of the verb form.

> Example: Unsheathing my rapier, I began **to grope** with it about the recess.

My Notes

After reading the sixth chunk of the story, I think my prediction was____ (correct or incorrect).

Now I think...

lasted for several minutes, during which, that I might hearken to it with the more satisfaction, I ceased my labours and sat down upon the bones. When at last the clanking subsided, I resumed the trowel, and finished without interruption the fifth, the sixth, and the seventh tier. The wall was now nearly upon a level with my breast. I again paused, and holding the flambeaux over the masonwork, threw a few feeble rays upon the figure within.

A succession of loud and shrill screams, bursting suddenly from the throat of the chained form, seemed to thrust me violently back. For a brief moment I hesitated—I trembled. Unsheathing my rapier, I began to grope with it about the recess; but the thought of an instant reassured me. I placed my hand upon the solid fabric of the catacombs, and felt satisfaction. I reapproached the wall; I replied to the yells of him who clamored. I reechoed—I aided—I surpassed them in volume and in strength. I did this, and the clamorer grew still.

Chunk 6

It was now midnight, and my task was drawing to a close. I had completed the eighth, the ninth, and the tenth tier. I had finished a portion of the last and the eleventh; there remained but a single stone to be fitted and plastered in. I struggled with its weight; I placed it partially in its destined position. But now there came from out the niche a low laugh that erected the hairs upon my head. It was succeeded by a sad voice, which I had difficulty in recognizing as that of the noble Fortunato. The voice said —

"Ha! ha! ha!—he! he!—a very good joke indeed—an excellent jest. We will have many a rich laugh about it at the palazzo— he! he! he!—over our wine—he! he! he!"

"The Amontillado!" I said.

"He! he! he!—he! he! he!— yes, the Amontillado. But is it not getting late? Will not they be awaiting us at the palazzo, the Lady Fortunato and the rest? Let us be gone."

"Yes," I said, "let us be gone."

"For the love of God, Montresor!"

"Yes," I said, "for the love of God!"

But to these words I hearkened in vain for a reply. I grew impatient. I called aloud—

"Fortunato!"

No answer. I called again—

"Fortunato!"

No answer still. I thrust a torch through the remaining aperture and let it fall within. There came forth in return only a jingling of the bells. My heart grew sick—on account of the dampness of the catacombs. I hastened to make an end of my labor. I forced the last stone into its position; I plastered it up. Against the new masonry I reerected the old rampart of bones. For the half of a century no mortal has disturbed them.

In pace requiescat![2]

[2] *In pace requiescat:* Rest in peace.

Opening the Cask

As you read "The Cask of Amontillado," list characteristics you discover or infer about Montresor and Fortunato. Stop after the third chunk of the text to list details you discover about the two characters. As you learn more about the two characters, add your information to the chart.

Montresor	Fortunato

Writing Prompt: "The Cask of Amontillado" begins with this sentence: "The thousand injuries of Fortunato, I had borne as I best could, but when he ventured upon insult, I vowed revenge." Using what you know about the two characters, write a creative story about one of these "injuries." Your story should include a well-developed conflict and resolution as well as dialogue and suspense to enhance the plot.

"The Cask of Amontillado" Story Diagram

SUGGESTED LEARNING STRATEGIES: Graphic Organizer, Marking the Text, Rereading, Skimming/Scanning

With a partner or in your small group, review these elements of the short story. Then, complete the story diagram, filling in the corresponding events from "The Cask of Amontillado."

1. **Setting** — Time and place in which the story happens.

2. **Exposition** — How the stage is set for the story. Characters are introduced, the setting is described, and the conflict begins to unfold.

3. **Complications** — Events that make the plot become more complex. While the characters struggle to find solutions to the conflict, suspense builds (also called rising action).

4. **Climax** — The point of greatest interest or suspense in a story. The climax is the turning point because the action reaches its peak and the outcome of the conflict is decided.

5. **Falling action** — The events between the climax and the resolution.

6. **Resolution/denouement** — The end of the story when loose ends are tied up.

7. **Characters** — People, animals, or imaginary creatures that take part in the action of the story. The short story usually centers on a **Main Character**. Also present are usually one or more **Minor Characters** who are not as complex, but whose thoughts, words, or actions move the story along.

8. **Theme** — The writer's main message about life. Theme is usually not stated directly and is left to the reader to figure out.

9. **Conflict(s)** —The struggle(s) or problem(s) in a story.

10. **Literary Elements Present**
    - **Point of view** — The perspective from which a narrative is told
    - **Verbal Irony** — When a speaker or narrator says one thing while meaning the opposite
    - **Foreshadowing** — The use of hints or clues in a narrative to suggest future action
    - **Motif** — A unifying element in an artistic work, especially any recurrent image, symbol, theme, character type, subject, or narrative detail

> **WORD CONNECTIONS**
>
> *Denouement* is a French term meaning "an untying" as in untying a plot.

"The Cask of Amontillado" Story Diagram

Short Story Diagram

Climax

Complications

Falling Action

Conflict

Exposition

Resolution/Denouement

Setting

Characters (Consider cause and effect. How do characters react to the situation? What causes those reactions?)

Theme

Other Literary Elements Present:

Irony in "The Cask of Amontillado"

You reviewed a definition of **irony** in the previous activity. One type of irony, *verbal* irony, occurs when a speaker or narrator says one thing while meaning the opposite.

For example, when Fortunato proposes a toast to the dead buried in the crypts around them, Montresor adds, "And I to your long life." Montresor is using verbal irony here, as he intends to end Fortunato's life very soon.

Provide some examples of your own:

Your example:

Your example:

WORD CONNECTIONS

The word **irony** has the Greek root *eiron*, referring to someone who, in speaking, conceals true thoughts or feelings.

Verbal Irony in "The Cask of Amontillado"

What is stated...	What it means...

Visualizing the Ending of "The Cask of Amontillado"

With your group, you will create a drawing to represent the ending of "The Cask of Amontillado." Reread the text and make notes on the elements that appeal to the senses in the passage, specifically the visual images.

Consider the following:

- What characters are present in the scene?

- What does this place look like?

- What type of clothing is mentioned in the text?

What visual elements in the text should be in your drawing, for example, a trowel, flambeaux, and so on?

With your group, fill out the following organizer. As your Reader reads the text aloud, the Writer will take notes on things to consider including in your drawing. Your group's Artist will decide how to set up the drawing in the most effective way.

After you complete your drawing, discuss the choices you made for the content of your drawing. Your Reader should record your answers to the reflection questions before you present your drawing to the class.

Writer — What We Could Include from the Text	Artist — How We Could Represent These Items in Our Picture

Reflection

1. Which details from the text did you choose to include in your drawing?

2. Which details from the text did you choose not to include? Why did you make this decision?

3. Why did you choose to set up your drawing the way you did?

Peer Interviews

SUGGESTED LEARNING STRATEGIES: Think-Pair-Share

Interview

Using the following questions, conduct an informal interview of your assigned partner. First, read through the questions and familiarize yourself with them. Then, create a statement that defines the focus of your interview. Finally, you and your partner will take turns interviewing each other. Take careful notes, and be prepared to share some of your partner's responses with the class.

The name of the person you are interviewing: _____

The focus of this interview is _____.

1. Describe a time when you were very excited about something but were disappointed about its outcome.

2. Describe an embarrassing event you either experienced or witnessed at a social event.

3. Describe a social event where you felt like an outsider.

Prediction: You will read a story entitled "The Stolen Party." Taking into consideration the prompts for your interview questions, predict what the story might be about.

My Notes

Short Story

> **ABOUT THE AUTHOR**
> Liliana Heker (b. 1943) is an Argentine journalist who also writes fiction. She has received a number of literary prizes in her country. In "The Stolen Party," Heker presents the events of a party through the eyes of a child.

The Stolen Party

by Liliana Heker

translated by Alberto Manguel

Mark and annotate the text so that you can discuss the conflict between mother and daughter.

Chunk 1

As soon as she arrived she went straight to the kitchen to see if the monkey was there. It was: what a relief! She wouldn't have liked to admit that her mother had been right. Monkeys at a birthday? her mother had sneered. Get away with you, believing any nonsense you're told! She was cross, but not because of the monkey, the girl thought; it's just because of the party.

"I don't like you going," she told her. "It's a rich people's party."

"Rich people go to Heaven too," said the girl, who studied religion at school.

"Get away with Heaven," said the mother.

The girl didn't approve of the way her mother spoke. She was barely nine, and one of the best in her class.

"I'm going because I've been invited," she said. "And I've been invited because Luciana[1] is my friend. So there."

"Ah yes, your friend," her mother grumbled. She paused. "Listen, Rosaura,"[2] she said at last. "That one's not your friend. You know what you are to them? The maid's daughter, that's what."

Rosaura blinked hard: she wasn't going to cry. Then she yelled: "Shut up! You know nothing about being friends!"

---

[1] **Luciana:** (Lū syə′nə)
[2] **Rosaura:** (Rō sah′rə)

Every afternoon she used to go to Luciana's house and they would both finish their homework while Rosaura's mother did the cleaning. They had their tea in the kitchen and they told each other secrets. Rosaura loved everything in the big house, and she also loved the people who lived there.

"I'm going because it will be the most lovely party in the whole world, Luciana told me it would. There will be a magician, and he will bring a monkey and everything."

The mother swung around to take a good look at her child, and pompously[3] put her hands on her hips.

Monkeys at a birthday? her mother had sneered. *Get away with you, believing any nonsense you're told!*

Rosaura was deeply offended. She thought it unfair of her mother to accuse other people of being liars simply because they were rich. Rosaura too wanted to be rich, of course. If one day she managed to live in a beautiful palace, would her mother stop loving her? She felt very sad. She wanted to go to that party more than anything else in the world.

"I'll die if I don't go," she whispered, almost without moving her lips.

And she wasn't sure whether she had been heard, but on the morning of the party she discovered that her mother had starched her Christmas dress. And in the afternoon, after washing her hair, her mother rinsed it in apple vinegar so that it would be all nice and shiny. Before going out, Rosaura admired herself in the mirror, with her white dress and glossy hair, and thought she looked terribly pretty.

Señora Ines[4] also seemed to notice. As soon as she saw her, she said:

"How lovely you look today, Rosaura."

Rosaura gave her starched skirt a light toss with her hands and walked into the party with a firm step. She said hello to Luciana and asked about the monkey. Luciana put on a secretive look and whispered into Rosaura's ear: "He's in the kitchen. But don't tell anyone, because it's a surprise."

Rosaura wanted to make sure. Carefully she entered the kitchen and there she saw it: deep in thought, inside its cage. It looked so funny that the girl stood there for a while, watching it, and later, every so often, she would slip out of the party unseen and go and admire it. Rosaura was the only one allowed into the kitchen. Señora Ines had said: "You yes, but not the others, they're much too boisterous, they might break something." Rosaura had never broken anything. She even managed the jug of orange juice, carrying it from the kitchen into the dining room. She held it carefully and didn't spill a single drop. And Señora Ines had said: "Are you sure you can

Chunk 2

---

[3] **pompously:** (pŏm′pəs lē), *adv.*: in a self-important way
[4] **Señora Ines:** (se nyōr′ă ē nes′)

GRAMMAR & USAGE

Heker uses the reciprocal pronoun *each other* in this sentence: "They had their tea in the kitchen and they told each other secrets." Writers use *each other* to describe interactions between two people and *one another* for three or more.

My Notes

Mark and annotate the text so that you can discuss Rosaura's attitude.

"The Stolen Party" — Close Reading

My Notes

Mark and annotate the text so that you can discuss the conflicts.

manage a jug as big as that?" Of course she could manage. She wasn't a butterfingers, like the others. Like that blonde girl with the bow in her hair. As soon as she saw Rosaura, the girl with the bow had said:

Chunk 3

"And you? Who are you?"

"I'm a friend of Luciana," said Rosaura.

"No," said the girl with the bow, "you are not a friend of Luciana because I'm her cousin and I know all her friends. And I don't know you."

"So what," said Rosaura. "I come here every afternoon with my mother and we do our homework together."

"You and your mother do your homework together?" asked the girl, laughing.

"I and Luciana do our homework together," said Rosaura, very seriously.

The girl with the bow shrugged her shoulders.

"That's not being friends," she said. "Do you go to school together?"

"No."

"So where do you know her from?" said the girl, getting impatient.

Rosaura remembered her mother's words perfectly. She took a deep breath.

"I'm the daughter of the employee," she said.

Her mother had said very clearly: "If someone asks, you say you're the daughter of the employee; that's all." She also told her to add "And proud of it." But Rosaura thought that never in her life would she dare say something of the sort.

"What employee?" said the girl with the bow. "Employee in a shop?"

"No," said Rosaura angrily. "My mother doesn't sell anything in any shop, so there."

"So how come she's an employee?" said the girl with the bow.

Just then Señora Ines arrived saying shh shh, and asked Rosaura if she wouldn't mind helping serve out the hot dogs, as she knew the house so much better than the others.

"See?" said Rosaura to the girl with the bow, and when no one was looking she kicked her in the shin.

Chunk 4

Apart from the girl with the bow, all the others were delightful. The one she liked best was Luciana, with her golden birthday crown; and then the boys. Rosaura won the sack race, and nobody managed to catch her when they played tag. When they split into two teams to play charades,

Mark and annotate the text so that you can discuss Rosaura's reactions.

all the boys wanted her for their side. Rosaura felt she had never been so happy in all her life.

But the best was still to come. The best came after Luciana blew out the candles. First the cake. Señora Ines had asked her to help pass the cake around, and Rosaura had enjoyed the task immensely, because everyone called out to her, shouting "Me, me!" Rosaura remembered a story in which there was a queen who had the power of life or death over her subjects. She had always loved that, having the power of life or death. To Luciana and the boys she gave the largest pieces, and to the girl with the bow she gave a slice so thin one could see through it.

After the cake came the magician, tall and bony, with a fine red cape. A true magician: he could untie handkerchiefs by blowing on them and make a chain with links that had no openings. He could guess what cards were pulled out from a pack, and the monkey was his assistant. He called the monkey "partner."

"Let's see here, partner," he would say, "Turn over a card." And, "Don't run away, partner: time to work now."

The final trick was wonderful. One of the children had to hold the monkey in his arms and the magician said he would make him disappear.

"What, the boy?" they all shouted.

"No, the monkey!" shouted the magician.

Rosaura thought that this was truly the most amusing party in the whole world.

The magician asked a small fat boy to come and help, but the small fat boy got frightened almost at once and dropped the monkey on the floor. The magician picked him up carefully, whispered something in his ear, and the monkey nodded almost as if he understood.

"You mustn't be so unmanly, my friend," the magician said to the fat boy.

"What's unmanly?" said the fat boy.

The magician turned around as if to look for spies.

"A sissy," said the magician. "Go sit down."

Then he stared at all the faces, one by one. Rosaura felt her heart tremble.

"You, with the Spanish eyes," said the magician. And everyone saw that he was pointing at her.

> ## GRAMMAR & USAGE
>
> **Independent** and **subordinate clauses** can be combined in a variety of ways with coordinating and subordinating conjunctions to form **compound** and **complex** sentences to express relationships among ideas.
>
> Example: Rosaura won the sack race [**independent clause**], and [**coordinating conjunction**] nobody managed to catch her [**independent clause**] when [**subordinating conjunction**] they played tag [**subordinate clause**]. This sentence, with two independent clauses and one dependent clause, is a **compound-complex** sentence.

My Notes

My Notes

Mark and annotate the details that convey Rosaura's feelings.

She wasn't afraid. Neither holding the monkey, nor when the magician made him vanish; not even when, at the end the magician flung his red cape over Rosaura's head and uttered a few magic words … and the monkey reappeared, chattering happily, in her arms. The children clapped furiously. And before Rosaura returned to her seat, the magician said:

"Thank you very much, my little countess."

She was so pleased with the compliment that a while later, when her mother came to fetch her, that was the first thing she told her.

Chunk 5

"I helped the magician and he said to me, 'Thank you very much, my little countess.'"

It was strange because up to then Rosaura had thought that she was angry with her mother. All along Rosaura had imagined that she would say to her: "See that the monkey wasn't a lie?" But instead she was so thrilled that she told her mother all about the wonderful magician.

Her mother tapped her on the head and said: "So now we're a countess!"

But one could see that she was beaming.

And now they both stood in the entrance, because a moment ago Señora Ines, smiling, had said: "Please wait here a second."

Her mother suddenly seemed worried.

"What is it?" she asked Rosaura.

"What is what?" said Rosaura. "It's nothing; she just wants to get the presents for those who are leaving, see?"

She pointed at the fat boy and at a girl with pigtails who were also waiting there, next to their mothers. And she explained about the presents. She knew, because she had been watching those who left before her. When one of the girls was about to leave, Señora Ines would give her a bracelet. When a boy left, Señora Ines gave him a yo-yo. Rosaura preferred the yo-yo because it sparkled, but she didn't mention that to her mother. Her mother might have said: "So why don't you ask for one, you blockhead?" That's what her mother was like. Rosaura didn't feel like explaining that she'd be horribly ashamed to be the odd one out. Instead she said:

"I was the best-behaved at the party."

And she said no more because Señora Ines came out into the hall with two bags, one pink and one blue.

First she went up to the fat boy, gave him a yo-yo out of the blue bag, and the fat boy left with his mother. Then she went up to the girl and gave her a bracelet out of the pink bag, and the girl with the pigtails left as well.

Finally she came up to Rosaura and her mother. She had a big smile on her face and Rosaura liked that. Señora Ines looked down at her, then looked up at her mother, and then said something that made Rosaura proud:

"What a marvelous daughter you have, Herminia."[5]

For an instant, Rosaura thought that she'd give her two presents: the bracelet and the yo-yo. Señora Ines bent down as if about to look for something. Rosaura also leaned forward, stretching out her arm. But she never completed the movement.

Chunk 6

Señora Ines didn't look in the pink bag. Nor did she look in the blue bag. Instead she rummaged[6] in her purse. In her hand appeared two bills.

"You really and truly earned this," she said handing them over. "Thank you for all your help, my pet."

Rosaura felt her arms stiffen, stick close to her body, and then she noticed her mother's hand on her shoulder. Instinctively she pressed herself against her mother's body. That was all. Except her eyes. Rosaura's eyes had a cold, clear look that fixed itself on Señora Ines's face.

Señora Ines, motionless, stood there with her hand outstretched. As if she didn't dare draw it back. As if the slightest change might shatter an infinitely[7] delicate balance.

---

[5] **Herminia:** (er mē nyā')
[6] **rummaged:** (rum'ijd), *v*.: searched thoroughly by moving things about
[7] **infinitely:** (in'fə nit lē): endlessly

My Notes

The theme of good versus evil that was established in "The Cask of Amontillado" is also seen in "The Stolen Party." How is the theme developed in each story?

Strategies Learning Log

Name of strategy:

Purpose of strategy:

How strategy was used:

How strategy helped you make meaning from the text, create a text, or orally present a text:

When you would use this strategy again:

Strategies Learning Log

Name of strategy:

Purpose of strategy:

How strategy was used:

How strategy helped you make meaning from the text, create a text, or orally present a text:

When you would use this strategy again:

Visualizing the Ending of "The Stolen Party"

Reread the final paragraphs of this story, when Señora Ines tries to hand Rosaura money instead of a gift like all the other children received.

"Rosaura felt her arms stiffen, stick close to her body, and then she noticed her mother's hand on her shoulder. Instinctively she pressed herself against her mother's body. That was all. Except her eyes. Rosaura's eyes had a cold, clear look that fixed itself on Señora Ines's face.

Señora Ines, motionless, stood there with her hand outstretched. As if she didn't dare draw it back. As if the slightest change might shatter an infinitely delicate balance."

This is a very powerful moment as all three characters appear to be frozen in time and space. How do you imagine this final scene in the story? Regardless of your artistic abilities, one of the most important reading skills to learn and practice is visualizing what you read. On separate paper, draw what you imagine this final scene looks like. You can focus on whatever you think is most important.

Next, review your drawing and look back at the excerpt from the story. What particular words and phrases helped you create your picture?

Now, imagine what might happen immediately after the scene you have just drawn. If the story were to contain one more scene, what would it look like? Consider what might happen to the money. Who, if anyone, would end up with it? Think through these things; then draw your scene on separate paper.

Writing Prompt: After creating your scene, write a continuation of the narrative to match your vision. Be sure to continue the conflict and perhaps devise an alternative resolution. Use dialogue if possible.

Point of View in "The Stolen Party"

ACADEMIC VOCABULARY

Point of view is the perspective from which a narrative is told.

WORD CONNECTIONS

The word *omniscient* has two Latin roots: *omni-*, meaning "all" or "everything," and *-sci-*, meaning "knowing" or "knowledge."

The root *omni-* also occurs in *omnivorous* and *omnipotent*.

The root *sci-* occurs in *science*, *conscious*, *conscience*, and *conscientious*.

Examine and discuss the differences among the three points of view:

- **First Person:** The narrator is a character in the story and refers to himself or herself as "I."
- **Third-Person Omniscient:** This type of narrator is not a character, but is all-knowing and is able to recount the background and inside thoughts and feelings of any character.
- **Third-Person Limited:** Like the omniscient narrator, this narrator is not a character in the story, but rather provides the reader the inside thoughts of only one character, and none of the thoughts of any of the other characters.

Now, use your understanding of point of view to transform each excerpt into the other two points of view.

Excerpt 1

First Person: I ran into my ex-girlfriend Lisa. I did not want to see her again. She always wants to get back with me, and I just want to move on.

Third-Person Limited:

Third-Person Omniscient:

Excerpt 2

First Person:

Third-Person Limited: The city skyline covered the horizon. From the balcony of her high-priced apartment that she shared with Jake, Sarah looked out and wondered if she was happy. Something seemed to be missing. Jake looked over to her and Sarah looked away quickly, hoping that she had not given away her private thoughts.

Third-Person Omniscient:

Excerpt 3

First Person:

Third-Person Limited:

Third-Person Omniscient:

The robber looked over his potential prey for the evening. They all seemed like easy marks to him. *Who would it be*, he wondered.

Feeling someone's eyes on her pocketbook, Jane held it closer to her body. She would not be robbed again, after that last time.

Point of View in "The Stolen Party"

Reflect: What are the benefits and limitations of each type of narration?

First-Person Point of View	Third-Person Limited	Third-Person Omniscient
Benefits:	Benefits:	Benefits:
Limitations:	Limitations:	Limitations:

"The Stolen Party" Story Diagram

SUGGESTED LEARNING STRATEGIES: Graphic Organizer, Marking the Text, Rereading

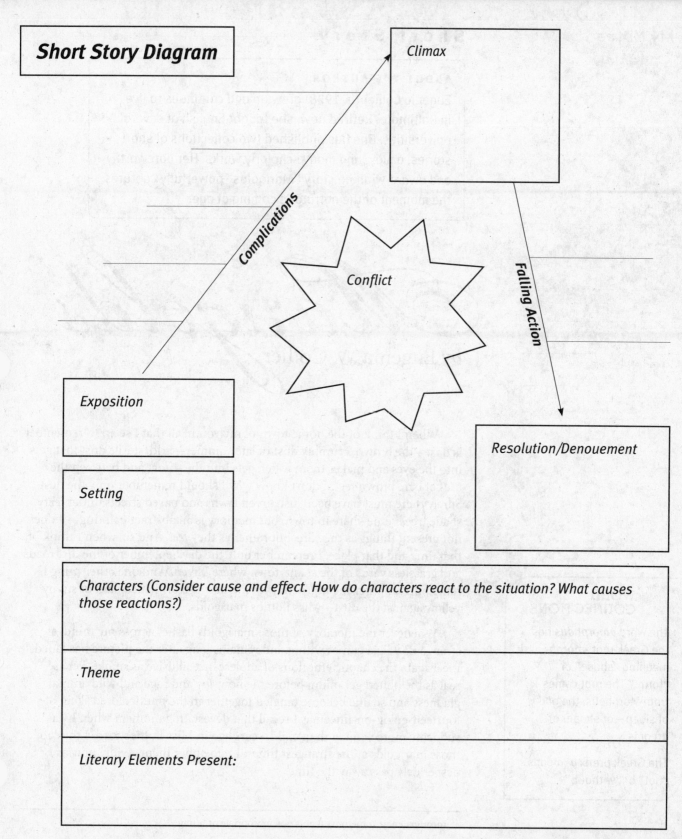

Short Story Diagram

Climax

Complications

Conflict

Falling Action

Exposition

Setting

Resolution/Denouement

Characters (Consider cause and effect. How do characters react to the situation? What causes those reactions?)

Theme

Literary Elements Present:

SIFTing through "Marigolds"

My Notes

Short Story

ABOUT THE AUTHOR

Eugenia Collier (b. 1928) grew up and continues to live in Baltimore. Retired now, she taught English at several universities. She has published two collections of short stories, a play, and many scholarly works. Her noteworthy and award-winning story "Marigolds" powerfully captures the moment of the narrator's coming of age.

Marigolds

by Eugenia W. Collier

When I think of the home town of my youth, all that I seem to remember is dust—the brown, crumbly dust of late summer—arid, sterile dust that gets into the eyes and makes them water, gets into the throat and between the toes of bare brown feet. I don't know why I should remember only the dust. Surely there must have been lush green lawns and paved streets under leafy shade trees somewhere in town; but memory is an abstract painting—it does not present things as they are, but rather as they *feel*. And so, when I think of that time and that place, I remember only the dry September of the dirt roads and grassless yards of the shantytown where I lived. And one other thing I remember, another incongruency[1] of memory—a brilliant splash of sunny yellow against the dust—Miss Lottie's marigolds.

Whenever the memory of those marigolds flashes across my mind, a strange nostalgia comes with it and remains long after the picture has faded. I feel again the chaotic emotions of adolescence, illusive as smoke, yet as real as the potted geranium before me now. Joy and rage and wild animal gladness and shame become tangled together in the multicolored skein of fourteen-going-on-fifteen as I recall that devastating moment when I was suddenly more woman than child, years ago in Miss Lottie's yard. I think of those marigolds at the strangest times; I remember them vividly now as I desperately pass away the time.

WORD CONNECTIONS

The word *amorphous* has the Greek root -*morph*-, meaning "shape" or "form." The root comes from Morpheus, the god of sleep—or shaper of dreams.

The Greek prefix *a*- means "not" or "without."

---

[1] **incongruency**: something that is not appropriate or fitting

I suppose that futile waiting was the sorrowful background music of our impoverished little community when I was young. The Depression that gripped the nation was no new thing to us, for the black workers of rural Maryland had always been depressed. I don't know what it was that we were waiting for; certainly not for the prosperity that was "just around the corner," for those were white folks' words, which we never believed. Nor did we wait for hard work and thrift to pay off in shining success, as the American Dream promised, for we knew better than that, too. Perhaps we waited for a miracle, amorphous[2] in concept but necessary if one were to have the grit to rise before dawn each day and labor in the white man's vineyard until after dark, or to wander about in the September dust offering some meager share of bread. But God was chary[3] with miracles in those days, and so we waited—and waited.

We children, of course, were only vaguely aware of the extent of our poverty. Having no radios, few newspapers, and no magazines, we were somewhat unaware of the world outside our community. Nowadays we would be called culturally deprived and people would write books and hold conferences about us. In those days everybody we knew was just as hungry and ill clad as we were. Poverty was the cage in which we all were trapped, and our hatred of it was still the vague, undirected restlessness of the zoo-bred flamingo who knows that nature created him to fly free.

As I think of those days I feel most poignantly the tag end of summer, the bright, dry times when we began to have a sense of shortening days and the imminence of the cold.

By the time I was fourteen, my brother Joey and I were the only children left at our house, the older ones having left home for early marriage or the lure of the city, and the two babies having been sent to relatives who might care for them better than we. Joey was three years younger than I, and a boy, and therefore vastly inferior. Each morning our mother and father trudged wearily down the dirt road and around the bend, she to her domestic job, he to his daily unsuccessful quest for work. After our few chores around the tumbledown shanty, Joey and I were free to run wild in the sun with other children similarly situated.

For the most part, those days are ill-defined in my memory, running together and combining like a fresh watercolor painting left out in the rain. I remember squatting in the road drawing a picture in the dust, a picture which Joey gleefully erased with one sweep of his dirty foot. I remember fishing for minnows in a muddy creek and watching sadly as they eluded my

---
[2] **amorphous**: without shape or form
[3] **chary**: ungenerous, wary

GRAMMAR & USAGE

Formal diction sometimes requires the use of the **subjunctive** form of the verb to express a doubt, a wish, a possibility, or a situation contrary to fact.

The narrator in "Marigolds" uses the subjunctive to express a wish or possibility in this clause:

... if one **were** to have the grit to rise before dawn each day....

Use this model to write your own sentence expressing a wish or a possibility in either Lizabeth's or Miss Lottie's voice.

My Notes

cupped hands, while Joey laughed uproariously. And I remember, that year, a strange restlessness of body and of spirit, a feeling that something old and familiar was ending, and something unknown and therefore terrifying was beginning.

One day returns to me with special clarity for some reason, perhaps because it was the beginning of the experience that in some inexplicable[4] way marked the end of innocence. I was loafing under the great oak tree in our yard, deep in some reverie which I have now forgotten, except that it involved some secret, secret thoughts of one of the Harris boys across the yard. Joey and a bunch of kids were bored now with the old tire suspended from an oak limb, which had kept them entertained for a while.

"Hey, Lizabeth," Joey yelled. He never talked when he could yell. "Hey, Lizabeth, let's go somewhere."

I came reluctantly from my private world. "Where you want to go? What you want to do?"

The truth was that we were becoming tired of the formlessness of our summer days. The idleness whose prospect had seemed so beautiful during the busy days of spring now had degenerated to an almost desperate effort to fill up the empty midday hours.

"Let's go see can we find some locusts on the hill," someone suggested.

Joey was scornful. "Ain't no more locusts there. Y'all got 'em all while they was still green."

The argument that followed was brief and not really worth the effort. Hunting locust trees wasn't fun anymore by now.

"Tell you what," said Joey finally, his eyes sparkling. "Let's us go over to Miss Lottie's."

The idea caught on at once, for annoying Miss Lottie was always fun. I was still child enough to scamper along with the group over rickety fences and through bushes that tore our already raggedy clothes, back to where Miss Lottie lived. I think now that we must have made a tragicomic spectacle, five or six kids of different ages, each of us clad in only one garment—the girls in faded dresses that were too long or too short, the boys in patchy pants, their sweaty brown chests gleaming in the hot sun. A little cloud of dust followed our thin legs and bare feet as we tramped over the barren land.

---

[4] **inexplicable:** unable to be explained or understood

My Notes

When Miss Lottie's house came into view we stopped, ostensibly[5] to plan our strategy, but actually to reinforce our courage. Miss Lottie's house was the most ramshackle of all our ramshackle homes. The sun and rain had long since faded its rickety frame siding from white to a sullen gray. The boards themselves seemed to remain upright not from being nailed together but rather from leaning together, like a house that a child might have constructed from cards. A brisk wind might have blown it down, and the fact that it was still standing implied a kind of enchantment that was stronger than the elements. There it stood and as far as I know is standing yet—a gray, rotting thing with no porch, no shutters, no steps, set on a cramped lot with no grass, not even any weeds—a monument to decay.

In front of the house in a squeaky rocking chair sat Miss Lottie's son, John Burke, completing the impression of decay. John Burke was what was known as queer-headed. Black and ageless, he sat rocking day in and day out in a mindless stupor, lulled by the monotonous squeak-squawk of the chair. A battered hat atop his shaggy head shaded him from the sun. Usually John Burke was totally unaware of everything outside his quiet dream world. But if you disturbed him, if you intruded upon his fantasies, he would become enraged, strike out at you, and curse at you in some strange enchanted language which only he could understand. We children made a game of thinking of ways to disturb John Burke and then to elude his violent retribution.

But our real fun and our real fear lay in Miss Lottie herself. Miss Lottie seemed to be at least a hundred years old. Her big frame still held traces of the tall, powerful woman she must have been in youth, although it was now bent and drawn. Her smooth skin was a dark reddish brown, and her face had Indian-like features and the stern stoicism that one associates with Indian faces. Miss Lottie didn't like intruders either, especially children. She never left her yard, and nobody ever visited her. We never knew how she managed those necessities which depend on human interaction—how she ate, for example, or even whether she ate. When we were tiny children, we thought Miss Lottie was a witch and we made up tales that we half believed ourselves about her exploits. We were far too sophisticated now, of course, to believe the witch nonsense. But old fears have a way of clinging like cobwebs, and so when we sighted the tumbledown shack, we had to stop to reinforce our nerves.

"Look, there she is," I whispered, forgetting that Miss Lottie could not possibly have heard me from that distance. "She's fooling with them crazy flowers."

---

[5] **ostensibly:** for the pretended reason

My Notes

"Yeh, look at 'er."

Miss Lottie's marigolds were perhaps the strangest part of the picture. Certainly they did not fit in with the crumbling decay of the rest of her yard. Beyond the dusty brown yard, in front of the sorry gray house, rose suddenly and shockingly a dazzling strip of bright blossoms, clumped together in enormous mounds, warm and passionate and sun-golden. The old black witch-woman worked on them all summer, every summer, down on her creaky knees, weeding and cultivating and arranging, while the house crumbled and John Burke rocked. For some perverse reason, we children hated those marigolds. They interfered with the perfect ugliness of the place; they were too beautiful; they said too much that we could not understand; they did not make sense. There was something in the vigor with which the old woman destroyed the weeds that intimidated us. It should have been a comical sight—the old woman with the man's hat on her cropped white head, leaning over the bright mounds, her big backside in the air—but it wasn't comical, it was something we could not name. We had to annoy her by whizzing a pebble into her flowers or by yelling a dirty word, then dancing away from her rage, reveling in our youth and mocking her age. Actually, I think it was the flowers we wanted to destroy, but nobody had the nerve to try it, not even Joey, who was usually fool enough to try anything.

"Y'all git some stones," commanded Joey now and was met with instant giggling obedience as everyone except me began to gather pebbles from the dusty ground. "Come on, Lizabeth."

I just stood there peering through the bushes, torn between wanting to join the fun and feeling that it was all a bit silly.

"You scared, Lizabeth?"

I cursed and spat on the ground—my favorite gesture of phony bravado. "Y'all children get the stones, I'll show you how to use 'em."

I said before that we children were not consciously aware of how thick were the bars of our cage. I wonder now, though, whether we were not more aware of it than I thought. Perhaps we had some dim notion of what we were, and how little chance we had of being anything else. Otherwise, why would we have been so preoccupied with destruction? Anyway, the pebbles were collected quickly, and everybody looked at me to begin the fun.

"Come on, y'all."

We crept to the edge of the bushes that bordered the narrow road in front of Miss Lottie's place. She was working placidly, kneeling over the flowers, her dark hand plunged into the golden mound. Suddenly *zing*—an expertly aimed stone cut the head off one of the blossoms.

"Who out there?" Miss Lottie's backside came down and her head came up as her sharp eyes searched the bushes. "You better git!"

We had crouched down out of sight in the bushes, where we stifled the giggles that insisted on coming. Miss Lottie gazed warily across the road for a moment, then cautiously returned to her weeding. *Zing*—Joey sent a pebble into the blooms, and another marigold was beheaded.

Miss Lottie was enraged now. She began struggling to her feet, leaning on a rickety cane and shouting. "Y'all git! Go on home!" Then the rest of the kids let loose with their pebbles, storming the flowers and laughing wildly and senselessly at Miss Lottie's impotent rage. She shook her stick at us and started shakily toward the road crying, "Git 'long! John Burke! John Burke, come help!"

Then I lost my head entirely, mad with the power of inciting such rage, and ran out of the bushes in the storm of pebbles, straight toward Miss Lottie, changing madly, "Old witch, fell in a ditch, picked up a penny and thought she was rich!" The children screamed with delight, dropped their pebbles, and joined the crazy dance, swarming around Miss Lottie like bees and changing, "Old lady witch!" while she screamed curses at us. The madness lasted only a moment, for John Burke, startled at last, lurched out of his chair, and we dashed for the bushes just as Miss Lottie's cane went whizzing at my head.

I did not join the merriment when the kids gathered again under the oak in our bare yard. Suddenly I was ashamed, and I did not like being ashamed. The child in me sulked and said it was all in fun, but the woman in me flinched at the thought of the malicious attack that I had led. The mood lasted all afternoon. When we ate the beans and rice that was supper that night, I did not notice my father's silence, for he was always silent these days, nor did I notice my mother's absence, for she always worked until well into evening. Joey and I had a particularly bitter argument after supper; his exuberance[6] got on my nerves. Finally I stretched out upon the pallet in the room we shared and fell into a fitful doze. When I awoke, somewhere in the middle of the night, my mother had returned, and I vaguely listened to the conversation that was audible through the thin walls that separated our

---

[6] **exuberance**: extreme good cheer or high spirits

SIFTing through "Marigolds"

rooms. At first I heard no words, only voices. My mother's voice was like a cool, dark room in summer—peaceful, soothing, quiet. I loved to listen to it; it made things seem all right somehow. But my father's voice cut through hers, shattering the peace.

"Twenty-two years, Maybelle, twenty-two years," he was saying, "and I got nothing for you, nothing, nothing."

"It's all right, honey, you'll get something. Everybody out of work now, you know that."

"It ain't right. Ain't no man ought to eat his woman's food year in and year out, and see his children running wild. Ain't nothing right about that."

"Honey, you took good care of us when you had it. Ain't nobody got nothing nowadays."

"I ain't talking about nobody else, I'm talking about *me*. God knows I try." My mother said something I could not hear, and my father cried out louder, "What must a man do, tell me that?"

"Look, we ain't starving. I get paid every week, and Mrs. Ellis is real nice about giving me things. She gonna let me have Mr. Ellis's old coat for you this winter—"

"Damn Mr. Ellis's coat! And damn his money! You think I want white folks' leavings? Damn, Maybelle"—and suddenly he sobbed, loudly and painfully, and cried helplessly and hopelessly in the dark night. I had never heard a man cry before. I did not know men ever cried. I covered my ears with my hand but could not cut off the sound of my father's harsh, painful, despairing sobs. My father was a strong man who could whisk a child upon his shoulders and go singing through the house. My father whittled toys for us, and laughed so loud that the great oak seemed to laugh with him, and taught us how to fish and hunt rabbits. How could it be that my father was crying? But the sobs went on, unstifled, finally quieting until I could hear my mother's voice, deep and rich, humming softly as she used to hum to a frightened child.

The world had lost its boundary lines. My mother, who was small and soft, was now the strength of the family; my father, who was the rock on which the family had been built, was sobbing like the tiniest child. Everything was suddenly out of tune, like a broken accordion. Where did I fit into this crazy picture? I do not now remember my thoughts, only a feeling of great bewilderment and fear.

Long after the sobbing and humming had stopped, I lay on the pallet, still as stone with my hands over my ears, wishing that I too could cry and be comforted. The night was silent now except for the sound of the crickets and of Joey's soft breathing. But the room was too crowded with fear to allow me to sleep, and finally, feeling the terrible aloneness of 4 A.M., I decided to awaken Joey.

"Ouch! What's the matter with you? What you want?" he demanded disagreeably when I had pinched and slapped him awake.

"Come on, wake up."

"What for? Go 'way."

I was lost for a reasonable reply. I could not say, "I'm scared and I don't want to be alone," so I merely said, "I'm going out. If you want to come, come on."

The promise of adventure awoke him. "Going out now? Where to, Lizabeth? What you going to do?"

I was pulling my dress over my head. Until now I had not thought of going out. "Just come on," I replied tersely

I was out the window and halfway down the road before Joey caught up with me.

"Wait, Lizabeth, where you going?"

I was running as if the Furies[7] were after me, as perhaps they were—running silently and furiously until I came to where I had half known I was headed: to Miss Lottie's yard.

The half-dawn light was more eerie than complete darkness, and in it the old house was like the ruin that my world had become—foul and crumbling, a grotesque caricature. It looked haunted, but I was not afraid, because I was haunted too.

"Lizabeth, you lost your mind?" panted Joey.

I had indeed lost my mind, for all the smoldering emotions of that summer swelled in me and burst—the great need for my mother who was never there, the hopelessness of our poverty and degradation, the bewilderment of being neither child nor woman and yet both at once, the fear

My Notes

---

[7] **Furies**: in classical mythology, three spirits of revenge who pursued and punished wrongdoers.

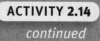

My Notes

unleashed by my father's tears. And these feelings combined in one great impulse toward destruction.

"Lizabeth!"

I leaped furiously into the mounds of marigolds and pulled madly, trampling and pulling and destroying the perfect yellow blooms. The fresh smell of early morning and of dew-soaked marigolds spurred me on as I went gearing and mangling and sobbing while Joey tugged my dress or my waist crying, "Lizabeth, stop, please stop!"

And then I was sitting in the ruined little garden among the uprooted and ruined flowers, crying and crying, and it was too late to undo what I had done. Joey was sitting beside me, silent and frightened, not knowing what to say. Then, "Lizabeth, look."

I opened my swollen eyes and saw in front of me a pair of large, calloused feet; my gaze lifted to the swollen legs, the age-distorted body clad in a tight cotton nightdress, and then the shadowed Indian face surrounded by stubby white hair. And there was no rage in the face now, now that the garden was destroyed and there was nothing any longer to be protected.

"M-miss Lottie!" I scrambled to my feet and just stood there and stared at here, and that was the moment when childhood faded and womanhood began. That violent, crazy act was the last act of childhood. For as I gazed at the immobile face with the sad, weary eyes, I gazed upon a kind of reality which is hidden to childhood. The witch was no longer a witch but only a broken old woman who had dared to create beauty in the midst of ugliness and sterility. She had been born in squalor and lived in it all her life. Now at the end of that life she had nothing except a falling-down hut, a wrecked body, and John Burke, the mindless son of her passion. Whatever verve there was left in her, whatever was of love and beauty and joy that had not been squeezed out by life, had been there in the marigolds she had so tenderly cared for.

Of course I could not express the things that I knew about Miss Lottie as I stood there awkward and ashamed. The years have put words to the things I knew in that moment, and as I look back upon it, I know that that moment marked the end of innocence. Innocence involves an unseeing acceptance of things at face value, an ignorance of the area below the surface. In that

My Notes

humiliating moment I had looked beyond myself and into the depths of another person. This was the beginning of compassion, and one cannot have both compassion and innocence.

The years have taken me worlds away from that time and that place, from the dust and squalor of our lives, and from the bright thing that I destroyed in a blind, childish striking out at God knows what. Miss Lottie died long ago and many years have passed since I last saw her hut, completely barren at last, for despite my wild contrition[8] she never planted marigolds again. Yet, there are times when the image of those passionate yellow mounds returns with a painful poignancy. For one does not have to be ignorant and poor to find that his life is as barren as the dusty yards of our town. And I too have planted marigolds.

[8] **contrition**: sorrow or remorse for one's wrongs

SIFTing through "Marigolds"

The acronym SIFT stands for Symbol, Images, Figurative Language, and Tone or Theme. You can use this strategy to "sift" through the parts of a story in order to explore how a writer uses literary elements and stylistic techniques to convey meaning or theme.

Record examples from "Marigolds" of each of the SIFT elements in the graphic organizer.

Symbol:

Imagery:

Figurative Language:

Tone/Theme:

"Marigolds" is a story that examines the coming of age of a young girl, Lizabeth. In order to truly understand the story, as well as Lizabeth's transformation, you must clearly articulate the choices that she makes along the way, both within her own mind and between forces from the outside world. On the following chart, examine the internal and external conflicts Lizabeth faces.

LITERARY TERMS

An **internal conflict** occurs when a character struggles between opposing needs or desires or emotions within his or her own mind.

An **external conflict** occurs when a character struggles against an outside force. This force may be another character, a societal expectation, or something in the physical world.

Internal Conflicts

One side of the conflict	The other side of the conflict

External Conflicts

One side of the conflict	The other side of the conflict

Working with Cinematic Techniques: Part 1

ACADEMIC VOCABULARY

Cinematic techniques are the methods a director uses to communicate meaning and to evoke particular emotional responses in viewers.

You have spent a good deal of time visualizing three short stories. In Embedded Assessment 1, you will address film. One of the first steps in filmmaking is visualizing, in the form of storyboarding. To prepare to make a storyboard, examine these **cinematic techniques**.

Shots and Framing

Shot: a single piece of film uninterrupted by cuts.

Establishing Shot: often a long shot or a series of shots that sets the scene. It is used to establish setting and to show transitions between locations.

Long Shot (LS): a shot from some distance. If filming a person, the full body is shown. It may show the isolation or vulnerability of the character (also called a Full Shot).

Medium Shot (MS): the most common shot. The camera seems to be a medium distance from the object being filmed. A medium shot shows the person from the waist up. The effect is to ground the story.

Close Up (CU): the image takes up at least 80 percent of the frame.

Extreme Close Up: the image being shot is a part of a whole, such as an eye or a hand.

Two Shot: a scene between two people shot exclusively from an angle that includes both characters more or less equally. It is used in love scenes where interaction between the two characters is important.

Camera Angles

Eye Level: a shot taken from a normal height; that is, the character's eye level. Ninety to ninety-five percent of the shots seen are eye level, because it is the most natural angle.

High Angle: the camera is above the subject. This usually has the effect of making the subject look smaller than normal, giving him or her the appearance of being weak, powerless, and trapped.

Low Angle: the camera films subject from below. This usually has the effect of making the subject look larger than normal, and therefore strong, powerful, and threatening.

Camera Movements

Pan: a stationary camera moves from side to side on a horizontal axis.

Tilt: a stationary camera moves up or down along a vertical axis.

Zoom: a stationary camera where the lens moves to make an object seem to move closer to or further away from the camera. With this technique, moving into a character is often a personal or revealing movement, while moving away distances or separates the audience from the character.

Dolly/Tracking: the camera is on a track that allows it to move with the action. The term also refers to any camera mounted on a car, truck, or helicopter.

Boom/Crane: the camera is on a crane over the action. This is used to create overhead shots.

Lighting

High Key: the scene is flooded with light, creating a bright and open-looking scene.

Low Key: the scene is flooded with shadows and darkness, creating suspense or suspicion.

Bottom or Side Lighting: direct lighting from below or the side, which often makes the subject appear dangerous or evil.

Front or Back Lighting: soft lighting on the actor's face or from behind gives the appearance of innocence or goodness, or a halo effect.

Editing Techniques

Cut: most common editing technique. Two pieces of film are spliced together to "cut" to another image.

Fade: can be to or from black or white. A fade can begin in darkness and gradually assume full brightness (fade-in) or the image may gradually get darker (fade-out). A fade often implies that time has passed or may signify the end of a scene.

Dissolve: a kind of fade in which one image is slowly replaced by another. It can create a connection between images.

Wipe: a new image wipes off the previous image. A wipe is more fluid than a cut and quicker than a dissolve.

Flashback: cut or dissolve to action that happened in the past.

Shot-Reverse-Shot: a shot of one subject, then another, then back to the first. It is often used for conversation or reaction shots.

Working with Cinematic Techniques: Part 1

Cross Cutting: cut into action that is happening simultaneously. This technique is also called parallel editing. It can create tension or suspense and can form a connection between scenes.

Eye-Line Match: cut to an object, then to a person. This technique shows what a person seems to be looking at and can reveal a character's thoughts.

Sound

Diegetic: sound that could logically be heard by the characters in the film.

Non-Diegetic: sound that cannot be heard by the characters but is designed for audience reaction only. An example might be ominous music for foreshadowing.

Applying Cinematic Techniques

SUGGESTED LEARNING STRATEGIES: Close Reading, Graphic Organizer

Shots and Framing	Camera Angles	Camera Movements	Lighting	Editing	Music/Sound

Analysis: Choose the most significant cinematic technique from your notes above, and write an interpretive statement that explains the effect of this cinematic technique in the commercial.

Applying Cinematic Techniques

Storyboarding allows filmmakers to plan the details of the film, shot by shot, in advance, saving time and money. You have visualized a moment in several texts in this unit, beginning with the poem "A Poison Tree" (Activity 2.3). Take a moment to review the sketches you created. Think now about how you might expand that visualization of a single image into a sequence of five or six shots. Describe those shots in the storyboard below.

SHOT #

Framing: _____

Describe the Music/Sound:

Dialogue:

Lighting:

SHOT #

Framing: _____

Describe the Music/Sound:

Dialogue:

Lighting:

SHOT #

Describe the Music/Sound:

Dialogue:

Framing: _____

Lighting:

SHOT #

Describe the Music/Sound:

Dialogue:

Framing: _____

Lighting:

Reflection: Why did you choose the framing, lighting, and music that you did? What words or phrases from the poem made you picture this? Explain.

Creating a Storyboard

SUGGESTED LEARNING STRATEGIES: **Graphic Organizer, Sharing And Responding**

Assignment

Your assignment is to work collaboratively to transform a section of a printed text into a storyboard. You will also include a written explanation of the intended effects of your cinematic choices.

Steps

Planning

1. Revisit a short story from this unit that you could imagine as a film. As a group, select a small passage to transform into a storyboard of at least 20 shots. You will not be able to capture the entire story in your storyboard; choose a compelling section that contains many visual elements.

2. As director, decide how you would like to show your version of this text and the effect you want it to have on your audience. Present your ideas to your group, and reach a consensus about your focus.

Drafting

3. Brainstorm a sequence of shots. Consider framing, camera movement, lighting, sound, and editing in each shot. Use sticky notes to sketch out or describe each shot on the Storyboard Graphic Organizer. Be sure to consider the effect you are trying to create with each shot and the words or phrases that communicate your vision. Share this draft within your small group. Even if you plan photographs for your final draft, you should sketch what your photos will look like for this first draft. Decide how to share the responsibilities of producing each element of the storyboard. Create a draft.

Refining

4. As a group, share your ideas with another group. Solicit feedback on

   ▶ Clear sequence of ideas

   ▶ Effective use of cinematic techniques in relation to the story

   ▶ Accurate identification and application of cinematic techniques

   Use the notes generated during the peer group discussion, and revise your storyboard. Add an explanation of the intended effect of your choices. Be specific in terms of your framing, lighting, sound, and other choices, and be sure that your effect is consistent with your cinematic choices. Support your explanation with textual evidence from the short story.

Revising and Editing for Publication

5. Prepare your final draft. Choose a presentation method, such as mounting your frames onto poster board or creating a slide show. Label each frame with all the information required (shot type, angle, lighting, and sound), including intended effect of each shot.

↗**TECHNOLOGY TIP** Consider designing and publishing your work using a graphics or presentation software program.

SCORING GUIDE

Scoring Criteria	Exemplary	Proficient	Emerging
Storyboard **Display of Cinematic Elements**	A compelling section of the selected story is vividly demonstrated through a clear sequence of ideas. The storyboard contains visually appealing frames that skillfully use images to convey a variety of cinematic elements. Each frame is completely and precisely labeled with information about shot type, angle, lighting, and sound.	An appropriate section of the selected story is demonstrated through an organized sequence of ideas. The storyboard contains frames that adequately use images to convey several cinematic elements. Each frame is accurately labeled with information about shot type, angle, lighting, and sound.	The selected section of the story may be inappropriate or may not demonstrate a logical sequence of ideas. The frames of the storyboard are insufficient. Images convey a limited number of cinematic elements. Frames may be labeled inconsistently and/or inaccurately.
Storyboard **Explanatory Text**	The written explanation provides a clear and detailed explanation that uses precise textual evidence to insightfully connect the cinematic choices to short story elements and intended effects.	The written explanation demonstrates a logical understanding of the effect of cinematic elements in relationship to short story elements; cinematic choices are supported by textual evidence.	The written explanation demonstrates a limited understanding of the effect of cinematic choices in relationship to short story elements. Textual support is lacking.
Evidence of Collaboration	The product demonstrates extensive evidence of successful planning and collaboration.	The product shows evidence of adequate planning and collaboration.	Inadequate planning and collaboration are evident.
Additional Criteria			

Comments:

Learning Focus:

What Is Your Style?

Whether it is the clothes you wear, how you walk and talk, or the way you decorate your room, you have your own unique **style**. How you choose to present yourself in a variety of situations reflects your individual style. This concept of style is similar in literary works.

Style in a written text can be investigated from a number of vantage points. It may be seen, for instance, in the way in which an author's **diction**, **imagery**, and **rhetorical devices** create a particular effect.

But what about film? In past units, you have viewed film much like a narrative, with plot, characters, conflicts, etc. Now, you will expand your view of film by approaching this visual medium through the lens of the director as author. Thus, you will begin to see the explicit connections between an author's choices of literary techniques and a director's choices of cinematic techniques. You can see some of these comparisons below.

▶ Tone/Mood   may be represented by   Lighting and Sound

▶ Diction   may be represented by   Dialogue

▶ Imagery   may be represented by   Symbolism, Costuming, Setting

▶ Organization   may be represented by   Storyboarding

▶ Syntax   may be represented by   Editing

▶ Point of view   may be represented by   Framing, Shot Type, and Camera Movement

Just as you analyze a short story to understand how its literary elements work together, so too you can analyze a film and how its cinematic elements work together to tell a story. Analyzing style takes this analysis one step further in that it allows you to understand and appreciate the creative craft of the author or director. Authors and directors choose to include certain elements to create certain effects, and these choices in turn reflect the style of the creator. Understanding style in literature is to have a larger understanding of not just the story, but also the craftsmanship of creation.

The imaginative and unusual worlds created by the director Tim Burton in his feature films provide the viewer with clear examples of a unique approach to telling a story. You may already enjoy the films of Tim Burton, and perhaps even appreciate them for their distinctive style of storytelling. Identifying and analyzing the elements of style will give you a vocabulary for explaining your understanding and appreciation of a contemporary, nonprint, literary text.

Film 101

SUGGESTED LEARNING STRATEGIES: **Close Reading, Graphic Organizer**

In the remainder of this unit, you will be viewing film as text. Consider your history of viewing film, and complete the following survey citing specific examples and experiences.

1. Approximately how many movies do you watch a month (on DVD or cable or in a theater)?

 **WORD CONNECTIONS**

The relationship in an analogy may show an object and its description; for example, film : award-winning. Complete the following analogy.

film : award-winning :: _____ : best-selling.

2. What are your favorite types of movies? Explain.

3. What are your least favorite types of movies? Explain.

4. List in order the top five best films ever made, in your opinion.

5. What kind of movies do your parents or guardians like to watch? How often do you watch movies with them?

6. What are the differences between watching a movie at home and watching in a theater?

7. What kind of movies do you watch in school?

8. What are you normally asked by the teacher to do while or after watching a film?

Reading a text and viewing a film have similarities and differences. In addition, the author of a text or the director of a film can affect his/her audience through common and/or dissimilar tools, strategies, and methods. Consider the roles of both creator and audience member and fill out the following graphic organizer. You might consider the following prompts to focus your answers:

- What can a director do that an author cannot, and vice versa?
- What tools and strategies do authors and directors share? What tools and strategies are different?
- Are you more entertained by reading books or by watching movies? Why?
- Why might a teacher ask you to read a book rather than watch a movie?
- Is the suggestion that one "should always read the book before watching the movie" valid? Why or why not?

Movie   **Text**

Film in Context: An Authorial Study

Director Tim Burton's life is as unique as his filming style. With an understanding of what has influenced him, we can begin to understand the directorial choices he has made. However, before we venture into the wild and fantastic world of Tim Burton, we must first review a key term: theme.

Theme is not the same as a **subject**, which can be expressed in a word or two: courage, survival, war, pride, etc. The theme is the idea the author wishes to convey about that subject. It is expressed as a sentence or general statement about life or human nature. A literary work may have more than one theme, and most themes are not directly stated but rather are implied. The reader must think about all the elements of the work and use them to make inferences, or reasonable guesses, about themes in a work. An example of a theme on the subject of pride might be that pride often precedes a fall.

Read carefully the short article entitled "Hollywood Outsider Tim Burton" from CBS News (March 5, 2006). While you read, record two or three possible subjects that might arise in Burton's films that reflect some of his beliefs and experiences.

SUBJECTS:

1.

2.

3.

Once you have created a class list, choose one of the subjects and turn it into a theme statement. Remember that themes must be inferred. You must think about what you have read and make a reasonable guess as to what Burton might believe.

THEME STATEMENT:

> **LITERARY TERMS**
>
> **Theme** is the central message of a literary work.

Hollywood Outsider

TIM BURTON

from cbsnews.com

The Corpse Bride is a ghoulish animated glee about a shy boy who marries a dead girl by mistake. It's full of crumbling bones, and dead people stealing the show. It all may sound strange, but not to those who know Tim Burton, the director who earned an Oscar nomination for best animated feature.

"Tim's bottled something magical, and I'm drinking it," said Johnny Depp, the voice of Victor, the groom.

"I've always been interested in the juxtaposition of what people say is fantasy versus reality or what's normal versus abnormal," said Burton. "They always seem different to me."

It's a vision that's as dark and oddly appealing as Burton himself is when you sit down with him, as Mika Brzezinski did for a rare interview.

"I did have somebody say their dog liked my work once," he recalled. "I thought it was quite interesting."

"That's weird. I was watching *Corpse Bride* this morning and my dog kept going up to the TV," said Mika.

"That's amazing," Burton replied. "Because somebody's dog says they liked *Nightmare Before Christmas*, too. To me, those are the best compliments because you know they're pure.

Film critic Roger Ebert has been following Burton's career ever since Burton made a very big splash 20 years ago as a very young filmmaker. Burton made such cult favorites as *Edward Scissorhands*, *Beetlejuice*, and *Big Fish*.

"If you go back through all his pictures you find nothing that is conventional," said Ebert. "You find worlds that come completely out of his imagination, as in *Big Fish*, or *Pee Wee's Big Adventure*, one of his early films. His *Batman* pictures have a very distinctive look and feel."

Not to mention successful. *Batman* is well up there on the list of Hollywood's top grossing films.

"Tim is visually astounding, in the way he approaches material," said Danny DeVito, who played the Penguin in *Batman Returns* and also the ringmaster in Burton's 2004 movie *Big Fish*.

"Even when you read the script of *Big Fish*, which is really a terrific script, you don't really get into the world that he's creating until you take that step with him, that first step into a world he's created in his mind," said DeVito.

GRAMMAR & USAGE

In the first paragraph, the writer uses the phrase "but not to those who know Tim Burton." This phrase contrasts with the statement just before it: "It may all sound strange."

A **contrasting expression**, which is set off with commas, gives emphasis to both points.

My Notes

LITERARY TERMS

A **biography** is a description or account of someone else's life or significant events from that person's life. In contrast, an **autobiography** is an account written by a person about his or her own life.

My Notes

DeVito even cast Burton in one of his own movies, *Hoffa*. Burton was, where else, in the coffin.

"His sort of interests, which are more than slightly off center, and a little outside, his interpretation of them does appeal to the masses, which ultimately I think is a very good sign," said Depp.

Burton's creative, quirky, fantastical world, along with his outsider take on life, has won him many fans.

Fans love Burton's creative, quirky, fantastical world, along with his outsider take on life. Among young adults who've grown up with his movies, Burton is a cult hero with a celebrity rare for a director.

In a way, Burton's drawings tell his story. By his own account, he was an odd and solitary kid growing up in Burbank, California, with little use for school or parents. He lived with his grandmother as a teenager, and spent his days drawing and dreaming and watching old monster movies. He even lived near a cemetery.

"I did grow up watching monster movies and I did enjoy playing (in the cemetery), but I thought most kids did. It didn't seem that strange to me."

Are you lashing back from being a tortured child?

"Of course. That's part of what's great about having drawing or writing as an outlet. It's a good way to exorcise those things."

Burton's preoccupation with death and monsters was evident from the start. His drawing talent won him a scholarship to nearby CalArts, founded by Walt and Roy Disney. After that, he landed a job as an animator, working on Disney classics like *The Fox and the Hounds*.

At age 26, he made a short film for Disney called *Frankenweenie*, about a little boy's efforts to revive his dead dog. The Disney folks felt it was too scary too release, but its unique style opened doors.

Next came *Pee Wee's Big Adventure*, which became a cult classic, and that led to *Beetlejuice,* a sleeper hit that received critical raves and earned tons of money for Warner Brothers.

And that led to his first really big budget movie, *Batman*. It was a smash. Suddenly, Tim Burton had Hollywood clout.

The movie he chose to make next was *Edward Scissorhands*, probably Burton's most personal film. It's about a creative misfit in a world that oddly mirrors the one Burton grew up in. But it almost didn't get made.

Despite the clout he garnered, movie executive still had trouble giving control to a guy who didn't even comb his hair.

"What they like about you they fear about you," said Burton. "They think you're a somewhat strange person, so they're always a little bit worried."

To play Edward Scissorhands, Burton chose Johnny Depp, who's now shooting Disney's sequel to *Pirates of the Caribbean* in the Bahamas.

"We connected on a number of levels," said Depp. "And it was the beginning of that interesting shorthand that exists between Tim and me."

For Burton, the connection with Depp was immediate and deep.

"He's just somebody who likes to transform," Burton said of his friend. "He's more like an old fashioned Boris Karloff- or Lon Chaney-style actor than he is like a leading man. I enjoy people like that. They're always surprising."

Depp and Burton have gone on to make many movies together, including *Ed Wood*, Burton's loving tribute to the man considered by many Hollywood insiders to be the worst director of all time.

"He deserves to be loved, there's a kind of purity to Ed Wood, which, in terms of intent, is not dissimilar to Tim," said Depp.

"I definitely identified with him," Burton said of Ed Wood. "I grew up seeing his movies and seeing how special they were. Just being in the industry you think there's a real fine line between success and failure, and what makes an artist or not.

Ed Wood may or may not have been an artist, but he was obsessed with movie making. One of his more famous stunts took place in his movie *Plan 9 from Outer Space*, which featured a very old and very ill Bela Lugosi, who died while the movie was being made. Wood got his dentist to fill in for Lugosi.

"The reason (Burton) wanted to make *Ed Wood* is that Ed Wood had so much fun making movies," said Ebert. "And that's where Ed Wood and Tim Burton connect. Tim Burton makes films that are a lot better, but he doesn't make them with any more love."

My Notes

Film in Context: An Authorial Study

My Notes

Burton's real life these days seems almost, dare we say it, normal. He lives in England with actress Helena Bonham Carter, and their young son, Billy.

The two often work together. She played a witch in *Big Fish*, Charlie Bucket's mother in *Charlie and the Chocolate Factory*, and she's the voice of the "Corpse Bride."

"It's actually quite nice," said Burton. "She knows what it's all about so there's no ego, no problem whatsoever."

One could argue Burton's life is almost like a fairy tale.

"I'm going to turn into a frog and jump off the stage now," said Burton.

With your classmates, identify and discuss the essential features of a biography that are present in this article.

You will now be assigned one of the following topics:

> Johnny Depp
>
> Vincent Price
>
> Edgar Allan Poe
>
> Gothic Literature

For your investigation, you must research your assigned topic, using a minimum of three Internet sources. You will become an expert on your topic and be responsible for teaching your peers what you have learned. Be sure to create a bibliography of your sources. When conducting research, use text features such as captions, illustrations, headings, sidebar information, and footnotes to help you identify information to include in your notes. When you have compiled enough information, respond to the following two questions in preparation for your presentation. You may use the graphic organizer for help.

1. Summarize what you know about the individual/subject you were asked to research

2. Draw connections between your individual/subject and the ideas your class uncovered regarding Tim Burton (hint: this might take some additional research!)

Summary of Topic

Connections to Tim Burton

Bibliography of Sources

Source 1:

Source 2:

Source 3:

Reflection: Evaluate your research process. What did you learn about research, and how will you apply that knowledge to future research tasks? Use the subjunctive stem, "If I had the opportunity to make changes, ..."

Film in Context: An Authorial Study

Take notes while you listen to your classmates report on their research.

Subject 1: _____

Subject 2: _____

Subject 3: _____

Writing Prompt: Summarize the influence of these individuals and genres on the contemporary works of Tim Burton.

Setting the Mood: Wonka Two Ways

You have uncovered and presented a variety of influences on Tim Burton's unique **style**. You will now have an opportunity to see that style in action through a comparative study between text and film. Both authors and directors thoughtfully consider the **mood** and **tone** they create. Therefore it is important to understand these terms.

By carefully considering the author's choice of words and detail to create a mood, a reader can often uncover the tone of a piece. Similarly, a director can make choices to create a mood and tone. Complete the following steps to compare a written text with a film text.

In passage 1 from *Charlie and the Chocolate Factory*, you will examine the mood. Annotate words and phrases that help to identify the atmosphere or predominant emotion in the text. List those words in the space provided. After you have completed your list of words and phrases, come up with one or two words to describe the mood of the passage.

> ## LITERARY TERMS
>
> **Mood** is the atmosphere or predominant emotion in a literary work.
>
> **Tone** is the writer's or speaker's attitude toward a subject, character, or audience. Tone can be serious, humorous, sarcastic, indignant, objective, etc.

Words/Phrases	Mood

My Notes

Novel Excerpt

From # CHARLiE and the CHOCOLaTE FaCTORY

by Roald Dahl

PASSAGE 1

The whole of this family—the six grownups (count them) and little Charlie Bucket—live together in a small wooden house on the edge of a great town.

The house wasn't nearly large enough for so many people, and life was extremely uncomfortable for them all. There were only two rooms in the place altogether, and there was only one bed. The bed was given to the four old grandparents because they were so old and tired. They were so tired, they never got out of it.

Grandpa Joe and Grandma Josephine on this side, Grandpa George and Grandma Georgina on this side.

Mr. and Mrs. Bucket and little Charlie Bucket slept in the other room, upon mattresses on the floor.

In the summertime, this wasn't too bad, but in the winter, freezing cold drafts blew across the floor all night long, and it was awful.

There wasn't any question of them being able to buy a better house—or even one more bed to sleep in. They were far too poor for that.

Mr. Bucket was the only person in the family with a job. He worked in a toothpaste factory, where he sat all day long at a bench and screwed the little caps onto the tops of the tubes of toothpaste after the tubes had been filled. But a toothpaste cap-screwer is never paid very much money, and poor Mr. Bucket, however hard he worked, and however fast he screwed on the caps, was never able to make enough to buy one-half of the things that so large a family needed. There wasn't even enough money to buy proper food for them all. The only meals they could afford were bread and margarine for breakfast, boiled potatoes and cabbage for lunch, and cabbage soup for supper. Sundays were a bit better. They all looked forward to Sundays because then, although they had exactly the same, everyone was allowed a second helping.

The Buckets, of course, didn't starve, but every one of them—the two old grandfathers, the two old grandmothers, Charlie's father, Charlie's mother, and especially little Charlie himself—went about from morning till night with a horrible empty feeling in their tummies.

Charlie felt it worst of all. And although his father and mother often went without their own share of lunch or supper so that they could give it to him, it still wasn't nearly enough for a growing boy. He desperately wanted something more filling and satisfying than cabbage and cabbage soup. The one thing he longed for more than anything else was . . . CHOCOLATE.

In passage 2, you will consider tone. Highlight words that help to identify the author's attitude toward the children he describes. List those words in the space provided. Then, come up with one or two words that describe the tone of the passage.

Words/Phrases	Tone

My Notes

Novel Excerpt

ABOUT THE AUTHOR

Roald Dahl (1916 – 1990) was born in Wales to Norwegian parents. The stories he heard as a child greatly influenced his love of stories and books. Dahl wrote stories for adults and children. Many of his children's stories came about from the bedtime stories he made up for his daughters. *James and the Giant Peach* was his first book, followed by *Charlie and the Chocolate Factory*, both of which enjoyed huge success in the United Kingdom and the United States.

From # CHARLIE and the CHOCOLATE FACTORY

by Roald Dahl

PASSAGE 2

The very next day, the first Golden Ticket was found. The finder was a boy called Augustus Gloop, and Mr. Bucket's evening newspaper carried a large picture of him on the front page. The picture showed a nine-year-old boy who was so enormously fat he looked as though he had been blown up with a powerful pump. Great flabby folds of fat bulged out from every part of his body, and his face was like a monstrous ball of dough with two small greedy curranty eyes peering out upon the world. The town in which Augustus Gloop lived, the newspaper said, had gone wild with excitement over their hero. Flags were flying from all the windows, children had been given a holiday from school, and a parade was being organized in honor of the famous youth.

"I just *knew* Augustus would find a Golden Ticket," his mother had told the newspapermen. "He eats so *many* candy bars a day that it was almost *impossible* for him *not* to find one. Eating is his hobby, you know. That's *all* he's interested in. But still, that's better than being a *hooligan* and shooting off *zip guns* and things like that in his spare time, isn't it? And what I always say is, he wouldn't go on eating like he does unless he *needed* nourishment, would he? It's all *vitamins,* anyway. What a *thrill* it will be for him to visit Mr. Wonka's Marvelous factory! We're just as *proud* as can be!"

ADMIT ★ ONE ★

1517441154

My Notes

"What a revolting woman," said Grandma Josephine.

"And what a repulsive boy," said Grandma Georgina.

… Suddenly, on the day before Charlie Bucket's birthday, the newspapers announced that the second Golden Ticket had been found. The lucky person was a small girl called Veruca Salt who lived with her rich parents in a great city far away. Once again, Mr. Bucket's evening newspaper carried a big picture of the finder. She was sitting between her beaming father and mother in the living room of their house, waving the Golden Ticket above her head, and grinning from ear to ear.

Veruca's father, Mr. Salt, had eagerly explained to the newspapermen exactly how the ticket was found. "You see, fellers," he had said, "as soon as my little girl told me that she simply *had* to have one of those Golden Tickets, I want out into the town and started buying up all the Wonka candy bars I could lay my hands on. *Thousands* of them, I must have bought. *Hundreds* of thousands! Then I had them loaded onto trucks and sent directly to my *own* factory. I'm in the peanut business, you see, and I've got about a hundred women working for me over at my joint, shelling peanuts for roasting and salting. That's what they do all day long, those women, they sit there shelling peanuts. So I says to them, 'Okay, girls,' I says, 'from now on, you can stop shelling peanuts and start shelling the wrappers off these crazy candy bars instead!' And they did. I had every worker in the place yanking the paper off those bars of chocolate full speed ahead from morning till night.

"But three days went by, and we had no luck. Oh, it was terrible! My little Veruca got more and more upset each day, and every time I went home she would scream at me, "*Where's my Golden Ticket! I want my Golden Ticket!*" And she would lie for hours on the floor, kicking and yelling in the most disturbing way. Well, sir, I just hated to see my little girl feeling unhappy like that, so I vowed I would keep up the search until I'd got her what she wanted. Then suddenly . . . on the evening of the fourth day, one of my women workers yelled, 'I've got it! A Golden Ticket!' And I said, 'Give it to me, quick!' and she did, and I rushed it home and gave it to my darling Veruca, and now she's all smiles, and we have a happy home once again."

"That's even worse than the fat boy," said Grandma Josephine.

"She needs a real good spanking," said Grandma Georgina.

Setting the Mood: Wonka Two Ways

You will now watch the beginning of Tim Burton's *Charlie and the Chocolate Factory.* While viewing, pay special attention to the ways in which a director's ability to create various moods leads to the shifting tone of the film. Consider these two questions as you watch the film:

1. How does Burton create mood and tone? What does a director have at his disposal that an author does not? (In addition to dialogue/text, a director can use lighting, costuming, sound, color, etc.)

2. In terms of mood and tone, is the film version similar to the written version? What specific instances contribute to the mood/tone?

FILM NOTES:

	MOOD	TONE
LIGHTING		
COSTUMES		
COLOR		
SOUND		

Revisiting "Wonka": Application of Film Terms

SUGGESTED LEARNING STRATEGIES: Close Reading, Drafting, Graphic Organizer, Quickwrite, Role Playing

Your teacher will give your group an index card with cinematic terms on it. In your group, take on the role of director, cameraman, or actors and create a scenario in which you apply the terms.

1. Describe the scene you and your group plan to demonstrate using your assigned cinematic techniques.

2. After you have presented your scene and viewed a clip from *Charlie and the Chocolate Factory*, draft a **quickwrite** in which you respond to the following questions:

   • In your scenario, what effect did you want to have on your audience?

   • What effect do you think Burton wants to have in this scene in the film?

   • What choices did you make in your direction to achieve your desired effect?

   • What choices does Burton make?

3. To elaborate on the concept of cinematic techniques, create a graphic organizer in your Vocabulary Notebook, with one section identifying film technques and another describing the intended and actual effect of that technique.

Working with Cinematic Techniques: Part 2

Use the graphic organizer to take notes as you view the film clip.

Charlie and the Chocolate Factory	Observations: Note what you observe in this scene — camera movement, angles, shots, sound, lighting, setting, characters, etc.	Interpretation: What can you infer from your observations?
First viewing — without sound		
Second viewing — with sound		
Final viewing (Optional)		

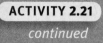

1. How does the director use sound (diegetic and non-diegetic) to enhance this scene?

2. What is the effect of dialogue on the scene?

3. Why does the author use a flashback scene? What does the director accomplish in doing so?

Reading Film: *Edward Scissorhands*

Segment of Film	Observations: What is happening in this scene?	Interpretation: What can you infer or predict based on your observations?
The Opening Credits: Images, Shapes, Music		
The Frame Story: Grandmother with Granddaughter		

Segment One: Opening Titles

1. Describe the **tone** in this scene. What type of movie does it remind you of?

2. How does the lighting help create the mood of this opening?

Segment Two: Frame Story — Grandmother with Granddaughter

1. How has the music changed between the opening credits and this scene? Why?

2. What does the camera do when it leaves the room where the story is being told? Why do you think the director does this?

3. What do you think this film will be about? On what do you base your prediction?

Discussion Questions for the Home Base Group

1. What do you know about Peg from this segment?

2. How has the director already established a connection between Edward and Kim?

3. How do you feel about Edward? What do you think will happen to him?

4. How do you feel about the town? Why do you feel this way?

Notes for Jigsaw Discussion of Key Sequence

In the graphic organizer below, note the places where you see particularly interesting or effective examples of your assigned cinematic element. You may need to put your notes on a separate sheet of paper.

Framing/Angles	Lighting	Camera Movement	Music/Sound	Editing

Analytical Statement with Textual Support

As you develop your analytical statement, it is important to understand the following terms:

Author's Purpose: The intended effect or meaning created or suggested by the use of a device (literary, rhetorical, or cinematic)

Effect: The result or influence of using a specific device

Take notes on the graphic organizer about the specific cinematic technique you studied, its effect, and an example from the film.

Purpose of the cinematic element

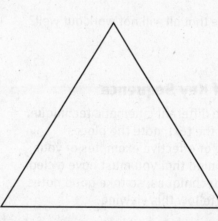

Example(s) of this cinematic element   Effect(s) of this cinematic choice

One way to pull your observations together for an analytical statement is to follow the model below:

Tim Burton, in *Edward Scissorhands*, uses _____

(cinematic element) in order to _____

(achieve what purpose). For example, _____

_____

_____

(evidence from the text to support the topic sentence).

Reading Film: Screening Day B

Discussion Questions for the Home Base Group

1. Why do the townspeople welcome Edward so quickly into their lives?

2. How does the town seem to change after Edward's arrival?

3. Kim's reaction to Edward is played for humor, but in what way is hers the most natural or realistic response?

4. What hints in this segment indicate that all will not work out well?

Notes for Jigsaw Discussion of Key Sequence

Today, you will become an expert on a different cinematic technique. While re-viewing the key sequence of the text, note the places where you see particularly interesting or effective examples of your assigned cinematic element. Keep in mind that you must have a clear understanding of all of the cinematic techniques, so take good notes during the jigsaw discussion that will follow this viewing.

Framing/Angles	Lighting	Camera Movement	Music/Sound	Editing

Analytical Statement with Textual Support and Reflective Commentary

In this writing exercise, you will add reflective commentary to your analytical statement. Remember that the reflective commentary comes after the example on purpose! The job of the commentary is to show your understanding of the relationship between your example and your original claim. You can make a comment, explain the connection, illustrate the point you made, or perhaps prompt a realization in the mind of the reader. In other words, if your example is the "what," then the reflective commentary is the "so what."

ACADEMIC VOCABULARY

Commentary is your explanation of the importance or relevance of your example and the way your example supports your analysis.

To make your analysis, complete this statement:

Tim Burton, in *Edward Scissorhands*, uses _____ in order

(*cinematic element*)

to _____.

(*achieve what purpose*)

For example, _____.

(*Provide evidence from the text to support the topic sentence.*)

_____.

_____.

(*reflective commentary*)

Director's Chair: Visualizing a Scene

Dialogue from *Edward Scissorhands*

KIM

You're here. They didn't hurt you, did they? Were you scared? I tried to make Jim go back, but you can't make Jim do anything. Thank you for not telling them about me.

EDWARD

You are welcome.

KIM

It must have been awful when they told you whose house it was.

EDWARD

I knew it was Jim's house.

KIM

You did?

EDWARD

Yes.

KIM

Well, then why did you do it?

EDWARD

Because you asked me to.

(Jim calls out for Kim, who runs outside to see him. Edward watches them together and then stalks off down the hallway, tearing the wallpaper with his hands.)

Imagine how the preceding scene might be filmed by Tim Burton.
Predict how he might sequence the shots, and craft a storyboard that
will capture the essence of the sequence.

SHOT #

Describe the Music/Sound:

Dialogue:

Framing: Lighting:

SHOT #

Describe the Music/Sound:

Dialogue:

Framing: Lighting:

SHOT #

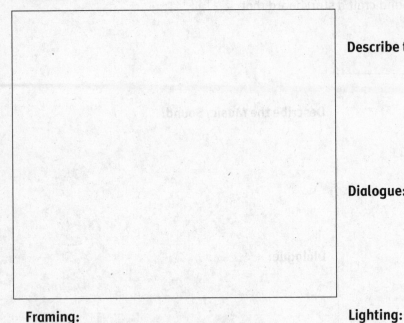

Describe the Music/Sound:

Dialogue:

Framing:

Lighting:

SHOT #

Describe the Music/Sound:

Dialogue:

Framing:

Lighting:

SHOT #

Describe the Music/Sound:

Dialogue:

Framing: **Lighting:**

SHOT #

Describe the Music/Sound:

Dialogue:

Framing: **Lighting:**

Reflection Questions:

Look back through your shots and, on separate paper, answer these questions.

- Why did you choose the framing, lighting, and music that you did?

- What words or phrases from the screenplay made you picture the scene as you did?

- How did the scenes you have already seen in the movie help you make your choices?

- How does this scene in Burton's film compare to the one that you envisioned? Explain.

Reading Film: Screening Day C

SUGGESTED LEARNING STRATEGIES: Close Reading, Discussion Groups, Graphic Organizer, Notetaking

GRAMMAR & USAGE

When you write your paragraph of analysis, it is important to use **parallel structure**, that is, to express similar ideas in the same grammatical form. In the following examples, the parallel structures are in boldface type.

The speaker **cajoled, remonstrated**, and **threatened**, but the audience remained unmoved.

Lincoln stressed "...a government **of the people, by the people**, and **for the people** shall not perish from the earth." Gettysburg Address

"**I came, I saw, I conquered**," wrote Julius Caesar.

Discussion Questions for the Home Base Group

1. Is Edward behaving any differently now than he did before? What is different about the town's treatment of him?

2. What is the effect of the scene with Kim dancing in the ice crystals? How have her feelings about Edward changed? Why?

3. How has Edward tried to fit in? Why has he failed? What does the "ethics lesson" reveal about Edward?

Notes for Jigsaw Discussion of Key Sequence

Note the places where you see particularly interesting or effective uses of your assigned cinematic element. Again, keep in mind that you must have a clear understanding of all of the cinematic techniques, so take good notes during the jigsaw discussion.

Framing/Angles	Lighting	Camera Movement	Music/Sound	Editing

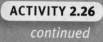

Analytical Statement with Textual Support, Reflective Commentary and Closure

Tim Burton, in *Edward Scissorhands*, uses _____ in order

(cinematic element)

to _____ .

(achieve what purpose)

For example, _____ .

(Provide evidence from the text to support the topic sentence.)

_____ .

_____ .

(reflective commentary)

_____

(sentence of closure)

Writing Prompt: With your writing group, create a well-developed paragraph analyzing the element that you focused on for the film segment. Remember to use parallel structure in your writing.

**ACTIVITY
2.27**

Reading Film: Screening Day D

SUGGESTED LEARNING STRATEGIES: **Close Reading, Discussion Groups, Graphic Organizer, Notetaking, Sharing And Responding**

Discussion Questions for the Home Base Group

1. Does Edward's action seem justified?

2. How does Edward appear to feel about Jim's death? How does Kim appear to feel?

3. Why do you think Edward cuts his clothes off?

4. Most fairy tales have a lesson or a moral to teach. What do you think Kim wants her granddaughter to learn from her story?

Notes for Jigsaw Discussion of the Key Sequence

Note the places where you see particularly interesting or effective uses of your assigned cinematic element. Again, keep in mind that you must have a clear understanding of all of the cinematic techniques, so take good notes during the jigsaw discussion.

Framing/Angles	Lighting	Camera Movement	Music/Sound	Editing

Writing Prompt: Write a well-developed paragraph analyzing Burton's use of a cinematic element in *Edward Scissorhands*. Include all the features that you have practiced, including analytical statements with textual support, reflective commentary, and closure.

Independent Viewing

SUGGESTED LEARNING STRATEGIES: Close Reading, Double-Entry Journal, Graphic Organizer, Notetaking

Use the following double-entry journal individually to identify film techniques and their intended effects. You will use these examples in your final writing assessment, so try to identify as many examples as you can.

Film Technique and Example: (Framing/Angles, Lighting, Camera Movement, Music/Sound, and Editing)	Intended Effect
1. **Dolly/Tracking:** We see the movement of the fish through its own eyes rather than an omniscient (all-seeing) observer.	1. Establishes a first person point of view and helps the viewer to understand the perspective of the animal as a character rather than an object.

Film Technique and Example: (Framing/Angles, Lighting, Camera Movement, Music/Sound, and Editing)	Intended Effect

Closing Question: After viewing the film(s), what similarities in style and/or theme did you notice in relation to the other films you watched? Record your ideas on a separate piece of paper for a class discussion.

Portfolio Activity: Film Style

There are six common literary elements to consider when examining an author's *style* in a text: tone, diction, imagery, syntax, organization, and point of view. Some of these terms will be familiar to you from previous years, some were introduced this year, and some might be brand new. Consider what you already know about these elements, and read the definitions provided. Then fill in the right side of the chart with an example from your viewing that is used for the same purpose. Hint: The first one is from a lesson in this unit.

Style Device	Cinematic Technique
Tone: The writer's or speaker's attitude toward a subject, character, or audience; it is conveyed through the author's choice of words and detail. **Mood:** The atmosphere or predominant emotion in a literary work.	
Diction: Word choice intended to convey a certain effect.	
Imagery: The descriptive words or phrases a writer uses to represent persons, objects, actions, feelings, and ideas by appealing to the senses.	
Organization: The narrative structure of a piece— how a text begins and ends, is sequenced, paced, or arranged.	
Syntax: The arrangement of words and the order of grammatical elements in a sentence.	
Point of View: The perspective from which a narrative is told.	

Portfolio Activity: Film Style

Now consider all of the films you have viewed in class. Fill in the graphic organizer below with similarities and differences in character, theme, and, especially, cinematic techniques. You might want to enlarge the Venn diagram or create your own organizer on a separate page.

Film:

Film:

Film:

Creating a Draft

SUGGESTED LEARNING STRATEGIES: **Close Reading, Marking the Draft,
Sharing and Responding, Revising**

Use the following outline to guide you as you craft your first draft of a
multiple-paragraph analytical essay. Use the space in the outline for
your notes.

Introduction

Should contain a lead or hook that grabs the reader's attention. Use
the subjunctive form to compose a rhetorical question expressing a
possibility as a hook.

Should provide a context for the reader (theme) of the movies you will
discuss, connecting to two cinematic elements.

Should provide a thesis that interprets Burton's use of your two
specified elements.

Should connect to larger themes.

Body Paragraph 1

Focus on one cinematic element and explore its effect in multiple films.

GRAMMAR & USAGE

Consider creating a
compound sentence
by joining independent
clauses with a **conjunctive
adverb**. A conjunctive
adverb joins the clauses
and also indicates the
relationship between
them.

These are some common
conjunctive adverbs:
*consequently, however,
instead, otherwise,
therefore, in addition,
nevertheless.*

Notice the punctuation
and the placement of the
conjunctive adverb in the
following examples:

> He was an accomplished
> speaker; **however,** he
> did not impress the
> audience.

> He was an accomplished
> speaker; he did not,
> **however,** impress the
> audience.

Creating a Draft

Body Paragraph 2

Focus on another cinematic element and explore its effect in multiple films.

Conclusion

Let the following questions shape your concluding thoughts:

- What did you say in regard to Burton's style in this essay?
- Do the cinematic elements you discuss connect to a larger theme?
- What does this interpretive analysis mean?
- Why does it matter?

Writing a Style Analysis Essay

SUGGESTED LEARNING STRATEGIES: Graphic Organizer, Prewriting, Marking The Draft, Outlining, Sharing and Responding, Self Editing

Assignment

Your assignment is to write an essay analyzing the cinematic style of director Tim Burton. Your essay will focus on the ways in which the director uses stylistic techniques across films to achieve a desired effect.

Steps

Prewriting

1. Review the graphic organizers and double-entry journals you have completed throughout the unit, and consider the multiple examples of Tim Burton's stylistic choices. Make a list of the stylistic elements you can incorporate into your essay. Narrow your list to include only three or four stylistic techniques for which you have clear examples.

2. Create a thesis statement in which you identify the stylistic techniques you will discuss. Then, use a prewriting strategy (e.g., mapping, webbing, or outlining) to develop the details and examples you can include to support each topic. You might consider talking to your Writing Group to refine your thinking about the examples you can include for each stylistic element.

Drafting

3. Draft your essay. Consult your mapping plan and outline. Use ample support for each of your topics. Continue to refer to your graphic organizers and double-entry journal for assistance.

Revising

4. Create manipulative cards on which you write your thesis statement, topics, and supporting details. Consider the relationship between your thesis and topics, and experiment with rearranging the order of your topics or details by shifting the position of the cards.

5. Next, share your draft with your Writing Group. Your peers should consult the Scoring Guide to guide their responses and suggestions with a focus on your essay's ideas, organization, and use of language.

6. Consider the results of your manipulative exercise and writing group discussion, and incorporate desired changes into your new draft.

Editing for Publication

7. Use your available resources (e.g., spell check, dictionaries, Editor's Checklist) to edit for correctness of grammar and conventions and prepare your essay for publication.

8. If you are handwriting your essay, remember to write clearly and legibly.

Writing a Style Analysis Essay

SCORING GUIDE

Scoring Criteria	Exemplary	Proficient	Emerging
Ideas	The writer insightfully identifies and analyzes Burton's stylistic techniques employing textual support from multiple films. The analysis displays an in-depth understanding of how Burton achieves his intended effect on the audience.	The writer clearly identifies and describes Burton's stylistic techniques using support from more than one film. The analysis displays a clear understanding of how Burton achieves his intended effect on the audience.	The writer demonstrates a limited understanding of Burton's stylistic techniques; support is insufficient or inaccurate. The analysis displays a misunderstanding of how Burton achieves the intended effect on the audience and/or may be replaced with plot summary.
Organization	The essay is multi-paragraphed and logically organized to enhance the reader's understanding. It includes an innovative introduction with an insightful lead or hook and strong thesis, coherent body paragraphs, and a perceptive conclusion. Effective transitions exist throughout and add to the essay's coherence.	The essay is multi-paragraphed and organized. It includes an introduction with a lead or hook and clear thesis, detailed body paragraphs, and a conclusion. Transitions create coherence.	Organization is attempted, but key components are lacking. It may include an introduction with an unfocused thesis, undeveloped body paragraphs, and/or inadequate conclusion. Transitions, if attempted, do little to create coherence.
Use of Language	Diction is appropriate for an academic audience. The essay demonstrates a sophisticated use of terminology to knowledgeably discuss film.	Diction is mostly appropriate for an academic essay. The essay demonstrates a basic use of terminology to discuss film.	Diction is informal or inappropriate for an academic essay. The essay may demonstrate limited or inaccurate use of terminology to discuss film.
Conventions	Writing is virtually error-free	Writing is generally error-free.	Writing contains errors that distract from meaning.

SCORING GUIDE

Scoring Criteria	Exemplary	Proficient	Emerging
Evidence of Writing Process	There is extensive evidence that the essay reflects the various stages of the writing process.	There is evidence that the essay reflects stages of the writing process.	There is little or no evidence that the essay has undergone stages of the writing process.
Additional Criteria			

Comments:

Reflection

An important aspect of growing as a learner is to reflect on where you have been, what you have accomplished, what helped you to learn, and how you will apply your new knowledge in the future. Use the following questions to guide your thinking and to identify evidence of your learning. Use separate notebook paper.

Thinking about Concepts

1. Using specific examples from this unit, respond to the Essential Questions:
   - How do authors and directors use specific techniques to achieve a desired effect?
   - What are the essential features of an effective style analysis?

2. Consider the new academic vocabulary from this unit (**Point of View, Style, Cinematic Techniques, Effect, Commentary**) as well as academic vocabulary from previous units, and select 3-4 terms of which your understanding has grown. For each term, answer the following questions:
   - What was your understanding of the term before you completed this unit?
   - How has your understanding of the term evolved throughout the unit?
   - How will you apply your understanding in the future?

Thinking about Connections

3. Review the activities and products (artifacts) you created. Choose those that most reflect your growth or increase in understanding.

4. For each artifact that you choose, record, respond to, and reflect on your thinking and understanding, using the following questions as a guide:
   a. What skill/knowledge does this artifact reflect, and how did you learn this skill/knowledge?
   b. How did your understanding of the power of language expand through your engagement with this artifact?
   c. How will you apply this skill or knowledge in the future?

5. Create this reflection as Portfolio pages—one for each artifact you choose. Use the model in the box for your headings and commentary on questions.

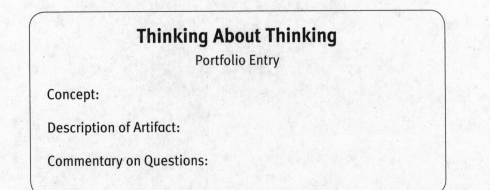

Thinking About Thinking
Portfolio Entry

Concept:

Description of Artifact:

Commentary on Questions:

Exploring Poetic
Voices

Essential Questions

 What is poetry?

 What can a writer learn from studying an author's craft and style?

Unit Overview

Poetry most poignantly conveys the power of words, of feelings, and of images. Since we are surrounded by poetry in its various forms on a daily basis—for example, popular music, billboards, and advertising jingles, it is important to understand the fundamentals of the genre. At the same time, you should appreciate and enjoy poetry independently, free from teacher interpretation. As Walt Whitman noted in his poem, "Song of Myself,"

Stop this day and night with me and you shall possess the origin of all poems,

You shall possess the good of the earth and sun (there are millions of suns left)

You shall no longer take things at second or third hand, nor look through eyes of the dead, nor feed on the spectres in books,

You shall not look through my eyes either, nor take things from me,

You shall listen to all sides and filter them from yourself.

—Walt Whitman, *Leaves of Grass*

185

Exploring Poetic Voices

Contents

Goals

▶ To develop the skills and knowledge to analyze and craft poetry

▶ To analyze the function and effects of figurative language

▶ To write original poems that reflect personal voice, style, and an understanding of poetic elements

▶ To write a style analysis essay

▶ To present an oral interpretation of a poem

ACADEMIC VOCABULARY

Poetic Structure

Diction

Imagery

Figurative Language

Syntax

Texts not included in these materials.

Learning Focus:

What Does My Voice Represent?

We have all had a song, whether we like it or not, get stuck in our heads. It plays over and over and over. Maybe the tune is catchy or maybe the lyrics are contagious; songs are poetry set to music, and lyrics —words— infectiously express an artist's voice. In this unit, you will discover **voice**, a very powerful tool, and you will be exposed to a variety of **poetic voices** that explore coming-of-age issues. Furthermore, you will analyze how poetry frees an artist to express perspectives on personal experiences, community, and societal issues.

As you examine the work of published poets, you will sharpen your ability to read, interpret, and critique poems. You will explore the function and effect of poetic devices (i.e., **poetic structure, figurative language, diction, imagery**). In addition, you will gain a sense of how specific poetic language reinforces ideas and themes, and you will gain a sense of what others' voices can represent.

Careful attention to another's work will help you to explore your own poetic voice, creating original poems that emulate the style and craft of published poets. Once you understand how authors use poetic devices for specific effect, you will be able to use those same devices to create poems that express your feelings about coming of age. As the first half of the unit ends, you will construct an anthology that showcases a collection of your original poems. This task will give you an opportunity to reflect on and critique the stylistic choices you make as a writer, and, as a result, your voice just may contagiously remain in someone else's head!

Independent Reading: Several of the poems in this unit focus on issues of growth, self-realization, and expression. For your own reading, you may want to look for a collection of poems or a story written in poetic form that relates to similar issues that are important to you.

Previewing the Unit

SUGGESTED LEARNING STRATEGIES: Close Reading, KWL Chart, Marking the Text, Skimming/Scanning, Summarizing/Paraphrasing, Think-Pair-Share

Essential Questions

1. What is poetry?

2. What can a writer learn from studying an author's craft and style?

Unit Overview and Learning Focus

Predict what you think this unit is about. Use the words or phrases that stood out to you when you read the Unit Overview and the Learning Focus.

Embedded Assessment 1

What knowledge must you have (what do you need to know) to succeed on Embedded Assessment 1? What skills must you have (what must you be able to do)?

What Is Poetry?

SUGGESTED LEARNING STRATEGIES: Close Reading, Marking the Text, Metacognitive Markers, Quickwrite, Think-Pair-Share

Poets' Perspectives About Poetry

1.	"We don't read and write poetry because it's cute. We read and write poetry because we are members of the human race. And the human race is filled with passion. And medicine, law, business, engineering, these are noble pursuits and necessary to sustain life. But poetry, beauty, romance, love, these are what we stay alive for." *Dead Poets Society*
2.	"Poetry is what gets lost in translation." —Robert Frost
3.	"Poetry is just the evidence of life. If your life is burning well, poetry is just the ash." —Leonard Cohen
4.	"Out of the quarrel with others we make rhetoric; out of the quarrel with ourselves we make poetry." —W.B. Yeats
5.	"Poetry is a packsack of invisible keepsakes." —Carl Sandburg
6.	"Poetry is man's rebellion against being what he is." —James Branch Cabell
7.	"Poetry is the revelation of a feeling that the poet believes to be interior and personal which the reader recognizes as his own." —Salvatore Quasimodo
8.	"Poetry is plucking at the heartstrings, and making music with them." —Dennis Gabor
9.	"Mathematics and poetry are . . . the utterance of the same power of imagination, only that in the one case it is addressed to the head, in the other, to the heart." —Thomas Hill
10.	"Poetry is an orphan of silence. The words never quite equal the experiences behind them." —Charles Simic

Essential Question: What is poetry?

Poetry

by Pablo Neruda

> **ABOUT THE AUTHOR**
>
> Chilean author Pablo Neruda (1904–1973) contributed his first poem to a literary journal when he was sixteen and published his first collection of poems the following year. Throughout his life, his poems reflected his world and his work. He wrote political poems, an epic poem about the South American continent, and a series of odes that reflect everyday life—things, events, relationships. In 1971, he was awarded the Nobel Prize in Literature.

And it was at that age . . . poetry arrived
in search of me. I don't know, I don't know where
it came from, from winter or a river.
I don't know how or when,
no they were not voices, they were not   5
words, nor silence,
but from a street I was summoned,
from the branches of night,
abruptly from the others,
among violent fires   10
or returning alone,
there I was without a face
and it touched me.

I did not know what to say, my mouth
had no way   15
with names,
my eyes were blind,
and something started in my soul,
fever or forgotten wings,
and I made my own way,   20
deciphering[1]
that fire,

---

[1] **deciphering:** figuring out the meaning of something that's not clear

My Notes

and I wrote the first faint line,
faint, without substance, pure
25 nonsense,
pure wisdom
of someone who knows nothing,
and suddenly I saw
the heavens
30 unfastened and open,
planets,
palpitating[2] plantations,
shadow perforated,[3]
riddled
35 with arrows, fire, and flowers,
the winding night, the universe.

And I, infinitesimal[4] being,
drunk with the great starry
void,
40 likeness, image of mystery,
felt myself a pure part
of the abyss,
I wheeled with the stars,
my heart broke loose on the wind.

WORD CONNECTIONS

The word *abyss* (a bottomless depth) contains the Greek prefix *a-*, which means "without" or "the absence of." This common prefix occurs in other English words like *amoral, apolitical,* and *asocial.*

---

[2] **palpitating**: pulsating or throbbing rapidly
[3] **perforated**: pierced with holes
[4] **infinitesimal**: so small as to be almost nothing

While reading the poem aloud, direct your attention to the following stylistic techniques:

Repetition

Verb Choice

Anaphora

Form

Quickwrite: Revisit the poetry quotations, your classroom discussions, and Neruda's poem and explore the unit's essential question, "What is poetry?"

> **LITERARY TERMS**
>
> **Repetition** is the use of any element of language—a sound, a word, a phrase, a line, or a stanza—more than once.
>
> **Anaphora** is a particular kind of repetition in which the same word or group of words is repeated at the beginnings of two or more successive clauses or lines.
>
> **Form** refers to the particular structure or organization of a work.

Use your ideas about poetry to complete the frame poem below.

A Poem About a Poem

by _____

Poetry is _____

Poetry is like _____

Poetry is about _____

Poetry is as important as _____

Poetry is as pointless as _____

Poetry means _____

Poetry is _____

A Writer Speaks About Poetry

My Notes

Essays

> **ABOUT THE AUTHOR**
> Susan Wooldridge is a teacher of creative writing. Her work has been published in numerous journals, though she is best known for her collection of essays, *poemcrazy*. As an observer of nature and the world around her, she is inspired in her writing by everyday events and shares her stories in a distinctive writing style.

From poemcrazy

by Susan Goldsmith Wooldridge

3

collecting words and creating a wordpool

I have a strong gathering instinct. I collect boxes, hats, rusty flattened bottlecaps for collages and creek-worn sticks to color with my hoard of Berol prismacolor pencils. When I was a kid I'd lie in bed imagining I was a squirrel who lived in a hollow tree, foraging for acorns, twigs and whatever it takes to make squirrel furniture.

Most of us have collections. I ask people all the time in workshops, Do you collect anything? Stamps? Shells? '57 Chevys? Raccoons? Money? Leopards? Meteorites? Wisecracks? What a coincidence, I collect them, too. Hats, coins, cougars, old Studebakers. That is, I collect the words. Pith helmet, fragment, Frigidaire, quarrel, love seat, lily. I gather them into my journal.

The great thing about collecting words is they're free; you can borrow them, trade them in or toss them out. I'm trading in (and literally composting) some of my other collections—driftwood, acorns and bits of colored Easter egg shell—for words. Words are lightweight, unbreakable, portable, and they're everywhere. You can even make them up. *Frebrent, bezoncular, zurber*. Someone made up the word *padiddle*.

A word can trigger or inspire a poem, and words in a stack or thin list can make up poems.

Because I always carry my journal with me, I'm likely to jot down words on trains, in the car, at boring meetings (where I appear to be taking notes), on hikes and in bed.

I take words from everywhere. I might steal *steel*, spelled both ways. *Unscrupulous.* I'll toss in *iron*, *metal* and *magnolias.* Whatever flies into my mind. *Haystack, surge, sidewinder.* A sound, *splash.* A color, *magenta.* Here's a chair. *Velvet. Plush.*

Dylan Thomas loved the words he heard and saw around him in Wales. "When I experience anything," he once said, "I experience it as a thing and a word at the same time, both equally amazing." Writing one ballad, he said, was like carrying around an armload of words to a table upstairs and wondering if he'd get there in time.

Words stand for feelings, ideas, mountains, bees. Listen to the sound of words. I line up words I like to hear, *Nasturtiums buzz blue grass catnip catalpa catalog.*

I borrow words from poems, books and conversations. Politely. Take *polite.* If I'm in a classroom, I just start chalking them onto the board. I don't worry about spelling or meaning. *Curdle. Cantankerous. Linoleum. Limousine.* Listen. *Malevolent. Sukulilli,* the Maidu Indian word for silly. *Magnet cat oven taste tilt titter.*

I call gathering words this way creating a *wordpool.* This process helps free us to follow the words and write poems. In Paradise, California, my students and I looked up insects in a field guide with names like *firebrat, jumping bristletail* and *slantfaced grasshopper.* Then, moving around the room, I asked each person for one word, *any* word.

Everyone started tossing out words. *Tabulate. Magnify. Silence.* We could see the weight and value of each one. Someone said the word *no.* We put yes up there to balance it. Scott said *hate* and then *demolish.* We added *love* and *create* after talking about the importance of opposites. Then we looked for the opposite of *brick, idea, jealousy, tumbleweed* and *cloud.* We piled dozens of words on the board,

toe joust marvel
apparatus dome click
tubed tailstripes
flabbergast horse thought
cumulus cumulo nimbus
nom de plume zodiac zirconium flicker
slip spin serendipity
obsession pyromaniac two-tailed thrips
adobe hypothermia
frost dragon confetti tapioca
observe slither slink snuggle snooze

The rhythm, the music in the words, the circle of voices around the room, the associations, the well of minds casting out words like water in a fountain, words next to words in new ways and the look of them spreading across and down the page takes us to the state of mind poems come from.

A Writer Speaks About Poetry

My Notes

I encourage people to toss foreign words into the wordpool. Just the sound can move us into another world very swiftly, like *avra*, breeze in Greek, or *petra*, rock. Add *petrified* and the Maidu word for water that sounds like a spring murmuring, *momoli*. Include place names like the ones I collected in Wales, *Abergavenny, Linthill* and *Skrinklehaven*.

Listed and tossed out this way, words begin to fall into poems by themselves. We put them together in unexpected ways, like *zodiac flicker, tree thought, tumbleweed sadness, magenta jealousy, cloud brick, summer ice, tapioca slithers.*

When I'm playing with words, I don't worry about sounding dumb or crazy. And I don't worry about whether or not I'm writing "a poem." *Word pool. World pool, wild pool, whipoorwill, swing.* Words taken out of the laborious structures (like this sentence) where we normally place them take on a spinning life of their own.

PRACTICE

Write words down. *Flap tip lob. Elope. Scrounge.*

Look around and steal some words. *Lamborghini. Jute. Wombat.*

Go ahead and make up a word. *Losoonie. Flapoon. Noplat.*

Be sloppy. Don't think. You can't make a mistake, there aren't any wrong words. *Phantom strut tumble porch. Dragoon.*

Don't worry too much about meaning for now. Words carry meaning along with them. Put words down and meaning will begin to rush in.

Give each word a color. *Vermilion regret.*

List the senses and give each sense a color. *Peach hearing.*

Toss in words from foreign languages. *Ciao.*

Go for sound: *hum, fizz, fiddle, fandango, zigzag, ziggurat, folderol, armadillo. Tintinabulation.*

Collect field guides. I often bring an insect, rock or butterfly book to workshops and we list words like *window winged moth, globular springtail* or *porphyry*, a purple rock named for the Latin and Greek word for "purple."

My friend Tom's Ford pickup repair manual is chock full of great words: *luminosity probe, diesel throttle control tool, acceleration pump link, swivel, internal vent valve, choke hinge pin. . . .*

Look for a Magnetic Poetry Kit of words that stick to the refrigerator. My friend Arielle got a kit and told me, "Things just come out of you." She wrote about her family's twenty-one-year-old cat, Jumbo,

> white puppy petal
> you gorgeous milk fluff
> sleep all day lick
> tiny love from time
> and dream

(word magnet tiles: hero, innocent, respect, look, delicious, hope, mutual, kiss, must, smile, beauty, nice, like, sweet, good, trust, embrace, spirit, belong)

5

most mad and moonly

Things I love have a way of turning up in my life in unexpected ways. In high school I idolized e. e. cummings because he was irreverent and made me feel free. He played with language and broke all the rules, nourishing my *Catcher in the Rye*, antiestablishment side.

I memorized most of "What of a much of a which of a wind" and several other Cummings poems. My favorite for years was "Somewhere I have never traveled," with the unexpected line that moved me most, "and no one, not even the rain, has such small hands."

During my freshman year of college in New York City I met a Columbia student named Simon Roosevelt, who played Lysander in a production of *A Midsummer Night's Dream*. I painted viney leaves for the set as part of a stage crew that played loud rock music all hours of the night. I helped mend and fit costumes, happiest hanging out behind the scenes. Simon and I went to movies and studied together in the Columbia library. One evening I noticed a worn photo of e. e. cummings in Simon's wallet. "He was my grandfather," Simon told me. e. e. cummings—who died while I was in high school—was turning up again in my world. Life can be like a poem that way, with the unexpected appearing in the room, not just on the page.

cummings plays with words, spacing and capital letters, often putting all the punctuation somewhere unexpected. He experiments with opposites. His poems are both goofy and profound, soft and sharp at the same time, tender and fierce. "What of a much of a which of a wind" opens gently, but soon we're shocked as the wind "bloodies with dizzying leaves the sun / and yanks immortal stars awry."

cummings's words, often like the trail of an acrobat tumbling down the page, invite us to put our *own* words down. Filled with open, white space, his poems leave room for us to enter. We feel we can do this too. cummings's writing inspired a passion in me to create my own world, poke around and explore my boundaries, see how many shades of unnamed color and sound I might find there.

I write this in the car as we zoom home from Berkeley approaching— believe it or not—the "Cummings skyway." Here's Crockett, where the world opens up like a cummings poem into sky, water, sun, ships, and we soar over the Carquinez Strait high in ocean air on a towering erector-set bridge. Back home, my teenage daughter saunters into my room with her hair in a high bun, shoulders low, lips pouting, hips swaying. She's a feminist high-fashion model named Tangerine Valentino. Now she swivels out, ignoring my applause, creating a character sketch for her drama class.

My Notes

My Notes

cummings reminds me to allow poems to swagger, soar or tiptoe in unexpectedly. I need to be open and ready for them. Poems aren't written from ideas, like essays, and they're not overly controlled. In a poem's "most mad and moonly" spell, out of time, I can break rules and expectations about who I am as well as about writing.

My journal has a memorial page both for e. e. cummings and for his grandson Simon, killed on his red motorcycle the year after we met. At Simon's memorial service someone read a cummings poem that helped us with our shock and sadness,

> love is more thicker than forget
> more thinner than recall
> more seldom than a wave is wet
> more frequent than to fail
>
> it is most mad and moonly
> and less it shall unbe
> than all the sea which only
> is deeper than the sea
>
> love is less always than to win
> less never than alive
> less bigger than the least begin
> less littler than forgive
>
> it is most sane and sunly
> and more it cannot die
> than all the sky which only
> is higher than the sky.

The unexpected brings us light and darkness, joy and sorrow, life and death. And it brings discovery. Some of our most important discoveries are made when we're not looking.

PRACTICE

Read some poems by e. e. cummings.

Let a poem write itself as if you were taking dictation from your pen.

Break words up.

> Frag
>
>   men
>
>   t

Let yourself be like a kid. Write your name some way you've never written it before. Draw your name. Use colored pens or pencils.

Go somewhere outside and turn over a stone.

List in detail what's under the stone that you didn't expect.

Notice three new things in someone's face. Write down what you've seen.

Notice anything that spirals, from the corkscrew to the pasta to the weather patterns on the news.

Write a series of images without stopping. Make some of them absurd. *The snow is black today. It's been raining paint. My dog is singing* La Bohème.

Give colors to ideas and abstractions. *Blue love. Chartreuse agreements. Silver deliberation. Magenta pride.*

Be open to unexpected words and adventures. Spend time being in a state of quiet expectation and see what (or who) comes your way.

My Notes

6

gas, food, longing

I could glimpse the Hudson River bordering New Jersey when I lived in the Barnard College dorm. This glimpse filled me with longing for I wasn't sure what—maybe a houseboat on the river, a village life I loved or the person I knew I could be.

One weekend I went to a van Gogh exhibit at the Guggenheim Museum. As I rounded a curve in the gallery I saw a painting called *The Sower*. A faceless man, solid as the tree leaning toward him, scatters seeds near a river lit by a huge sun, palpable as a grapefruit in a green sky.

Staring at the painting, I almost stopped breathing. The simple figure in sunset seeding the earth expressed all my feelings of longing, hope and promise. I felt van Gogh had painted the inside of *me*. *I* was the peasant expectantly seeding the field. *I* was the glimpse of river like a blue path. *I* was the low sun about to sink from sight. *I* was the seed in a dark hand waiting to be tossed home. Though it cost more than I could afford, I bought a print of *The Sower* at the show and hung it on a straw mat in my pale green dorm room. The painting made me feel less alone, though I never lost that longing. Even now on the freeway sometimes I'll read the signs as, "Gas, Food, *Longing*."

I still have that print. Tattered and ripped, it's tacked to a wall in my garage, so many years later. I can't throw it out. When I left Barnard and met my future husband, Kent, I was delighted to see a paler version of my *Sower* hanging in his apartment.

For years I've collected paintings on postcards my friend Deborah sends me. I have a large shoebox full. There's Ivan Albright's door, crumbling and bedecked with fading roses like a poem that makes me feel loss and regret.

Albright gave his painting a name that's a poem fragment in itself, *That Which I Should Have Done I Did Not Do.* There's a Magritte room that makes me feel expansive with its clouds for walls, giant comb and shaving brush. Once a student saw this painting and, using the word tickets, wrote, "Suddenly my walls disappear."

In workshops I give each student a postcard to transform into a painting with words. Creating an image with words can express a feeling with color flooding in, as van Gogh's painting does for me.

Image is the root word of imagination. It's from Latin *imago*, "picture," how you see things. Images carry feelings. Saying, "I'm angry," or "I'm sad," has little impact. Creating images, I can make you feel how I feel.

When I read the words of a young student named Cari— "I'm a rose in the shape of a heart / with nineteen days of nothing / but the pouncing of shoes on my dead petals"—I experience desperation through her image.

Cari doesn't even have to name the feeling—nineteen days, a pale green sky, a pouch of seed held against a sower's heart.

Writing poems using images can create an experience allowing others to feel what we feel. Perhaps more important, poems can put us in touch with our own often buried or unexpected feelings.

Shoua discovered her frustration by using the image of a man shooting pool,

> I hear bang, click, shoosh
> feeling like the white ball
> that does all the work.

Tori used images from a landscape to indicate hopelessness,

> the clouds collapsed,
> they're touching the ground
> trying to come alive,
> but they can't.

Sometime word tickets magically fit with the images in the paintings. One of Tori's words was *jingle*. It helped her convey her developing feeling of hope,

> the glowing water shows shadow
> till we all hear
> the *jingle* of dawn.

Images we create in our poem can not only help us discover our feelings, but can help us begin to transform them.

PRACTICE

Make a wordpool of feeling words, going for opposites: *psychotic stable laughable sober drab vibrant bored blissful frantic calm fragile invincible.*

Find a postcard of a painting, a reproduction in a magazine or book, or a poster on a wall. Any painting will do.

Choose a feeling. Look closely at your painting and find a detail that seems to express your feeling, perhaps one color or the gesture of someone's arm. Perhaps a jug in the corner. Let your words paint the feeling. *I feel as still as a white water jug.*

Say your painting is a landscape. You feel *powerless*. What does that gray cloud look like that expresses your feeling? You might write that the cloud is dissolving, losing its shape. Or you feel *powerful*. Now the cloud is gathering electricity to snap out as lightning.

You might feel *unimportant*, like that tiny leaf on top of the tree, lost in all the others. You might feel like you're *fading* like the last bit of pink light on top of the mountain.

Choose a variety of paintings so you can begin to express the full range of your feelings in one or several poems.

My Notes

7

being here

Once I heard poet Gary Snyder say, "Poetry has an interesting function. It helps people *be* where they are." It's hard to write a poem about a place, an experience or even a state of mind without fully *being* there. When I'm fully present describing a place in a poem it helps bring my reader there too.

I need to breathe in the air, hear the sounds, feel the ground under my feet and join a place to fully describe it. If it's winter, my footprints need to sink in snow or mud beside weblike bird tracks. I need to get wet or muddy, smell, taste and look at things closely. It's important for me to use all my senses in poems: sight, touch smell, taste, hearing and the sixth sense, intuition or "dreamsense" as my friend Mark Rodriguez calls it.

Yesterday morning, on a walk, my writing partner Elizabeth and I got so caught up talking about our kids we barely noticed we were walking along the creek. To write poems I need to be alone. When I avoid being alone I avoid poetry and the messages it brings me.

Alone I open my senses, listen to my surroundings, take in the smells, the light and the way a sycamore curves over the creek like a pale rainbow. "Everything's got to do with listening," the poet W. S. Merwin said of a poem he wrote about the wind. Many of my poems come from what I notice when I'm alone.

Writer Louis Owens says that to most Native Americans, paying this kind of attention is a responsibility. "Our job is to be an awake people . . . utterly conscious, to attend to our world."

This noon I'm on the upper park rim trail on a pockmarked rock. It rained yesterday and there's a veil of mud over the lava cap on the ridge. My dog, Emma, explores as I peer over star thistle at retreating clouds. Thin winter grass is poking up and it's mid-November. Soon I'll find miner's lettuce to feed my kids along with the curly dock I gather for my daughter and me. Everyone else thinks it's too sour.

To experience a place I need to walk in it as often as I can. Abenaki native poet Joseph Bruchac says, "We need to walk to know sacred places, those around us and those within. We need to walk to remember the songs."

Now I've climbed up the hill about fifty feet and I'm sitting against an oak. I'm holding two large acorn caps like small pipe bowls. Here's one of the acorns, long, greenish brown. I rub off the tiny point and polish the acorn with my fingers. Later at home, two acorns will wobble around on the kitchen table shining like bullets.

Bird song. Sweet air. I feel the crumbly oak bark against my back. A darting bird's just above me and I hear thrumming wings. The oak helps me trust and wait and breathe and bend. I feel my body and mind taking in the tree. Soon I'll see what words come.

For now, I'll just be *here*, alone, watching and listening.

PRACTICE

All my poems are suggested by real life and therein have a firm foundation. . . . No one can imitate when you write of the particular, because no others have experienced exactly the same thing. —Goethe

Walk somewhere alone. Listen. Write about what's around you, using all of your senses.

It's important to narrow everything down, make it as specific as you can, down to the tip of a blade of grass, or you'll leave the reader out. For emotion to arise, writing has to be very specific—describing a particular moment or experience in a particular place.

A useful daily practice is to sit (or walk) with a notebook and focus on what's happening right now, in minute detail. "Inside a moment," Emily Dickinson wrote, "centuries of June."

Wherever you are, if it's warm enough, take off your shoes. Breathe deeply. What can you smell?

Look to your right. What's there? Feel your body and mind taking it in.

Look straight down. Notice a color, texture, shape.

Look straight up. Do you see acoustical tiles or blue sky or antique white plaster? Is there a spider up there in a corner webbing herself over? Leave her there, but describe her exactly on paper.

William Blake thought that art and science exist in the organization of "Minute Particulars." Blake saw "a World in a Grain of Sand."

Listen. Do you hear a coffeemaker? Freeway sounds? Tree frogs?

Place your right hand down. What do you feel? A nubby cushion, a chair? Your knee in frayed leggings?

Look closely at something you see all the time. Write as if you've never seen this before.

Keep writing. If you focus on your surroundings, the words may just help you be there. But if they want to take you somewhere else, follow them.

My Notes

My Notes

8

it looks like

When my son, Daniel, was small he would often compare the way one thing looked to another. Passing a peach cannery I said, "See the smoke coming out of that chimney?" Daniel responded, "Just yike a cigarette." He was always saying, "*It yooks yike, it yooks yike.*" When his sister, Elisabeth, was born, Dan saw her swaddled with only her head visible and remarked, "She yooks yike a hot dog."

When we transplanted a small tree from a pot to a hole in the ground, Daniel said, "The world will be its new pants." As we drove toward the coast one day and saw cows on the hillside, Elisabeth said, "They yook yike popcorn."

I think we naturally see things metaphorically. We're always comparing the way one thing looks to another. Comparison is built into our language. I've noticed that on a highway a hairpin turn, from above, *looks like* a hairpin. Cattails in a swampy area along Lonestar Road *look like* cat's tails. In my garden foxglove looks like a wee "folk's glove," with a pouch for a tiny hand. Georgia O'Keeffe said she painted individual flowers and made them huge so we'd be forced to look closely and notice what flowers really look like. Whether she intended this or not, O'Keeffe's paintings lend themselves to metaphor. Inside her white flower I see

> a gown with long white sleeves,
> a curled satin slipper with grey on the toe,
> a Chinese lantern on low,
> a bowl of silver bells, ringing.

Wilfred Funk writes in *Word Origins and Their Romantic Stories* that originally all words were poems, since our language is based, like poems, in metaphor. The names of flowers makes this easier to see. This flower looks like a shooting star. Maybe the next time I see one I'll make the shift from simile to full metaphor and think, This flower *is* a shooting star, or a bird's-eye, a paintbrush, butter and eggs.

In some words we can still see the poem/metaphor, especially flowers and trees like ladyslipper, redbud, spinster blue-eyed Mary. My married name, Wooldridge, must have come from the image of lambs on a ridge.

Metaphor is a bridge bringing things together. The world is a stage. Life is a dream. The navel is a belly button. When she lived in Athens years ago, a friend Sally tells me, some of the delivery bikes had the word METAPHOR printed on their sides—probably a company name. In Greek *metaphor* literally means to bear or carry over.

Sometimes part of writing a poem is as simple as looking carefully and bringing things together through simile and metaphor. This bit of moon looks like a canoe. The moon *is* a cradle, a wolf's tooth, a fingernail, snow on a curved leaf or milk in the bottom of a tipped glass.

PRACTICE

Take an object and think about what it *looks like*. Describe exactly what you see.

Look around you. Does your lampshade look like a ballerina's illuminated pink pleated skirt? Not exactly, but it's a start. Let yourself go for the farfetched and the ridiculous when you make comparisons.

If you can find a flower, look inside. What does it look like?

Find a painting, abstract or realistic. Choose a detail and stare at it. Focusing on that detail, write,

> I see
> It looks like
> it looks like
> I see
> It looks like (repeat)

For more practice, list what you see around you and write down what it looks like.

> The pine tree looks like a torpedo
> That folded piece of paper looks like a flattened sail
> The curled telephone cord looks like an earthworm
> That man's curly hair looks like. . .
> The moth's wing . . .

Keep going.

After Reading

What insights about writing does Susan Wooldridge suggest?

Literary Devices Scavenger Hunt

Personal Poetry Glossary

Literary Device	Definition	Example from the Text and Explanation of Function and Use	Original Example for My Writer's Toolbox
Refrain			
Tone			
Imagery			
Diction			
Hyperbole			
Allusion			
Connotation			

Extended Metaphor		
Symbol		
Onomatopoeia		
Alliteration		
Rhyme		
Theme		
Anaphora		
Assonance		
Consonance		

Literary Devices Scavenger Hunt

WORD CONNECTIONS

Hyperbole contains the Greek prefix *hyper-*, which means "excessive," or "more than normal." This prefix appears in such words as *hyperactive*, *hypersensitive*, *hypertension*, and *hypertext*.

Select a term from the preceding chart that is of particular interest to you, and create a graphic representation that captures the essence of the term.

Literary Device _____

SUGGESTED LEARNING STRATEGIES: Freewriting, Marking the Text, Notetaking, Questioning the Text, Think-Pair-Share, Close Reading

Poetry

ABOUT THE AUTHOR
Born in 1943 in Knoxville, Tennessee, Nikki Giovanni is a popular poet and professor of English. Over the years, she has won numerous writing awards. One of her recurring themes, presented through a variety of styles and topics, is love. Once known as "the priestess of Black poetry," she has more recently been called a "national treasure" and named an Oprah Winfrey "Living Legend."

NIKKI ROSa

by Nikki Giovanni

childhood remembrances are always a drag

if you're Black

you always remember things like living in Woodlawn

with no inside toilet

and if you become famous or something   5

they never talk about how happy you were to have

your mother

all to yourself and

how good the water felt when you got your bath

from one of those   10

big tubs that folk in Chicago barbecue in

and somehow when you talk about home

it never gets across how much you

understood their feelings

My Notes

LITERARY TERMS
An **autobiography** is written by a person who is telling his or her life's story. What elements in this poem make it autobiographical?

LITERARY TERMS

The term *free verse* describes poetry without a fixed pattern of meter and rhyme.

My Notes

15   as the whole family attended meetings about Hollydale

and even though you remember

your biographers never understand

your father's pain as he sells his stock

and another dream goes

20   and though you're poor it isn't poverty that

concerns you

and though they fight a lot

it isn't your father's drinking that makes any difference

but only that everybody is together and you

25   and your sister have happy birthdays and very good

Christmases

and I really hope no white person ever has cause

to write about me

because they never understand

30   Black love is Black wealth and they'll

probably talk about my hard childhood

and never understand that

all the while I was quite happy.

Structure in Poetry

Poetry

ABOUT THE AUTHOR

Gwendolyn Brooks (1917–2000) grew up and lived her life in Chicago. While still in her teens, she published poems in an African American newspaper in Chicago. It wasn't long before her poetry became recognized nationally, and she won the Pulitzer Prize for Poetry in 1950, the first African American to win a Pulitzer. Poetry was the focus of Brooks's life, and she continued to be a prolific writer as well as a teacher and advocate of poetry. She taught creative writing at a number of colleges and universities. Her publications and awards were numerous, including an appointment as Consultant in Poetry to the Library of Congress in 1985.

We Real Cool

Prose: *The Pool Players. Seven at the Golden Shovel.* We real cool. We Left school. We Lurk late. We Strike straight. We Sing sin. We Thin gin. We Jazz June. We Die soon.

As you read "We Real Cool," pay attention to its poetic structure.

by Gwendolyn Brooks

The Pool Players.
Seven at the Golden Shovel.

We real cool. We
Left school. We

Lurk late. We
Strike straight. We

Sing sin. We
Thin gin. We

Jazz June. We
Die soon.

My Notes

ACADEMIC VOCABULARY

Poetic structure refers to the poet's organization of words, lines, and images and ideas.

LITERARY TERMS

Rhythm in poetry is the pattern of stressed and unstressed syllables.

Rhyme scheme refers to the consistent pattern of rhyme throughout a poem.

A **stanza** is a group of lines, usually similar in length and pattern, that form a unit within a poem.

Author's purpose: What message about life is Brooks sending to young people with this poem?

How do the structure (free verse, line breaks, stanzas) and musical devices (consonance, assonance, and alliteration) create an effect?

Exploring Diction and Imagery

Before Reading

Freewrite: Choose a hobby, topic, or interest about which you are passionate, and explain why.

After Reading

Use the Title/Author/Genre (TAG) sentence stem to write an analytical statement examining the author's use of diction or imagery. (For example, Hirsch's poem, "Fast Break" uses the imagery/diction of... to convey...).

ACADEMIC VOCABULARY

Diction refers to a writer's choice of words.

Imagery refers to descriptive or figurative language that appeals to the senses and is used to create word pictures.

LITERARY TERMS

Voice is a writer's distinctive use of language.

My Notes

Poetry

> **ABOUT THE AUTHOR**
> Edward Hirsch (b. 1950) is a professor of English and a published author of many poems, essays, and books. His collection of verse, *Wild Gratitude*, was awarded the National Book Critics Circle Award in 1986. Hirsh has also earned a Guggenheim Fellowship and a MacArthur Foundation Fellowship. One of Hirsch's most popular books has been his surprise best-seller, *How to Read a Poem and Fall in Love with Poetry*.

FAST BREAK

In Memory of Dennis Turner, 1946–1984

by Edward Hirsch

A hook shot kisses the rim and
hangs there, helplessly, but doesn't drop,

and for once our gangly starting center
boxes out his man and times his jump

perfectly, gathering the orange leather
from the air like a cherished possession

and spinning around to throw a strike
to the outlet who is already shoveling

an underhand pass toward the other guard
scissoring past a flat-footed defender

who looks stunned and nailed to the floor
in the wrong direction, trying to catch sight

of a high, gliding dribble and a man
letting the play develop in front of him

in slow motion, almost exactly
like a coach's drawing on the blackboard,

both forwards racing down the court
the way that forwards should, fanning out

and filling the lanes in tandem, moving
together as brothers passing the ball

between them without a dribble, without
a single bounce hitting the hardwood

until the guard finally lunges out
and commits to the wrong man

while the power-forward explodes past them
in a fury, taking the ball into the air

by himself now and laying it gently
against the glass for a lay-up,

but losing his balance in the process,
inexplicably falling, hitting the floor

with a wild, headlong motion
for the game he loved like a country

and swiveling back to see an orange blur
floating perfectly though the net.

Extended Metaphor and Symbol

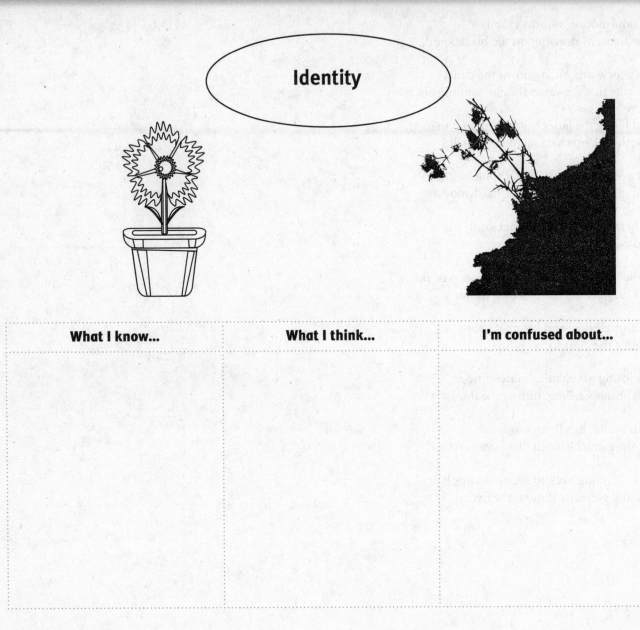

What I know...	What I think...	I'm confused about...

Summary of Identity:

Writing Prompt: After reading the poem "Identity," write an original
poem using metaphors, symbols, or repetition to reinforce an idea
or concept. You may want to begin with this line: I am like a .... Use
figurative language to create an imaginative image of yourself.

by Julio Noboa Polanco

My Notes

> **ABOUT THE AUTHOR**
> Julio Noboa Polanco was born in New York and
> has worked as an educational advocate for Latino
> communities in several cities. His focus has been on
> Latino history and heritage, and he writes his poetry in
> both Spanish and English.

Let them be as flowers
always watered, fed, guarded, admired,
but harnessed to a pot of dirt.

I'd rather be a tall, ugly weed,
clinging on cliffs, like an eagle   5
wind-wavering above high, jagged rocks.

To have broken through the surface of stone,
to live, to feel exposed to the madness
of the vast, eternal sky.
To be swayed by the breezes of an ancient sea,   10
carrying my soul, my seed,
beyond the mountains of time or into the abyss of the bizarre.

I'd rather be unseen, and if
then shunned by everyone,
than to be a pleasant-smelling flower,   15
growing in clusters in the fertile valley,
where they're praised, handled, and plucked
by greedy human hands.

I'd rather smell of musty, green stench
than of sweet, fragrant lilac.   20
If I could stand alone, strong and free,
I'd rather be a tall, ugly weed.

ACADEMIC VOCABULARY

Figurative language is
language that uses figures
of speech, words, or phrases
that describe one thing in
terms of another and are
not meant to be interpreted
literally.

Hyperbolic Me with Allusions

My Notes

EGO TRIPPING

(there may be a reason why)

by Nikki Giovanni

I was born in the congo
I walked to the fertile crescent and built
   the sphinx
I designed a pyramid so tough that a star
   that only glows every one hundred years falls
   into the center giving divine perfect light
I am bad

I sat on the throne
   drinking nectar with allah
I got hot and sent an ice age to europe
   to cool my thirst
My oldest daughter is nefertiti
   the tears from my birth pains
   created the nile
I am a beautiful woman

I gazed on the forest and burned
   out the sahara desert
   With a packet of goat's meat
   and a change of clothes
I crossed it in two hours
I am a gazelle so swift
   so swift you can't catch me

   For a birthday present when he was three
I gave my son hannibal an elephant
   He gave me rome for mother's day
My strength flows ever on

My son noah built new/ark and
I stood proudly at the helm
    as we sailed on a soft summer day
I turned myself into myself and was
    jesus
    men intone my loving name
    All praises All praises
I am the one who would save

I sowed diamonds in my back yard
My bowels delivered uranium
    The filings from my fingernails are
    semi-precious jewels
    On a trip north
I caught a cold and blew
My nose giving oil to the arab world
I am so hip even my errors are correct
I sailed west to reach east and had to round off
    the earth as I went
    The hair from my head thinned and gold was laid
    across three continents

I am so perfect, so divine so ethereal[1] so surreal
I cannot be comprehended except by my permission

I mean . . . I . . . can fly
    like a bird in the sky. . .

---

[1] **ethereal:** not of the earth; heavenly

My Notes

SUGGESTED LEARNING STRATEGIES: Graphic Organizer, Marking the Text, Think Aloud, Think-Pair-Share

ABOUT THE AUTHOR

Born in Harlem in New York, Audre Lorde (1934–1992) was a poet and essayist. Her first poem was published in *Seventeen* magazine while she was in high school. Lorde's writing, especially her poetry, explores personal, political, and social issues, focusing on the emotions of relationships, especially in urban life. She had been the New York State poet laureate when she died.

My Notes

Poetry

Hanging Fire

by Audre Lorde

I am fourteen
and my skin has betrayed me
the boy I cannot live without
still sucks his thumb
in secret
how come my knees are
always so ashy
what if I die
before the morning comes
and momma's in the bedroom
with the door closed.

I have to learn how to dance
in time for the next party
my room is too small for me
suppose I die before graduation
they will sing sad melodies
but finally
tell the truth about me
There is nothing I want to do
and too much
that has to be done
and momma's in the bedroom
with the door closed.

Nobody even stops to think
about my side of it
I should have been on Math Team
my marks were better than his
why do I have to be
the one
wearing braces
I have nothing to wear tomorrow
will I live long enough
to grow up
and momma's in the bedroom
with the door closed.

What I know...	What I think...	I'm confused about...

1. Audre Lorde's poem, "Hanging Fire" is about...

2. List questions you would like to ask Audre Lorde:

3. **Writing Prompt:** Explain a theme of Audre Lorde's poem, "Hanging Fire."

GRAMMAR & USAGE

The purpose of punctuation is to help a reader understand the writer's phrasing and emphasis on specific words. Audre Lorde's poem has almost no punctuation. How does the lack of punctuation affect your reading and understanding of this poem?

My Notes

WORD CONNECTIONS

The origin of *ode* is the Greek word *oide*, for a song.

A related spelling, *-ody*, is found in *melody*, *parody*, *rhapsody*.

Poetry

ABOUT THE AUTHOR

Pablo Neruda (1904–1973) was born in Chile. He began writing at an early age and published his first literary work as a teenager. Neruda spent much of his life living in different countries, and his writing reflects the political and social matters of his time.

ODE TO MY SOCKS

by Pablo Neruda
translated by Robert Bly

Mara Mori brought me
a pair of socks
which she knitted herself
with her sheepherder's hands,
two socks as soft as rabbits.
I slipped my feet into them
as if they were two cases
knitted with threads of twilight and goatskin,
Violent socks,
my feet were two fish made of wool,
two long sharks
sea blue, shot through
by one golden thread,
two immense blackbirds,
two cannons,
my feet were honored in this way
by these heavenly socks.

My Notes

They were so handsome for the first time

my feet seemed to me unacceptable

like two decrepit firemen,

firemen unworthy of that woven fire,

of those glowing socks.

Nevertheless, I resisted the sharp temptation

to save them somewhere as schoolboys

keep fireflies,

as learned men collect

sacred texts,

I resisted the mad impulse to put them

in a golden cage and each day give them

birdseed and pieces of pink melon.

Like explorers in the jungle

who hand over the very rare green deer

to the spit and eat it with remorse,

I stretched out my feet and pulled on

the magnificent socks and then my shoes.

The moral of my ode is this:

beauty is twice beauty

and what is good is doubly good

when it is a matter of two socks

made of wool in winter.

My Notes

Poetry

> **ABOUT THE AUTHOR**
> Sandra Cisneros (b. 1954) grew up in Chicago and now lives in San Antonio, Texas. Cisneros has written extensively about the experiences of growing up as a Latina. In talking about her writing, Cisneros says she creates stories from things that have touched her deeply; "...in real life a story doesn't have shape, and it's the writer that gives it a beginning, a middle, and an end."

Abuelito Who

by Sandra Cisneros

Abuelito[1] who throws coins like rain
and asks who loves him
who is dough and feathers
who is a watch and glass of water
whose hair is made of fur
is too sad to come downstairs today
who tells me in Spanish you are my diamond
who tells me in English you are my sky
whose little eyes are string
can't come out to play
sleeps in his little room all night and day
who used to laugh like the letter k
is sick
is a doorknob tied to a sour stick
is tired shut the door
doesn't live here anymore
is hiding underneath the bed
who talks to me inside my head
is blankets and spoons and big brown shoes
who snores up and down up and down up and down again
is the rain on the roof that falls like coins
asking who loves him
who loves him who?

---

[1] **Abuelito:** Spanish term for "grandfather"

Coming of Age in Sonnets

Sonnet

My Notes

> **ABOUT THE AUTHOR**
> Little is known about the early life of William Shakespeare (1564–1616) except that he was born and grew up in Stratford-on-Avon in England. He is considered one of the greatest playwrights who ever lived. In addition to thirty-seven plays (comedies, tragedies, and histories), he also wrote a series of 154 sonnets in a style that has become known as the Shakespearean sonnet, which includes three quatrains and a couplet.

Sonnet 18

by William Shakespeare

Shall I compare thee to a summer's day?
Thou[1] art more lovely and more temperate.
Rough winds do shake the darling buds of May,
And summer's lease hath all too short a date.
Sometime too hot the eye of heaven shines,
And often is his gold complexion dimmed;
And every fair from fair sometime declines,
By chance, or nature's changing course untrimmed.[2]
But thy eternal summer shall not fade
Nor lose possession of that fair thou ow'st;[3]
Nor shall death brag thou wand'rest in his shade,
When in eternal lines to time thou grow'st,
So long as men can breathe or eyes can see,
So long lives this, and this gives life to thee.

> **LITERARY TERMS**
>
> A **quatrain** is a four-line stanza in a poem.
>
> A **couplet** is two consecutive lines of verse with end rhyme. A couplet usually expresses a complete unit of thought.
>
> **Iambic pentameter** describes a rhythmic pattern: five feet (or units) of one unstressed syllable followed by a stressed syllable.

1. What is the purpose of each quatrain?

2. How does the couplet bring closure to ideas presented in the poem?

3. How does the poem address the thematic concept of coming of age?

---

[1] **thee, thou:** you
[2] **untrimmed:** stripped of beauty
[3] **fair thou ow'st:** beauty you possess

Creating a Poetry Anthology

SUGGESTED LEARNING STRATEGIES: **Marking the Draft, Sharing and Responding, Self-Editing/Peer Editing**

Assignment

Your assignment is to create a thematic poetry anthology with an introduction to the collection, seven or eight original poems with complementary visuals, and a reflection explaining the style and content of the work.

Steps

Planning and Drafting the Collection

1. Revisit the poems you generated throughout this unit. Select ones you think will work well for this assignment. If necessary, draft additional poems using the various structures (sonnet, free verse, catalogue, ode).

2. Revise your poems for purposeful use of figurative language and literary devices to capture your theme.

3. Share your poems with your peers and solicit feedback for revision on:
   ▶ Refining line breaks, stanza, refrains.
   ▶ Adding, deleting, or reordering lines.
   ▶ Adding in or refining figurative language and poetic devices.

4. Annotate each poem by marking the text and creating marginal notes identifying the literary devices and explaining their effect.

5. Think about the imagery and symbolism in your poems. Find pictures or make sketches to represent the thematic concepts.

6. Reread, revise, and edit your poems to prepare final drafts for publication. Be sure each poem contains an appropriate title.

Planning and Drafting the Introduction and Reflection

7. Write a brief autobiography to introduce your poetry anthology. Focus on what the reader needs to know about you to better understand your poems.

8. Write a reflection to explain your favorite selections, and discuss the style and form used to capture the ideas in your poems. What was your intended effect on the reader? How did you design your poems to accomplish this? Discuss your creative process and what inspires you as a poet.

Refining the Anthology for Publication

9. Consult the Scoring Guide, and review your poetry anthology in its entirety to revise and edit each section, preparing for publication.

10. Create a cover with a unique title and thematic visual.

11. Organize your anthology and bind it in this order: cover page, table of contents, introduction, annotated original poems with visuals, and reflection.

....

⤴**TECHNOLOGY TIP** You may want to use a software program to create your anthology. Many word processing programs have attractive templates for creating booklets, or you can design your own.

SCORING GUIDE

Scoring Criteria	Exemplary	Proficient	Emerging
Original Poems	The collection of poems displays skillful use of format and structure to capture key ideas within the poetic form (i.e., line breaks, stanzas, refrain, title, etc.). The poetry contains knowledgeable use of word choice, figurative language, and literary devices to reinforce the thematic concept and have an impact on the reader. Each poem contains an insightful connection to the thematic concept of the unit appealing to the universal level.	The collection of poems contains a clear format or structure appropriate to the poetic form (i.e., line breaks, stanzas, refrain, etc.). The poetry contains appropriate word choice, figurative language, and literary devices that reinforce the thematic concept of the collection. Each poem contains an appropriate connection to the thematic concept of the unit.	The poems presented do not contain a clear format or structure. If devices are present, the poems in this collection contain a limited understanding of these literary devices and how they are used to add meaning to the text. The poems do not show a connection to the thematic concepts addressed within the unit.
Annotated Poems	The poet marks the poems, identifies literary devices used, and provides insightful analysis of the function and purpose of the device and its impact on the reader.	The poet is able to identify, appropriately label some of the literary devices used, and analyze the literary devices' function and purpose in marginal notes.	The poet is unable to identify the literary devices used and/ or does not provide appropriate analysis of the function and purpose of the devices.
Introduction	The engaging introduction highlights significant and influential moments of the poet's life that thoroughly provide the reader an insight about the poet's collection of work.	The introduction is clear and contains relevant information about the poet's life that helps the reader better understand the collection of work.	The introduction is unfocused and vaguely discusses the life and work of the poet. The reader is unable to draw connections between the life events shared and the collection of poems.

SCORING GUIDE

Scoring Criteria	Exemplary	Proficient	Emerging
Reflection	The reflection insightfully explains and provides examples of the poet's purpose, creative process, challenges encountered, and use of symbolic visuals. It clarifies learning within the unit on poetic form, style, and content.	The reflection insightfully explains and provides examples of the poet's purpose, creative process, challenges encountered, and use of symbolic visuals. It reveals learning in some or all aspects of poetic form, style, and content.	The reflection is unclear and/or incomplete. It does not adequately explain the process, product, or learning of poetic form, style, and content.
Organization and Presentation	The poetry anthology is a polished collection of work that contains: • a creative cover page with an insightful title • an accurate table of contents • a well written introduction • insightful annotated original poems with symbolic visuals to support the ideas in the poem • a thoughtful reflection.	The poetry anthology is an organized collection of work that contains: • a cover page and title • a table of contents • a clear introduction • annotated original poems with complementary visuals • a clear reflection.	The poetry anthology is not well organized or may contain some or all of the following: • a missing or vague cover page, no title • a missing or inaccurate table of contents • a missing or limited introduction • a limited number of poems that are not annotated or are missing complementary visuals • a missing or limited reflection.
Additional Criteria			

Comments:

Learning Focus:

A Signature Style

What is a signature style in writing? Is a signature style one that reveals a clear understanding of self? Is a signature style one that is emulated by others? During the second half of this unit, you will choose a published author whose signature style speaks to you. In your analysis of this writer's work, you will distinguish between a thematic concept, a subject of a text, and a theme—the author's underlying message about life inferred by the reader. Independently, you will know when, why, and how to use strategies to interpret and critique a poet's work. To deepen your understanding of the poet's work, you will conduct research to learn about the poet's life.

You will demonstrate your analysis at the end of the unit by creating a literary analysis essay. You will use the writing process to explain your poet's thematic ideas and style. As you develop your essay, you will create complex thesis and topic sentences, and you will seamlessly embed quotations. In addition to writing your analysis, you will present a poem of your choice to your peers. This presentation will allow you to show what you have learned about your author, about theme, and about the significance of the poet's style. This in turn will help you to understand the power of style in your own writing as you continue to encounter and create new texts.

SUGGESTED LEARNING STRATEGIES: **Close Reading, Paraphrasing, Predicting**

ABOUT THE AUTHOR
Dwight Okita (b. 1958) was born and continues to live in Chicago. His first book of poems, *Crossing with the Light*, was published in 1992. He continues to be an active writer, working on poetry, stage plays, a screenplay, and fiction—both stories and novels.

My Notes

Poetry

In Response to Executive Order 9066:
All Americans of Japanese Descent Must Report to Relocation Centers

by Dwight Okita

Dear Sirs:
Of course I'll come. I've packed my galoshes
and three packets of tomato seeds. Denise calls them
love apples. My father says where we're going
5   they won't grow.

I am a fourteen-year-old girl with bad spelling
and a messy room. If it helps any, I will tell you
I have always felt funny using chopsticks
and my favorite food is hot dogs.
10 My best friend is a white girl named Denise—
we look at boys together. She sat in front of me
all through grade school because of our names:
O'Connor, Ozawa. I know the back of Denise's head very well.

I tell her she's going bald. She tells me I copy on tests.
15 We're best friends.

I saw Denise today in Geography class.
She was sitting on the other side of the room.
"You're trying to start a war," she said, "giving secrets
away to the Enemy.[1] Why can't you keep your big
20 mouth shut?"

I didn't know what to say.
I gave her a packet of tomato seeds
and asked her to plant them for me, told her
when the first tomato ripened
25 she'd miss me.

Writing Prompt: Follow your teacher's instructions to construct a paragraph analyzing the function of connotation in "In Response to Executive Order 9066."

---

[1] **Enemy:** the Japanese, who were at war against the United States in World War II.

Tone Deaf—Exercises on Tone in Poetry

"Smells Like Teen Spirit" is a song originally written by and recorded by Nirvana. Later, Tori Amos recorded it with her own signature style. Listen to both artists' versions of the song, and use the graphic organizer below to note words or phrases that may describe the tone that the artist conveys in the song.

Nirvana's Version: "Smells Like Teen Spirit"	Tori Amos's Version: "Smells Like Teen Spirit"
Comments About Tone:	Comments About Tone:

1. What are the differences between these two versions of one song?

2. What tone (attitude) does each artist create? Incorporate phrases and images from the song to support your opinion.

3. Where do you see or hear a shift? Explain.

Writing Prompt: Follow your teacher's directions to write a style analysis paragraph identifying the tone and explain how it shifts between the two songs.

SUGGESTED LEARNING STRATEGIES: **Marking the Text, Skimming, Think-Pair-Share, TP-CASTT**

My Notes

Poetry

ABOUT THE AUTHOR
Anne Sexton (1928–1974) discovered her poetic voice as an adult when she joined writing groups and met other poets who encouraged her work. She published several successful collections of poetry and was awarded a Pulitzer Prize for Poetry in 1967. Much of her work explores personal issues or issues specific to women.

YOUNG

by Anne Sexton

A thousand doors ago
when I was a lonely kid
in a big house with four
garages and it was summer
5   as long as I could remember,
I lay on the lawn at night,
clover wrinkling under me,
the wise stars bedding over me,
my mother's window a funnel
10   of yellow heat running out,
my father's window, half shut,
an eye where sleepers pass,
and the boards of the house
were smooth and white as wax
15   and probably a million leaves
sailed on their strange stalks
as the crickets ticked together
and I, in my brand new body,
which was not a woman's yet,
20   told the stars my questions
and thought God could really see
the heat and the painted light,
elbows, knees, dreams, goodnight.

TP-CASTT Analysis

Title of Poem:

Author:

Title: Make a prediction. What do you think the title means before you read the poem?

Paraphrase: Restate the main ideas of the poem in your own words.

Connotation: What words or phrases suggest something beyond their literal meanings? What do you think the poet is saying in this poem? Go beyond the literal meanings (denotation) or the plot of the poem.

Attitude: Describe the speaker's attitude. Use specific adjectives to describe your ideas.

Shifts: Describe where the poem appears to shift, either in subject, speaker, or tone.

Title: Re-examine the title. What do you think it means now in the context of the poem?

Theme: What do you think is the underlying message about life expressed in this poem?

Reflection: How does the TP-CASTT strategy assist you to make meaning of a complex poem?

> **WORD CONNECTIONS**
>
> In analyzing analogies, look at the parts of speech in the word pairs. Parts of speech are consistent within an analogy; for example, if an adjective is used in one pair, the second pair also will use an adjective. Look at this analogy:
>
> carpenter : hammer :: musician : piano. Complete the following analogy.
>
> youth: child :: adult :
>
> _____

Poetry Café

TP-CASTT Analysis

Title of Poem:

Author:

Title: Make a prediction. What do you think the title means before you read the poem?

Paraphrase: Restate the main ideas of the poem in your own words.

Connotation: What words or phrases suggest something beyond their literal meanings? What do you think the poet is saying in this poem? Go beyond the literal meaning or the plot of the poem.

Attitude: Describe the speaker's attitude toward the subject. Use specific adjectives to describe your ideas.

Shifts: Describe where the poem appears to shift, either in subject, speaker, or tone.

Title: Re-examine the title. What do you think it means now in the context of the poem?

Theme: What do you think is the underlying message about life the author is expressing in this poem?

Combing

by Gladys Cardiff

ABOUT THE AUTHOR

Gladys Cardiff (b. 1942) is an American poet and writer of Irish, Welsh, and Cherokee descent. Her poetry tends to reflect her heritage. She has published two books of poems, *To Frighten a Storm* and *A Bare Unpainted Table*. She is an associate professor of poetry, American literature, and Native American literature at Oakland University.

Bending, I bow my head
And lay my hand upon
Her hair, combing, and think
How women do this for
Each other. My daughter's hair 5
Curls against the comb.
Wet and fragrant— orange
Parings. Her face, downcast,
Is quiet for one so young.

I take her place. Beneath 10
My mother's hands I feel
The braids drawn up tight
As a piano wire and singing,
Vinegar-rinsed. Sitting
before the oven I hear 15
The orange coils tick
The early hour before school.

She combed her grandmother
Mathilda's hair using
A comb made out of bone. 20
Mathilda rocked her oak-wood
Chair, her face downcast,
intent on tearing rags
In strips to braid a cotton
Rug from bits of orange 25
And brown. A simple act,

Preparing hair. Something
Women do for each other,
Plaiting the generations.

My Notes

Poetry

> **ABOUT THE AUTHOR**
>
> William Wordsworth (1770–1850) was a British poet who lived in the Lake District in Northern England. He was an innovator in that he wrote lyric poetry in the language of ordinary people rather than in the "poetic" diction that was common at the time. He wrote about his love of nature in a way that later came to be known as Romanticism.

I Wandered Lonely as a Cloud

by William Wordsworth

I wandered lonely as a cloud
That floats on high o'er vales and hills,
When all at once I saw a crowd,
A host, of golden daffodils;
5   Beside the lake, beneath the trees,
Fluttering and dancing in the breeze.

Continuous as the stars that shine
And twinkle on the milky way,
They stretched in never-ending line
10   Along the margin of a bay:
Ten thousand saw I at a glance,
Tossing their heads in sprightly dance.

The waves beside them danced; but they
Outdid the sparkling waves in glee:
15   A poet could not but be gay,
In such a jocund company:
I gazed—and gazed—but little thought
What wealth the show to me had brought:

For oft, when on my couch I lie
20   In vacant or in pensive mood,
They flash upon that inward eye
Which is the bliss of solitude;
And then my heart with pleasure fills,
And dances with the daffodils.

Poetry

My Notes

ABOUT THE AUTHOR

Langston Hughes (1902–1967) was born in the Midwest but came to New York to attend Columbia University. He became a prominent figure in the period of American literature known as the Harlem Renaissance. Much of his work—poetry, prose, and plays—evoked life in the Harlem section of New York. In fact, he was known as the "poet laureate of Harlem." In his work, he focused on the struggles and feelings of ordinary individuals.

HARLEM

by Langston Hughes

What happens to a dream deferred?

Does it dry up
like a raisin in the sun?
Or fester like a sore—
And then run?   5
Does it stink like rotten meat?
Or crust and sugar over—
like a syrupy sweet?

Maybe it just sags
like a heavy load.   10

Or does it explode?

My Notes

Poetry

> **ABOUT THE AUTHOR**
> Emily Dickinson (1830–1886) lived her entire life in her
> father's house in Amherst, Massachusetts. She was
> somewhat reclusive, yet her imagination was extremely
> active. Using her own peculiar style of punctuation and
> capitalization, she wrote more than 1,700 short poems,
> of which only a few were published (anonymously) in her
> lifetime. The others were found after her death. She is
> regarded as one of America's greatest poets.

"HOPE" IS THE THING WITH FEATHERS

by Emily Dickinson

"Hope" is the thing with feathers—
That perches in the soul—
And sings the tune without the words—
And never stops—at all—

5　And sweetest—in the Gale—is heard—
And sore must be the storm—
That could abash the little Bird
That kept so many warm—

I've heard it in the chillest land—
10　　And on the strangest Sea—
Yet, never, in Extremity,
It asked a crumb— of Me.

Poetry

> **ABOUT THE AUTHOR**
> Daniel Halpern (b. 1945) is a literary editor, translator,
> and writer. He has published eight collections of his own
> poetry. He has also edited two collections of international
> short stories and several collections of writings on a
> variety of topics, such as nature and artists.

Scars

by Daniel Halpern

They are the short stories of the flesh,
can evoke the entire event
in a moment–the action, the scent
and sound–place you there a second time.

It's as if the flesh decides to hold   5
onto what threatens its well-being,
They become part of the map marking
the pain we've had to endure.

If only the heart were so ruthless,
willing to document what it lived   10
by branding even those sensitive
tissues so information might flow back.

It's easy to recall what doesn't heal,
more difficult to call back what leaves
no mark, what depends on memory   15
to bring forward what's been gone so long,

The heart's too gentle. It won't hold
before us what we may still need to see.

My Notes

My Notes

Poetry

ABOUT THE AUTHOR
Essex Hemphill (1957–1995) was a poet, essayist, and editor. He began writing when he was fourteen, and, over time, he published three volumes of poetry. His poetry also appeared in a variety of magazines and in several films and documentaries. Some of his poems, like "American Hero," reflect on self-acceptance and social acceptance or denial.

AMERICAN HERO

by Essex Hemphill

I have nothing to lose tonight.
All my men surround me, panting,
as I spin the ball above our heads
on my middle finger.
5   It's a shimmering club light
and I'm dancing, slick in my sweat.
Squinting, I aim at the hole
fifty feet away. I let the tension go.
Shoot for the net. Choke it.
10   I never hear the ball
slap the backboard. I slam it
through the net. The crowd goes wild
for our win. I scored
thirty-two points this game
15   and they love me for it.
Everyone hollering
is a friend tonight.
But there are towns,
certain neighborhoods
20   where I'd be hard pressed
to hear them cheer
if I move on the block.

SUGGESTED LEARNING STRATEGIES: Graphic Organizer, Quickwrite

Poetry

"Poetry, to me, is the association of disassociated ideas. I like clear simple images, clear simple metaphors, making clear simple statements about not-so-clear, not-so-simple human beings." – Nikki Giovanni

The BEEP BEEP Poem
by Nikki Giovanni

```
i should write a poem
but there's almost nothing
that hasn't been said,
and said and said
beautifully, ugly, blandly                         5
excitingly
        stay in school
        make love not war
        death to all tyrants
        where have all the flowers gone            10
and don't they understand at kent state¹
the troopers will shoot . . . again

i could write a poem
because i love walking
 in the rain                                        15
and the solace² of my naked
body in a tub of warm water
cleanliness may not be next
to godliness but it sure feels
 good                                               20

i wrote a poem
for my father but it was so constant³
i burned it up
he hates change
and i'm baffled by sameness                         25

i composed a ditty
about encore american and worldwide news
```

---

¹ **kent state:** on May 4, 1970, National Guard troops fired at student protestors at Kent State University in Ohio, killing four students and wounding nine others.
² **solace:** comfort in times of disappointment
³ **constant:** unchanging, faithful, dependable

My Notes

but the editorial board
said no one would understand it
30 as if people have to be tricked
into sensitivity
though of course they do

i love to drive my car
hours on end
35 along back country roads
i love to stop for cider and apples and acorn squash
three for a dollar
i love my CB when the truckers talk
and the hum of the diesel in my ear
40 i love the aloneness of the road
when I ascend[4] the descending curves
the power within my toe delights me
and i fling my spirit down the highway
i love the way i feel
45 when i pass the moon and i holler to the stars
i'm coming through

    Beep Beep

k i d n a p p o e m

ever been kidnapped
by a poet
if i were a poet
i'd kidnap you
5 put you in my phrases and meter
you to jones beach
or maybe coney island
or maybe just to my house
lyric you in lilacs
10 dash you in the rain
blend into the beach
to complement my see
play the lyre for you
ode you with my love song
15 anything to win you
wrap you in the red Black green
show you off to mama
yeah if i were a poet i'd kid
nap you

---

[4] **ascend:** move upward; rise to a higher level

Writing Prompt: Write a short poem expressing a wish for yourself.
Model Giovanni's phrasing "If I were a ..."

Style Chart

Poet or Lyricist: _____ Nikki Giovanni _____

Author's Style	Example from the Poems/ Song Lyrics	Analysis

Syntax Surgery

Poet or Lyricist: _____

Author's Style	Example from the Poems/ Song Lyrics	Analysis

ACADEMIC VOCABULARY

Syntax refers to the arrangement of words and the order of grammatical elements in a sentence; the way in which words are put together to make meaningful elements, such as phrases and clauses.

Criteria for thesis statement:

- Include title, author, genre
- Identify the stylistic technique and its effect

Example:

> In "The Beep Beep Poem," Giovanni's artful use of diction causes the reader to ponder considerably before gaining clarity.

Generate a working thesis on your poet or lyricist. Mark the text to identify where you have met the criteria of a strong thesis.

GRAMMAR & USAGE

A verb form must **agree** in number (singular or plural) with its subject. Notice that in the sample thesis statement the singular verb *causes* agrees with the singular subject *use*:

In "The Beep Beep Poem," Giovanni's artful **use** of diction **causes** the reader to ponder considerably before gaining clarity.

If needed, use the space below to revise your thesis statement to incorporate missing criteria or strengthen your thesis.

Generating a Rhetorical Plan

Model outline of analysis of Giovanni's style:

Thesis: *In "The Beep Beep Poem," Giovanni's artful use of diction causes the reader to ponder considerably before gaining clarity.*

- **Topic Sentence 1:** Giovanni's connotations are elusive because they comprise various shades of suggestion making a simple object a complex idea.

  Possible examples for support:

- **Topic Sentence 2:** Giovanni weaves formal and informal diction together seamlessly to assert an informed, yet humble opinion.

  Possible examples for support:

As you work on your rhetorical plan, consider—and use—the grammatical knowledge and skills you have studied and practiced throughout this unit.

Your Outline:

I. Thesis

II. Topic Sentence 1:
Possible examples:

III. Topic Sentence 2:
Possible examples:

Analyzing and Presenting a Poet

SUGGESTED LEARNING STRATEGIES: Drafting, TP-CASTT, Marking
the Text, Self-Editing, Oral Interpretation, Sharing and Responding

Assignment

Your assignment is to analyze a collection of work from a poet, and write a
style-analysis essay. You will then select one of the poems you analyzed and
present an oral interpretation of the poem to the class.

Steps

Planning

1. Review the list of poets provided by your teacher and briefly research
   potential poets for this assignment. Select a poet that is of interest to
   you.

2. Read through a collection of the poet's work and choose three to five
   poems to analyze for this task. Mark and annotate the texts using
   TP-CASTT or another strategy.

Drafting

3. Review the analyzed poems and look for recurring patterns within the
   text. Generate a working thesis that identifies the author's stylistic
   technique and its effect.

4. Create an outline to organize and structure ideas for the essay.

5. Generate a first draft to develop the ideas from the outline.

Revising

6. Review and evaluate your draft by color-coding the text to identify
   elements of organization listed in the Scoring Guide. Revise your draft
   and add any missing elements into it to ensure that ideas flow coherently.

7. Share your draft with your peers and get feedback to revise for the
   following:

   - Analysis of style.

   - Clarity of ideas.

   Review the suggestions from your peers and consult the Scoring Guide to
   revise accordingly.

Editing for Publication

8. Reread and edit your draft for seamless integration of quotations and for
   correct grammar, punctuation, and spelling. If you are handwriting your
   essay, write legibly.

9. Create an appropriate title, and prepare a final draft for publication.

....

TECHNOLOGY TIP If you are using word processing software to create your
essay, use its spell-check features to help you create a publishable final
product. Also, consult a style manual such as that published by the
Modern Language Association or *The Chicago Manual of Style* to find
general guidelines for formatting your essay.

Planning and Rehearsing for Presentation

10. Select the poem that most intrigues you and prepare an oral interpretation of the poem. Mark and annotate this poem for purposeful use of movement, gestures, inflection, props, sound effects, etc.

11. Rehearse your oral interpretation in a mirror, and practice within a group of your peers. Ask for suggestions to refine your oral interpretation.

12. Use the format below to organize your performance:

    • Brief introduction of the poet and his or her style.

    • Oral interpretation of the poem.

    • Brief rationale for your oral interpretation.

13. Check that your presentation has a logical progression of ideas and a clearly stated point of view.

14. Consult the Scoring Guide criteria, and use peer feedback to refine your presentation.

Analyzing and Presenting a Poet

SCORING GUIDE

Scoring Criteria	Exemplary	Proficient	Emerging
Ideas	The essay demonstrates an insightful analysis of the poet/lyricist's style. It makes relevant connections within the text at a sophisticated level.	The presentation and essay demonstrate an accurate analysis of the poet/lyricist's style.	The presentation and essay demonstrate a sustained misinterpretation of the text and/or a lack of appropriate analysis, relying primarily on summary.
Organization	The essay's structure contains: • a well-written introduction with an engaging lead, TAG, and a sophisticated thesis • coherent and concise body paragraphs with complex topic sentences, strong textual support, and insightful commentary • effective transitions that show relationship between ideas • a reflective conclusion that extends the key ideas of the essay.	The essay's structure contains: • an introduction with a clear lead, TAG, and thesis • coherent body paragraphs with topic sentences, adequate textual support, and relevant commentary • transitions that show a relationship between ideas • a logical conclusion that extends the key ideas of the essay.	The essay's structure may or may not contain: • a limited introduction with an unfocused lead, inaccurate TAG, and/or an unclear thesis • incoherent body paragraphs with topic sentences that do not support the thesis, inadequate textual support, and irrelevant commentary • inappropriate transitions • a limited conclusion that is repetitive and/or does not extend the ideas presented in the essay.
Use of Language	The writing contains a clear, consistent academic voice and seamless integration of quotations woven in with commentary.	The writing contains an academic voice and integration of quotations with commentary.	Writing may contain inconsistent/inappropriate voice, ineffective sentence structure (run-ons, fragments), and/or freestanding quotations not connected with commentary.
Evidence of Writing Process	The writing demonstrates thoughtful planning, significant revision, and careful editing in preparing a publishable draft.	The writing demonstrates planning, revision, and editing in preparing a publishable draft.	The writing lacks evidence of planning, revision, and/or editing. The draft is not ready for publication.

SCORING GUIDE

Scoring Criteria	Exemplary	Proficient	Emerging
Presentation	The oral interpretation of the poem is convincingly performed with skillful use of movement, gestures, inflection, props, and/or sound effects.	The oral interpretation of the poem is performed with purposeful use of movement, gestures, inflection, props, and/or sound effects.	The oral interpretation lacks movement, gestures, inflection, props, and/or sound effects, or the performance elements may be distracting.
	The brief introduction and rationale enlighten the audience, communicating a deep understanding of the poem.	The brief introduction and rationale inform the audience, communicating a clear understanding of the poem.	The brief introduction and rationale do little to communicate a clear understanding of the poem or may be missing.
	Focused rehearsal is evident.	Adequate rehearsal is evident.	There is little or no evidence of rehearsal.
Additional Criteria			

Comments:

Reflection

An important aspect of growing as a learner is to reflect on where you have been, what you have accomplished, what helped you to learn, and how you will apply your new knowledge in the future. Use the following questions to guide your thinking and to identify evidence of your learning. Use separate notebook paper.

Thinking about Concepts

1. Using specific examples from this unit, respond to the Essential Questions:

   • What is poetry?

   • What can a writer learn from studying an author's craft and style?

2. Consider the new academic vocabulary from this unit (**Diction, Imagery, Poetic Structure, Figurative Language, Syntax**) as well as academic vocabulary from previous units and select 3-4 terms of which your understanding has grown. For each term, answer the following questions:

   • What was your understanding of the word before you completed this unit?

   • How has your understanding of the term evolved throughout the unit?

   • How will you apply your understanding in the future?

Thinking about Connections

3. Review the activities and products (artifacts) you created. Choose those that most reflect your growth or increase in understanding.

4. For each artifact that you choose, record, respond to, and reflect on your thinking and understanding, using the following questions as a guide:

   a. What skill/knowledge does this artifact reflect, and how did you learn this skill/knowledge?

   b. How did your understanding of the power of language expand through your engagement with this artifact?

   c. How will you apply this skill or knowledge in the future?

5. Create this reflection as Portfolio pages—one for each artifact you choose. Use the model in the box for your headings and commentary on questions.

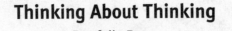

Thinking About Thinking
Portfolio Entry

Concept:

Description of Artifact:

Commentary on Questions:

Interpreting
Drama Through
Performance

Essential Questions

❓ What are the essential features of an effective drama and/or dramatic performance?

❓ How have the strategies I have learned this year helped me to be a better reader, writer, speaker, and listener?

Unit Overview

"All the world's a stage and all the men and women merely players…"

—*William Shakespeare (1564–1616)*

In this line from *As You Like It*, William Shakespeare reminds us of the connection between drama and our lives. One of his most famous plays is *The Tragedy of Romeo and Juliet*, a "coming of age" drama widely read by students. The play has everything an Elizabethan or a modern audience could ask for—romance, combat, comedy, and death. Over the centuries, the play has inspired artists, musicians, choreographers, and filmmakers. It has even been the basis for different texts such as the musical *West Side Story* and the action film *Romeo Must Die*. Shakespeare's language, his insight into human nature, and his creative sense of theater are the qualities that make his plays memorable. By speaking lines, performing scenes, hearing the language, and viewing various directors' interpretations, your experience with *Romeo and Juliet* will bring the play to life.

Contents

Goals

▶ To engage in authentic research related to performing *Romeo and Juliet*

▶ To explore multiple interpretations of *Romeo and Juliet* through performance and film

▶ To examine the "coming of age" concept in context of the play

▶ To be intentional in the use of strategies and to evaluate how well they work

▶ To reflect on one's growth as a learner

ACADEMIC VOCABULARY

Drama

Tragedy

Theatrical Elements

Interpretation

Metacognition

*Texts not included in these materials.

Learning Focus:

Expressing Your Vision of Shakespeare

Just as reading another writer's poetry and writing your own poetry are entirely different experiences, reading a play and performing someone else's play are demanding and rewarding in different ways. Performers have many tools by which they convey dramatic interpretations. Perhaps you found it challenging and satisfying to express your personal and unique voice through poetry. Performance is another opportunity to express your interpretation of words and ideas.

Actually performing a drama allows you to understand more deeply the multiple layers of dramatic interaction—from dealing with physical movement as you wield props to memorizing lines and communicating the emotions of the characters. Your involvement with the reality of a play allows you to make a text come alive for yourself and for viewers.

Shakespeare's understanding of human nature is timeless. In the course of this unit, you will strive to get inside the minds of the characters in *Romeo and Juliet*. You have already learned how to use different voices in different situations. Shakespearean text is often difficult for modern readers, but the words coupled with clear voices and actions guide an audience's understanding. The characters find themselves in situations where they are not always able to express their true voices. As a reader and performer, you will look for the subtext beneath the words the characters say.

Interpretation of a work of literature comes from a desire to convey an understanding of the work itself through close readings and a thoughtful appreciation of the author's purpose. Film interpretations allow you to see how different directors and actors bring their own interpretations to Shakespeare's words and ideas.

Directors use theatrical elements such as set design, props, costumes, music and other sounds, lighting, and editing to express a vision or interpretation of Shakespeare's words and ideas. As you deliver Shakespeare's dramatic language, you will practice a deliberate vocal delivery and careful blocking of movement to match the words to the actions. Understanding Shakespeare's sense of inverted syntax and the comedy of puns, as well as all the figurative language of the poetry, will help you perform the text.

Independent Reading: In this unit, you will study one of Shakespeare's most famous tragedies. For independent reading, look for another play, perhaps one by Shakespeare. You might also consider a collection of short stories or informational text about Shakespeare's life and influence on literature.

Previewing the Unit

SUGGESTED LEARNING STRATEGIES: Think-Pair-Share, Close Reading, Summarizing/Paraphrasing, Graphic Organizer

Essential Questions

1. What are the essential features of an effective drama and/or dramatic performance?

2. How have the strategies I have learned this year helped me to be a better reader, writer, speaker, and listener?

Unit Overview and Learning Focus

Predict what you think this unit is about. Use the words or phrases that stood out to you when you read the Unit Overview and the Learning Focus.

Embedded Assessment

What knowledge must you have (what do you need to know)? What skills must you have (what will you need to do to complete the Embedded Assessment successfully)? Write your responses below.

Mask Monologues

> **LITERARY TERMS**
>
> A **monologue** is a dramatic speech delivered by a character.

Look closely at the pictures provided by your teacher and consider the following:

- The person's gender, age, and ethnicity
- His or her facial expression
- The kind of person you think he or she is; what he or she might sound like; what he or she might talk about; what body movements or gestures he or she would use

Write a short **monologue** in the voice of the person to deliver to others. Cover topics that you think the person would discuss as you try to "speak for" him or her.

What I look like:

What I might say or talk about:

How I might move:

Then, hold up your mask in front of your face as you deliver the *monologue* to others. Speak at an appropriate volume. Allow your audience to pose questions that you answer in the voice of your "masked" character. You will have a chance to pose questions to other students' characters.

Next, read the poem "We Wear the Mask" by Paul Laurence Dunbar and use the SIFT strategy to guide your marking of the text. Discuss the poem, including its relevance to the monologue activity you completed earlier. Consider the following questions: How do we wear masks in our daily lives? What do people really know about us if we wear a mask to hide our true feelings? How do you think this poem may relate to the play *Romeo and Juliet*?

WE WEAR THE MASK

by Paul Laurence Dunbar

> **ABOUT THE AUTHOR**
>
> The son of former slaves, Paul Laurence Dunbar
> (1872–1906) was the first African American writer to
> earn his living solely by writing poetry and fiction.
> He was also the first to gain a national audience of
> mostly white readers.

We wear the mask that grins and lies,

It hides our cheeks and shades our eyes—

This debt we pay to human guile[1];

With torn and bleeding hearts we smile,

And mouth with myriad[2] subtleties.   5

Why should the world be over-wise,

In counting all our tears and sighs?

Nay, let them only see us, while

    We wear the mask.

We smile, but, O great Christ, our cries   10

To thee from tortured souls arise.

We sing, but oh the clay is vile[3]

Beneath our feet, and long the mile;

But let the world dream other-wise,

    We wear the mask.   15

---

[1] **guile**: deception
[2] **myriad**: countless
[3] **vile**: repulsive or wretched

My Notes

Symbols:

Images:

Figures of Speech:

Tone and Theme:

Who's Who in Verona

ACADEMIC VOCABULARY

A **drama** is a play written for stage, radio, film, or television, usually about a serious topic or situation.

1. Create a graphic organizer, such as a word map, on separate paper and then brainstorm all of the words and phrases you can think of that are associated with **drama**. As your class discusses this academic vocabulary term, take notes and be sure to save your work in your vocabulary notebook for later use.

2. Next, consider the essential question "What are the essential features of an effective drama and/or dramatic performance?"

3. To preview *The Tragedy of Romeo and Juliet*, your teacher will give you a card with a character's name and description on it. You will then "become" the character and work in a group to create a tableau. A *tableau* is a purposeful arrangement of characters frozen as if in a painting or a photograph. In your tableau, convey as much information as you can about the characters and their relationships.

4. Read your card aloud to the others in the group, along with any additional information from the cast of characters in your copy of *Romeo and Juliet*.

5. Practice arranging yourselves according to your descriptions. Assign one student the role of director so he or she can give the group feedback to help you create the effect you want. Think about the following as you prepare your tableau:

    • Body positions (who you stand next to, distance, and how you pose)

    • Postures

    • Facial expressions

    • Gestures

    • Simple props to convey your character

6. After you have rehearsed, pose your tableau. Create a freeze-frame image for your classmates. Then either step out of the tableau one at a time and tell why you chose to place yourself as you did, or have your director explain your group's choices.

WORD CONNECTIONS

An analogy may help understanding with a second word that describes the first. For example, a tableau may present a striking scene of a group of people. Complete the following analogy.

tableau : group :: flock :

_____

Write a sentence describing the relationship of the two sets of words.

7. Using what you learned from the tableau and the *Dramatis Personae* (Cast of Characters) in your edition of *Romeo and Juliet*, write each of the characters listed below under the correct family heading. Highlight or draw asterisks next to the names of the two **protagonists**.

LITERARY TERMS

Protagonists are the main, or most important, characters in a play.

Prince Escalus	Romeo	Juliet
Benvolio	Mercutio	Tybalt
Count Paris	Nurse	Friar Lawrence
Lord Capulet	Lady Capulet	Apothecary (druggist)
Lord Montague	Lady Montague	Peter
Sampson	Balthasar	Abraham

Capulet	Montague	Unaffiliated

8. To help you keep track of the characters, create a bookmark to use while you are reading *Romeo and Juliet*. Fold a sheet of paper in half lengthwise, and write the Capulets on one side, the Montagues on the other side, and unaffiliated characters inside. Write what you know about each character.

9. On separate paper, reflect on how well your group worked together. Describe the effective speaking and listening skills that members of your group practiced, and explain why they were effective.

The Prologue: So Much from One Sonnet

ACADEMIC VOCABULARY

A **tragedy** is a dramatic play that tells the story of a main character, usually of a noble class, who meets an untimely and unhappy death or downfall, often because of a specific character flaw or twist of fate.

GRAMMAR & USAGE

The general sentence pattern in modern English is subject-verb-complement. Shakespeare frequently uses **inverted order**, in which the verb precedes the subject.

Example: LADY MONTAGUE: "*O where is* (verb) *Romeo?* (subject). *Saw* (verb) *you* (subject) *him today?*"

The story of *Romeo and Juliet* was well known to those who attended the play in Shakespeare's day. The audience knew the end result would be a **tragedy**. The Prologue served as an introductory speech where an actor, in this case probably just one man called the "Chorus," provided the audience with a brief outline for the plot.

In this case, the Prologue is a 14-line poem with a defined structure that is called a Shakespearean **sonnet**. Using what you learned about sonnets in Unit 3, label the lines of the Prologue to show its **rhyme scheme**.

Listen to the Prologue as it is read aloud. Close your eyes and envision an actor speaking the words. In the space below, describe how the Prologue aids your understanding of the play.

from *The Tragedy of Romeo and Juliet*
by Willliam Shakespeare

ABOUT THE AUTHOR

William Shakespeare (1564–1616) is considered one of the most gifted and perceptive writers in the English language. He left his home in Stratford-upon-Avon for London, where he pursued a career as an actor. He was more successful as a playwright and poet, however, producing more than three dozen plays, which are still performed centuries after his death.

Enter Chorus

Two households, both alike in dignity,

In fair Verona, where we lay our scene,

From ancient grudge break to new mutiny,

Where civil blood makes civil hands unclean.

From forth the fatal loins of these two foes   5

A pair of star-crossed lovers take their life,

Whose misadventured piteous overthrows

Doth with their death bury their parents' strife.

The fearful passage of their death-marked love,

And the continuance of their parents' rage,   10

Which, but their children's end, naught could remove,

Is now the two hours' traffic of our stage;

The which if you with patient ears attend,

What here shall miss, our toil shall strive to mend.

WORD CONNECTIONS

Prologue contains the root *-log-*, from the Greek word *logos*, meaning *word*. This root also appears in *dialogue*, *catalogue*, and *eulogy*. The prefix pro- means "before."

The Prologue: So Much from One Sonnet

Shakespeare's plays and poems are written in Modern English, although the language sounds quite different from the English we speak today. It is possible to understand Shakespeare's language if you know a few strategies.

Go back and read through the Prologue and underline words that you do not know. Try to guess at the meanings, if using context clues help. Then, use a dictionary to determine the meaning of the unfamiliar words. Write a synonym for each unknown word. For example, the word *mutiny* appears in line 3. One dictionary defines it as a noun that means "an open rebellion against authorities, especially by soldiers or sailors against their officers." A mutiny is a rebellion, so you may write *rebellion* above *mutiny*.

1. Review your word map for *drama*. You have probably seen the graphic representation of drama—the comedy and tragedy masks. Sketch those masks beside each other on the same sheet of paper. Underneath **Tragedy**, write a bulleted list of words that come to mind. You might find some of these words in the Prologue.

Based on what you have learned from the Prologue, why do you think *Romeo and Juliet* is called a tragedy?

Later in this unit, you will be acting scenes from the play. Practicing reading aloud in unison with your classmates can help you get used to speaking Shakespeare's words. After you participate in several choral readings of the Prologue, rate your comfort level with saying Shakespeare's words, with 1 being "I do not feel comfortable at all" and 10 being "I'm ready for Broadway!"

1   2   3   4   5   6   7   8   9   10

2. Explain your self-rating:

An important skill in drama is the ability to memorize lines. This is another method that can help you get used to Shakespeare's language. To practice this skill, you will memorize the Prologue.

Memorizing is easier than it seems; you have memorized hundreds of lines from TV shows, movies, jokes, and songs. This is no harder; it just takes a little patience and practice.

Start slowly and work on a line or two at a time and visualize what is happening in each line. Practice by saying the lines into a tape recorder or writing them down. Say them aloud to yourself until you can finally write or say the entire Prologue without help.

Below you will find the Prologue, but some of the words are left out. Once you think you know the Prologue, fill in the blanks. Keep trying until you know the Prologue and can fill in all the blanks.

Two _____, both alike in _____,

In fair _____, where we _____ our scene,

From ancient _____ break to new _____,

Where civil _____ makes civil _____ unclean.

From forth the fatal _____ of these two _____

A _____ of _____ lovers take their life;

Whose _____ piteous overthrows

Doth with their death _____ their parents' _____.

The fearful _____ of their death-marked _____,

And the continuance of their parents' _____,

Which, but their _____ end, naught could _____,

Is now the two hours' _____ of our _____;

The which if you with _____ ears attend,

What here shall _____, our toil shall strive to _____.

Essential Question 2: How have the strategies I have learned this year helped me to be a better reader, writer, speaker, and listener? What is your initial response to this question?

A Sorrowful Son, a Dutiful Daughter

In Act 1, Romeo's parents are concerned about their son because he has been behaving strangely. After the street brawl in Act I, Scene 1, Lady Capulet asks Romeo's friend Benvolio:

> "O, where is Romeo? Saw you him today?
>
> Right glad I am he was not at this fray."

Notice the way Lady Capulet reverses the order of the subject and the verb in her second question. We would probably say, "I am glad" not "glad I am." We would also say, "Did you see him today?" instead of "Saw you him today?" Putting the verb before the subject is called *inversion*.

1. Try rewriting these inverted sentences the way we would say them today.

   • Pining over unreturned love is our hero Romeo.

   • A promise to stay pure has his love made.

Romeo's friend Benvolio tries to cheer up his love-sick friend, but Romeo is not interested in his solutions. He says to Benvolio:

> "Farewell. Thou canst not teach me to forget."

Thou and *canst* are archaic, or old, forms of words. *Thou* means *you*; *canst* means "can." Romeo is saying, "Goodbye. You cannot teach me to forget."

2. Using *can* as a model, try to determine the meanings of these words used in Shakespeare's day.

canst	can
didst	
hadst	
wouldst	
dost	

In Act 1, Scene 1, Benvolio proposes that Romeo compare Rosaline with the other lovely girls at the feast. Don't let Benvolio's words *thee* and *thy* confuse you; these are archaic forms of *you* and *your*. Benvolio is saying, "I will make you think your swan is a crow."

> "Compare her face with some that I shall show,
>
> And I will make thee think thy swan a crow."

3. Use this glossary to update the lines from the play that follow by writing the more modern word above the older one in the sentences below.

thee: you

thy: your

hath: has

art: are

thou: you

mine: my

Dost thou not laugh?

This love that *thou hast* shown/*Doth* add more grief to too much of *mine* own.

Why, Romeo, *art thou* mad?

Ay, *mine* own fortune in my misery.

4. When we first meet Juliet (Act I, Scene 4), she is an obedient and courteous daughter. When her mother tells her that Paris is interested in her, Juliet answers that she will honor her mother's wishes and consider him. In this conversation, Shakespeare uses figurative language (metaphor, simile, personification) to paint word pictures of characters. Look for three comparisons that the Nurse and Lady Capulet use to describe Paris vividly. What does each say about Paris?

To what is Paris compared?	What does this comparison tell you about Paris?

5. Work in pairs to discuss what Lady Capulet and the Nurse value about Paris. Does this match what you would look for?

A Timeline of Events

SUGGESTED LEARNING STRATEGIES: Graphic Organizer,
Discussion Groups

Scholars have indicated that the action of this play occurs in a short period of time. At the end of each act or major plot event, take notes in the following chart to help you review and summarize the play.

Day	Act(s)/Scene(s)	Setting(s)	Plot Events
Sunday a.m.			
p.m.			
Monday a.m.			
p.m.			
Tuesday a.m.			
p.m.			
Wednesday a.m.			
p.m.			
Thursday a.m.			
p.m.			
Early Friday a.m.			

You Are Cordially Invited

Below are famous lines from *Romeo and Juliet*. Choose one that appeals to you and practice saying it quietly. When the line feels familiar, rehearse it again, using movement, gestures, inflection, and intonation to convey the feelings behind it.

- How does this rehearsal help you make sense of the line?
- Which character do you think said the line, and what do you think it means in the play?

> **WORD CONNECTIONS**
>
> **Intonation** contains the root *-ton-*, from the Greek word *tonos*, meaning "a stretching tone or pitch." The root also appears in the words *tonic* and *astonish*. The suffix *-ation* indicates that the word is a noun.

	Spoken by:
"O Romeo, Romeo! Wherefore art thou Romeo?"	
"Oh, I am fortune's fool!"	
"Good night, good night! Parting is such sweet sorrow."	
"But, soft! What light through yonder window breaks? It is the East, and Juliet is the sun!"	
"What's in a name? That which we call a rose By any other name would smell as sweet."	
"A plague o' both your houses!"	
"O happy dagger! This is thy sheath; there rest, and let me die."	
"My only love sprung from my only hate! Too early seen unknown and known too late!"	
"O true apothecary! Thy drugs are quick. Thus with a kiss I die."	
"For never was a story of more woe Than this of Juliet and her Romeo."	

In *Romeo and Juliet*, the nobles speak in poetry, using **formal diction**, while the servants speak in prose, using **informal diction**. Keep the level of language in mind as you create an invitation from Lord Capulet to the feast (Act I, Scene 2).

> **LITERARY TERMS**
>
> **Diction** is a writer or speaker's choice of words.

Comparing Film Interpretations: An Old Accustomed Feast

SUGGESTED LEARNING STRATEGIES: Graphic Organizer, Close Reading, Revisiting Prior Work, Notetaking, Drafting

ACADEMIC VOCABULARY

An **interpretation** is the act of making meaning from something, such as a text. **Theatrical elements** are physical, visual, and oral means the director uses to convey meaning.

Your teacher will show you the same scene from at least two different film **interpretations** of *Romeo and Juliet*. An interpretation is based on the reader, actor, or director's own experiences as well as on the actual words of the text. As you watch, write notes in the chart below, paying attention to the **theatrical elements** of costumes and music in each version. Ask yourself, "Why would the director choose those costumes and music for the first meeting between Romeo and Juliet?"

Act I, Scene 5: The Capulets' party — first meeting between Romeo and Juliet

Version: Director's Name	Costumes: Colors, Style	Music: Vocals, Instruments, Lyrics	What is the effect of the director's choices?

In Unit 2, you considered the similarities and differences between reading a text and viewing a film. Now consider the similarities and differences between viewing a film and watching a live performance. Fill out the following graphic organizer. Consider the following prompts to help focus your answers:

- What can a film do that live performance cannot and vice versa?

- What tools and strategies do directors of plays and directors of films share? What tools and strategies are different?

- Are you more entertained by watching movies or watching live performances? Why?

Movie　　　　　　　　　**Live Performance**

Comparing Film Interpretations: An Old Accustomed Feast

You have seen two interpretations of the same scene from *Romeo and Juliet*. **Interpretation** is an academic vocabulary word for this unit. Work with a partner to come up with your own definition and an original sentence that uses this word.

Theatrical elements include sets, props, costumes, lighting, and sound effects—anything that helps bring a story to life on the stage. On separate paper, create a graphic organizer to help you remember these elements. Use theatrical elements as the main topic, with costumes and music as the secondary topics. You will be adding additional theatrical elements as you continue reading *Romeo and Juliet*.

Think again about the Essential Question, "What are the essential features of an effective drama and/or dramatic performance?" Review your initial response and add any new thoughts in the space below.

Writing Prompt: What is the essence of the first meeting between Romeo and Juliet? On a separate sheet of paper, write a piece that explains which interpretation more effectively captures the essence of the first meeting between Romeo and Juliet. Your writing should include a thesis or analytical statement along with textual support from your notes and reflective commentary. Be sure to make specific references to theatrical elements from the film, such as costumes, music, props, and actions.

Persuasive Prompt

SUGGESTED LEARNING STRATEGIES: **Brainstorming, Graphic Organizer, Drafting, Sketching**

Below is a writing prompt based on ideas from Act I of *Romeo and Juliet*. Read the prompt and think about the writing strategies you can use. Think carefully about how best to proceed.

Before you begin writing, look over the writing strategies and identify the ones that you plan to use for prewriting, drafting, revising, and editing. Then respond to the writing prompt.

Name of Strategy	Why I Plan to Use This Strategy

Writing Situation

Your best friend has met a boy or girl at a party and has fallen in love. You know that your friend's family will be set against the relationship because the boy or girl is from a family with a different set of values. Your best friend is unhappy about the situation; he or she does not want to give up the relationship, but how can it continue if the family is against it? Think about reasons your friend might use to convince his or her family to accept the relationship.

Writing Prompt: Write a letter to your best friend with suggestions that may convince family members to allow her or him to date the boy or girl. Keep your audience's concerns in mind as you think through your writing plan. Also consider the persuasive appeals you learned in Unit I.

Persuasive Prompt

ACADEMIC VOCABULARY

Metacognition is the ability to know and be aware of one's own thought processes. It is a tool that helps students identify and evaluate their learning goals.

In your vocabulary notebook, use roots and affixes to determine the meaning of the academic vocabulary word **metacognition**. Create a visual representation of metacognition and write a caption below your sketch. Save the sketch in your vocabulary notebook for later use.

After you write your letter, decide how effective the strategies that you selected were and note if you used strategies that you had not originally planned to use. You may use these ratings and descriptions:

1. The strategy worked well for the assignment; I would use it again for a similar writing task.

2. The strategy worked pretty well, but I found that I needed other strategies to complete the task.

3. The strategy did not work well for this writing task; it might work better for a different writing task.

4. The strategy did not work well for me; in fact, I may never use this strategy again.

5. Although I thought I might, I did not use this strategy after all.

Strategy	Rating/Description	Notes/Explanation

Developing Dramaturges

Review everything you have heard, read, or learned about Shakespeare, Elizabethan England, and the play *Romeo and Juliet*. There are many interesting topics to research, such as male actors playing the parts of girls or girls marrying at age 14. From your recent exposure to the play and other background information, generate a list of topics that you find interesting.

List topics that you are interested in:

Choose the topic that most interests you at this point:

Is it about Shakespeare, Elizabethan England, or the play itself?

On a separate sheet of paper, create a KWHL chart for the topic that most interests you, filling in the first three columns.

1. Your teacher will have you share your topic and one of the questions with the class. Then give your questions to somebody who is interested in that topic and have them answer the questions as best they can. They may not know all the answers, since you have not yet researched most topics related to the author and the play. The idea here is to find topics that are interesting that you will want to research. You will, in turn, answer someone else's questions.

2. In addition, try to offer ideas for how the other student can find out more information about his or her topic, and he or she will try to give you additional ideas.

Developing Dramaturges

Share one of your questions and its possible answer with the whole class. Take notes below while others are presenting topics.

Interesting topics I heard from others:

You will now take on the role of *dramaturge*, an important member of an acting company. The dramaturge helps the director make informed decisions by providing pertinent information related to the play. Add *dramaturge* to your word map for *drama*, and write an explanation of the role.

1. Using the appropriate style as directed by your teacher, research your topic of interest and prepare to share your findings with your classmates. Keep in mind that the information you and your classmates learn from each other will help you better understand the play and will enhance your performance of a scene from the play.

2. Keep track of your sources so you can create a bibliography or works cited page later. In addition, make notes about your research process and focus questions for a later reflection. As you continue your research, consider the quantity and quality of information you are finding. Do not be afraid to modify your process or change your focus questions to achieve better results.

I Pray You, Speak Plainly, Please

Below are some chunks of text from Act II, Scene 2 of *Romeo and Juliet*. With a friend, translate the lines into the other forms below or forms suggested by your teacher. After you read the examples, think of at least one other format for translation, such as a foreign language or a secret code.

Translation Formats

Standard English: The widely accepted way of speaking.

Computer messaging: Instant Messenger and e-mail chat.

Examples:

Original Text:
O Romeo, Romeo! Wherefore art thou Romeo?
Deny thy father and refuse thy name!
Or, if thou wilt not, be but sworn my love,
And I'll no longer be a Capulet.

Standard English:
O Romeo, Romeo. Why does your name have to be Romeo? Give up your father and your name; or if you can't, then tell me you love me and I will marry you and no longer be a Capulet.

Computer messaging:
O R. R.! Why r u a R.? Deny ur father and refuse ur name. Or, tell me u luv me 2 n I will no longer b a C.

Other:

I Pray You, Speak Plainly, Please

1. JULIET: "What's in a name? That which we call a rose
By any other name would smell as sweet."

Standard English:

Other translation of your choice:

2. ROMEO: "With love's light wings did I o'er-perch these walls;
For stony limits cannot hold love out"

Standard English:

Other translation of your choice:

3. JULIET: "Or if thou think'st I am too quickly won,
I'll frown, and be perverse, and say thee nay,
So thou wilt woo; but else, not for the world.
In truth, fair Montague, I am too fond,
And therefore thou mayst think my 'havior light;"

Standard English:

Other translation of your choice:

4. ROMEO: "O blessed, blessed night! I am afeard,
Being in night, all this is but a dream,
Too flattering-sweet to be substantial."

Standard English:

Other translation of your choice:

Choose one of these sets of lines and rehearse saying it in a translation
of your choice. Get feedback on your pitch (how high or low your voice
is) and the rate or speed at which you speak.

Comparing Film Interpretations:
The Balcony Scene

You will view at least two different film versions of the same famous scene from *Romeo and Juliet*. This scene is the balcony scene in which Romeo and Juliet first declare their love for each other. Watch closely and take notes on the chart provided below.

1. The focus of this chart is staging. In other words, look closely at where the actors stand on the stage or set and how they move in relation to one another and to the props and objects around them. Look closely at the *mise en scène*, or "everything in the scene." As you view the scene, write your responses to the questions below.

Version: Director's Name and Year	Set Design: What does it look like? What does the set look and feel like? How does its design affect the way the actors move?	Movements of Actors on Stage or Set Why did the director place the actors where he did? (blocking)	Effect of the Director's Choices

The importance of this scene is that it is the first time the young couple declare their love for each other, after knowing each other for a very short period of time.

2. Discuss with a small group how the staging of this scene adds to its emotional impact. How does the way the director staged the scene help you to understand it better? Which version seems more effective and why? How could you achieve a similar effect with the resources available to you?

3. You can see that the two film clips have similarities and differences. Write a short essay in which you compare the two films, considering the set design, actors' movements, and other theatrical elements. Begin by thinking about how you want to organize your writing. There are two ways you could organize the points of comparison:

Subject-by-subject: Discuss all the elements (set design, actor movement, music, props, etc.) of one film version first and then discuss the elements of the other.

Feature-by-feature: Go back and forth in your discussion of the two film interpretations, comparing and contrasting each element.

Remember to use transition words to help your reader follow your ideas.

> ### GRAMMAR & USAGE
> The reciprocal pronoun *one another* describes interactions among three or more people. Use *each other* to describe interactions between two people.

Transition Words and Phrases for Comparison:

also	in the same way	likewise	similarly
in addition	moreover	another	

Transition Words and Phrases for Contrast:

but	however	in contrast	instead	yet
although	nevertheless	on the other hand		

Strategies Reflection: As you have been doing throughout the unit, plan which strategies you will use and then reflect on how well they worked for you.

Poetry, Paraphrased

LITERARY TERMS

Imagery is language that appeals to the senses, particularly the sense of sight.

A **metaphor** is a figure of speech that compares two or more unlike things. Metaphors do not use the words *like* or *as* to make the comparison.

Hyperbole is a figure of speech that uses exaggeration to express a strong feeling.

An **allusion** refers to a literary, historical, or cultural moment, figure, or event.

Personification is a figure of speech that describes an object as if it were a living creature.

One reason Shakespeare's plays are so well loved is the poetic language that he uses. Every scene of *Romeo and Juliet* is enriched by the use of poetic devices you learned in Unit 3. Choose one of the following literary devices and find an example and comment on its effect: **imagery, metaphor, hyperbole, allusion,** and **personification.**

Literary device:

Example in Act II, Scene 3:

Effect of the literary device on the scene:

Paraphrasing, or restating in your own words, is a strategy that can help you gain understanding of the play. A paraphrased text will be about as long as the original text. Work with a partner to paraphrase the dialogue in Act II, Scene 3, between Romeo and the Friar that begins with Romeo's line, "Thou chid'st me oft for loving Rosaline" and ends at the close of Scene 3.

Both partners should write the entire dialogue on separate paper. Then with your partner, rehearse saying the dialogue in different ways.

Finally, reflect on how the strategies you used helped you understand the scene.

Writing Prompt: Choose at least ten lines of dialogue, and transform the interaction into an email or an instant message conversation. Your content will be similar, but your syntax and voice will change. Be sure to use the proper structure for your format.

Foiled Again

SUGGESTED LEARNING STRATEGIES: Graphic Organizer,
Think-Pair-Share

You may have noticed Shakespeare's use of wordplay in *Romeo and Juliet*. For example, Shakespeare makes liberal use of **puns**, or plays on words that have two meanings. In Act II, Scene 4, Mercutio and Romeo engage in an exchange in which Mercutio scolds Romeo for giving his friends "the counterfeit" the night before. Romeo, still on top of the world after spending the evening with his new love Juliet, goes along with Mercutio's joke. The next several lines capitalize on the dual meanings of *counterfeit* and *slip*.

> **WORD CONNECTIONS**
>
> Many writers, including Shakespeare, are known for their wordplay. The word *repartee* is a French word that describes a type of wordplay with witty replies or retorts.

1. Why do you think puns are known as "thinking man's humor?"

2. In this scene, the wordplay between Romeo and Mercutio helps characterize their friendship and reveals contrasts between them. Compare the characters in the chart below.

Mercutio	Romeo

When a character in a text is seemingly the opposite of another character, yet complements that character, we say he or she is a **character foil.** Use your comparison chart to show how Mercutio serves as a *character foil* for Romeo.

> **LITERARY TERMS**
>
> A **character foil** is a person who, in contrast to the main character—the protagonist—accentuates the main character's distinctive qualities or characteristics.

Short Shrift: A Quick Wedding

The art of visualizing is the ability to picture what something looks like. Consider the following questions and then fill in the chart below with your ideas.

Shakespeare does not write a scene for the wedding of Romeo and Juliet. Why does the wedding take place off-stage?

If the wedding were added to the action of the play, how would you show it in two different time periods—Shakespeare's and now? Describe in detail your choices below and justify them in the space provided.

Time Period: Shakespeare's Time

Costumes: Colors and styles for all three characters (Draw, describe, or cut out pictures.)	Music: Instruments, vocals, artists, specific songs, etc.	Staging: What would the set look like?
Intended effect?	Intended effect?	Intended effect?

Time Period: Now

Costumes: Colors and styles for all three characters (Draw, describe, or cut out pictures.)	Music: Instruments, vocals, artists, specific songs, etc.	Staging: What would the set look like?
Intended effect?	Intended effect?	Intended effect?

Short Shrift: A Quick Wedding

Wedding Vows

Writing Prompt: Shakespeare did not stage Romeo and Juliet's vows, but you can imagine what the characters said. Reread lines in Act II that help you get a sense of the protagonists' voices. Take notes about the way they talk to and about each other. Then, on a separate sheet of paper, write a script with wedding vows for the star-crossed lovers. In your script, include descriptions of gestures, movement, and staging that evoke a definite tone or mood.

Causes and Consequences

1. How does the concept of coming of age relate so far to Romeo? What about Juliet?

2. Does the emotional behavior of Romeo and Juliet have more to do with their age or with love at first sight? Why do you say that?

3. Why do the Friar and the Nurse, adults who care deeply about the young lovers, allow Romeo and Juliet to act so quickly?

Acting Companies

SUGGESTED LEARNING STRATEGIES: Drafting, Brainstorming, Discussion Groups

Performance Scenes

Your acting company will perform a scene from *Romeo and Juliet*. See the list of possible scenes below. Your teacher may add to or delete from this list. Some of the scenes include long speeches from which lines may be cut with your teacher's direction and approval. In addition, a few research topics are provided for your group's dramaturge.

Act and Scene	Description	Characters	Research Topics for the Dramaturge
Act III, Scene 1 Begin — TYBALT: Follow me close, for I will speak to them. End — ROMEO: O, I am fortune's fool! **104 lines**	Mercutio, Tybalt, and Romeo engage in a fight in the street.	Mercutio Tybalt Romeo Benvolio	Fencing, banishment laws
Act III, Scene 5 Begin — LADY CAPULET: Marry, my child, early next Thursday morn ... End — LADY CAPULET: Talk not to me, for I'll not speak a word. **98 lines**	Juliet, her parents, and the Nurse argue about her proposed marriage to Paris.	Lady Capulet Juliet Capulet Nurse	Courtship customs, females' rights
Act IV, Scene 3 Begin — JULIET: Farewell! — God knows when we shall meet again. End — JULIET: Romeo, I come! this do I drink to thee. **45 lines**	Juliet drinks the Friar's potion.	Juliet	Burial vaults, herbal potions

Acting Companies

Act and Scene	Description	Characters	Research Topics for the Dramaturge
Act IV, Scene 5 Begin — NURSE: I must needs wake her. End — FRIAR: Move them no more by crossing their high will.	The Nurse thinks Juliet is dead, and she informs the household. **91 lines**	Nurse Capulet Lady Capulet Friar Paris	Funeral customs, astrology
Act V, Scene 3 Begin — ROMEO: For here lies Juliet, and her beauty makes / This vault a feasting presence full of light. End — JULIET: This is thy sheath; there rest, and let me die.	Romeo and Juliet commit suicide. Note: The exchange between Friar Lawrence and Balthasar may be deleted from this scene **90 lines**	Romeo Juliet Friar Lawrence Balthasar	Burial customs
Act V, Scene 3 Begin — PRINCE: What misadventure is so early up, ... End — PRINCE: For never was a story of more woe / Than this of Juliet and her Romeo.	All is revealed and resolved. Note: Friar Lawrence has a long speech that could be cut or edited. **126 lines**	Prince Capulet Lady Capulet First Watch Montague Friar Lawrence Balthasar Page	Statues as memorials, famous feuds and truces

In Shakespeare's day, acting companies named themselves just as bands do today. Sometimes the acting companies honored their patron (the person who provided financial support) in their name. Shakespeare belonged first to the Lord Chamberlain's Men and later to the King's Men.

1. Your acting company should think of a name that reflects the characteristics of your group. Try to incorporate something you have learned about Shakespeare, the Renaissance, Elizabethan theater, or *Romeo and Juliet* into your company's name.

   Once you reach an agreement, write, sign, and turn in a contract like the one below to your teacher.

   We, the _____ (name of acting company), pledge to

   plan, rehearse, and perform _____ (act and scene)

   from William Shakespeare's *The Tragedy of Romeo and Juliet*.

Cast:

(Name of student) as (name of character)

Director:

Dramaturge:

Date of performance:

2. Once you know the role you will play, read the rest of the play, paying attention to what your character says and does. Take notes as you read. You may also need to do research in preparation for the performance.

3. With your acting company, brainstorm people whom you could invite to your performance and then prepare invitations. Keep your audience's interests in mind as you create the invitation.

"A Plague o' Both Your Houses!"

Quickwrite: Before you read Act III, Scene 1, think about action scenes that you have seen on TV or in video games or movies. On a separate sheet of paper, quickwrite about action scenes that involve fighting. Use the following questions to guide your thinking, but do not limit yourself to answering just these questions:

- Why do people fight?
- Who usually wins in a fight? Why?
- Under what circumstances would you fight?
- What are the consequences of fighting?

While you are reading Act III, Scene 1, try to imagine the action in your head and think about why the characters are doing what they are doing.

Character	How is he behaving?	Why is he behaving in this way? What is his motivation?
Romeo		
Mercutio		
Tybalt		
Benvolio		

Reread the Prince's decision at the end of the scene. How does the Prince feel? What thoughts may be going through his mind? Pretend you are a director and make notes on the script below to indicate how you want the actor playing the Prince to deliver the lines. Begin by identifying where you would have the Prince pause for effect. Using pauses and silence is part of vocal variety, just as pitch, rate and intonation are. Include in your planning all the elements of visual delivery (gestures, posture, movement, eye contact, facial expression and props) and vocal delivery (volume, pitch, rate, pauses, vocal variety, and pronunciation/articulation). You will use these notations later to mark your text for the performance of your scene from the play.

Act III, Scene 1

PRINCE: And for that offence

Immediately we do exile him hence.

I have an interest in your hate's proceeding,

My blood for your rude brawls doth lie a-bleeding;

But I'll amerce you with so strong a fine   5

That you shall all repent the loss of mine.

I will be deaf to pleading and excuses;

Nor tears nor prayers shall purchase out abuses.

Therefore use none. Let Romeo hence in haste,

Else, when he's found, that hour is his last.   10

Bear hence this body and attend our will.

Mercy but murders, pardoning those that kill.

2. After you have heard some oral interpretations of this speech, note how they differ. What does the speaker do and to what effect? Which interpretation best expresses your ideas of how the Prince must be feeling at this moment? Why?

"A Plague o' Both Your Houses!"

3. After you have read Act III, Scene 1, analyze the arguments made by each side. The Prince must sentence Romeo to some kind of punishment for killing Tybalt.

- What punishment for Romeo does Lady Capulet demand?

- What punishment does Lord Montague suggest?

- What is the Prince's decree or decision?

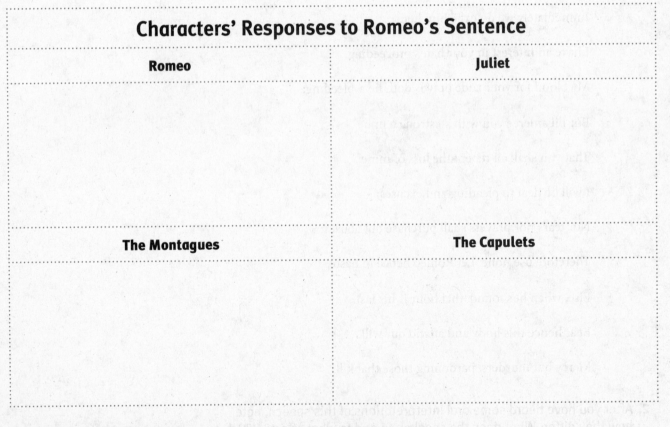

Characters' Responses to Romeo's Sentence

Romeo	Juliet
The Montagues	**The Capulets**

Writing Prompt: Do you think this is a fair punishment for the crime? Choose one of the characters above and, on a separate sheet of paper, work with your acting company to write his or her response to the Prince's decree. Use RAFT to help you form your response.

Comparing Film Interpretations: "And Fire-eyed Fury Be My Conduct Now"

SUGGESTED LEARNING STRATEGIES: Graphic Organizer, Discussion Groups, Drafting

From the opening of the play, the conflict between the Capulets and the Montagues has inspired "fire-eyed fury," or anger that has erupted into violence and murder. As you watch at least two interpretations of Act III, Scene 1, pay attention to the portrayals of the major characters. Take notes on any shifts in the emotions of the characters and consider how the director presents the shift.

Director: /

	Romeo	Mercutio	Tybalt
How does the character behave? (Consider visual and vocal delivery to show emotion.)			
Why does the character behave this way?			
What causes the shift in behavior?			
How does the character's behavior change?			
Why does the character behave in this new way?			

How does the director signal change in the mood of the scene? Consider any changes in set, props, costumes, music and other sounds, lighting, and editing.

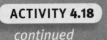

Comparing Film Interpretations: "And Fire-eyed Fury Be My Conduct Now"

Director:

	Romeo	Mercutio	Tybalt
How does the character behave? (Consider visual and vocal delivery to show emotion.)			
Why does the character behave this way?			
What causes the shift in behavior?			
How does the character's behavior change?			
Why does the character behave in this new way?			
How does the director signal a change in the mood of the scene? Consider any changes in set, props, costumes, music and other sounds, lighting, and editing.			

In your acting company, discuss the mood created in these film interpretations, then brainstorm ways that your company could create a similar mood with the resources you have available.

Writing Prompt: On separate paper, write an essay that explains which film version more powerfully conveys the seriousness of "fire-eyed fury." Be sure to provide textual support and reflective commentary. Be mindful of the strategies you use in the writing process.

Emotional Roller Coaster

SUGGESTED LEARNING STRATEGIES: Graphic Organizer

Coming of age stories involve young characters who are just learning how to deal with the intense emotions and experiences of young adulthood. At times the characters seem to be on an emotional roller coaster. In Act III, Romeo and Juliet both experience a broad range of emotions. For example, one minute Juliet is anxiously awaiting a message from her love, and the next she is grieving the death of her cousin.

Create a list of significant events in each character's story so far (you might update your timeline chart from Activity 4.6). Number them in a key below the graph. Next, plot the numbers of the events on the emotional graph below. When you have finished reading Act III, connect the points you have plotted for each character's emotions.

Juliet's Emotions

Angry

Sad

Happy

Calm

Key: Incidents in the story that reveal Juliet's emotions

1.

2.

3.

4.

5.

Emotional Roller Coaster

When Juliet first receives the news about Tybalt's fate, she reacts with a wide range of feelings. The figurative language she uses to describe Romeo in Act III, Scene 2, shows her confusion. Identify the oxymorons that Juliet uses to describe Romeo (see the speech beginning with "O serpent heart . . . "). An ***oxymoron*** is an expression that combines contradictory ideas into a single, unusual expression; for example, "cold fire" or "sweet sorrow."

In the space below, illustrate or create a symbolic representation of the descriptions she uses.

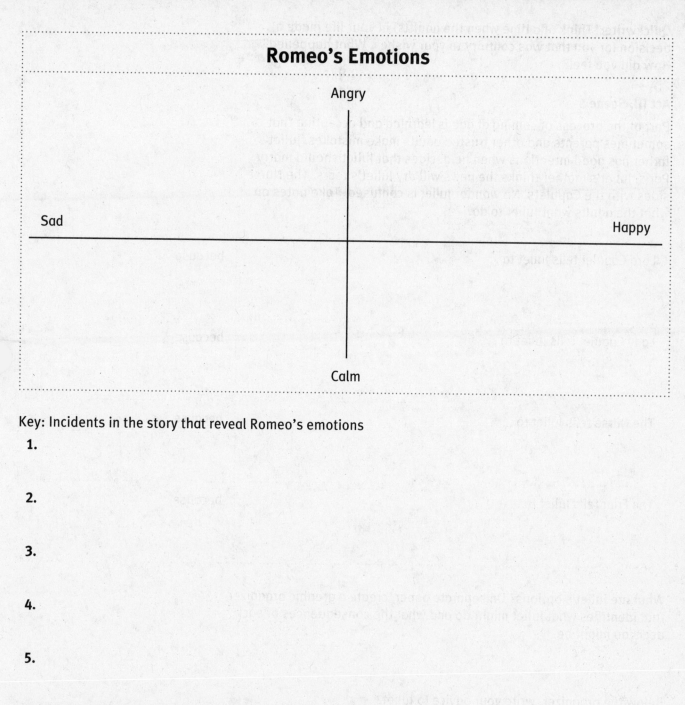

Romeo's Emotions

Angry

Sad

Happy

Calm

Key: Incidents in the story that reveal Romeo's emotions

1.

2.

3.

4.

5.

Look back at the graphs you have drawn. What do the characters' ranges of emotion reveal about them and their situations?

"But Now I'll Tell Thee Joyful Tidings, Girl"

Quickwrite: Think of a time when the adult(s) in your life made a decision for you that was contrary to your wishes. What happened? How did you feel?

Act III, Scene 5

Part of the process of coming of age is learning and accepting that sometimes parents and other trusted adults make mistakes. Juliet's father has good intentions when he decides that Juliet should marry Paris. Juliet's mother thinks the news will dry Juliet's tears. The Nurse sides with the Capulets. No wonder Juliet is confused! Take notes on what the adults want Juliet to do.

Lord Capulet tells Juliet to . . .		because
Lady Capulet tells Juliet to . . .		because
The Nurse tells Juliet to . . .		because
The Friar tells Juliet to . . .		because

What are Juliet's options? On separate paper, create a graphic organizer that identifies what Juliet might do and what the consequences of each decision might be.

Below the organizer, write your advice to Juliet.

"And, If Thou Darest, I'll Give Thee Remedy"

SUGGESTED LEARNING STRATEGIES: Oral Interpretation, Marking the Text, Graphic Organizer

1. Write your own explanation of **subtext** and give an example.

2. Why is it important to keep the subtext in mind when you are performing a scene?

3. In Act IV, Scene 1, Juliet has a conversation with Paris during which she must hide her true feelings. Using sticky notes, mark the text by writing the subtext—Juliet's true thoughts—which you find "between the lines."

4. Your teacher will ask your acting company to pantomime either the things Juliet would rather do than marry Paris or the Friar's plan for Juliet. Remember that in a pantomime, you act out something without using words. Your audience must guess the action from your movements and expressions.

What Juliet Would Rather Do Than Marry Paris	Pantomime Plan (Movements, expressions, gestures)

Steps in the Friar's Plan for Juliet	Pantomime Plan (Movements, expressions, gestures)

"And, If Thou Darest, I'll Give Thee Remedy"

Quickwrite: Evaluate the Friar's plan for Juliet. Be sure to explain the subtext of his plan. Does it seem wise? Why or why not?

"… I Needs Must Act Alone"

In Act IV, Scenes 2–3, Juliet must conceal her emotions once again. Role-play parts of the scenes, having one of the actors say Juliet's lines while another actor stands nearby and pantomimes Juliet's true feelings. Discuss what the scenes suggest about Juliet and her family.

Work with your acting company to create a graphic organizer that shows all the characters with whom Juliet has interacted. Show on your organizer those with whom she speaks in her true voice and those with whom she "wears a mask." For each, explain why. Describe the most important event in Act IV, Scene 3.

A close reading reveals that Juliet has much to fear if she follows the Friar's plan. Read carefully Juliet's soliloquy from Act IV, Scene 3, which appears on the next page. Underline all the potential outcomes that frighten Juliet. In the margin, summarize Juliet's fears.

Highlight the words and phrases that you associate with death. In the margin, write which sense each word appeals to (sight, hearing, taste, touch, smell). What is the effect of all this death imagery?

Quickwrite: Do you think Juliet made a good decision in drinking the potion? Why or why not?

> **WORD CONNECTIONS**
>
> *Soliloquy* contains the root -*sol*- from the Latin word *soli*, meaning "one, alone, or lonely." This root also appears in *solo, solitary,* and *solitude*.

My Notes

Drama

From ROMEO

AND JULIET

by William Shakespeare

Juliet

Farewell! — God knows when we shall meet again.

I have a faint cold fear thrills through my veins

That almost freezes up the heat of life.

I'll call them back again to comfort me.

5   Nurse! — What should she do here?

My dismal scene I needs must act alone.

Come, vial.

What if this mixture do not work at all?

Shall I be married then to-morrow morning?

10   No, no! This shall forbid it. Lie thou there.

[Laying down her dagger.]

What if it be a poison, which the friar

Subtly hath ministere'd to have me dead,

Lest in this marriage he should be dishonoured,

Because he married me before to Romeo?

15   I fear it is; and yet, methinks, it should not,

I will not entertain so bad a thought.

For he hath still been tried a holy man.

How if, when I am laid into the tomb,

I wake before the time that Romeo

20   Come to redeem me? There's a fearful point!

Shall I not, then, be stifled in the vault,

To whose foul mouth no healthsome air breathes in,

And there die strangled ere my Romeo comes?

Or, if I live, is it not very like,

The horrible conceit of death and night,   25

Together with the terror of the place,

As in a vault, an ancient receptacle

Where, for this many hundred years, the bones

Of all my buried ancestors are packed;

Where bloody Tybalt, yet but green in earth,   30

Lies fest'ering in his shroud; where, as they say,

At some hours in the night spirits resort—

Alack, alack, is it not like that I,

So early waking—what with loathsome smells,

And shrieks like mandrakes torn out of the earth,   35

That living mortals, hearing them, run mad—

O, if I wake, shall I not be distraught,

Environed with all these hideous fears,

And madly play with my forefathers' joints,

And pluck the mangled Tybalt from his shroud,   40

And, in this rage, with some great kinsman's bone

As with a club dash out my desp'rate brains?

O, look! Methinks I see my cousin's ghost

Seeking out Romeo, that did spit his body

Upon a rapier's point. Stay, Tybalt, stay!   45

Romeo, I come! This do I drink to thee.

[Throws herself on the bed.]

Writing Prompt: Choose an example of a subjunctive possibility
from Juliet's speech, and rewrite it in modern English.

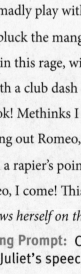

After your group has read the previous scene, individually choose one part that you feel is important. Imagine that you are directing an actor. What would you tell her to do in order to create an effective performance?

Rewrite part of the speech here. Then review the essential features of an effective dramatic performance. Mark the speech, indicating how the actor should use vocal delivery and visual delivery to convey the essence of the speech.

Trade papers with a classmate and follow each other's directions in a rehearsal. Practice a few times until you each feel that your partner is delivering the lines the way you want.

Writing Prompt: Reflect on your experiences both as a director and an actor. Which did you prefer? Why? Write your response on a separate sheet of paper.

Shakespeare in Art

SUGGESTED LEARNING STRATEGIES: Close Reading, Graphic
Organizers, Discussion Groups

Shakespeare's works have inspired artists for over four hundred years. As you examine a piece of art inspired by the tragedy of *Romeo and Juliet,* think about the connections between the drama and the artwork and how the artist achieves them.

Name of painting:

Artist:

Part of *Romeo and Juliet* depicted:

Which Characters Appear?	What Are the Characters Doing?	How Do the Characters Appear to Feel?

How Would You Describe the Grouping of the Characters?	Why Do You Think the Artist Chose to Group the Characters in This Way?

Shakespeare in Art

How Would You Describe the Setting?

What Effect Is Created by This Setting?

What Colors are Used in the Painting?

What Effect Do You Think the Artist was Trying to Achieve by Using These Colors?

What Feelings Does the Painting Evoke in You?	What About the Painting Evokes These Feelings?

Meet with your acting company to discuss how you can apply your thoughts about the artwork you analyzed to your own performance. Discuss what visual and emotional effects you want to achieve and how you might use elements such as the placement of the actors (blocking), simple sets and props, and color to create them. Be sure to take notes during this discussion.

"Then I Defy You, Stars!"

1. You have read most of *Romeo and Juliet* with your class, so you should be ready to read Act V on your own. First, think about the reading strategies you have used in the past and identify which you intend to use. After reading Act V, reflect on the effectiveness of those strategies in the space provided below.

2. Rather than marry Paris, Juliet decides to drink the Friar's potion so she will appear dead and then be interred in her family's vault. When Romeo hears news of Juliet's death, he, too, makes a difficult decision. As you read Act V, Scene 1, look for evidence that tells you what Romeo intends to do.

3. Based on the details you identified, what is Romeo's plan?

4. What does Romeo mean when he says, "Then I defy you, stars!"?

5. What are Romeo's options? On separate paper, create a graphic organizer such as a bubble cluster, and brainstorm every option you can see for Romeo and the possible outcomes of each option.

Comparing Film Interpretations: "Thus with a Kiss I Die"

SUGGESTED LEARNING STRATEGIES: **Quickwrite, Close Reading, Graphic Organizer, Drafting**

In Shakespeare's time, the stage would have looked similar to the drawing below. The theater in London where many of Shakespeare's productions were staged is the Globe Theatre. Modern-day stages are not so different, though seating for the audience is arranged differently.

Stage directions written into a play are usually given from the point of view of an actor facing the audience.

Comparing Film Interpretations:
"Thus with a Kiss I Die"

Look at the stage directions below and imagine you are an actor facing the audience.

Using the information already provided for you, label areas of the stage:

Upstage

Stage Right

Stage Left

Center Stage

Downstage

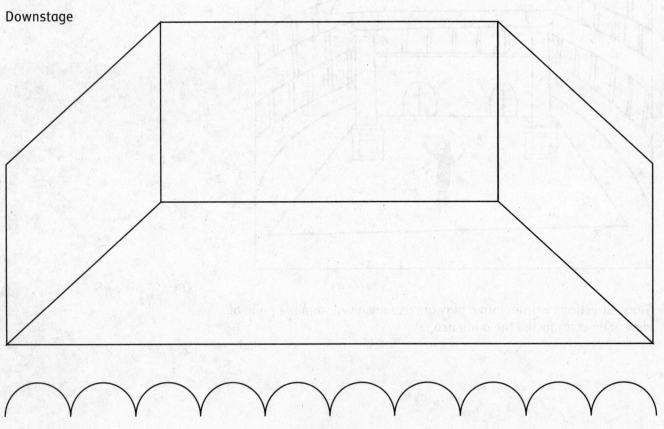

Audience

Find an area in your classroom and pretend it is your stage. See if you can identify the different areas of the stage.

The Tragedy of Romeo and Juliet has been performed countless times since Shakespeare's company first staged the drama, in part because audiences around the world respond emotionally to the young lovers who cannot be together.

1. What emotions does Act V of *Romeo and Juliet* create in you?

2. List the props you would need to create your vision of this scene.

3. The scene when Romeo and Juliet die is obviously one of the most important scenes in the play. Think about how you might stage this scene. Draw a diagram of your set and mark where your actors and props would be.

What Kind of Lighting Would You Use to Create the Effect You Want?	What Kind of Music Would You Use to Create the Effect You Want?

↗TECHNOLOGY TIP If appropriate resources are available, work with peers to capture your ideas for staging a scene by filming short enactments or your discussions of props and staging.

As you watch film interpretations of the deaths of Romeo and Juliet, take notes on what each film does to create an emotional response. Think about all the theatrical elements directors use to create their intended effect:

- Actors' visual delivery (gestures, posture, movement, eye contact, facial expression)
- Actors' vocal delivery (volume, pitch, rate, pauses, vocal variety, pronunciation/articulation)
- Costumes/Props
- Setting
- Music/Sounds
- Lighting
- Editing

Title / Director	Intended Effect	How Director Creates Effect

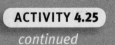

Comparing Film Interpretations:
"Thus with a Kiss I Die"

Title / Director	Intended Effect	How Director Creates Effect

LITERARY TERMS

Dramatic irony occurs when the audience knows something that a character does not.

Some directors emphasize **dramatic irony** in this scene. Explain any example of dramatic iron that you noticed. What knowledge did you have that the characters did not? How did your knowledge affect the way you felt during the scene?

Writing Prompt: Write a piece that explains which interpretations of *Romeo and Juliet* you found effective. Be sure to make specific references to theatrical elements, such as costumes, props, gestures, music, and other details to support your response.

"Some Shall Be Pardoned, and Some Punished"

SUGGESTED LEARNING STRATEGIES: Discussion Groups, Drafting, Graphic Organizer, Paraphrasing

Review what you know about tragedy. Revisit any notes you have taken about tragedy and add to and refine them, showing how your understanding has grown after reading *Romeo and Juliet*.

> **LITERARY TERMS**
>
> A **theme** is a central idea or message of a literary work. Unlike a topic (for example, love, revenge, or death), a statement of theme is a complete thought; for example, not every love story is meant to have a happy ending.

Now that you have read *Romeo and Juliet*, consider the important **themes** that Shakespeare's play suggests. A literary work can have more than one theme, and the author does not generally directly state a theme but rather implies it. List several thematic statements about the subjects that Shakespeare treats in the play.

Which of these themes is most relevant to teenagers today? Explain.

"Some Shall Be Pardoned, and Some Punished"

During your reading of *Romeo and Juliet* you have considered the causes of Romeo's and Juliet's deaths. The major causes leading to their untimely demise are as follows:

- Romeo's and Juliet's youth and inexperience,
- The interference of the adults in the play,
- The influence of fate and/or chance on the lives of the characters.

Now look back through the play to locate actions and lines that support each of these causes. Use the chart below to organize your findings.

Youth and Inexperience	Adults' Interference	Fate/Chance
Act I	Act I	Act I
Act II	Act II	Act II
Act III	Act III	Act III

Youth and Inexperience	Adults' Interference	Fate/Chance
Act IV	Act IV	Act IV
Act V	Act V	Act V

Thesis Statement: After compiling your evidence and thinking about the causes of the deaths of Romeo and Juliet, write a thesis statement that addresses the question: Who or what is responsible for the deaths of Romeo and Juliet?

Now write topic sentences that address three possible causes of Romeo's and Juliet's deaths. Put the causes in order from least to most important.

Cause 1 (least important)

Cause 2 (important)

Cause 3 (most important)

Use the following outline to draft your essay:

Introduction

Lead or hook to grab the reader's attention

TAG (Title, Author, Genre) and minimal plot summary

Thesis—your opinion on the subject that you are trying to prove

Body Paragraphs

Topic sentences in each body paragraph that express ideas in support of your thesis.

Evidence from the text that supports your topic sentence

Commentary or explanations of the significance of your evidence

Conclusion

Summary of your main points

Expression of your own thoughts

Brief considerations of related questions, such as:

How does a major theme of the play relate to the causes of the characters' deaths?

What lesson can be learned from the characters' fates?

What was Shakespeare trying to tell us about life through this story?

Timed Writing

At the end of *Romeo and Juliet*, the Prince states that some characters will be pardoned and others punished. You have considered the actions of Romeo and Juliet themselves, the adults in their lives, and fate or chance. Which do you think is primarily to blame for the deaths of Romeo and Juliet? Write your thesis here.

Compose a persuasive essay in which you argue that one of the three causes is the most important. Discuss each of the causes. Show which is the most important by organizing your essay from least to most important. Use transitions to reflect your organization. Also, consider the five elements of argumentation (hook, claim, concessions/refutations, support, and summary/call to action). Look at the Scoring Criteria on the next page to help guide your writing.

Writing Prompt: For Embedded Assessment 1, you will be presenting a Shakespearean scene. Work with your classmates to write two class advertisements for your performance. Use language and images to attract your audience. If possible, add sound to your advertisements, and film them for presentation to the class.

"Some Shall Be Pardoned, and Some Punished"

Scoring Criteria	Exemplary	Proficient	Emerging
Ideas and Organization	Essay opens with a clearly stated purpose that grabs readers' attention. Author provides opinions and supports them with evidence from the play. Author concludes with a thought-provoking ending.	Essay contains an opening with a clear purpose. Author states clear opinions and supports them with evidence from the play and concludes by giving the reader a sense of closure.	The essay lacks a clear purpose and opinions, as well as relevant evidence from the play. The conclusion does not address ideas expressed in essay.
Use of Language (Persuasive Techniques)	The author's skillful use of persuasive techniques works effectively to sway the reader. The author has a clear sense of effective tone for that audience.	The author uses persuasive techniques in an attempt to sway the reader. The author is aware of and uses an appropriate tone for that audience.	The author lacks appropriate techniques of persuasion and appropriate tone for the audience.
Conventions	The writer demonstrates strong control and mastery of standard conventions. Either no errors appear, or they are so slight that they do not interfere with meaning.	The writer demonstrates control of standard writing conventions. Though some errors may appear, they do not seriously impede readability.	There are frequent errors in standard conventions that seriously interfere with meaning.
Additional Criteria			

Comments:

Presenting a Shakespearean Scene

SUGGESTED LEARNING STRATEGIES: Discussion Groups, Oral Interpretation

Assignment

Your assignment is to work with your acting company to interpret, rehearse, and perform a scene from *The Tragedy of Romeo and Juliet*. In addition to the performance, actors, the director, and the dramaturge will prepare notebooks to accompany the scene.

Steps

Planning

1. When you formed your acting companies, you selected roles and a scene from the play to perform for the class. As you prepare for the performance, each member of the company must prepare a staging notebook specific to his or her role. (The content will be determined by the role of director, actor, or dramaturge.)

2. Review the essential features of an effective dramatic performance. Discuss how your acting company will integrate those features into your performance.

3. Begin the process by rereading your selected scene, getting comfortable saying the lines, and understanding the action in the scene. Plan appropriate visual and vocal delivery.

4. Remember, the goal is to interpret a scene. The acting company's success depends on how well members work together to create a polished and interesting performance.

5. The director will guide the acting company, making lists of props, costume pieces, and background music that will enhance the performance. The dramaturge will provide needed background information to enhance your performance.

Rehearsing

6. Rehearse your scene several times, using the strategies you have learned in this unit. The director's feedback and the dramaturge's research should enhance the acting company's performance.

7. If possible, videotape one of your rehearsals to help you improve the quality of the performance. Pay attention to your positions on stage, the pacing of your speeches, and the volume at which you speak. If videotaping is not practical, ask another group to watch and provide feedback on how you might improve your performance. Consult the Scoring Guide to help facilitate your rehearsals.

Presenting a Shakespearean Scene

Performing

8. Perform your scene on the agreed-upon day. The director will introduce the scene, and, after the performance, the dramaturge will explain how the performance reflects his or her research.

Reflecting

9. After your performance, write a metacognitive reflection of the entire process including the scene analysis, rehearsals, and performance itself. Include your commentary on the challenges you faced, how you worked to overcome them, and your evaluation of the final performance. You may want to revisit the Scoring Guide to ensure your understanding of the criteria for this piece.

↗TECHNOLOGY TIP If appropriate resources are available, film your rehearsals for use in critiquing and improving your performance. Pay particular attention to speaking skills and delivery of your lines.

Director's Notebook

In preparation for your acting company's performance of a scene from *Romeo and Juliet*, you will create a staging notebook. Completing each item listed below will help you understand the scene and your responsibilities in the scene.

Text

Type or paste a copy of your scene on white paper. Leave plenty of room in the margins to take notes about the visual and vocal delivery by each character. Actors will take notes about their own characters, based on your direction, but you should have notes about all the characters. Plan to sit near your acting company during the performance and be prepared to feed lines to the actors if they forget.

Diagram of the Set

You will need to draw the set, so be sure to ask your teacher where you will be performing your scene. Include a sketch of the set from the audience's perspective as well as an aerial view (a view from above).

Lighting and Sound

Create a plan for lighting that will enhance your acting company's performance. Also list any sound effects or music that your group will use. For both lighting and sound, include an explanation as to why you think your choices are appropriate for your scene.

Props

Make a list of the props for your scene and where you will get them.

Introduction

Write an introduction for the scene and memorize it. You will present this introduction before your acting company performs.

Meeting Log

After every meeting, you will be responsible for writing a dated log that records how the meeting went. Some questions you might answer in your log include the following:

- What did the group accomplish?
- What obstacles were identified?
- Which problems have been resolved? How?
- What needs to be done before and at the next meeting?

Presenting a Shakespearean Scene

Actor's Notebook

To help you prepare for your performance of a scene from *Romeo and Juliet*, you will create a staging notebook. Completing each of the items listed below should help you understand your scene and your part in the scene.

Text

Type or paste a copy of your scene on white paper. Highlight your own lines, and paraphrase them to help you understand them. There should be plenty of room in the margins for you to take notes about vocal and visual delivery. Write down everything that you and your director decide you should do to convey your interpretation of your character.

Costume

You will need to decide on an appropriate costume for your character. This page of your staging notebook will have two parts: the first part will show your ideal costume, and the second part will show your real costume.

- Your **ideal costume** is the one you would wear if you had all the resources you could wish for. You can draw, trace, or cut a picture out of a magazine for your ideal costume.

- Your **real costume** might be very simple, but it should reflect the character in some recognizable way. You may draw, trace, or attach a picture of yourself wearing your real costume.

Explain why the costume is appropriate for your character.

Character Analysis

Write a character analysis or explain your interpretation of your character.

- If you write a character analysis, choose a genre that will allow you to convey your character's thoughts, desires, actions, and obstacles.

- If you explain your artistic interpretation, think of a way to express these concerns visually. For example, you might draw an outline of a body and write your analysis on the corresponding body parts:

Head: thoughts of your character

Heart: desires of your character

Arms: actions of your character

Legs: obstacles for your character

Dramaturge's Notebook

Research Questions

As soon as your acting company has selected its scene, you will need to generate research questions related to the scene. These questions might address the context of the play, or they might focus on the history of its performance. You might need to research references made in the play or the meanings of unfamiliar words or phrases. In short, your assignment is to answer questions so that your company's performance is as authentic as possible.

Notes

Conduct research to answer questions and take careful notes.

Bibliography

Create a bibliography of the works you consulted in your research.

Suggestions

Based on your research findings, prepare a list of suggestions for the director and the actors. Present them to the group and be prepared to explain your reasons for the suggestions.

Explanation

Write an explanation of how your research helped the acting company interpret its scene. Memorize this explanation and present it after your group's performance.

Reflection

Write a reflection considering the research for your role as dramaturge. Did the process work effectively? Did you modify your major research question during research? How would you change the process for future research?

SCORING GUIDE

Scoring Criteria	Exemplary	Proficient	Emerging
Staging Notebook	The staging notebook demonstrates an insightful understanding of the scene and of the student's responsibilities. Each required entry is complete and detailed. The format of the notebook is exceptionally neat, organized, and well presented.	The staging notebook demonstrates a clear understanding of the scene and of the student's responsibilities. Required entries are complete. The format of the notebook is organized.	The staging notebook inadequately demonstrates an understanding of the scene and of the student's responsibilities. Required entries may be incomplete or missing. The format of the notebook is disorganized and difficult to follow.
Performance	The groups' interpretation of the scene is insightful, and the intended effect is clearly communicated to the audience. Participants demonstrate a polished performance by: • skillfully using various theatrical elements; • strategically using all elements of vocal delivery to effectively fulfill their role within the acting company; • effectively using elements of visual delivery to create focus and maintain energy for the scene.	The groups' interpretation of the scene is plausible, and the intended effect is communicated to the audience. Participants demonstrate an organized performance by: • adequately using various theatrical elements; • knowledgeably using elements of vocal delivery to appropriately portray their character(s) or to communicate information related to their role within the acting company; • using elements of visual delivery to create coherence for the scene.	The groups' interpretation of the scene may be unclear, and/or the intended effect is not successfully communicated to the audience. Participants demonstrate a disorganized performance and may: • not utilize various theatrical elements; • not use elements of vocal delivery to portray their character(s) or to communicate information related to their role within the acting company; • use elements of visual delivery that are unclear or detract from the quality of the scene.
Evidence of Collaboration	Throughout the entire process of planning and presenting, the group cooperates and works successfully to maintain purpose and to achieve goals. The equal sharing of responsibility is evident.	Throughout the process of planning and presenting, the group works together adequately to maintain purpose and achieve goals. The sharing of responsibility is mostly balanced.	Throughout the process of planning and presenting, the group members' cooperation is lacking, which impedes their ability to maintain a purpose or achieve goals. Responsibilities may not be equally divided.

SCORING GUIDE

Scoring Criteria	Exemplary	Proficient	Emerging
Reflective Text	The writer's metacognition demonstrates a thorough and detailed analysis of the entire process including analyzing, rehearsing, and performing the scene. It includes insightful commentary on challenges faced, how they were overcome, and an evaluation of the final performance.	The writer's metacognition demonstrates adequate analysis of the process of analyzing, rehearsing, and performing the scene. It includes commentary on challenges faced, how they were overcome, and an evaluation of the final performance.	The writer's metacognition demonstrates inadequate analysis of the process of analyzing, rehearsing, and performing the scene. Commentary on the challenges faced, how they were overcome, and an evaluation of the final performance may be weak or missing. Analysis and evaluation may be replaced by summary.
Additional Criteria:			

Comments:

Learning Focus:

Measuring My Growth

You and your group have presented your interpretation of a scene from a Shakespearean play, which is quite an accomplishment. Some parts of the assignment may not have gone as you had planned, while other parts may have gone better than you expected. One thing is certain—you learned along the way. You probably learned about the play itself as well as the playwright and the different contexts of his work, but more importantly, you may have learned about yourself.

You have used reading, writing, speaking, and listening skills to help you learn about and perform Shakespeare's drama. Now is your opportunity to take a close look at your growth as a learner, a reader, a writer, and a communicator. The second part of the unit focuses on **metacognition**. Metacognition is the ability to evaluate your growth and recognize the strategies that contributed to it so that you can continue to meet new learning goals.

You will have several opportunities to reflect on the learning strategies that are effective for you. Metacognition is an important skill to master because while your teachers and others may guide your education, ultimately you need to know and understand your strengths and challenges as a learner.

Reflecting on Growth: Speaking and Listening

SUGGESTED LEARNING STRATEGIES: **Revisiting Prior Work, Graphic Organizer**

Think about your acting company's presentation of a scene from *Romeo and Juliet*. Now take some time to reflect on the presentation and your part in it.

What did you do well?	
Next time, what would you do differently?	
What did you learn about yourself?	
What did you learn about working with others?	
How did you grow or change as a result of the experience?	

You have had many opportunities for speaking and performing in front of an audience this year. Review your portfolio for activities in which you spoke to or performed for others. In this unit, you engaged in role playing, participated in a dress rehearsal, and performed a scene from a play.

Complete the graphic organizer about yourself as a speaker and/or performer.

In the past, as a speaker or performer I was...	
When I had to speak or perform before an audience, I felt...	
While I spoke or performed, I used to...	
Now, as a speaker or performer, I am...	
Now when I have to speak or perform before an audience, I feel...	
In the future, when I speak or perform, I will...	

Part of the experience of performing scenes is serving as audience for your classmates' performances. Give yourself a rating, with 10 being the best score, as a listener/audience member.

| 1 | 2 | 3 | 4 | 5 | 6 | 7 | 8 | 9 | 10 |

Why did you give yourself this rating?

Working collaboratively also requires listening. Rate yourself as a listener in your acting company.

| 1 | 2 | 3 | 4 | 5 | 6 | 7 | 8 | 9 | 10 |

Why did you give yourself this rating?

How would you rate yourself as a listener in other activities you have completed?

| 1 | 2 | 3 | 4 | 5 | 6 | 7 | 8 | 9 | 10 |

Why did you give yourself this rating?

What can you do to be a better listener?

Which speaking and listening strategies have helped you most? Explain.

Reflecting on Growth: Reading and Writing

Identify activities from the unit that fit the descriptors listed at the bottom of the page. Write the activity in the Title(s) column. Then choose a descriptor that describes your response(s) to the activities. You can use the same activity more than once.

Type of Activity	Title(s)	Descriptor Words*	Strategies Used
Activities Where Your Feelings Changed as You Worked			
Activities Where Your Feelings Changed After You Finished Working			
Activities That the Class and/or Teacher Seemed to Enjoy But You Did Not			
Activities That Were Very Challenging			

*Descriptor Words

curiosity	doubt	humor	surprise	fear
unwillingness	boredom	confidence	realization	confusion
amazement	empathy	joy	intimidation	awakening
anger	serenity	anticipation	engagement	compassion
disdain	dread	frustration	questioning	encouragement
delight	nostalgia	comfort	reminding	connection
disengagement	agitation	beauty	regret	admiration

On separate paper, write a response to an activity and text that you completed in this unit. Try to trace your connection (or lack of it) to this activity throughout the whole process of completing the task. In your response, discuss the strategies you used and their effect on the activity. You are not writing a review of the activity (saying whether or not it was good) but focusing on your response to that activity and text.

After writing your response, answer the following reflection questions.

1. As you review the challenging activities you listed on the previous page, what did strategies add to the activity, if anything? Explain.

2. You may have used some strategies more than others in this unit. Which strategies did you use most often? Why?

3. What pieces of work, if any, do you plan to include in your portfolio as measurements of growth during this unit? Why did you select those pieces? How do they reflect your growth? Fill in the organizer below.

Name of Activity or Activities	Reason for Including This Activity in the Portfolio as an Example of Growth

4. In which strategies do you feel you have improved the most in this unit?

5. Which strategies, if any, are not comfortable for you at this point? Why?

Writing a Metacognitive Reflection

SUGGESTED LEARNING STRATEGIES: **Drafting, Revising**

Assignment

Your assignment is to write a reflective essay about your growth as a reader, writer, speaker, and listener. Your essay should include examples of reading, writing, speaking, listening, and collaborative strategies you have used this year. You should also explain how those strategies helped you to improve your ability to read and comprehend challenging texts as well as write and present original texts.

Steps

Planning

1. Review the activities you completed this year. Also, refer to your list of strategies you have used this year. Be sure to consider strategy learning logs and end-of-unit reflections, as well as the pieces you have saved in your portfolio throughout the year.

2. Identify two or three strategies from each category (Reading, Writing, Speaking and Listening, Collaborative) that you used often and found to be most helpful in your tasks.

3. Using a prewriting strategy of your choice, develop a plan for a reflective essay in which you describe yourself as a reader, a writer, a speaker and a listener.

Drafting

4. Draft your essay. Include examples of your strengths, the challenges and obstacles you have encountered, and the strategies you have used to overcome them. Be sure to identify the strategies you have used, their effectiveness, and reasons you think they worked well for you. Use your portfolio as a resource and provide specific examples of texts you have read and created. Conclude by describing how you will meet new challenges and opportunities as a speaker, listener, and writer. Consult the Scoring Guide to review criteria.

Revising and Publishing

5. When you revise and edit your essay, make sure that your references to specific texts and assignments are accurate.

6. Share your metacognitive reflection with an audience of your choice.

Writing a Metacognitive Reflection

SCORING GUIDE

Scoring Criteria	Exemplary	Proficient	Emerging
Evidence of Metacognition	The text insightfully and descriptively discusses the writer's strengths and the obstacles/challenges encountered in reading, writing, speaking, and listening. It provides reflective commentary on the effectiveness of strategies used as a reader, speaker, listener, and writer and demonstrates a perceptive analysis of strategies the student will apply in the future.	The text discusses the writer's strengths and the obstacles/challenges encountered in reading, writing, speaking, and listening. The text evaluates the effectiveness of particular strategies as a reader, speaker, listener, and writer. Commentary also shows an adequate evaluation of the strategies the student will apply in the future.	The text attempts to discuss the writer's strengths and the obstacles/challenges encountered in reading, writing, speaking, and listening. Commentary does little to explain the strategies to support experiences with challenging texts and opportunities as a speaker, listener, and writer. Parts of the reflective evaluation and evidence of personalized strategies to apply in the future may be missing.
Examples of Strategy Application	Specific and varied examples of texts the writer read and created and examples of speaking and listening opportunites support the identified strategies. They directly connect to the writer's analysis.	Clear examples of texts the writer read and created and examples of speaking and listening opportunities support the identified strategies. They relate to the writer's analysis.	Examples are difficult to identify from the description the student provides.
Organization	The text is multi-paragraphed and logically organized to enhance reader's understanding.	The essay is multi-paragraphed and organized in a coherent manner.	Organization is attempted, but key components are lacking in coherence.

SCORING GUIDE

Scoring Criteria	Exemplary	Proficient	Emerging
Additional Criteria			

Comments:

Reflection

An important aspect of growing as a learner is to reflect on where you have been, what you have accomplished, what helped you to learn, and how you will apply your new knowledge in the future. Use the following questions to guide your thinking and to identify evidence of your learning. Use separate notebook paper.

Thinking about Concepts

1. Using specific examples from this unit, respond to the Essential Questions:

   - What are the essential features of an effective drama and/or dramatic performance?

   - How have the strategies I have learned this year helped me to be a better reader, writer, speaker, and listener?

2. Consider the new academic vocabulary from this unit (Drama, Tragedy, Theatrical Elements, Interpretation, Metacognition) as well as academic vocabulary from previous units, and select 3–4 terms of which your understanding has grown. For each term, answer the following questions:

   - What was your understanding of the term before you completed this unit?

   - How has your understanding of the term evolved throughout the unit?

   - How will you apply your understanding in the future?

Thinking about Connections

3. Review the activities and products (artifacts) you created. Choose those that most reflect your growth or increase in understanding.

4. For each artifact that you choose, record, respond to, and reflect on your thinking and understanding, using the following questions as a guide:

   a. What skill/knowledge does this artifact reflect, and how did you learn this skill/knowledge?

   b. How did your understanding of the power of language expand through your engagement with this artifact?

   c. How will you apply this skill or knowledge in the future?

5. Create this reflection as Portfolio pages—one for each artifact you choose. Use the model in the box for your headings and commentary on questions.

Thinking About Thinking
Portfolio Entry

Concept:

Description of Artifact:

Commentary on Questions:

Coming of Age Amidst
Controversy

Essential Questions

? What are the essential elements of an effective informative presentation?

? What impact does historical, cultural, geographical, and social context have on a novel and on the reaction of readers to it?

Unit Overview

In this unit, you will encounter a longer, more complex text that deals with the concept of coming of age. Like Romeo and Juliet, who are confronted with prejudice in their world, Jem and Scout in Harper Lee's novel *To Kill a Mockingbird* confront prejudice in their community. Jem and Scout are more fortunate than Romeo and Juliet because their father is a model of tolerance, rationality, and compassion. The two children learn from their father and from their experiences how best to live in a less-than-perfect world. In your reading, you will trace a sustained development of character, setting, conflict, and you will examine how these relate to theme. Also, you will consider how social, cultural, geographical, and historical context can affect both the writer's construction of a text and the readers' responses to it.

Unit 5

Coming of Age Amidst Controversy

Goals

- To gather and synthesize information for an oral presentation on the social, cultural, historical, and geographical context of the novel

- To explore the significance of setting, conflict, and the growth of characters in relation to the theme of coming of age

- To extrapolate from a short passage the larger themes and literary elements of the novel

ACADEMIC VOCABULARY

Context

Annotated Bibliography

Thematic Statement

Characterization

Audience Analysis

Contents

*Texts not included in these materials.

Learning Focus:

Setting the Context

The novel *To Kill a Mockingbird*, by Harper Lee, is the perfect combination of engaging story-telling and hard-edged social commentary. Recognizing injustices through the eyes of an innocent narrator makes those injustices all the more memorable. The novel is very much about the "coming of age" theme you have studied all year, but it's also about a controversial event that creates turmoil in a fictional community—an event that reflects the tensions that defined a certain time and place in real American history.

Have you ever wondered where authors get inspiration for the things they write? Or how "real" a work of fiction might be? Or why a novelist sets a story in a particular time and place? Have you ever questioned why someone might want to ban a book that others think everyone should read? Research is the way to get answers to these kinds of questions.

Understanding the social, cultural, historical, and geographical context of a novel's setting, as well as the time period in which the novel was written, allows for a greater understanding of the immediate and long-lasting impact of a novel in the society in which it is published.

Presenting information to your classmates is a challenging and rewarding endeavor. As you present your research on social, cultural, historical, and geographical issues of the novel's context, you will enable your classmates to make connections between the novel and the real world it represents. One way to enhance your presentation is to understand what your audience knows and wants to know about the subject. As with any presentation, an audience analysis helps you to tailor the presentation to the needs of your classmates. After your presentation, it is also important to evaluate how effective you were at helping your audience to understand the issues explored in the novel and their relevance both to the author's contemporary readers and to readers of today.

As this level ends, you will also have an opportunity to think about how cultural, historical, and contemporary contexts reflect themes such as "coming of age." Theme is present in all genres, from poetry and film to drama and the novel.

Independent Reading: Reading in this unit focuses on a novel that explores issues such as prejudice, community, tolerance, and coming of age. For independent reading, look for a text that expands your understanding of one of these themes. You could also select historical fiction that helps illuminate the connection between historical context and the construction of a fictional work.

SUGGESTED LEARNING STRATEGIES: Close Reading, KWL Chart, Marking the Text, Skimming/Scanning, Summarizing/Paraphrasing, Think-Pair-Share

Essential Questions

1. What are the essential elements of an effective informative presentation?

2. What impact does historical, cultural, geographical, and social context have on a novel and on the reaction of readers to it?

Unit Overview and Learning Focus

Predict what you think this unit is about. Use the words or phrases that stood out to you when you read the Unit Overview and the Learning Focus.

Embedded Assessment 1

What knowledge must you have (what do you need to know) to succeed on Embedded Assessment 1? What skills must you have (what must you be able to do)?

Exploring My Opinions

WORD CONNECTIONS

The word *prejudice* means a preconceived idea or judgment. The Latin prefix *pre-* means "before." The Latin root *-judic-* means to "judge" or "decide." Other words using this root include *judge* and *judicial*.

Opinionnaire

Respond to the following statements by placing either **A** (Agree) or **D** (Disagree) next to each one to indicate your feelings. Your response should simply be your first impression in response to each statement. You can also jot down comments about a statement, examples to support your point of view, or mixed feelings you have about the statement. Be prepared to present your perspectives to your classmates.

A = Agree   **D** = Disagree

Beginning of Unit   **Conclusion of Unit**

1. All men and women are treated equally in society.

2. Girls should act like girls, and boys should act like boys.

3. In society, it's okay to be different from what others consider normal.

4. People are either all good or all evil; there is no in-between.

5. Some words are so offensive that they should never be stated or written.

6. Under our justice system, all citizens are treated fairly in our courts of law.

7. This old saying still applies in society today: "Sticks and stones may break my bones, but words will never hurt me."

8. Speaking standard English proves that a person is smart.

9. A hero is born, not made.

10. We should follow only the laws in society that make sense to us.

11. Education gives everyone an equal opportunity to succeed.

12. When the law does not succeed in punishing a criminal, citizens should be able to punish the criminal themselves.

13. If someone is on trial for murder, that person is probably guilty.

14. Killing under any circumstance is wrong.

15. Good parents set limits for their children.

16. Every individual in society is prejudiced about something.

After you have responded to the questionnaire and discussed your responses, work in pairs or small groups to sort the sixteen questions into general topic areas, such as justice or education.

A Time and a Place

To develop some understanding of the **context** for the novel *To Kill a Mockingbird*, view the photographs your teacher has provided. Note your observations and questions on the graphic organizer.

> **ACADEMIC VOCABULARY**
>
> **Context** refers to the circumstances or conditions in which something takes place.

Photo #	Observation: Note the details of the image in the photograph.	Reflection: What is your response to the images in the photograph?	Questions: What questions come to mind that might lead to further exploration or research?
1	The bomb is wood stove	They can't do better :(	Couldn't they find a better wood stove
3	Colored waiting room	People were so against colored :(	Why was it rike that
1	Haha... naked kid	family tightly packed :-/	better medical
4	working tireless ly	no better jobs :(	are they colored
5	tent!	Better homes, :(	no better homes?

You have viewed photographs to give you a context for the novel *To Kill A Mockingbird*, which you are about to read. But what exactly is context? With a partner, brainstorm what you already know about the idea of context. Then, find out its meaning and derivation in a dictionary. Create a web graphic organizer below, exploring the relationships of historical, cultural, social, and geographical settings to context.

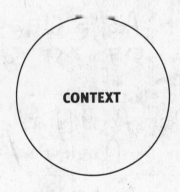

Once you have investigated the idea of context, add branches for historical, cultural, social, and geographical aspects. What does each term incorporate?

Putting the Text in Context

SUGGESTED LEARNING STRATEGIES: Close Reading, KWHL Chart, Marking the Text, Skimming/Scanning

Reflecting on the images from the gallery walk and other information from your class discussion, fill out the first two columns of the chart below.

K: What do I know about life in the South during the 1930s?	W: What do I want to know about life in the South during the 1930s?	H: How will I find information? (Which resources, web pages, texts, methods, etc.)	L: What have I learned about life in the South during the 1930s?
The econo- my was very Poor and People were very racist	Why the economy was so bad.	@wikipedia.org /wiki/Great Depression shmoop.com	Stock Market crash because of "black Tuesty heavy industry cities were hit the most. worst market crash in all of American history. large business bad stock.

My Notes

What were Jim Crow laws? As you read the following article, mark the text to identify the words and phrases that help you to define the meaning of the term *Jim Crow* and understand its importance in American history.

Informational Text

JIM CROW:
SHORTHAND FOR SEPARATION

by Rick Edmonds

"Jim Crow" the term, like Jim Crow the practice, settled in over a long period of time. By the 1950s, *Jim Crow* was the colloquialism whites and blacks routinely used for the complex system of laws and customs separating the races in the South. Hardly anyone felt a particular need to define it or explore its origins.

The term appears to date back at least to the eighteenth century, though there is no evidence that it refers to an individual. Rather it was a mildly derogatory slang for a black everyman (Crow, as in black like a crow.) A popular American minstrel song of the 1820s made sport of a stereotypic Jim Crow. "Jump Jim Crow" was a sort of jig. By the mid-1800s, a segregated rail car might be called the "Jim Crow." As segregation laws were put into place—first in Tennessee, then throughout the South—after Reconstruction, such diverse things as separate public facilities and laws restricting voting rights became known collectively as Jim Crow.

A bit like "political correctness" in recent years, the term was particularly popular with opponents of the practice. It was a staple of NAACP conversations of the '30s and '40s. Ralph Bunche once said he would turn down an appointment as ambassador of Liberia because he "wouldn't take a Jim Crow job." A skit at Morehouse College during Martin Luther King's student days portrayed a dramatic "burial" of Jim Crow. And . . . at the eventful Republican National Convention of 1964 in San Francisco, picketers outside the hall chanted, "Jim Crow (clap, clap) must go." . . .

From material in *American Heritage Dictionary, Safire's Political Dictionary,* and *From Slavery to Freedom.*

Use text features such as boldface type or italics to aid your comprehension of the text. Work with other members of your group to scan the following laws. Use the bold type as a guide to create a list of possible categories into which you might sort the laws.

Once you have arrived at four or five categories, read the entire text of each law, and put the law into one of the categories you have created. You might need to create more or change or delete categories. Also, note in the margin any questions you may have. Discuss your responses as you read and categorize. Be prepared to share your categories and your reactions and questions with the whole class.

Sample Jim Crow Laws

Created by the Interpretive Staff of the Martin Luther King, Jr., National Historic Site

1. **Nurses** No person or corporation shall require any white female nurse to nurse in wards or rooms in hospitals, either public or private, in which negro men are placed. *Alabama*

2. **Buses** All passenger stations in this state operated by any motor transportation company shall have separate waiting rooms or space and separate ticket windows for the white and colored races. *Alabama*

3. **Restaurants** It shall be unlawful to conduct a restaurant or other place for the serving of food in the city, at which white and colored people are served in the same room, unless such white and colored persons are effectually separated by a solid partition extending from the floor upward to a distance of seven feet or higher, and unless a separate entrance from the street is provided for each compartment. *Alabama*

4. **Pool and Billiard Rooms** It shall be unlawful for a negro and white person to play together or in company with each other at any game of pool or billiards. *Alabama*

5. **Intermarriage** The marriage of a person of Caucasian blood with a Negro, Mongolian, Malay, or Hindu shall be null and void. *Arizona*

6. **Intermarriage** All marriages between a white person and a negro, or between a white person and a person of negro descent to the fourth generation inclusive, are hereby forever prohibited. *Florida*

7. **Education** The schools for white children and the schools for negro children shall be conducted separately. *Florida*

8. **Mental Hospitals** The Board of Control shall see that proper and distinct apartments are arranged for said patients, so that in no case shall Negroes and white persons be together. *Georgia*

My Notes

WORD CONNECTIONS

Legal documents use many foreign words and phrases, including *quid pro quo* and *ipso facto*. *Quid pro quo* is Latin and describes giving something of value to get something else of value in return. *Ipso facto* means "by the fact itself." It may be used to describe factual evidence.

9. **Barbers** No colored barber shall serve as a barber [to] white women or girls. *Georgia*

10. **Burial** The officer in charge shall not bury, or allow to be buried, any colored persons upon ground set apart or used for the burial of white persons. *Georgia*

11. **Restaurants** All persons licensed to conduct a restaurant shall serve either white people exclusively or colored people exclusively and shall not sell to the two races within the same room or serve the two races anywhere under the same license. *Georgia*

12. **Amateur Baseball** It shall be unlawful for any amateur white baseball team to play baseball on any vacant lot or baseball diamond within two blocks of a playground devoted to the Negro race, and it shall be unlawful for any amateur colored baseball team to play baseball in any vacant lot or baseball diamond within two blocks of any playground devoted to the white race. *Georgia*

13. **Parks** It shall be unlawful for colored people to frequent any park owned or maintained by the city for the benefit, use and enjoyment of white persons. . .and unlawful for any white person to frequent any park owned or maintained by the city for the use and benefit of colored persons. *Georgia*

14. **Reform Schools** The children of white and colored races committed to the houses of reform shall be kept entirely separate from each other. *Kentucky*

15. **Circus Tickets** All circuses, shows, and tent exhibitions, to which the attendance of. . .more than one race is invited or expected to attend shall provide for the convenience of its patrons not less than two ticket offices with individual ticket sellers, and not less than two entrances to the said performance, with individual ticket takers and receivers, and in the case of outside or tent performances, the said ticket offices shall not be less than twenty-five (25) feet apart. *Louisiana*

16. **The Blind** The board of trustees shall. . .maintain a separate building. . . on separate ground for the admission, care, instruction, and support of all blind persons of the colored or black race. *Louisiana*

17. **Railroads** All railroad companies and corporations, and all persons running or operating cars or coaches by steam on any railroad line or track in the State of Maryland, for the transportation of passengers, are hereby required to provide separate cars or coaches for the travel and transportation of the white and colored passengers. *Maryland*

18. **Promotion of Equality** Any person. . .who shall be guilty of printing, publishing or circulating printed, typewritten or written matter urging or presenting for public acceptance or general information, arguments or suggestions in favor of social equality or of intermarriage between whites

and negroes, shall be guilty of a misdemeanor and subject to fine not exceeding five hundred (500.00) dollars or imprisonment not exceeding six (6) months or both. *Mississippi*

19. **Intermarriage** The marriage of a white person with a negro or mulatto or person who shall have one-eighth or more of negro blood, shall be unlawful and void. *Mississippi*

20. **Hospital Entrances** There shall be maintained by the governing authorities of every hospital maintained by the state for treatment of white and colored patients separate entrances for white and colored patients and visitors, and such entrances shall be used by the race only for which they are prepared. *Mississippi*

21. **Prisons** The warden shall see that the white convicts shall have separate apartments for both eating and sleeping from the negro convicts. *Mississippi*

22. **Education** Separate free schools shall be established for the education of children of African descent; and it shall be unlawful for any colored child to attend any white school, or any white child to attend a colored school. *Missouri*

23. **Intermarriage** All marriages between. . .white persons and negroes or white persons and Mongolians. . .are prohibited and declared absolutely void. . . . No person having one-eighth part or more of negro blood shall be permitted to marry any white person, nor shall any white person be permitted to marry any negro or person having one-eighth part or more of negro blood. *Missouri*

24. **Education** Separate rooms [shall] be provided for the teaching of pupils of African descent, and [when] said rooms are so provided, such pupils may not be admitted to the school rooms occupied and used by pupils of Caucasian or other descent. *New Mexico*

25. **Textbooks** Books shall not be interchangeable between the white and colored schools, but shall continue to be used by the race first using them. *North Carolina*

26. **Libraries** The state librarian is directed to fit up and maintain a separate place for the use of the colored people who may come to the library for the purpose of reading books or periodicals. *North Carolina*

27. **Transportation** The. . . Utilities Commission. . . is empowered and directed to require the establishment of separate waiting rooms at all stations for the white and colored races. *North Carolina*

28. **Teaching** Any instructor who shall teach in any school, college or institution where members of the white and colored race are received and enrolled as pupils for instruction shall be deemed guilty of a misdemeanor, and upon conviction thereof, shall be fined in any sum not

My Notes

WORD CONNECTIONS

The word *transportation* means "a method of moving passengers or goods from one place to another." The Latin prefix *trans-* means "across" or "beyond." The Latin root *-port-* means "to carry" or "to bear."

The root *-port-* is found in many other English words, such as *portable, portfolio, import, export, report,* and *support.*

Some of the words in which the prefix *trans-* appears are *transfer, transform, transition, translate,* and *transparent.*

My Notes

less than ten dollars ($10.00) nor more than fifty dollars ($50.00) for each offense. *Oklahoma*

29. **Fishing, Boating, and Bathing** The [Conservation] Commission shall have the right to make segregation of the white and colored races as to the exercise of rights of fishing, boating and bathing. *Oklahoma*

30. **Telephone Booths** The Corporation Commission is hereby vested with power and authority to require telephone companies. . . to maintain separate booths for white and colored patrons when there is a demand for such separate booths. That the Corporation Commission shall determine the necessity for said separate booths only upon complaint of the people in the town and vicinity to be served after due hearing as now provided by law in other complaints filed with the Corporation Commission. *Oklahoma*

31. **Lunch Counters** No persons, firms, or corporations, who or which furnish meals to passengers at station restaurants or station eating houses, in times limited by common carriers of said passengers, shall furnish said meals to white and colored passengers in the same room, or at the same table, or at the same counter. *South Carolina*

32. **Libraries** Any white person of such county may use the county free library under the rules and regulations prescribed by the commissioners court and may be entitled to all the privileges thereof. Said court shall make proper provision for the negroes of said county to be served through a separate branch or branches of the county free library, which shall be administered by [a] custodian of the negro race under the supervision of the county librarian. *Texas*

33. **Education** [The County Board of Education] shall provide schools of two kinds; those for white children and those for colored children. *Texas*

34. **Railroads** The conductors or managers on all such railroads shall have power, and are hereby required, to assign to each white or colored passenger his or her respective car, coach or compartment. If the passenger fails to disclose his race, the conductor and managers, acting in good faith, shall be the sole judges of his race. *Virginia*

35. **Theaters** Every person. . .operating. . .any public hall, theatre, opera house, motion picture show or any place of public entertainment or public assemblage which is attended by both white and colored persons, shall separate the white race and the colored race and shall set apart and designate. . .certain seats therein to be occupied by white persons and a portion thereof, or certain seats therein, to be occupied by colored persons. *Virginia*

36. **Intermarriage** All marriages of white persons with Negroes, Mulattos, Mongolians, or Malayans hereafter contracted in the State of Wyoming are and shall be illegal and void. *Wyoming*

WORD CONNECTIONS

The word *provision* begins with the Latin prefix *pro-*, meaning "before" or "for." The root *-vis-* means "see."

The Latin word *provisio* means "a foreseeing." The word *provision* means "something provided or supplied for the future."

Some of the words in which the root *-vis-* (and its alternate spelling *-vid-*) appear include *vision*, *visible*, *visualize*, *video*, and *evident*.

Preparing for Research

SUGGESTED LEARNING STRATEGIES: Think-Pair-Share

1. Form groups of three to plan, organize, and prepare a research project, which you will present in Embedded Assessment 1. Your group will investigate the historical, cultural, social, or geographical *context* of the novel *To Kill a Mockingbird*. Using the information from your viewing of 1930s photographs, your reading of Jim Crow laws, and your thinking on the KWHL chart, choose a research topic.

2. List possible topics to investigate and present with a Guiding Question for research:

3. List possible focus questions for your investigation of the Guiding Question:

> **WORD CONNECTIONS**
>
> An analogy may use both words and phrases. For example, Jim Crow laws : segregation as negligence : accident. This analogy shows a cause-effect relationship. Write two additional cause-effect analogies, either on your own or as part of a class activity. Use both phrases and words.

4. Prepare a group proposal sheet with the following information:
   - Group members' names (no more than three members)
   - Topic expressed as a universal question or Guiding Question. Focus areas: related questions that fall within the overall topic area (Example: What kinds of jobs did women hold in the 1930s?)
   - Possible resources you might use to find answers to your questions
   - Individual responsibilities at this point (who will look for what, including visuals)

5. Find and collect resources about your topic. Your group must find five sources of information. You must use at least three different types of sources (e.g., magazine, reference source, Internet) in the presentation.

Collecting Resources

You and your group have collected sources to research your topic in preparation for a presentation to your classmates.

First, evaluate the relevance of the sources you have collected. Then select five sources, keeping in mind that you must reference at least three different types (e.g., magazine article, reference source, Internet) in your presentation.

For each source you use, you will create an **annotated bibliography** entry in the MLA format. Annotated bibliographies are tools for tracking and processing your research work. Entries typically consist of two parts: a *bibliographic citation* for the source and an *annotation* (a brief summary of or commentary about the source).

For this task, the annotation will consist of three elements:

- A summary of the information you found in the source
- An assessment of the degree to which the source was helpful in your research
- A reflection on how the information might be used in your presentation.

Below are sample formats and entries. Your teacher may provide resources that have more examples.

For an Article:

Author(s). "Title of Article." *Magazine Title*. Publication date or issue: page number.

Sample Entry with Annotation:

Edmonds, Rick. "Jim Crow: Shorthand for Separation." *FORUM Magazine*. Summer 1999: 7.

Edmonds reviews the origins of the term "Jim Crow" and the significance of Jim Crow laws and customs as a social factor in the South. He also traces how awareness of the term's meaning has changed over time as our society has become more politically correct. This source was helpful for understanding how racial attitudes led to the creation of separate-but-equal laws. We might use it to show how political the term became in the 1930s through 1960s.

ACADEMIC VOCABULARY

A **bibliography** is a list of the sources used for research. This list may also be called a Works Cited list. An **annotated bibliography** includes comments or summaries about each of the sources and the information found there.

For a Web site:

Author(s). "Name of Page." Date of Posting/Revision. Name of Institution/Organization Affiliated with the Site. Date of access. <electronic address>.

Sample Entry:

Martin Luther King, Jr., *National Historic Site*. "Jim Crow Laws." 15 Nov. 2004. National Parks Service. 5 January 2008. <http://www.nps.gov/malu/documents/jim_crow_laws.htm>.

Annotation: This site gave a shocking list of laws that existed across the South—but also in other states (such as Arizona and Wyoming). It shows how Jim Crow regulated things ranging from the use of public facilities and transportation to marriage and schools. We might use it to engage our audience with some shocking examples—or to challenge their belief that this only happened in the South.

Once you have completed your annotated entries, compile a complete annotated bibliography as a group, placing the entries in alphabetical order. Use the next page to write your annotated bibliography.

Use the MLA format to create a complete bibliographic citation for each source. Include an annotation of each source based on your research group's understanding and discussion.

Collecting Resources

Annotated Bibliography

Source 1: Citation:

Annotation:

Source 2: Citation:

Annotation:

Source 3: Citation:

Annotation:

Source 4: Citation:

Annotation:

Source 5: Citation:

Annotation:

Writing Prompt: Individually, craft a one-page paper that uses information you have gained from your research to answer the question guiding your group's research. You may also address some or all of your group's focus questions. Be sure to cite information from your sources appropriately.

Audience Analysis

Whether you are writing a paper or preparing a presentation, knowing who your audience will be is one of the most important steps toward planning your final product. For your presentation, complete an **audience analysis** by answering these questions.

1. What do you want your classmates—your audience—to get from your presentation?

2. What background knowledge or assumptions does your audience have about your subject?

   How will this background affect the types of information and vocabulary you use as you present?

3. How might your audience's values, opinions, and beliefs affect their perspective towards your subject?

4. What audio/visual components can you include in your presentation to engage your audience and convey your information effectively?

5. What connections can you make between your subject and your target audience to make your topic relevant to them?

6. What additional materials will you need to present your subject successfully?

> ### ACADEMIC VOCABULARY
>
> An **audience analysis** is an evaluation of the characteristics and knowledge of the people who will read a work or hear a speech. Examples of information that might be useful would be average age, prior experience with your topic, or formal education about the topic.

Audience Analysis

Levels of Questioning

1. Work collaboratively to write questions about your topic. Your presentation will be the "text," so the questions will guide both the structure and organization of your speech and the audience's notetaking on your presentation.

   - Level 1 questions reveal key factual information in your presentation.
   - Level 2 questions should push listeners to consider how prevailing attitudes (towards race, class, gender, etc.) affect social practices.
   - Level 3 questions should prompt the audience to consider connections beyond the presentation, such as to their personal experience, current social issues, or other texts they have encountered.

You might use questions you previously generated if you think they will work to organize your information for your audience. However, you still need a balance of Level 1, 2, and 3 questions in your presentation.

Level of Questions	Questions on Your Topic
Level 1 **Questions of Fact:** **What does the text say?** For example: Which states had laws restricting interracial marriage? In what three major ways did Jim Crow laws affect schools?	1. 2. 3.
Level 2 **Questions of Interpretation:** **The how or why of the text** For example: How were the laws enforceable? What do people mean today when they refer to something as being "Jim Crow"?	1. 2. 3.

Level 3 **Questions That Go Beyond the Text: Why does it matter?** For example: How could the United States have ever allowed Jim Crow laws to exist? Are racist laws still a major factor in the United States today?	1. 2. 3.

2. Once you have generated questions for your presentation, review your *audience analysis* on the previous page. Then answer the following questions.

   • What is the purpose of an audience analysis?

   • How can it help you evaluate what information to include in your presentation?

   • How can it help you choose which questions to use to organize and structure your presentation?

   • How can it help you to create an engaging presentation?

3. Based on your audience analysis and your answers to the questions above, design a notetaking handout, in the form of a graphic organizer, for your classmates to use while you present your topic. Design your handout so that classmates will have ample room to record answers to a limited number of questions that will best help them to understand the topic of your group's presentation of the 1930s South.

On the back of your organizer, be sure to leave ample space for the audience to take notes on connections they make while reading *To Kill a Mockingbird*.

Historical Investigation and Presentation

SUGGESTED LEARNING STRATEGIES: **Drafting, Notetaking, Rehearsal**

Assignment

Your assignment is to work collaboratively to investigate the historical, cultural, social, or geographical *context* of the novel *To Kill a Mockingbird*. You will make an oral presentation of your findings, with audio or visual support, and you will prepare a notetaking handout for your audience to use.

Planning

1. Review your work on the skills and knowledge required of the investigation and presentation in order to identify key expectations for your presentation. Review your group proposal and, if necesssry, revise how you will share the responsibilities of the investigation and presentation.

Drafting and Creating

2. Draft your presentation outline or script covering the following:

   ▶ Thesis regarding the significance of your topic and its importance in the historical, social, cultural, or geographical context of the 1930s or the 1960s.

   ▶ Key questions that will guide the structure of your presentation

   ▶ Transitions to link your points together.

   Place your information on 3 x 5 note cards. Include the following with your outline:

   ▶ Audio-visual resources you will use and their placement in the presentation

   ▶ A speaking plan for who will cover what during the presentation

3. Decide on an interactive way to present your research to the class (e.g., digital slides, a Web page, online blog, tri-fold presentation board). Update your group proposal to include a plan of what you will do in your presentation and the materials you need to be successful. If you create PowerPoint slides, consult a style manual such as that published by The Modern Language Association to help you format your presentation.

4. Finalize a one-page graphic organizer handout of questions for your classmates to use to take notes on your presentation. The title of your organizer may be your guiding question. Choose a few other questions designed to help listeners identify information relevant to that question.

Rehearsal and Performance

5. Review the guidelines for effective public speaking that you generated in Unit 1 and your self-evaluation as a speaker from Unit 4. Using these, determine your goals for improvement. Refine each group member's roles and responsibilities.

6. Plan the oral components of your presentation, and rehearse. Consult the Scoring Guide for specific criteria, and use peer feedback to refine your presentation.

7. Deliver your presentation to your class.

Presentation Follow-up

As you read and study *To Kill A Mockingbird*, take notes on how your topic (or another that interests you more) surfaces in the novel. Record both textual evidence and personal commentary. After you have finished the novel, you will connect the information you have presented to your understanding of the novel.

TECHNOLOGY TIP If you have the appropriate resources, consider recording your rehearsals for use in reviewing your performance. You may also want to record your notes and commentary for later use.

SCORING GUIDE

Scoring Criteria	Exemplary	Proficient	Emerging
Presentation: **Analysis of the Subject**	The presentation is thoughtfully and effectively organized. It demonstrates a comprehensive understanding of significant aspects of the topic and its relevance to the novel.	The presentation is organized and displays a solid understanding of the topic. The connection between the topic and the novel as a whole is clear to the audience.	The presentation is somewhat organized. The information presented demonstrates a limited understanding of the topic and fails to make any connection to the novel as a whole.
Presentation: **Use of Media**	The presentation skillfully uses a variety of audio/visual resources to keep the audience engaged. The audio/visual selections are thoughtfully chosen and demonstrate critical thinking.	The presentation uses some audio/visual components to engage the audience. The selections are relevant and creative and serve the purpose of the presentation.	The presentation may or may not contain audio/visual components to supplement the information. The materials chosen are not relevant or are distracting and fail to serve the group's purpose.
Presentation: **Oral Delivery**	The presenters demonstrate effective oral communication skills. Each group member participates equally. The presentation actively engages audience members. It is is well-planned and successfully coordinated.	The presenters display adequate oral communication skills. All members participate, but the balance may be unequal. The presentation is engaging. Adequate collaboration is evident.	The presenters lack adequate oral communication skills. Some group members participate little or not at all. The presentation lacks energy and enthusiasm and is unengaging.
Audience Guide	The graphic organizer is clearly organized with thoughtful questions to focus the information for viewers. The layout skillfully provides space for recording information and reflecting on its importance. It contains no errors.	The graphic organizer is adequately organized with questions to help focus information for viewers. The layout provides space for recording information and reflecting on its importance. It contains no errors.	The graphic organizer lacks clear organization or may confuse viewers. The layout is inadequate for following and recording information, or it provides no space for reflection. It may contain errors.
Additional Criteria			

Comments:

Learning Focus:

How Do a Million Little Parts Equal a Whole?

In earlier units, you've studied the ways in which authors and directors use stylistic choices to suggest meaning in their texts. But how do choices work with a text as complicated as a novel? Does every word really matter when there are 60,000 of them? Is everything really a symbol of something more? As you begin the second part of this unit, you'll immerse yourself in the world of Scout Finch, the narrator of *To Kill a Mockingbird*. As you do so, though, you'll go beyond the story of what happens to Scout and the folks of Maycomb, Alabama, to focus as well on *how* Harper Lee tells the story. In particular, you'll explore how the setting, conflict, and characters develop themes within the text.

As you read Part One of the novel, you'll apply various strategies for active reading:

▶ Visualizing the Text

▶ Marking/Annotating the Text

▶ Making Connections

▶ Making Predictions

▶ Drawing Inferences

▶ Questioning the Text

▶ Diffusing Vocabulary

As you move into Part Two of the novel, you'll become more independent in your reading, while class activities will focus more on analyzing the language used to tell the story. Like a detective, you'll interpret quotations and passages as clues to the novel's thematic meaning. You'll develop a thematic statement and write a literary analysis explaining how the meaning of a passage contributes to the meaning of the novel as a whole. It's a way to end the year by applying all the skills you've developed as a reader and writer—and by grappling with the ways texts challenge us to question the world around us.

Reflecting on Growth: Researching and Presenting

SUGGESTED LEARNING STRATEGIES: Graphic Organizer

You have engaged in a number of activities as a researcher. Being an effective researcher requires several key skills. These skills are listed below. For each of these skills, review your work from this unit and from the year as a whole to find evidence of your practice of the skill. Then discuss your current level of mastery of the skill, citing examples to support your evaluation.

- Assessing your current knowledge of your subject and identifying areas to address through research:

- Defining and revising research questions to guide research:

- Identifying and evaluating potential sources of information:

- Using strategies to monitor comprehension while engaging with complex texts:

- Using strategies to organize, restructure, and synthesize text content from research sources:

- Effectively incorporating and citing information from outside sources in your own texts:

Think about your group's presentation of your research topic. Take some time to reflect on the presentation and your part in it.

What did you do well?	
Given another opportunity to present, what would you do differently?	
What did you learn about organizing information?	
What did you learn about how to effectively engage an audience?	
How have you most improved as a researcher this year?	
What goals do you have for improving as a researcher?	

A Scouting Party

SUGGESTED LEARNING STRATEGIES: Diffusing the Text, Graphic Organizer, Previewing, Quickwrite, Think Aloud, Think-Pair-Share, Visualizing, Notetaking, Marking the Text

View the opening clip of *To Kill a Mockingbird*, and note your observations on this graphic organizer. After watching the opening credits, share your findings in groups of three. Add your groups' findings to your graphic.

First Viewing of the Opening Credits of *To Kill a Mockingbird*

What did you observe? What images did you see on screen?	What did you notice about the lighting?	What did you notice about the sound?	Based on your observations, what predictions can you make?

View the opening credits again. This time each member of your small group should take notes on one element in one column. After the second viewing, share and note your observations.

From the sound and the images, what can you infer about the *point of view* from which this story will be told?

Something to Ponder: When this film was made, color film technology was available. The director made a conscious decision to shoot this film in black and white. Why do you think the director might have made this choice?

As your teacher reads the opening of *To Kill a Mockingbird*, highlight the part that indicates the story is a **flashback**. In addition, note what you are learning about the narrator and her perspective, both from what she talks about and from the language she uses to do so. Finally, make a list below of the characters who are introduced in Chapter 1.

> ### LITERARY TERMS
> A **flashback** is an interruption in the sequence of events to relate events that occurred in the past.

Facts about the narrator	Character names

Quickwrite: What *perspective* is established in the opening credits of the film that contrasts with the perspective that opens the novel?

My Notes

Visualizing the Characters

As you read, highlight all the images and details that describe what the children look like and are doing.

Novel

> **ABOUT THE AUTHOR**
>
> American writer Nelle Harper Lee (b. 1926) was born and grew up in Alabama. As an adult, she moved to New York City, where she wrote and published several short stories. She then took a year off from work to write *To Kill a Mockingbird*, using her father as a model for Atticus Finch.
>
> *To Kill a Mockingbird* won much acclaim when it was published and a Pulitzer Prize in 1961. Harper Lee has never written another novel.

from # To Kill a
MOCKINGBIRD

by Harper Lee

Early one morning as we were beginning our day's play in the back yard, Jem and I heard something next door in Miss Rachel Haverford's collard patch. We went to the wire fence to see if there was a puppy—Miss Rachel's rat terrier was expecting—instead we found someone sitting looking at us. Sitting down, he wasn't much higher than the collards. We stared at him until he spoke:

"Hey."

"Hey yourself," said Jem pleasantly.

"I'm Charles Baker Harris," he said, "I can read."

"So what?" I said.

"I just thought you'd like to know I can read. You got anything needs readin' I can do it…."

"How old are you," asked Jem, "four-and-a-half?"

"Goin' on seven."

"Shoot no wonder, then," said Jem, jerking his thumb at me. "Scout yonder's been readin' ever since she was born, and she ain't even started to school yet. You look right puny for goin' on seven."

"I'm little but I'm old," he said.

Jem brushed his hair back to get a better look. "Why don't you come over, Charles Baker Harris?" he said. "Lord, what a name."

"'s not any funnier'n yours. Aunt Rachel says your name's Jeremy Atticus Finch."

Jem scowled. "I'm big enough to fit mine," he said. "Your name's longer'n you are. Bet it's a foot longer."

"Folks call me Dill," said Dill, struggling under the fence.

"Do better if you go over it instead of under it," I said. "Where'd you come from?"

Dill was from Meridian, Mississippi, was spending the summer with his aunt, Miss Rachel, and would be spending every summer in Maycomb from now on. His family was from Maycomb County originally, his mother worked for a photographer in Meridian, had entered his picture in a Beautiful Child contest and won five dollars. She gave the money to Dill, who went to the picture show twenty times on it.

"Don't have any picture shows here, except Jesus ones in the courthouse sometimes," said Jem. "Ever see anything good?"

Dill had seen *Dracula*, a revelation that moved Jem to eye him with the beginning of respect. "Tell it to us," he said.

Dill was a curiosity. He wore blue linen shorts that buttoned to his shirt, his hair was snow white and stuck to his head like duck-fluff; he was a year my senior but I towered over him. As he told us the old tale his blue eyes would lighten and darken; his laugh was sudden and happy; he habitually pulled at a cowlick in the center of his forehead.

When Dill reduced *Dracula* to dust, and Jem said the show sounded better than the book, I asked Dill where his father was: "You ain't said anything about him."

"I haven't got one."

"Is he dead?"

"No . . ."

"Then if he's not dead you've got one, haven't you?"

After Reading

After you have read the conversation, visualize and sketch the scene and the characters on another sheet of paper. How would they be standing in relation to each other? What features would you emphasize? Where are they?

GRAMMAR & USAGE

Relative clauses can be **restrictive** (essential) or **nonrestrictive** (nonessential). Notice the use and punctuation of the adjective clauses in the following examples:

Nonrestrictive: She gave the money to Dill, **who went to the picture show twenty times on it.**

Restrictive: He wore blue linen shorts **that buttoned to his shirt....**

In your writing, use commas to set off nonrestrictive adjective clauses in complex sentences.

My Notes

Visualizing Setting

GRAMMAR & USAGE

In the second sentence of the second paragraph, notice that the author uses a series without a conjunction before the last item. This effect is called **asyndeton**.

My Notes

As your teacher reads aloud this passage, underline or highlight images and words—adjectives and verbs in particular—that create a vivid picture of the town where the novel takes place. Consider what effect the author wants to create in this description, then answer the questions on the next page.

from ***To Kill a Mockingbird***, Chapter 1

Maycomb was an old town, but it was a tired old town when I first knew it. In rainy weather the streets turned to red slop; grass grew on the sidewalks, the courthouse sagged in the square. Somehow, it was hotter then: a black dog suffered on a summer's day; bony mules hitched to Hoover carts flicked flies in the sweltering shade of the live oaks on the square. Men's stiff collars wilted by nine in the morning. Ladies bathed before noon, after their three-o'clock naps, and by nightfall were like soft teacakes with frostings of sweat and sweet talcum.

People moved slowly then. They ambled across the square, shuffled in and out of the stores around it, took their time about everything. A day was twenty-four hours long but seemed longer. There was no hurry, for there was nowhere to go, nothing to buy and no money to buy it with, nothing to see outside the boundaries of Maycomb County. But it was a time of vague optimism for some of the people: Maycomb County had recently been told that it had nothing to fear but fear itself.

1. Which **images** help you to visualize life in Maycomb? Write several of the images that enable you to "see" the town.

2. Write down specific words or **diction** that create a picture. What effect is created by these words? What does this effect suggest is Scout's attitude toward the town she grew up in?

3. Write an interpretive statement about the specific effect the **diction** and **imagery** create in this passage about the setting. An interpretive statement can be used as a topic sentence because it presents an assertion about a specific topic.

My Notes

Reread this passage that introduces the Radley place. Underline or highlight sensory images and words—adjectives and verbs in particular—that create a vivid picture of the house. Consider what effect the author wants to create in this description.

from **To Kill a Mockingbird**, Chapter 1

The Radley Place jutted into a sharp curve beyond our house. Walking south, one faced its porch; the sidewalk turned and ran beside the lot. The house was low, was once white with a deep front porch and green shutters, but had long ago darkened to the color of the slate-gray yard around it. Rain-rotted shingles drooped over the eaves of the veranda; oak trees kept the sun away. The remains of a picket drunkenly guarded the front yard—a "swept" yard that was never swept—where johnson grass and rabbit-tobacco grew in abundance.

GRAMMAR & USAGE

Notice the punctuation in the final sentence of the excerpt: the **quotation marks** around *swept* indicate irony, and the **dashes** emphasize the parenthetical nature of the information.

1. Which images help you to visualize the Radley place? In the My Notes space, write several of the images that help you to "see" the house.

2. Write down specific words or diction that create a picture. What effect is created by these words? What does this effect suggest is Scout's attitude towards the Radley place?

3. Write an *interpretive sentence* about the specific effect the *diction* and *imagery* create in this passage about the setting.

Brief Review of the Elements of a Paragraph

- Topic sentence (an *interpretive sentence* about effect)
- Evidence from the text to support *claims made*
- Reflective commentary on the *evidence*
- Sentence of closure

Writing Prompt: Write a paragraph explaining how the diction and imagery in the description of either the town of Maycomb or the Radley place creates a certain effect. Your *topic sentence* (an interpretive statement) must state the effect created by the words and images in the passage.

Main Idea and Detail Notes

As you read the novel, take notes on Boo Radley whenever he is mentioned. Include page numbers for your notes. Look for any changes in the way that Jem and Scout react to Boo, and make note of these changes.

Incidents Involving Boo Radley	Details from the Text

Strategies Reflection

You have used several reading strategies as you have begun reading
To Kill a Mockingbird:

> Read-Aloud/Think-Aloud
>
> Marking the Text
>
> Annotating the Text
>
> Diffusing Vocabulary
>
> Close Reading
>
> Double Entry Journaling

Writing Prompt: Write a short paragraph starting with a *topic sentence*
on how effective these strategies are for you in making meaning of the
text. Which is most effective, which will you need more practice with,
and which do you feel confident about?

Making Connections

SUGGESTED LEARNING STRATEGIES: Oral Interpretation,
Think-Pair-Share

Reading Strategies

Good readers are strategic, and being strategic requires that readers use an array of strategies to make meaning from text. Making connections while reading is a strategy that keeps you engaged in the text and enables you to understand the text more deeply. These are some types of connections you can make while reading:

- Text-to-self: when the text makes you think of your own life.
- Text-to-text: when the text makes you think of another text.
- Text-to-world: when the text makes you think of world events.

As you read Chapters 2 and 3, fill in the circles with your own connections.

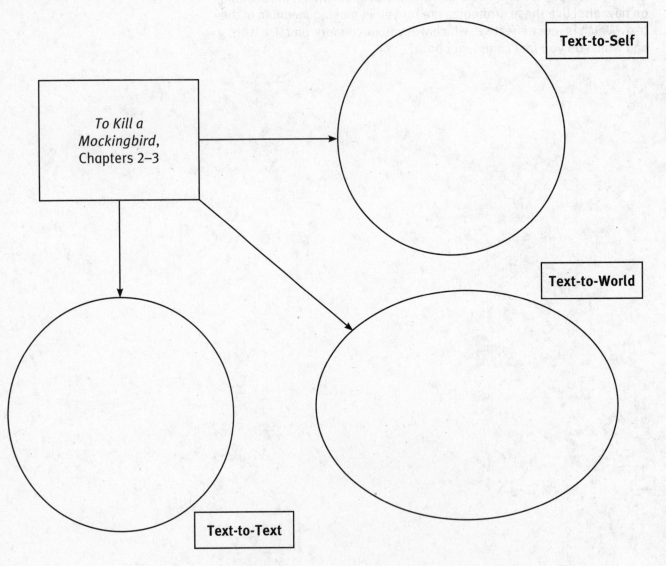

Making Predictions

SUGGESTED LEARNING STRATEGIES: Double-Entry Journals, Drafting, Notetaking, Predicting, Word Map

Good readers **make predictions** while they read, and then they confirm or negate these predictions based on the information in the text. The focus of this read-aloud/think-aloud will be to model the practice of predicting and then confirming or negating predictions as the chapter unfolds. As you read Chapters 4 and 5, record details about the growing relationship between Boo and the children, and predict what you think is likely to happen. Then, check these predictions as you go.

Incidents Involving Boo Radley	Predictions

ACADEMIC VOCABULARY

Characterization is the way a writer portrays a character.

In your Vocabulary Notebook, write all you know about the word **characterization**. What do you know about terms associated with characterization, with how characters are developed and how they function?

Writing Prompt: Write a diary entry in Boo's voice (use first-person point of view) commenting on the children's latest pranks. Be sure to communicate Boo's attitude toward the children through the diction and imagery you use to write about them. Think about how you could use the subjunctive mood to begin your diary entry; for example, "If I could talk to Jem and Scout, I would …"

The strategies I used to make meaning from this text are...

Drawing Inferences

SUGGESTED LEARNING STRATEGIES: Close Reading, Double-Entry Journal, Think-Pair-Share

Active readers *infer* much, or "read between the lines." You infer to discover character motivation and to consider the symbolic and thematic implications of textual details. As you read Chapters 6 and 7, identify textual details that suggest something more to you, and interpret what these suggestions are.

Incidents Involving Boo Radley	Making Inferences and Drawing Conclusions from Inferences

Lessons from the Neighborhood

LITERARY TERMS

A **motif** is a unifying element in an artistic work, especially any recurrent image, symbol, theme, character type, subject, or narrative detail.

Lessons from the Neighborhood — Who Is Arthur Radley?

1. In small groups, using the notes you have collected, answer the following questions to discuss the character of Boo Radley as a **motif**. Take notes in your double-entry journal about your conclusions.

   - Who is most affected by the contacts the children have had with Boo (Arthur Radley)? How do you know, and what has been the effect?

   - Review the rumors and gossip the children hear about Boo. What is the effect of all that stereotyping? What is the truth of the rumors, gossip, and stereotyping?

   - What has been Atticus's role in the children's relationship to Boo?

   - Discuss Harper Lee's purpose in including this story of the children and Boo Radley. What are the children learning from this experience as they come of age in Maycomb, Alabama?

2. Once you have discussed the questions above, synthesize all the incidents by writing an interpretive sentence that shows your understanding of how the relationship has changed from the beginning of the novel to now.

WORD CONNECTIONS

The word **synthesize**, which means "to combine parts or elements into a whole," has a Greek prefix, *syn-*, meaning "together" or "united," and the Greek root *thesis*, which is "something laid down, like a statement."

Questioning the Text

SUGGESTED LEARNING STRATEGIES: Questioning the Text, Close Reading

Levels of Questioning

Write three questions about Chapter 10 for each level of questioning.

Level of Questions	Your Questions
Level 1 **Questions of Fact:** **What did the text say?** For example: When did Atticus scold Scout for fighting?	1. 2. 3.
Level 2 **Questions of Interpretation:** **What does the text mean?** For example: Why does Jem encourage Scout to ask Atticus about Cecil Jacobs's comments instead of just explaining them to her?	1. 2. 3.

Questioning the Text

Level 3	1.
Questions That Go Beyond the Text: Why does it matter? For example: How do you explain racism to a child?	
	2.
	3.

The strategies I used to make meaning from this text are...

Examining the Title

Conduct a close reading of the passage below from Chapter 10. As you read, highlight references to the title and think about why Harper Lee chose this the title for her novel. Keep track of your ideas by noting your thoughts in the margin.

from ***To Kill a Mockingbird,*** Chapter 10

When he gave us our air rifles Atticus wouldn't teach us to shoot. Uncle Jack instructed us in the rudiments thereof; he said Atticus wasn't interested in guns. Atticus said to Jem one day, "I'd rather you shot at tin cans in the back yard, but I know you'll go after birds. Shoot all the bluejays you want, if you can hit 'em, but remember it's a sin to kill a mockingbird."

That was the only time I ever heard Atticus say it was a sin to do something, and I asked Miss Maudie about it.

"Your father's right," she said. "Mockingbirds don't do one thing but make music for us to enjoy. They don't eat up people's gardens, don't nest in corncribs, they don't do one thing but sing their hearts out for us. That's why it's a sin to kill a mockingbird."

1. How does Miss Maudie's information about mockingbirds add to Atticus's comment that "it's a sin to kill a mockingbird"?

2. Based on the passage above, predict what you think may happen in the novel.

3. A *motif* is a repeated image; expect to encounter more mentions of the mockingbird. As you do, note them in your double-entry journal, and think about how the image helps you understand Harper Lee's thinking when she named her novel.

GRAMMAR & USAGE

Most novels and short stories contain dialogue, as do some nonfiction forms, such as memoirs and biographies. In dialogue, the speaker's exact words are always enclosed in quotation marks. The rules for other punctuation marks with quotations include the following:

- A direct quotation can be set off from the rest of a sentence by a comma, a question mark, or an exclamation mark.

- Commas and periods are placed inside quotation marks.

- Colons and semicolons are placed outside closing quotation marks.

- Question marks and exclamation marks are placed inside if the quotation itself is a question or exclamation.

Pin the Quote on Atticus

WORD CONNECTIONS

The word **conceal** is formed from the Latin prefix *con-*, meaning "together," and the Latin verb *celare*, meaning "to hide."

Many English words have the prefix *con-*, including *conceited, conceive, concentrate*, and *concentric*.

GRAMMAR&USAGE

An independent clause is a group of words that contains a subject and a verb and can stand alone as a sentence. A sentence having more than one independent clause is a **compound sentence**. One way to combine two such clauses is to use a coordinating conjunction: *and, or, but*. Unless the clauses are both short and simple, you need to place a comma before the coordinating conjunction between the two independent clauses.

Example: I did not remember our mother, but Jem did....

Analysis begins with a close reading of the novel. Read the passage below from the beginning of Chapter 11. Apply all the strategies you have practiced—rereading, diffusing vocabulary, questioning the text, inferring, predicting, and marking the text—to show your understanding as you read.

from **To Kill a Mockingbird**, Chapter 11

When we were small, Jem and I confined our activities to the southern neighborhood, but when I was well into the second grade at school and tormenting Boo Radley became passé, the business section of Maycomb drew us frequently up the street past the real property of Mrs. Henry Lafayette Dubose. It was impossible to go to town without passing her house unless we wished to walk a mile out of the way. Previous minor encounters with her left me with no desire for more, but Jem said I had to grow up some time.

Mrs. Dubose lived alone except for a Negro girl in constant attendance, two doors up the street from us in a house with steep front steps and a dog-trot hall. She was very old; she spent most of each day in bed and the rest of it in a wheelchair. It was rumored that she kept a CSA pistol concealed among her numerous shawls and wraps.

Jem and I hated her. If she was on the porch when we passed, we would be raked by her wrathful gaze, subjected to ruthless interrogations regarding our behavior, and given a melancholy prediction on what we would amount to when we grew up, which was always nothing. We had long ago given up the idea of walking past her house on the opposite side of the street; that only made her raise her voice and let the whole neighborhood in on it.

We could do nothing to please her. If I said as sunnily as I could, "Hey, Mrs. Dubose," I would receive for an answer, "Don't you say hey to me, you ugly girl! You say good afternoon, Mrs. Dubose!"

She was vicious. Once she heard Jem refer to our father as "Atticus" and her reaction was apoplectic. Besides being the sassiest, most disrespectful mutts who ever passed her way, we were told that it was quite a pity our father had not remarried after our mother's death. A lovelier lady than our mother never lived, she said, and it was heartbreaking the way Atticus Finch let her children run wild. I did not remember our mother, but Jem did—he would tell me about her sometimes—and he went livid when Mrs. Dubose shot us this message.

1. On index cards, write quotations of important things Atticus says that teach Jem and Scout about people and life. Share a quote with the class, and discuss why you selected it before you place it on the Atticus outline. A sample index card has been prepared for you.

> "You just hold your head high and be a gentleman. Whatever she says to you, it's your job not to let her make you mad." (page 100)

2. What does this quotation reveal about Atticus?

3. Create a web of adjectives that describe Atticus's character:

Atticus's Character

Pin the Quote on Atticus

4. Select two adjectives from your web that are complementary yet not the same, and organize them into a coherent topic sentence with a subject (Atticus) and an opinion (character trait).

Write your topic sentences here:

Share your topic sentences with your neighbor.

5. Work collaboratively in small groups to find evidence from all the quotations you've gathered to support your claims.

Exploring the Issues in *To Kill a Mockingbird*

Review Embedded Assessment 2. What will you need to do to successfully complete this assessment?

Embedded Assessment 2 asks you to discuss the connection between a passage in the book and a central subject of the text. Create a web of the many thematic subjects Harper Lee explores in Part One of *To Kill a Mockingbird*. In addition to the central journey of Coming of Age, list the various subjects Scout, Jem, and Dill must come to terms with as they discover what coming of age means. You will add to this web as you read Part Two.

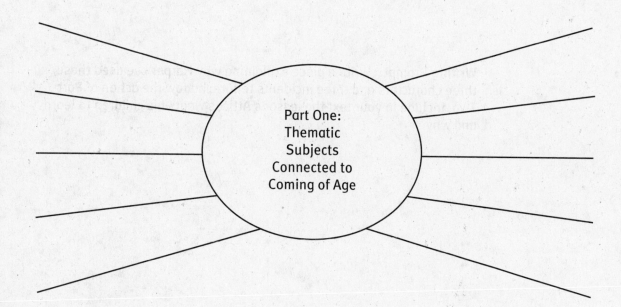

Part One:
Thematic
Subjects
Connected to
Coming of Age

Exploring the Issues in *To Kill a Mockingbird*

LITERARY TERMS

Foreshadowing is the use of hints or clues in a narrative to suggest future action.

Briefly summarize the incidents involving Cecil Jacobs, Francis Hancock, and Mrs. Dubose. How are these three incidents related? What might these characters and these incidents **foreshadow**?

- Scout and Cecil Jacobs:

- Scout and Francis Hancock:

- Jem and Scout and Mrs. Dubose:

Writing Prompt: Write a piece explaining why Harper Lee used these three characters and three incidents to foreshadow the action of Part Two. Include in your text the lessons Atticus wants his children to learn and why.

Changing the Scene

SUGGESTED LEARNING STRATEGIES: **Discussion Groups**

Part Two of *To Kill A Mockingbird* begins with two dramatic developments in Jem and Scout's life: the visit to First Purchase African M.E. Church and Aunt Alexandra's arrival for a prolonged stay.

The following questions will help you to consider how these developments contribute to the text's overall meaning. They will help you examine how setting, conflict, and character development within specific scenes function in connection with the rest of the text.

Question Set 1:

1. What details does Scout provide when describing Calpurnia's church? The events of the service? What do these reveal about the nature of the Quarters as a community, especially in contrast to life in Scout and Jem's own neighborhood?

2. This scene shows that Calpurnia is a **dynamic** rather than a **static** character. What is revealed about Calpurnia through the conflict with Lula? Through Scout's conversation with her following the service (e.g., linin', her "double life," her "command of two languages")?

3. Based on the events of this chapter, what values does Calpurnia seem to represent in the book? Find quotes that support your conclusion.

4. How do Calpurnia and the trip to her church influence Scout's perspective? Find quotes that support your conclusions regarding the impact of the church scene and the conversation on Scout's view of the world.

> **WORD CONNECTIONS**
>
> The word *dynamic* comes from the Greek word meaning "powerful." The root *dyna-* appears in *dynamo, dynamite,* and *dynasty.*
>
> *Static* also comes from a Greek word, *statikos,* referring to a stand or a pause or something firm or fixed. Other words in English with the root *-stat-* include *status, station, statistics,* and *statue.*

Changing the Scene

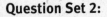

Question Set 2:

1. Describe the shift regarding Calpurnia that occurs in the first sentence of Chapter 13. How else is Calpurnia referred to during this chapter?

2. Why does Scout say "Aunt Alexandra fitted into the world of Maycomb like a hand into a glove"? How is this connected to the extended description of Maycomb's history in this chapter?

3. What is revealed about Aunt Alexandra through Scout's conversation with her about Cousin Lily and Cousin Joshua? Through Atticus's conversation with Scout and Jem on her behalf?

4. Based on the events of this chapter, what values does Aunt Alexandra represent? Find quotations that support your conclusion.

Now that you have examined the significance of setting and of characters in more detail, it's time to write thematic statements. A **thematic statement** articulates your interpretation of the text's central meaning or message. Earlier, you identified thematic subjects *To Kill a Mockingbird* explores, such as prejudice and courage. You may want to add more subjects to your classroom web. Your thematic statement would clarify what Harper Lee seems to be saying about these subjects.

For Embedded Assessment 2, you will analyze a passage and explain how it contributes to the meaning of the novel as a whole. You can focus on a character, conflict, or setting within the passage to develop your analysis. Based on your discussions in this activity, write a thematic statement for each of these three elements. You may use the following stems, but feel free to write your own.

> **ACADEMIC VOCABULARY**
>
> A **thematic statement** is an idea a writer wishes to convey about a subject.

1. Character: Aunt Alexandra's fascination with family history symbolizes

_____.

2. Conflict: The confrontation between Calpurnia and Lula shows that

_____.

3. Setting: The trip to Calpurnia's church reveals that

_____.

Exchange your thematic statements with a partner, and evaluate the statements using the following criteria:

- A thematic statement should not be stated as an order. (Example: "People should not be racist.")

- It should not be a cliché. (Example: "Blood is thicker than water.")

- It should not be restricted to the characters themselves. (Example: "Calpurnia looks beyond skin color.")

- It should not be stated as an absolute. (Example: "All white Southerners are racist.")

Revise your thematic statements based on your peer's feedback.

Comparing Print and Film Text

Reread Chapter 15. Your teacher will give you a particular character to observe. As you reread the chapter, complete the following chart for that character.

Then, your class will perform a Reader's Theater interpretation of the scene. Finally, your teacher will show you the film version of the scene. In each version, note how your character is portrayed and how this portrayal influences your perspective on the character. You will then compare the versions.

Name of Character _____	Notes from Novel	Notes from Reader's Theater	Notes from Film Clip
What your character says, and how			
What your character does			
Your character's appearance			
What others say **about** your character (you may look outside Chapter 15 for this information)			
What others say **to** your character, and how			

Reflect on your notes, focusing on differences and similarities between how the novel and the movie portray the scene.

1. How did the Reader's Theater interpretation affect your impressions of the chracters? Why?

2. In the film, how are framing, lighting, sound, and other **cinematic elements** used to communicate meaning in this scene? Describe how each element is used and its effect. See Activity 2.15 to review film terms.

   • **Angles and Framing** (high and low angles, long shot, medium shot, close-ups):

   • **Lighting** (high key and low key):

   • **Sound** (diegetic and non-diegetic):

   • **Other elements** (camera movement):

Comparing Print and Film Text

3. What changes in dialogue were made? Why? What is the effect of these changes?

4. Cite specific changes made in the transformation from print to film. Why might those changes have been made?

Writing Prompt: Explain the significance of conflict and setting in this scene. Then, choose a character and discuss the significance of his or her role in the outcome of the scene. How does this scene contribute to the meaning of the novel as a whole?

Analyzing Atticus's Closing Argument

from **To Kill a Mockingbird**, Chapter 20

My Notes

"Gentlemen," he was saying, "I shall be brief, but I would like to use my remaining time with you to remind you that this case is not a difficult one, it requires no minute sifting of complicated facts, but it does require you to be sure beyond all reasonable doubt as to the guilt of the defendant. To begin with, this case should never have come to trial. This case is as simple as black and white.

"The state has not produced one iota of medical evidence to the effect that the crime Tom Robinson is charged with ever took place. It has relied instead upon the testimony of two witnesses whose evidence has not only been called into serious question on cross-examination, but has been flatly contradicted by the defendant. The defendant is not guilty, but somebody in this courtroom is.

"I have nothing but pity in my heart for the chief witness for the state, but my pity does not extend so far as to her putting a man's life at stake, which she has done in an effort to get rid of her own guilt.

"I say guilt, gentlemen, because it was guilt that motivated her. She has committed no crime, she has merely broken a rigid and time-honored code of our society, a code so severe that whoever breaks it is hounded from our midst as unfit to live with. She is the victim of cruel poverty and ignorance, but I cannot pity her: she is white. She knew full well the enormity of her offense, but because her desires were stronger than the code she was breaking, she persisted in breaking it. She persisted, and her subsequent reaction is something that all of us have known at one time or another. She did something every child has done—she tried to put the evidence of her offense away from her. But in this case she was no child hiding stolen contraband: she struck out at her victim—of necessity she must put him away from her—he must be removed from her presence, from this world. She must destroy the evidence of her offense.

"What was the evidence of her offense? Tom Robinson, a human being. She must put Tom Robinson away from her. Tom Robinson was her daily reminder of what she did. What did she do? She tempted a Negro.

"She was white, and she tempted a Negro. She did something that in our society is unspeakable: she kissed a black man. Not an old Uncle, but a strong young Negro man. No code mattered to her before she broke it, but it came crashing down on her afterwards.

"Her father saw it, and the defendant has testified as to his remarks. What did her father do? We don't know, but there is circumstantial evidence to indicate that Mayella Ewell was beaten savagely by someone who led almost exclusively with his left. We do know in part what Mr. Ewell did: he did what any God-fearing, persevering, respectable white man would do under the

WORD CONNECTIONS

Circumstantial is an adjective meaning "having to do with certain facts or conditions." The prefix *circum-* derives from the Latin word *circum*, meaning "around." English has many words beginning with *circum-*. They include *circumference*, *circumnavigate*, and *circumvent.*

My Notes

circumstances—he swore out a warrant, no doubt signing it with his left hand, and Tom Robinson now sits before you, having taken the oath with the only good hand he possesses—his right hand.

"And so a quiet, respectable, humble Negro who had the unmitigated temerity to 'feel sorry' for a white woman has had to put his word against two white people's. I need not remind you of their appearance and conduct on the stand—you saw them for yourselves. The witnesses for the state, with the exception of the sheriff of Maycomb County, have presented themselves to you gentlemen, to this court, in the cynical confidence that their testimony would not be doubted, confident that you gentlemen would go along with them on the assumption—the evil assumption—that *all* Negroes lie, that *all* Negroes are basically immoral beings, that *all* Negro men are not to be trusted around our women, an assumption one associates with minds of their caliber.

"Which, gentlemen, we know is in itself a lie as black as Tom Robinson's skin, a lie I do not have to point out to you. You know the truth, and the truth is this: some Negroes lie, some Negroes are immoral, some Negro men are not to be trusted around women—black or white. But this is a truth that applies to the human race and to no particular race of men. There is not a person in this courtroom who has never told a lie, who has never done an immoral thing, and there is no man living who has never looked upon a woman without desire."

Atticus paused and took out his handkerchief. Then he took off his glasses and wiped them, and we saw another "first": we had never seen him sweat—he was one of those men whose faces never perspired, but now it was shining tan.

"One more thing, gentlemen, before I quit. Thomas Jefferson once said that all men are created equal, a phrase that the Yankees and the distaff side of the Executive branch in Washington are fond of hurling at us. There is a tendency in this year of grace, 1935, for certain people to use this phrase out of context, to satisfy all conditions. The most ridiculous example I can think of is that the people who run public education promote the stupid and idle along with the industrious—because all men are created equal, educators will gravely tell you, the children left behind suffer terrible feelings of inferiority. We know all men are not created equal in the sense some people would have us believe—some people are smarter than others, some people have more opportunity because they're born with it, some men make more money than others, some ladies make better cakes than others—some people are born gifted beyond the normal scope of most men.

GRAMMAR & USAGE

Parallel structure is the use of the same grammatical structures—words, phrases, or clauses—to balance related ideas. Writers perform this balancing act because it makes their writing more effective. Readers can see the commonalities and relationships clearly when the structures are parallel.

Example: . . . the assumption . . . *that all Negroes lie, that all Negroes are basically immoral beings, that all Negro men are not to be trusted around our women.* . . . (parallel adjective clauses)

"But there is one way in this country in which all men are created equal—there is one human institution that makes a pauper the equal of a Rockefeller, the stupid man the equal of an Einstein, and the ignorant man the equal of any college president. That institution, gentlemen, is a court. It can be the Supreme Court of the United States or the humblest J.P. court in the land, or this honorable court which you serve. Our courts have their faults, as does any human institution, but in this country our courts are the great levelers, and in our courts all men are created equal.

"I'm no idealist to believe firmly in the integrity of our courts and in the jury system—that is no ideal to me, it is a living, working reality. Gentlemen, a court is no better than each man of you sitting before me on this jury. A court is only as sound as its jury, and a jury is only as sound as the men who make it up. I am confident that you gentlemen will review without passion the evidence you have heard, come to a decision, and restore this defendant to his family. In the name of God, do your duty."

Atticus's voice had dropped, and as he turned away from the jury he said something I did not catch. He said it more to himself than to the court. I punched Jem. "What'd he say?"

"'In the name of God, believe him,' I think that's what he said."

When you have read this passage, analyze Atticus's speech for the rhetorical structures and devices he uses to convince the reader. Highlight the five elements of an argument (hook, claim, concessions/refutations, support, and summary/call to action).

My Notes

WORD CONNECTIONS

Legal arguments often use a persuasive technique of *ad hominem*, which is Latin for "argument against the person." An *ad hominem* appeal points out that a person may be disposed to take a particular position. Find an example of *ad hominem* in the excerpt from Chapter 20 of *To Kill a Mockingbird*.

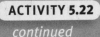
Perform a close reading of Atticus's famous closing statement. Use the
SMELL strategy to analyze the quality and credibility of his evidence for
this particular audience.

S = Sender-Receiver relationship. Atticus is the sender. The jury and the audience are
the receivers. What is the relationship among Atticus, the jury, and the audience? Whom
does Atticus mean to influence with his statement? What attitudes and assumptions
does his target audience hold towards his subject? Towards Atticus himself?

M = Message. What is Atticus's message? Summarize the statements made in his
closing argument.

E = Emotional strategies. Does Atticus use any statements that are meant to get an
emotional reaction from his audience? Explain. If so, what is the desired effect?

L = Logical strategies. Does Atticus use any statements or appeals that are logical?
Explain. How does the logic (or its absence) affect the message?

L = Language. Look for specific words and phrases chosen by Atticus, and consider
how the language affects his message.

As you watch the film version of the courtroom scene, fill out the chart below, looking for specific elements from the scene.

What images does the director present to the audience in this scene?	What images does the director consciously choose NOT to present to the audience?	What did you notice about the relationship between the speech and the images?	What changes or deletions did you notice in the text of Atticus's speech?

Discussion Questions:

1. How do the director's choices affect the way we respond to the scene?

2. How do the changes in the text of the speech affect the message of the speech (if they do)?

3. Why do you think the director changed the speech in this way (other than to shorten it)?

Writing Prompt: Write a paragraph analyzing the use of appeals in Atticus's closing argument. In your paragraph, relate your analysis to the ideas of justice and equality.

Reflection on the Verdict

Socratic Seminar: Your teacher will place you in a group. Your group will be given a question regarding the verdict to begin the discussion. Write the question below, and write your initial response. Reread or scan the last pages of Chapter 22 and the first six pages of Chapter 23, as you think about your answer and as you begin to talk in your Socratic circles.

Writing Prompt: Use **RAFT** to write a piece that expresses your reaction (as a character) to the verdict convicting Tom.

ROLE	AUDIENCE	FORMAT	TOPIC
Scout	Readers of the *Maycomb Tribune*	Letter to the editor	The Tom Robinson verdict
Jem	A friend in some other part of the country	Personal letter	
Atticus	A paper in some other part of the country	Other:	
Tom Robinson	Other:		
Judge Taylor			
Other:			

SUGGESTED LEARNING STRATEGIES: Discussion Groups,
Graphic Organizer

As you discuss these questions, consider the significance of Chapter 24 to the meaning of the novel as a whole. Consider, also, the different perspectives on racial equality represented by each of the characters who appear in the scene.

1. What values does Mrs. Grace Merriweather seem to represent in the novel? Is there anything ironic about her name? Find textual evidence to support your answer.

2. What is the effect of revealing Tom Robinson's death during this scene? Why do you think the author chose to do so here instead of elsewhere?

3. Does your impression of Aunt Alexandra change in this chapter from the impressions you had of her earlier the book? Is she a *static character* or a *dynamic character*? Explain your answer.

4. How does Scout's perspective on what it means to be a lady evolve during this scene? Find textual evidence to support your answer.

After you have completed your discussions, choose the question you most strongly responded to, and use it as a starting point for a thematic statement. Incorporate the idea of coming of age into your statement. Be prepared to share this with your discussion group.

With your group members, make a list of all the characters who appear in this chapter. Next, rank them in terms of the level of racism they seem to portray. Create a graphic organizer to represent your conclusions using whatever visual layout seems most insightful. For each character, include a quotation (possibly from another chapter, if necessary) that represents his or her attitude towards race and racial equality. Be prepared to explain your organizer to your classmates. Make notes below; then use separate paper to create your graphic organizer.

Character names:

Rank:

Potential Quotes:

Exploring Insights

SUGGESTED LEARNING STRATEGIES: **Close Reading,
Questioning the Text**

Each of the following quotations links to the novel's exploration of what it means to come of age. After each quote, explain which thematic subject(s) (from the class list) you think it best links to, and explain why.

"He jerked his head at Dill: 'Things haven't caught up with that one's instinct yet. Let him get a little older and he won't get sick and cry. Maybe things'll strike him as being—not quite right, say, but he won't cry, not when he gets a few years on him.'"

—Dolphus Raymond to Jem, Dill, and Scout, Chapter 20

"'This is their home, sister,' said Atticus. 'We've made it this way for them, they might as well learn to cope with it.'"

—Atticus to Alexandra, Chapter 22

"The older you grow the more of it you'll see. The one place where a man ought to get a square deal is in a courtroom, be he any color of the rainbow, but people have a way of carrying their resentments right into a jury box."
—Atticus to Jem, Chapter 23

"As you grow older, you'll see white men cheat black men every day of your life, but let me tell you something and don't you forget it—whenever a white man does that to a black man, no matter who he is, how rich he is, or how fine a family he comes from, that white man is trash."
—Atticus to Jem, Chapter 23

"There was no doubt about it, I must soon enter this world, where on its surface fragile ladies rocked slowly, fanned gently, and drank cool water."
—Scout, Chapter 24

Writing Prompt: Choose a quotation and write about what it means, how it relates to coming of age, and how it connects to one of the thematic subjects presented in the novel.

Standing in Borrowed Shoes

SUGGESTED LEARNING STRATEGIES: Graphic Organizer,
Think-Pair-Share

"Atticus was right. One time he said you never really know a man until you stand in his shoes and walk around in them."

In the chart below, define each of the terms. Then work in a small group to list all the primary (major) and secondary (minor) characters you can identify from the novel. When you have finished, compare your list with that of other groups to determine which characters should be added or deleted based on their importance in the story. Then, make notes on how the secondary, or minor, characters represent certain thematic subjects in the novel.

Primary Characters:	Secondary Characters:

Working with a partner, create a character profile poster. Your poster should include the following elements:

- A picture or graphic representation
- A physical description from the novel
- A list of several adjectives describing his or her personality, values, and/or motives
- An explanation of the function he or she serves in advancing the novel's plot
- A quotation about him or her from another character
- A quotation by him or her that reveals the character's values

These profiles will go up on the wall in a class collage, so make your poster visually appealing! Be prepared to present your poster to your classmates, explaining the information you have included.

Scout and Boo

"If there's just one kind of folks, why can't they get along with each other? If they're alike, why do they go out of their way to despise each other? Scout, I think I'm beginning to understand something. I think I'm beginning to understand why Boo Radley's stayed shut up in the house all this time . . . it's because he wants to stay inside."

—Jem to Scout, Chapter 23

Using notes from your double-entry journal on Boo and from the text of *To Kill a Mockingbird*, fill out the following grid:

Scout's mental picture of Boo before Chapter 29	
The reality of Boo	
Scout's vision of Boo after she meets him	

Quickwrite: After her encounter with Boo, how does Scout's changed perception of him connect to your broader understanding of what it means to come of age? How does this understanding link to Atticus's closing words, "Most people are [real nice], Scout, when you finally see them"?

Analyzing a Passage from
To Kill a Mockingbird

SUGGESTED LEARNING STRATEGIES: **Close Reading, Drafting,
Marking the Text, Revising**

Assignment

Your assignment is to write a literary essay that analyzes a short passage
that depicts a key scene from *To Kill a Mockingbird*. Your analysis must
discuss the passage in terms of the literary elements of the novel – setting,
conflict, or character—and explain how that passage relates to the thematic
development of the work as a whole.

Steps

Prewriting

1. Select a passage from the novel that illustrates a defining moment in a
   setting, conflict, or development of character as it pertains to the overall
   thematic concept: coming of age.

2. Make a photocopy of the passage, and do a close reading on your copy.
   Mark and annotate the text to make sure you understand it and its
   significance in terms of the themes of the novel. You will attach this copy
   of the passage to your essay.

3. Review your annotations and explore the significance of this passage.
   Generate a working thematic statement that identifies the significance of
   the passage as it relates to the theme.

4. In pairs, share a summary of your analyzed text and your thematic
   statement, using the criteria established in Activity 5.20 to evaluate
   the statement's effectiveness. Use the feedback of your peers to revise
   accordingly.

Drafting and Revision

5. Create a topic outline for your essay that contains the thematic
   statement, supporting topic sentences, and textual support in the form of
   direct and indirect quotations and paraphrasing. Share your outline with
   your writing partner.

6. Write your first draft and incorporate your writing partner's suggestions.

7. Gather in writing groups to share your passages and your first draft.
   Analyze drafts for the following:

   ▶ Organizational structure of a literary analysis: look for effective
     three-fold transition sentences.

   ▶ Interpretation of the text: claim, evidence, commentary, and closure in
     each paragraph; clarity of ideas.

   As you share and respond in your writing groups, you may want to
   consult the Scoring Guide criteria.

8. Revise your draft for seamless integration of quotations using this strategy: introduce the quote, use the quote, and explain the quote. Share your draft in your writing group to ensure that quotes flow within the context of the essay and are properly cited. Mark the text as you read to make sure each source is adequately introduced, correctly cited, and effectively extended with commentary.

9. Read through your draft, and generate a list of possible titles for your essay that capture key ideas, words, or phrases. Select a memorable title that captures the essence of your essay.

Editing for Publication

10. Proofread your essay, and mark the text making final edits in grammar, punctuation, and spelling. Prepare for submission by using publication software to type and edit your draft for spelling and grammar. Consult an appropriate style manual to find general guidelines for formatting your essay.

SCORING GUIDE

Scoring Criteria	Exemplary	Proficient	Emerging
Ideas	The writer insightfully links the chosen passage to a thematic interpretation of coming of age as well as elements of literature. Supporting details from *To Kill a Mockingbird* richly enhance the understanding of the writer's position. All commentary relates directly back to the thesis.	The writer adequately links the chosen passage to a thematic interpretation of coming of age as well as elements of literature. Supporting details from *To Kill a Mockingbird* are relevant to understanding the writer's position. Most commentary relates directly back to the thesis, but some commentary may lack development.	The writer attempts to link the chosen passage to a thematic interpretation of coming of age and/or elements of literature. Supporting details from *To Kill a Mockingbird* may be present but may lack development or may not be concrete enough to give a full understanding of the writer's position. Commentary may not relate directly to the thesis. The writer may replace commentary with plot summary.
Organization	The essay is multi-paragraphed and logically organized to enhance the reader's understanding. Transitions establish fluent connections between the ideas. It includes an innovative introduction with an insightful lead and a strong thesis, coherent body paragraphs, and a perceptive conclusion.	The essay is multi-paragraphed and organized. Transitions establish connections between ideas. It includes an introduction with a lead and a clear thesis, detailed body paragraphs, and a conclusion.	Organization is attempted, but key components are lacking. Transitions are absent or ineffective. It may include an introduction with an unfocused thesis, undeveloped body paragraphs, and/or an inadequate conclusion.
Use of Language	The writer shows command of language and employs purposeful, appropriate diction for an academic audience.	The writer's language is adequate, using diction that is appropriate for an academic essay, but may use some unsophisticated or incorrect words.	The writer's language is coherent yet simplistic, and may be inappropriate for an academic audience, using slang or informal word choice.

SCORING GUIDE

Scoring Criteria	Exemplary	Proficient	Emerging
Conventions	Writing is virtually error-free. The writer uses proper punctuation and capitalization to smoothly embed quotations into text.	Writing is generally error-free. The writer uses proper punctuation and capitalization to embed quotations into text.	Writing contains errors that at times distract from meaning. At times, the writer attempts proper punctuation and capitalization to incorporate quotations into text.
Evidence of Writing Process	The writing demonstrates thoughtful planning, significant revision, and careful editing in preparing a publishable draft.	The writing demonstrates planning, revision, and editing in preparing a publishable draft.	The writing lacks evidence of planning, revision, and/or editing. The draft is not ready for publication.
Additional Criteria			

Comments:

Essay

> **ABOUT THE AUTHOR**
> Nicholas Karolides is an author and editor of books for young adults. He has often written about the topics of the politics of suppression and censorship of literary works.

From

"IN DEFENSE OF
To Kill a Mockingbird"

by Nicholas J. Karolides, et al.

The critical career of *To Kill a Mockingbird* is a late twentieth-century case study of censorship. When Harper Lee's novel about a small southern town and its prejudices was published in 1960, the book received favorable reviews in professional journals and the popular press. Typical of that opinion, Booklist's reviewer called the book "melodramatic" and noted "traces of sermonizing," but the book was recommended for library purchase, commending its "rare blend of wit and compassion." Reviewers did not suggest that the book was young-adult literature, or that it belonged in adolescent collections; perhaps that is why no one mentioned the book's language or violence. In any event, reviewers seemed inclined to agree that *To Kill a Mockingbird* was a worthwhile interpretation of the South's existing social structures during the 1930s. In 1961 the book won the Pulitzer Prize Award, the Alabama Library Association Book Award, and the Brotherhood Award of the National Conference of Christians and Jews. It seemed that Harper Lee's blend of family history, local custom, and restrained sermonizing was important reading, and with a young girl between the ages of six and nine as the main character, *To Kill a Mockingbird* moved rapidly into junior and senior high school libraries and curriculum. The book was not destined to be studied by college students. Southern literature's critics rarely mentioned it; few university professors found it noteworthy enough to "teach" as an exemplary southern novel.

Contextualizing Controversy

GRAMMAR & USAGE

Verbs have **active** and **passive voice** in all six tenses. A passive-voice verb always contains a form of *be* with the past participle of the verb.

Examples:

- Active voice (past perfect): Things **had changed** in the South...

- Passive voice (past perfect): Things **had been changed**...

Note the following examples of passive-voice verbs on this page:

- Two national leaders... were assassinated....

- John F. Kennedy was killed...

These examples demonstrate one reason to use passive voice: when you want to emphasize the receiver of the action.

WORD CONNECTIONS

The word *psychological* is an adjective meaning "mental" or "of the mind." The prefix *psycho-* comes from the Greek word *psychē*, meaning "soul" or "spirit." Other words with the prefix *psycho-* include *psychoanalysis*, *psychobabble*, and *psychodrama*.

By the mid-sixties *To Kill a Mockingbird* had a solid place in junior and senior high American literature studies. Once discovered by southern parents, the book's solid place became shaky indeed. Sporadic lawsuits arose. In most cases the complaint against the book was by conservatives who disliked the portrayal of whites. Typically, the Hanover County School Board in Virginia first ruled the book "immoral," then withdrew their criticism and declared the ruckus "was all a mistake" (*Newsletter* [*on Intellectual Freedom*] 1966). By 1968 the National Education Association listed the book among those which drew the most criticism from private groups. Ironically it was rated directly behind *Little Black Sambo* (*Newsletter* 1968). And the seventies arrived.

Things had changed in the South during the sixties. Two national leaders who had supported integration and had espoused the ideals of racial equality were assassinated in southern regions. When John F. Kennedy was killed in Texas on November 27, 1963, many southerners were shocked. Populist attitudes of racism were declining, and in the aftermath of the tragedy southern politics began to change. Lyndon Johnson gained the presidency: blacks began to seek and win political offices. Black leader Martin Luther King had stressed the importance of racial equality, always using Mahatma Gandhi's strategy of nonviolent action and civil disobedience. A brilliant orator, King grew up in the South; the leader of the [Southern Christian Leadership Conference], he lived in Atlanta, Georgia. In 1968, while working on a garbage strike in Memphis, King was killed. The death of the 1965 Nobel Peace Prize winner was further embarrassment for white southerners. Whites began to look at public values anew, and gradually southern blacks found experiences in the South more tolerable. In 1971 one Atlanta businessman observed [in *Ebony*], "The liberation thinking is here. Blacks are more together. With the doors opening wider, this area is the mecca...." Southern arguments against *To Kill a Mockingbird* subsided. *The Newsletter* on *Intellectual Freedom* contained no record of southern court cases during the seventies or eighties. The book had sustained itself during the first period of sharp criticism; it had survived regional protests from the area it depicted.

The second onslaught of attack came from new groups of censors, and it came during the late seventies and early eighties. Private sectors in the Midwest and suburban East began to demand the book's removal from school libraries. Groups, such as the Eden Valley School Committee in Minnesota, claimed that the book was too laden with profanity (*Newsletter* 1978). In Vermont, New York, Reverend Carl Hadley threatened to establish a private Christian school because public school libraries contained such "filthy, trashy sex novels" as *A Separate Peace* and *To Kill a Mockingbird* (*Newsletter* 1980). And finally, blacks began to censor the book. In Warren, Indiana, three blacks resigned from the township Human Relations Advisory Council when the Warren County school administration refused to remove the book from Warren junior high school classes. They contended that the book "does psychological damage to the positive integration process and represents institutionalized racism" (*Newsletter* 1982). Thus, censorship of *To Kill a*

Mockingbird swung from the conservative right to the liberal left. Factions representing racists, religious sects, concerned parents, and minority groups vocally demanded the book's removal from public schools....

The censors' reactions to *To Kill a Mockingbird* were reactions to issues of race and justice. Their moves to ban the book derive from their own perspectives of the book's theme. Their "reader response" criticism, usually based on one reading of the book, was personal and political. They needed to ban the book because it told them something about American society that they did not want to hear. That is precisely the problem facing any author of realistic fiction. Once the story becomes real, it can become grim. An author will use first-person flashback in a story in order to let the reader lie in another time, another place. Usually the storyteller is returning for a second view of the scene. The teller has experienced the events before and the story is being retold because the scene has left the storyteller uneasy. As the storyteller recalls the past, both the listener and the teller see events in a new light. Both are working through troubled times in search of meaning. In the case of *To Kill a Mockingbird* the first-person retelling is not pleasant, but the underlying significance is with the narrative. The youthful personalities who are recalled are hopeful. Scout tells us of a time past when white people would lynch or convict a man because of the color of his skin. She also shows us three children who refuse to believe that the system is right, and she leaves us with the thought that most people will be nice if seen for what they are: humans with frailties. When discussing literary criticism, Theo D'Haen suggested [in *Text to Reader*] that the good literary work should have a life within the world and be "part of the ongoing activities of that world." *To Kill a Mockingbird* continues to have life within the world; its ongoing activities in the realm of censorship show that it is a book which deals with regional moralism. The children in the story seem very human; they worry about their own identification, they defy parental rules, and they cry over injustices. They mature in Harper Lee's novel, and they lose their innocence. So does the reader. If the readers are young, they may believe Scout when she says, "nothin's real scary except in books." If the readers are older they will have learned that life is scary, and they will be prepared to meet some of its realities.

Reflection

An important aspect of growing as a learner is to take the time to reflect. It is important to take into account where you have been, what you have accomplished, what helped you to learn, and how you will apply your new knowledge in the future. Use the following process to record your thinking and to identify evidence of your learning.

Thinking about Concepts

1. Using specific examples from this unit, respond to the following Essential Questions

   - What are the essential elements of an effective informative presentation?

   - What impact does historical, cultural, geographical, and social context have on a novel and on the reaction of readers to it?

2. Consider the new academic vocabulary from this unit (Context, Annotated Bibliography, Audience Analysis, Characterization, Thematic Statement) as well as academic vocabulary from previous units, and select 3 - 4 terms of which your understanding has grown. For each term, answer the following questions:

   - What was your understanding of the term before this unit?

   - How has your understanding of the word evolved throughout this unit?

   - How will you apply your understanding in the future?

Thinking about Connections

3. Reflecting on key concepts (Essential Questions, Academic Vocabulary, and Important Themes), select one or two concepts that reflect your most growth or greatest understanding. Then, find an example (or "artifact") from your work that can serve as evidence of your understanding of your selected concepts

4. For each artifact that you choose, record, respond to, and reflect on your thinking and understanding, using the following questions as a guide:

   a. What skill/knowledge does this artifact reflect, and how did you learn this skill/knowledge?

   b. How did your understanding of the power of language expand through your engagement with this artifact?

   c. How will you apply this skill or knowledge in the future?

5. Create this reflection as Portfolio pages—one for each artifact you choose. Use the model in the box for your headings and commentary on questions.

Thinking About Thinking

Portfolio Entry

Concept:

Description of Artifact:

Commentary on Questions:

Grammar Handbook

Part 1: Using Pronouns Clearly

Because a pronoun REFERS BACK to a noun or TAKES THE PLACE OF that noun, you have to use the correct pronoun so that your reader clearly understands which noun your pronoun is referring to. Therefore, pronouns should:

1. Agree in number

If the pronoun takes the place of a singular noun, you have to use a singular pronoun.

> If a student parks a car on campus, he or she has to buy a parking sticker.
> (**NOT:** If a student parks a car on campus, they have to buy a parking sticker.)

Remember: the words everybody, anybody, anyone, each, neither, nobody, someone, a person, etc. are singular and take singular pronouns.

> Everybody ought to do his or her best. (NOT: their best)
> Neither of the girls brought her umbrella. (NOT: their umbrellas)

NOTE: Many people find the construction "his or her" wordy, so if it is possible to use a plural noun as your antecedent so that you can use "they" as your pronoun, it may be wise to do so. If you do use a singular noun and the context makes the gender clear, then it is permissible to use just "his" or "her" rather than "his or her."

2. Agree in person

If you are writing in the "first person" (I), don't confuse your reader by switching to the "second person" (you) or "third person" (he, she, they, it, etc.). Similarly, if you are using the "second person," don't switch to "first" or "third."

> When a person comes to class, he or she should have his or her homework ready.
> (**NOT:** When a person comes to class, you should have your homework ready.)

3. Refer clearly to a specific noun.

Don't be vague or ambiguous.

> **NOT:** Although the motorcycle hit the tree, it was not damaged. (Is "it" the motorcycle or the tree?)
> **NOT:** I don't think they should show violence on TV. (Who are "they"?)
> **NOT:** Vacation is coming soon, which is nice. (What is nice, the vacation or the fact that it is coming soon?)
> **NOT:** George worked in a national forest last summer. This may be his life's work. (What word does "this" refer to?)
> **NOT:** If you put this sheet in your notebook, you can refer to it. (What does "it" refer to, the sheet or your notebook?)

Pronoun Case

Pronoun case is really a very simple matter. There are three cases.

- Subjective case: pronouns used as subject.
- Objective case: pronouns used as objects of verbs or prepositions.
- Possessive case: pronouns which express ownership.

Pronouns as Subjects	Pronouns as Objects	Pronouns that show Possession
I	me	my (mine)
you	you	your (yours)
he, she, it	him, her, it	his, her (hers), it (its)
we	us	our (ours)
they	them	their (theirs)
who	whom	whose

The pronouns **this, that, these, those,** and **which** do not change form.

Some problems of case:

1. **In compound structures, where there are two pronouns or a noun and a pronoun, drop the other noun for a moment. Then you can see which case you want.**

   Not: Bob and me travel a good deal.
   (Would you say, "me travel"?)
   Not: He gave the flowers to Jane and I.
   (Would you say, "he gave the flowers to I"?)
   Not: Us men like the coach.
   (Would you say, "us like the coach"?)

2. **In comparisons. Comparisons usually follow than or as:**

   He is taller than I (am tall).
   This helps you as much as (it helps) me.
   She is as noisy as I (am).

Comparisons are really shorthand sentences which usually omit words, such as those in the parentheses in the sentences above. If you complete the comparison in your head, you can choose the correct case for the pronoun.

   Not: He is taller than me.
   (Would you say, "than me am tall"?)

3. **In formal and semiformal writing:**

Use the subjective form after a form of the verb to be.

   Formal: It is I.
   Informal: It is me.

Use whom in the objective case.

   Formal: To whom am I talking?
   Informal: Who am I talking to?

Part 2: Appositives

An appositive is a noun or pronoun — often with modifiers — set beside another noun or pronoun to explain or identify it. Here are some examples of appositives (the **noun or pronoun will be in blue**, the **appositive will be in boldface**).

> Your friend **Bill** is in trouble.
>
> My brother's car, **a sporty red convertible with bucket seats**, is the envy of my friends.
>
> The chief surgeon, **an expert in organ-transplant procedures**, took her nephew on a hospital tour.

An appositive phrase usually follows the word it explains or identifies, but it may also precede it.

> **A bold innovator**, Wassily Kadinsky is known for his colorful abstract paintings.
>
> **The first state to ratify the U. S. Constitution**, Delaware is rich in history.
>
> **A beautiful collie**, Skip was my favorite dog.

Punctuation of Appositives

In some cases, the noun being explained is too general without the appositive; the information is essential to the meaning of the sentence. When this is the case, do not place commas around the appositive; just leave it alone. If the sentence would be clear and complete without the appositive, then commas are necessary; place one before and one after the appositive. Here are some examples.

> The popular US president **John Kennedy** was known for his eloquent and inspirational speeches.

Here we do not put commas around the appositive, because it is essential information. Without the appositive, the sentence would be, "The popular US president was known for his eloquent and inspirational speeches." We wouldn't know which president was being referred to.

> John Kennedy, **the popular US president**, was known for his eloquent and inspirational speeches.

Here we put commas around the appositive because it is not essential information. Without the appositive, the sentence would be, "John Kennedy was known for his eloquent and inspirational speeches." We still know who the subject of the sentence is without the appositive.

Part 3: What is the Difference Between Adjectives and Adverbs?

The Basic Rules: Adjectives

Adjectives modify nouns. To modify means to change in some way. For example:

- "I ate a meal." *Meal* is a noun. We don't know what kind of meal; all we know is that someone ate a meal.
- "I ate an enormous lunch." *Lunch* is a noun, and *enormous* is an adjective that modifies it. It tells us what kind of meal the person ate.

Adjectives usually answer one of a few different questions: "What kind?" or "Which?" or "How many?" For example:

- "The *tall* girl is riding a *new* bike." *Tall* tells us which girl we're talking about. *New* tells us what kind of bike we're talking about.
- "The *tough* professor gave us the *final* exam." *Tough* tells us what kind of professor we're talking about. *Final* tells us which exam we're talking about.
- "*Fifteen* students passed the midterm exam; *twelve* students passed the final exam." *Fifteen* and *twelve* both tell us how many students; *midterm* and *final* both tell us which exam.

So, generally speaking, adjectives answer the following questions: Which? What kind of? How many?

The Basic Rules: Adverbs

Adverbs modify verbs, adjectives, and other adverbs. (You can recognize adverbs easily because many of them are formed by adding -ly to an adjective, though that is not always the case.) The most common question that adverbs answer is **how**.

Let's look at verbs first.

- "She sang *beautifully.*" *Beautifully* is an adverb that modifies *sang*. It tells us **how** she sang.
- "The cellist played *carelessly.*" *Carelessly* is an adverb that modifies *played*. It tells us **how** the cellist played.

Adverbs also modify adjectives and other adverbs.

- "That woman is *extremely* nice." *Nice* is an adjective that modifies the noun *woman*. *Extremely* is an adverb that modifies *nice*; it tells us **how** nice she is. **How** nice is she? She's extremely nice.
- "It was a *terribly* hot afternoon." *Hot* is an adjective that modifies the noun *afternoon*. *Terribly* is an adverb that modifies the adjective *hot*. **How** hot is it? Terribly hot.

So, generally speaking, adverbs answer the question **how**. (They can also answer the questions **when**, **where**, and **why**.)

Part 4: Verbals

Gerunds

A gerund is a verbal that ends in -*ing* and functions as a noun. The term *verbal* indicates that a gerund, like the other two kinds of verbals, is based on a verb and therefore expresses action or a state of being. However, since a gerund functions as a noun, it occupies some positions in a sentence that a noun ordinarily would, for example: subject, direct object, subject complement, and object of preposition.

Gerund as subject:

- Traveling might satisfy your desire for new experiences. (**Traveling** is the gerund.)
- The study abroad program might satisfy your desire for new experiences. (The gerund has been removed.)

Gerund as direct object:

- They do not appreciate my singing. (The gerund is **singing**.)
- They do not appreciate my assistance. (The gerund has been removed)

Gerund as subject complement:

- My cat's favorite activity is sleeping. (The gerund is **sleeping**.)
- My cat's favorite food is salmon. (The gerund has been removed.)

Gerund as object of preposition:

- The police arrested him for speeding. (The gerund is **speeding**.)
- The police arrested him for criminal activity. (The gerund has been removed.)

A Gerund Phrase is a group of words consisting of a gerund and the modifier(s) and/or (pro)noun(s) or noun phrase(s) that function as the direct object(s), indirect object(s), or complement(s) of the action or state expressed in the gerund, such as:

The gerund phrase functions as the subject of the sentence.

Finding **a needle** <u>in a haystack</u> would be easier than what we're trying to do.

Finding (gerund) **a needle** (direct object of action expressed in gerund) <u>in a haystack</u> (prepositional phrase as adverb)

The gerund phrase functions as the direct object of the verb *appreciate*.

I hope that you appreciate **my** offering you *this opportunity*.

my (possessive pronoun adjective form, modifying the gerund)
offering (gerund)
you (indirect object of action expressed in gerund)
this opportunity (direct object of action expressed in gerund)

The gerund phrase functions as the subject complement.

Ned's favorite tactic has been **lying to** his constituents.

lying to (gerund)
his constituents (direct object of action expressed in gerund)

The gerund phrase functions as the object of the preposition *for*.

You might get in trouble for **faking** an illness *to avoid work*.

faking (gerund)
an illness (direct object of action expressed in gerund)
to avoid work (infinitive phrase as adverb)

The gerund phrase functions as the subject of the sentence.

Being the boss made Jeff feel uneasy.

Being (gerund)
the boss (subject complement for Jeff, via state of being expressed in gerund)

Punctuation
A gerund virtually never requires any punctuation with it.

Points to remember:
1. A gerund is a verbal ending in -ing that is used as a noun.
2. A gerund phrase consists of a gerund plus modifier(s), object(s), and/or complement(s).
3. Gerunds and gerund phrases virtually never require punctuation.

Participles
A participle is a verbal that is used as an adjective and most often ends in -*ing* or -*ed*. The term *verbal* indicates that a participle, like the other two kinds of verbals, is based on a verb and therefore expresses action or a state of being. However, since they function as adjectives, participles modify nouns or pronouns. There are two types of participles: present participles and past participles. Present participles end in -*ing*. Past participles end in -*ed*, -*en*, -*d*, -*t*, or -*n*, as in the words *asked*, *eaten*, *saved*, *dealt*, and *seen*.

- The *crying* baby had a wet diaper.
- *Shaken*, he walked away from the *wrecked* car.
- The *burning* log fell off the fire.
- *Smiling*, she hugged the *panting* dog.

A participial phrase is a group of words consisting of a participle and the modifier(s) and/or (pro)noun(s) or noun phrase(s) that function as the direct object(s), indirect object(s), or complement(s) of the action or state expressed in the participle, such as:

Example: **Removing** his coat, Jack rushed to the river.

The participial phrase functions as an adjective modifying *Jack*.

Removing (participle)
his coat (direct object of action expressed in participle)

> Example: Delores noticed her cousin **walking** along the shoreline.

The participial phrase functions as an adjective modifying *cousin*.
walking (participle)
along the shoreline (prepositional phrase as adverb)

> Example: Children **introduced to** music early develop strong intellectual skills.

The participial phrase functions as an adjective modifying *children*.
introduced (to) (participle)
music (direct object of action expressed in participle)
early (adverb)

> Example: **Having been** a gymnast, Lynn knew the importance of exercise.

The participial phrase functions as an adjective modifying *Lynn*.
Having been (participle)
a gymnast (subject complement for Lynn, via state of being expressed in participle)

Placement: In order to prevent confusion, a participial phrase must be placed as close to the noun it modifies as possible, and the noun must be clearly stated.

- *Carrying a heavy pile of books,* his foot caught on a step.
- *Carrying a heavy pile of books,* he caught his foot on a step.

In the first sentence there is no clear indication of who or what is performing the action expressed in the participle carrying. Certainly foot can't be logically understood to function in this way. This situation is an example of a **dangling modifier** error since the modifier (the participial phrase) is not modifying any specific noun in the sentence and is thus left "dangling." Since a person must be doing the carrying for the sentence to make sense, a noun or pronoun that refers to a person must be in the place immediately after the participial phrase, as in the second sentence.

Punctuation: When a participial phrase begins a sentence, a comma should be placed after the phrase.

- *Arriving at the store,* I found that it was closed.
- *Washing and polishing the car,* Frank developed sore muscles.

If the participle or participial phrase comes in the middle of a sentence, it should be set off with commas only if the information is not essential to the meaning of the sentence.

- Sid, *watching an old movie,* drifted in and out of sleep.
- The church, *destroyed by a fire,* was never rebuilt.

Note that if the participial phrase is essential to the meaning of the sentence, no commas should be used:

- The student *earning the highest grade point average* will receive a special award.
- The guy *wearing the chicken costume* is my cousin.

If a participial phrase comes at the end of a sentence, a comma usually precedes the phrase if it modifies an earlier word in the sentence but not if the phrase directly follows the word it modifies.

- The local residents often saw Ken wandering through the streets.
  (The phrase modifies *Ken*, not *residents*.)
- Tom nervously watched the woman, alarmed by her silence.
  (The phrase modifies *Tom*, not *woman*.)

Points to remember

1. A participle is a verbal ending in *-ing* (present) or *-ed*, *-en*, *-d*, *-t*, or *-n* (past) that functions as an adjective, modifying a noun or pronoun.

2. A participial phrase consists of a participle plus modifier(s), object(s), and/or complement(s).

3. Participles and participial phrases must be placed as close to the nouns or pronouns they modify as possible, and those nouns or pronouns must be clearly stated.

4. A participial phrase is set off with commas when it:
   (a) comes at the beginning of a sentence
   (b) interrupts a sentence as a nonessential element
   (c) comes at the end of a sentence and is separated from the word it modifies.

Infinitives

An infinitive is a verbal consisting of the word *to* plus a verb (in its simplest "stem" form) and functioning as a noun, adjective, or adverb. The term *verbal* indicates that an infinitive, like the other two kinds of verbals, is based on a verb and therefore expresses action or a state of being. However, the infinitive may function as a subject, direct object, subject complement, adjective, or adverb in a sentence. Although an infinitive is easy to locate because of the *to* + verb form, deciding what function it has in a sentence can sometimes be confusing.

- *To wait* seemed foolish when decisive action was required. (subject)
- Everyone wanted *to go*. (direct object)
- His ambition is *to fly*. (subject complement)
- He lacked the strength *to resist*. (adjective)
- We must study *to learn*. (adverb)

Be sure not to confuse an infinitive—a verbal consisting of *to* plus a verb—with a prepositional phrase beginning with *to*, which consists of *to* plus a noun or pronoun and any modifiers.

- **Infinitives:** to fly, to draw, to become, to enter, to stand, to catch, to belong
- **Prepositional Phrases:** to him, to the committee, to my house, to the mountains, to us, to this address

An Infinitive Phrase is a group of words consisting of an infinitive and the modifier(s) and/or (pro)noun(s) or noun phrase(s) that function as the actor(s), direct object(s), indirect object(s), or complement(s) of the action or state expressed in the infinitive, such as:

We intended **to leave early**.

The infinitive phrase functions as the direct object of the verb *intended*.

to leave (infinitive)
early (adverb)

I have a paper **to write before class**.

The infinitive phrase functions as an adjective modifying *paper*.

to write (infinitive)
before class (prepositional phrase as adverb)

Phil agreed **to give me** *a ride*.

The infinitive phrase functions as the direct object of the verb *agreed*.

to give (infinitive)
me (indirect object of action expressed in infinitive)
a ride (direct object of action expressed in infinitive)

They asked **me** to bring *some food*.

The infinitive phrase functions as the direct object of the verb *asked*.

me (actor or "subject" of infinitive phrase)
to bring (infinitive)
some food (direct object of action expressed in infinitive)

Everyone wanted **Carol** to be **the captain** *of the team*.

The infinitive phrase functions as the direct object of the verb *wanted*.

Carol (actor or "subject" of infinitive phrase)
to be (infinitive)
the captain (subject complement for Carol, via state of being expressed in infinitive)
of the team (prepositional phrase as adjective)

Actors: In these last two examples the actor of the infinitive phrase could be roughly characterized as the "subject" of the action or state expressed in the infinitive. It is somewhat misleading to use the word *subject*, however, since an infinitive phrase is not a full clause with a subject and a finite verb. Also notice that when it is a pronoun, the actor appears in the objective case (*me*, not *I*, in the fourth example). Certain verbs, when they take an infinitive direct object, require an actor for the infinitive phrase; others can't have an actor. Still other verbs can go either way, as the charts below illustrate.

Verbs that take infinitive objects without actors:			
agree	begin	continue	decide
fail	hesitate	hope	intend
learn	neglect	offer	plan
prefer	pretend	promise	refuse
remember	start	try	

Examples:

- Most students *plan* to study.
- We *began* to learn.
- They *offered* to pay.
- They *neglected* to pay.
- She *promised* to return.

In all of these examples no actor can come between the italicized main (finite) verb and the infinitive direct-object phrase.

Verbs that take infinitive objects with actors:			
advise	allow	convince	remind
encourage	force	hire	teach
instruct	invite	permit	tell
implore	incite	appoint	order

Examples:

- He *reminded* me to buy milk.
- Their fathers *advise* them to study.
- She *forced* the defendant to admit the truth.
- You've *convinced* the director of the program to change her position.
- I *invite* you to consider the evidence.

In all of these examples an actor is required after the italicized main (finite) verb and before the infinitive direct-object phrase.

Verbs that use either pattern:				
ask	expect	(would) like	want	need

Examples:

- I *asked* to see the records.
- I *asked* him to show me the records.
- Trent *expected* his group to win.
- Trent *expected* to win.
- Brenda *likes* to drive fast.
- Brenda *likes* her friend to drive fast.

In all of these examples the italicized main verb can take an infinitive object with or without an actor.

Punctuation: If the infinitive is used as an adverb and is the beginning phrase in a sentence, it should be set off with a comma; otherwise, no punctuation is needed for an infinitive phrase.

- To buy a basket of flowers, John had to spend his last dollar.
- To improve your writing, you must consider your purpose and audience.

Points to remember:

1. An infinitive is a verbal consisting of the word *to* plus a verb; it may be used as a noun, adjective, or adverb.
2. An infinitive phrase consists of an infinitive plus modifier(s), object(s), complement(s), and/or actor(s).
3. An infinitive phrase requires a comma only if it is used as an adverb at the beginning of a sentence.

Split infinitives

Split infinitives occur when additional words are included between *to* and the verb in an infinitive. Many readers find a single adverb splitting the infinitive to be acceptable, but this practice should be avoided in formal writing.

Examples:

- I like *to* on a nice day *walk* in the woods. (unacceptable)
  On a nice day, I like *to walk* in the woods. (revised)
- I needed *to* quickly *gather* my personal possessions. (acceptable in informal contexts)
  I needed *to gather* my personal possessions quickly. (revised for formal contexts)

Part 5: Prepositions for Time, Place, and Introducing Objects

One point in time

On is used with days:

- I will see you on Monday.
- The week begins on Sunday.

At is used with noon, night, midnight, and with the time of day:

- My plane leaves at noon.
- The movie starts at 6 p.m.

In is used with other parts of the day, with months, with years, with seasons:

- He likes to read in the afternoon.
- The days are long in August.
- The book was published in 1999.
- The flowers will bloom in spring.

Extended time

To express extended time, English uses the following prepositions: **since, for, by, from–to, from–until, during, (with)in**

- She has been gone since yesterday. *(She left yesterday and has not returned.)*
- I'm going to Paris for two weeks. *(I will spend two weeks there.)*
- The movie showed from August to October. *(Beginning in August and ending in October.)*
- The decorations were up from spring until fall. *(Beginning in spring and ending in fall.)*
- I watch TV during the evening. *(For some period of time in the evening.)*
- We must finish the project within a year. *(No longer than a year.)*

Place

To express notions of place, English uses the following prepositions: to talk about the point itself: **in**, to express something contained: **inside**, to talk about the surface: **on**, to talk about a general vicinity, **at**.

- There is a wasp in the room.
- Put the present inside the box.
- I left your keys on the table.
- She was waiting at the corner.

To introduce objects of verbs

English uses the following prepositions to introduce objects of the following verbs.

At: glance, laugh, look, rejoice, smile, stare
- She took a quick glance at her reflection.
  (*exception with* **mirror**: She took a quick glance in the mirror.)
- You didn't laugh at his joke.
- I'm looking at the computer monitor.
- We rejoiced at his safe rescue.
- That pretty girl smiled at you.
- Stop staring at me.

Of: approve, consist, smell
- I don't approve **of** his speech.
- My contribution to the article consists **of** many pages.
- He came home smelling **of** garlic.

Of (or about): dream, think
- I dream **of** finishing college in four years.
- Can you think **of** a number between one and ten?
- I am thinking **about** this problem.

For: call, hope, look, wait, watch, wish
- Did someone call **for** a taxi?
- He hopes **for** a raise in salary next year.
- I'm looking **for** my keys.
- We'll wait **for** her here.
- You go buy the tickets and I'll watch **for** the train.
- If you wish **for** an "A" in this class, you must work hard.

Part 6: Identifying Independent and Dependent Clauses

When you want to use commas and semicolons in sentences and when you are concerned about whether a sentence is or is not a fragment, a good way to start is to be able to recognize dependent and independent clauses. The definitions offered here will help you with this.

Independent Clause

An independent clause is a group of words that contains a subject and verb and expresses a complete thought. An independent clause is a sentence.

Jim studied in the Sweet Shop for his chemistry quiz.

Dependent Clause

A dependent clause is a group of words that contains a subject and verb but does not express a complete thought. A dependent clause cannot be a sentence. Often a dependent clause is marked by a **dependent marker word**.

When Jim studied in the Sweet Shop for his chemistry quiz . . . (What happened when he studied? The thought is incomplete.)

Dependent Marker Word

A dependent marker word is a word added to the beginning of an independent clause that makes it into a dependent clause.

When Jim studied in the Sweet Shop for his chemistry quiz, it was very noisy.

Some common dependent markers are: **after, although, as, as if, because, before, even if, even though, if, in order to, since, though, unless, until, whatever, when, whenever, whether,** and **while.**

Connecting Dependent and Independent Clauses

There are two types of words that can be used as connectors at the beginning of an independent clause: coordinating conjunctions and independent marker words.

1. Coordinating Conjunction

The seven coordinating conjunctions used as connecting words at the beginning of an independent clause are **and, but, for, or, nor, so,** and **yet.** When the second independent clause in a sentence begins with a coordinating conjunction, a comma is needed before the coordinating conjunction:

Jim studied in the Sweet Shop for his chemistry quiz, **but** it was hard to concentrate because of the noise.

2. Independent Marker Word

An independent marker word is a connecting word used at the beginning of an independent clause. These words can always begin a sentence that can stand alone. When the second independent clause in a sentence has an independent marker word, a semicolon is needed before the independent marker word.

Jim studied in the Sweet Shop for his chemistry quiz; **however**, it was hard to concentrate because of the noise.

Some common independent markers are: **also**, **consequently**, **furthermore**, **however**, **moreover**, **nevertheless**, and **therefore**.

Some Common Errors to Avoid

Comma Splices

A comma splice is the use of a comma between two independent clauses. You can usually fix the error by changing the comma to a period and therefore making the two clauses into two separate sentences, by changing the comma to a semicolon, or by making one clause dependent by inserting a dependent marker word in front of it.

Incorrect: I like this class, it is very interesting.

Correct: I like this class. It is very interesting.
- (or) I like this class; it is very interesting.
- (or) I like this class, and it is very interesting.
- (or) I like this class because it is very interesting.
- (or) Because it is very interesting, I like this class.

Fused Sentences

Fused sentences happen when there are two independent clauses not separated by any form of punctuation. This error is also known as a run-on sentence. The error can sometimes be corrected by adding a period, semicolon, or colon to separate the two sentences.

Incorrect: My professor is intelligent I've learned a lot from her.

Correct: My professor is intelligent. I've learned a lot from her.
- (or) My professor is intelligent; I've learned a lot from her.
- (or) My professor is intelligent, and I've learned a lot from her.
- (or) My professor is intelligent; moreover, I've learned a lot from her.

Sentence Fragments

Sentence fragments happen by treating a dependent clause or other incomplete thought as a complete sentence. You can usually fix this error by combining it with another sentence to make a complete thought or by removing the dependent marker.

Incorrect: Because I forgot the exam was today.

Correct: Because I forgot the exam was today, I didn't study.
- (or) I forgot the exam was today.

Part 7: Parallel Structure

Parallel structure means using the same pattern of words to show that two or more ideas have the same level of importance. This can happen at the word, phrase, or clause level. The usual way to join parallel structures is with the use of coordinating **conjunctions** such as "and" or "or."

Words and Phrases

With the -ing form (gerund) of words:

Parallel: Mary likes hiking, swimming, and bicycling.

With infinitive phrases:

Parallel: Mary likes **to hike, to swim,** and **to ride** a bicycle.
OR
Mary likes to **hike, swim,** and **ride** a bicycle.

(Note: You can use "to" before all the verbs in a sentence or only before the first one.)

Do not mix forms.

Example 1

Not Parallel:
Mary likes hiking, swimming, and **to ride** a bicycle.

Parallel:
Mary likes hiking, swimming, and riding a bicycle.

Example 2

Not Parallel:
The production manager was asked to write his report quickly, accurate **ly,** and **in a detailed manner.**

Parallel:
The production manager was asked to write his report quickly, accurately, and thoroughly.

Example 3

Not Parallel:
The teacher said that he was a poor student because he waited until the last minute to study for the exam, completed his lab problems in a careless manner, and **his motivation was** low.

Parallel:
The teacher said that he was a poor student because he waited until the last minute to study for the exam, completed his lab problems in a careless manner, and lacked motivation.

Clauses

A parallel structure that begins with clauses must keep on with clauses. Changing to another pattern or changing the voice of the verb (from active to passive or vice versa) will break the parallelism.

Example 1

Not Parallel:
The coach told the players **that they should get** a lot of sleep, **that they should not eat** too much, and to do some warm-up exercises before the game.

Parallel:
The coach told the players **that they should get** a lot of sleep, **that they should not eat** too much, and **that they should do** some warm-up exercises before the game.

OR

Parallel:
The coach told the players that they should **get** a lot of sleep, not **eat** too much, and **do** some warm-up exercises before the game.

Example 2

Not Parallel:
The salesman expected **that he would present** his product at the meeting, **that there would be** time for him to show his slide presentation, and **that questions would be asked** by prospective buyers. **(passive)**

Parallel:
The salesman expected **that he would present** his product at the meeting, **that there would be** time for him to show his slide presentation, and **that prospective buyers would ask** him questions.

Lists After a Colon

Be sure to keep all the elements in a list in the same form.

Example 1

Not Parallel:
The dictionary can be used for these purposes: to find **word meanings, pronunciations, correct spellings,** and **looking up irregular verbs**.

Parallel:
The dictionary can be used for these purposes: to find **word meanings, pronunciations, correct spellings,** and **irregular verbs**.

Proofreading Strategies to Try:

- Skim your paper, pausing at the words "and" and "or." Check on each side of these words to see whether the items joined are parallel. If not, make them parallel.
- If you have several items in a list, put them in a column to see if they are parallel.
- Listen to the sound of the items in a list or the items being compared. Do you hear the same kinds of sounds? For example, is there a series of "-ing" words beginning each item? Or do your hear a rhythm being repeated? If something is breaking that rhythm or repetition of sound, check to see if it needs to be made parallel.

Part 8: Introduction and General Usage in Defining Clauses

Relative pronouns are **that, who, whom, whose, which, where, when,** and **why.** They are used to join clauses to make a complex sentence. Relative pronouns are used at the beginning of the subordinate clause which gives some specific information about the main clause.

This is the house *that* Jack built.
I don't know the day *when* Jane marries him.
The professor, *whom* I respect, was tenured.

In English, the choice of the relative pronoun depends on the type of clause it is used in. There are two types of clauses distinguished: *defining (restrictive)* relative clauses and *non-defining (non-restrictive)* relative clauses. In both types of clauses the relative pronoun can function as a subject, an object, or a possessive.

Relative Pronouns in Defining Clauses

Defining relative clauses (also known as *restrictive relative clauses*) provide some essential information that explains the main clause. The information is crucial for understanding the sentence correctly and cannot be omitted. Defining clauses are opened by a relative pronoun and **ARE NOT** separated by a comma from the main clause.

The table below sums up the use of relative pronouns in defining clauses:

Function in the sentence	Reference to				
	People	Things/concepts	Place	Time	Reason
Subject	who, that	which, that			
Object	(that, who, whom)	(which, that)	where	when	why
Possessive	whose	whose, of which			

Examples

Relative pronoun used as a subject:

> This is the house *that* had a great Christmas decoration.
> It took me a while to get used to people *who* eat popcorn during the movie.

Relative pronoun used as an object:

1. As can be seen from the table, referring to a person or thing, the relative pronoun **may be omitted** in the object position:

    > This is the man (who / that) I wanted to speak to and whose name I'd forgotten.

    > The library didn't have the book (which / that) I wanted.

    > I didn't like the book (which / that) John gave me.

    > This is the house *where* I lived *when* I first came to the US.

2. In American English, *whom* is not used very often. **Whom** is more formal than *who* and is very often omitted in **speech**:

    > **Grammatically Correct:** The woman to *whom* you have just spoken is my teacher.

    > **Common in Speech:** The woman (*who*) you have just spoken to is my teacher.

However, *whom* may not be omitted if preceded by a preposition:

> I have found you the tutor <u>for</u> *whom* you were looking.

Relative pronoun used as a possessive:

Whose is the only possessive relative pronoun in English. It can be used with both people and things:

> The family *whose* house burnt in the fire was immediately given a suite in a hotel.
> The book *whose* author is now being shown in the news has become a bestseller.

General remarks: That, Who, Which compared

The relative pronoun *that* can only be used in defining clauses. It can also be substituted for *who* (referring to persons) or *which* (referring to things). *That* is often used in speech; *who* and *which* are more common in written English.

> William Kellogg was the man *that* lived in the late 19th century and had some weird ideas about raising children. (spoken, less formal)

William Kellogg was the man *who* lived in the late 19th century and had some weird ideas about raising children. (written, more formal)

Although your computer may suggest to correct it, referring to things, *which* may be used in the defining clause to put additional emphasis on the explanation. Again, the sentence with *which* is more formal than the one with *that*: Note that since it is the defining clause, there is NO comma used preceding *which*:

The café *that* sells the best coffee in town has recently been closed. (less formal)
The café *which* sells the best coffee in town has recently been closed. (more formal)

Some special uses of relative pronouns in defining clauses

that / who
Referring to people, both *that* and *who* can be used. *That* may be used to refer to someone in general:

He is the kind of person *that/who* will never let you down.
I am looking for someone *that/who* could give me a ride to Chicago.

However, when a particular person is being spoken about, *who* is preferred:

The old lady *who* lives next door is a teacher.
The girl *who* wore a red dress attracted everybody's attention at the party.

that / which
There are several cases when *that* is more appropriate and is preferred to *which*.

After the pronouns *all, any(thing), every(thing), few, little, many, much, no(thing), none, some(thing)*:

The police usually ask for every detail *that* helps identify the missing person. (*that* used as the subject)
Marrying a congressman is *all* (that) she wants. (*that* used as the object)

After verbs that answer the question **WHAT?** For example, *say, suggest, state, declare, hope, think, write*, etc. In this case, the whole relative clause functions as the object of the main clause:

Some people *say* (that) success is one percent of talent and ninety-nine percent of hard work.
The chairman *stated* at the meeting (that) his company is part of a big-time entertainment industry.

After the noun modified by an adjective *in the superlative degree*:

This is the *funniest* story (that) I have ever read! (*that* used as the object)

After ordinal numbers, e.g., *first, second, etc.*:

The first draft (that) we submitted was really horrible. (*that* used as the object)

If the verb in the main clause is a form of *BE*:

This is a claim that has absolutely no reason in it. (*that* used as the subject)

Relative Pronouns in Non-Defining Clauses
Non-defining relative clauses (also known as non-restrictive, or parenthetical, clauses) provide some additional information which is not essential and may be omitted without affecting the contents of the sentence. All relative pronouns EXCEPT "that" can be used in non-defining clauses; however, the pronouns MAY NOT be omitted. Non-defining clauses ARE separated by commas.

The table below sums up the use of relative pronouns in non-defining clauses:

Function in the sentence	Reference to				
	People	Things/concepts	Place	Time	Reason
Subject	who	which			
Object	who, whom	which	where	when	why
Possessive	whose	whose, of which			

a. **Relative pronoun used as a subject:**

The writer, **who** lives in this luxurious mansion, has just published his second novel.

b. **Relative pronoun used as an object:**

The house at the end of the street, **which** my grandfather built, needs renovating.

c. **Relative pronoun used as a possessive:**

William Kellogg, **whose** name has become a famous breakfast foods brand-name, had some weird ideas about raising children.

Some Special Uses of Relative Pronouns in Non-Defining Clauses

a. **which**
If you are referring to the previous clause as a whole, use *which*:
My friend eventually decided to get divorced, **which** upset me a lot.

b. **of whom, of which**
Use *of whom* for persons and *of which* for things or concepts after numbers and words such as *most, many, some, both, none*:
I saw a lot of new people at the party, some **of whom** seemed familiar.
He was always coming up with new ideas, most **of which** were absolutely impracticable.

Part 9: Sentence Types and Punctuation Patterns

To punctuate a sentence, you can use and combine some of these patterns.

Pattern One: Simple Sentence
This pattern is an example of a simple sentence:

Independent clause [.]

Example: Doctors are concerned about the rising death rate from asthma.

Pattern Two: Compound Sentence
This pattern is an example of a compound sentence with a coordinating conjunction:

Independent clause [,] coordinating conjunction **independent clause** [.]

There are seven coordinating conjunctions: and, but, for, or, nor, so, yet.

Example: Doctors are concerned about the rising death rate from asthma, but they don't know the reasons for it.

Pattern Three: Compound Sentence

This pattern is an example of a compound sentence with a semicolon.

> Independent clause [;] independent clause [.]

> Example: Doctors are concerned about the rising death rate from asthma; they are unsure of its cause.

Pattern Four: Compound Sentence

This pattern is an example of a compound sentence with an independent marker.

> Independent clause [;] independent marker [,] independent clause [.]

Examples of independent markers are the following: **therefore, moreover, thus, consequently, however, also.**

> Example: Doctors are concerned about the rising death rate from asthma; therefore, they have called for more research into its causes.

Pattern Five: Complex Sentence

This pattern is an example of a complex sentence with a dependent marker.

> *Dependent marker* dependent clause [,] Independent clause [.]

Examples of dependent markers are as follows: **because, before, since, while, although, if, until, when, after, as, as if.**

> Example: *Because* doctors are concerned about the rising death rate from asthma, they have called for more research into its causes.

Pattern Six: Complex Sentence

This pattern is an example of a complex sentence with a dependent marker following the independent clause.

> Independent clause dependent marker dependent clause [.]

> Example: Doctors are concerned about the rising death rate from asthma because it is a common, treatable illness.

Pattern Seven

This pattern includes an independent clause with an embedded non-essential clause or phrase. A non-essential clause or phrase is one that can be removed without changing the meaning of the sentence or making it ungrammatical. In other words, the non-essential clause or phrase gives additional information, but the sentence can stand alone without it.

> First part of an independent clause [,] non-essential clause or phrase, rest of the independent clause [.]

> Example: Many doctors, including both pediatricians and family practice physicians, are concerned about the rising death rate from asthma.

Pattern Eight

This pattern includes an independent clause with an embedded essential clause or phrase. An essential clause or phrase is one that cannot be removed without changing the overall meaning of the sentence.

> First part of an independent clause essential clause or phrase rest of the independent clause [.]

> Example: Many doctors who are concerned about the rising death rate from asthma have called for more research into its causes.

Part 10: Making Subjects and Verbs Agree

1. When the subject of a sentence is composed of two or more nouns or pronouns connected by *and*, use a plural verb.

    She and **her friends** <u>are</u> at the fair.

2. When two or more singular nouns or pronouns are connected by *or* or *nor*, use a singular verb.

    The book or **the pen** <u>is</u> in the drawer.

3. When a compound subject contains both a singular and a plural noun or pronoun joined by *or* or *nor*, the verb should agree with the part of the subject that is nearer the verb.

    The boy or **his friends** <u>run</u> every day.
    His friends or **the boy** <u>runs</u> every day.

4. *Doesn't* is a contraction of *does not* and should be used only with a singular subject. *Don't* is a contraction of *do not* and should be used only with a plural subject. The exception to this rule appears in the case of the first person and second person pronouns *I* and *you*. With these pronouns, the contraction *don't* should be used. [Note that formal writing generally avoids the use of contractions.]

    He doesn't <u>like</u> it.
    They don't <u>like</u> it.

5. Do not be misled by a phrase that comes between the subject and the verb. The verb agrees with the subject, not with a noun or pronoun in the phrase.

    One of the boxes <u>is</u> open
    The people who listen to that music <u>are</u> few.
    The team captain, as well as his players, <u>is</u> anxious.
    The book, including all the chapters in the first section, <u>is</u> boring.
    The woman with all the dogs <u>walks</u> down my street.

6. The words *each*, *each one*, *either*, *neither*, *everyone*, *everybody*, *anybody*, *anyone*, *nobody*, *somebody*, *someone*, and *no one* are singular and require a singular verb.

    Each of these hot dogs <u>is</u> juicy.
    Everybody <u>knows</u> Mr. Jones.
    Either <u>is</u> correct.

7. Nouns such as *civics*, *mathematics*, *dollars*, *measles*, and *news* require singular verbs.

    The news <u>is</u> on at six.

    Note: The word **dollars** is a special case. When talking about an amount of money, it requires a singular verb, but when referring to the dollars themselves, a plural verb is required.

    Five dollars <u>is</u> a lot of money.
    Dollars <u>are</u> often used instead of rubles in Russia.

8. Nouns such as *scissors*, *tweezers*, *trousers*, and *shears* require plural verbs. (There are two parts to these things.)

    These scissors <u>are</u> dull.
    Those trousers <u>are</u> made of wool.

9. In sentences beginning with *there is* or *there are*, the subject follows the verb. Since *there* is not the subject, the verb agrees with what follows.

There **are** many questions.
There **is** a question.

10. Collective nouns are words that imply more than one person but that are considered singular and take a singular verb, such as: *group*, *team*, *committee*, *class*, and *family*.

   The team **runs** during practice.
   The committee **decides** how to proceed.
   The family **has** a long history.
   My family **has never been able to agree**.

   In some cases, a sentence may call for the use of a plural verb when using a collective noun.

   The crew **are preparing** to dock the ship.

   This sentence is referring to the individual efforts of each crew member.

11. Expressions such as *with*, *together with*, *including*, *accompanied by*, *in addition to*, or *as well* do not change the number of the subject. If the subject is singular, the verb is too.

   The President, accompanied by his wife, **is** traveling to India.
   All of the books, including yours, **are** in that box.

Sequence of Tenses

Simple Present: They walk.

Present Perfect: They have walked.

Simple Past: They walked.

Past Perfect: They had walked.

Future: They will walk.

Future Perfect: They will have walked.

Problems in sequencing tenses usually occur with the perfect tenses, all of which are formed by adding an auxiliary or auxiliaries to the past participle, the third principal part.

   ring, rang, rung
   walk, walked, walked

The most common auxiliaries are forms of "be," "can," "do," "may," "must," "ought," "shall," "will," "has," "have," "had," and they are the forms we shall use in this most basic discussion.

Present Perfect

The present perfect consists of a past participle (the third principal part) with "has" or "have." It designates action which began in the past but which continues into the present or the effect of which still continues.

   1. Betty taught for ten years. (simple past)
   2. Betty has taught for ten years. (present perfect)

The implication in (1) is that Betty has retired; in (2), that she is still teaching.

   1. John did his homework. He can go to the movies.
   2. If John has done his homework, he can go to the movies.

Infinitives, too, have perfect tense forms when combined with "have," and sometimes problems arise when infinitives are used with verbs such as "hope," "plan," "expect," and "intend," all of which usually point to the future (I wanted to go to the movie. Janet meant to see the doctor.) The perfect tense sets up a sequence by marking the action which began and usually was completed before the action in the main verb.

1. I am happy to have participated in this campaign!
2. John had hoped to have won the trophy.

Thus the action of the main verb points back in time; the action of the perfect infinitive has been completed.

The past perfect tense designates action in the past just as simple past does, but the action of the past perfect is action completed in the past before another action.

1. John raised vegetables and later sold them. (past)
2. John sold vegetables that he had raised. (past perfect)

The vegetables were raised before they were sold.

1. Renee washed the car when George arrived. (simple past)
2. Renee had washed the car when George arrived. (past perfect)

In (1), she waited until George arrived and then washed the car. In (2), she had already finished washing the car by the time he arrived.

In sentences expressing condition and result, the past perfect tense is used in the part that states the condition.

1. If I had done my exercises, I would have passed the test.
2. I think George would have been elected if he hadn't sounded so pompous.

Future Perfect Tense

The future perfect tense designates action that will have been completed at a specified time in the future.

1. Saturday I will finish my housework. (simple future)
2. By Saturday noon, I will have finished my housework. (future perfect)

Part 11: Using Active Versus Passive Voice

In a sentence using **active voice**, the subject of the sentence performs the action expressed in the verb.

The dog *bit* the boy.

The arrow points from the subject performing the action (the dog) to the individual being acted upon (the boy). This is an example of a sentence using the active voice.

Scientists *have conducted* experiments to test the hypothesis.

Sample active voice sentence with the subject performing the action described by the verb.

Watching a framed, mobile world through a car's windshield *reminds* me of watching a movie or TV.

The active voice sentence subject (watching a framed, mobile world) performs the action of reminding the speaker of something.

Each example above includes a sentence subject performing the action expressed by the verb.

Examples:

	Active	Passive
Simple Present	• The company ships the computers to many foreign countries.	• Computers are shipped to many foreign countries
Present Progressive	• The chef is preparing the food.	• The food is being prepared.
Simple Past	• The delivery man delivered the package yesterday.	• The package was delivered yesterday.
Past Progressive	• The producer was making an announcement.	• An announcement was being made.
Future	• Our representative will pick up the computer.	• The computer will be picked up.
Present Perfect	• Someone has made the arrangements for us.	• The arrangements have been made for us.
Past Perfect	• They had given us visas for three months.	• They had been given visas for three months.
Future Perfect	• By next month we will have finished this job.	• By next month this job will have been finished.

Part 12: Irregular Verbs: Overview and List

In English, regular verbs consist of three main parts: the root form (present), the (simple) past, and the past participle. Regular verbs have an *-ed* ending added to the root verb for both the simple past and past participle. Irregular verbs do not follow this pattern, and instead take on an alternative pattern.

The following is a partial list of irregular verbs found in English. Each listing consists of the present/root form of the verb, the (simple) past form of the verb, and the past participle form of the verb.

List of Irregular Verbs in English

Present	Past	Past Participle
be	was, were	been
become	became	become
begin	began	begun
blow	blew	blown
break	broke	broken
bring	brought	brought
build	built	built
burst	burst	burst
buy	bought	bought
catch	caught	caught
choose	chose	chosen
come	came	come
cut	cut	cut

Present	Past	Past Participle
deal	dealt	dealt
do	did	done
drink	drank	drunk
drive	drove	driven
eat	ate	eaten
fall	fell	fallen
feed	fed	fed
feel	felt	felt
fight	fought	fought
find	found	found
fly	flew	flown
forbid	forbade	forbidden
forget	forgot	forgotten

Present	Past	Past Participle
forgive	forgave	forgiven
freeze	froze	frozen
get	got	gotten
give	gave	given
go	went	gone
grow	grew	grown
have	had	had
hear	heard	heard
hide	hid	hidden
hold	held	held
hurt	hurt	hurt
keep	kept	kept
know	knew	known
lay	laid	laid
lead	led	led
leave	left	left
let	let	let
lie	lay	lain
lose	lost	lost
make	made	made
meet	met	met
pay	paid	paid
quit	quit	quit
read	read	read
ride	rode	ridden
run	ran	run
say	said	said

Present	Past	Past Participle
see	saw	seen
seek	sought	sought
sell	sold	sold
send	sent	sent
shake	shook	sent
shine	shone	shone
sing	sang	sung
sit	sat	sat
sleep	slept	slept
speak	spoke	spoken
spend	spent	spent
spring	sprang	sprung
stand	stood	stood
steal	stole	stolen
swim	swam	swum
swing	swung	swung
take	took	taken
teach	taught	taught
tear	tore	torn
tell	told	told
think	thought	thought
throw	threw	thrown
understand	understood	understood
wake	woke (waked)	woken (waked)
wear	wore	worn
win	won	won
write	wrote	written

Commonly Confused Verbs

LIE versus LAY

Lie vs. Lay Usage		
Present	Past	Past Participle
lie, lying (to tell a falsehood)	I lied to my mother.	I have lied under oath.
lie, lying (to recline)	I lay on the bed because I was tired.	He has lain in the grass.
lay, laying (to put, place)	I laid the baby in her cradle.	We have laid the dishes on the table.

Example sentences:

After **laying** down his weapon, the soldier **lay** down to sleep.

Will you **lay** out my clothes while I **lie** down to rest?

SIT versus SET

Sit vs. Set Usage		
Present	Past	Past Participle
sit (to be seated or come to resting position)	I sat in my favorite chair.	You have sat there for three hours.
set (to put or place)	I set my glass on the table.	She has set her books on my desk again.

Example sentence:

Let's **set** the table before we **sit** down to rest.

RISE versus RAISE

Rise vs. Raise Usage		
Present	Past	Past Participle
rise (steady or customary upward movement)	The balloon rose into the air.	He has risen to a position of power.
raise (to cause to rise)	They raised their hands because they knew the answer.	I have raised the curtain many times.

Example sentence:

The boy **raised** the flag just before the sun **rose**.

Part 13: Capitalization and Punctuation

A Little Help with Capitals

If you have a question about whether a specific word should be capitalized that doesn't fit under one of these rules, try checking a dictionary to see if the word is capitalized there.

Use capital letters in the following ways:

The first words of a sentence

When he tells a joke, he sometimes forgets the punch line.

The pronoun "I"

The last time I visited Atlanta was several years ago.

Proper nouns (the names of specific people, places, organizations, and sometimes things)

Worrill Fabrication Company
Golden Gate Bridge
Supreme Court
Livingston, Missouri
Atlantic Ocean
Mothers Against Drunk Driving

Family relationships (when used as proper names)

I sent a thank-you note to Aunt Abigail, but not to my other aunts.
Here is a present I bought for Mother.
Did you buy a present for your mother?

The names of God, specific deities, religious figures, and holy books

God the Father
the Virgin Mary
the Bible
the Greek gods
Moses
Shiva
Buddha
Zeus

Exception: Do not capitalize the non-specific use of the word "god."

The word "polytheistic" means the worship of more than one god.

Titles preceding names, but not titles that follow names

She worked as the assistant to Mayor Hanolovi.
I was able to interview Miriam Moss, mayor of Littonville.

Directions that are names (North, South, East, and West when used as sections of the country, but not as compass directions)

The Patels have moved to the Southwest.
Jim's house is two miles north of Otterbein.

The days of the week, the months of the year, and holidays (but not the seasons used generally)

Halloween
October
Friday
winter
spring
fall

Exception: Seasons are capitalized when used in a title.

The Fall 1999 Semester

The names of countries, nationalities, and specific languages

Costa Rica
Spanish
French
English

The first word in a sentence that is a direct quote

Emerson once said, "A foolish consistency is the hobgoblin of little minds."

The major words in the titles of books, articles, and songs (but not short prepositions or the articles "the," "a," or "an," if they are not the first word of the title)

One of Jerry's favorite books is *The Catcher in the Rye*.

Members of national, political, racial, social, civic, and athletic groups

Green Bay Packers
African-Americans
Democrats
Friends of the Wilderness
Chinese

Periods and events (but not century numbers)

Victorian Era
Great Depression
Constitutional Convention
sixteenth century

Trademarks

Pepsi
Honda
IBM
Microsoft Word

Words and abbreviations of specific names (but not names of things that came from specific things but are now general types)

Freudian	UN
NBC	french fries
pasteurize	italics

Comma

Use a comma to join two independent clauses by a comma and a coordinating conjunction (*and, but, or, for, nor, so*).

Road construction can be inconvenient, but it is necessary.

The new house has a large fenced backyard, so I am sure our dog will enjoy it.

Use a comma after an introductory phrase, prepositional phrase, or dependent clause.

To get a good grade, you must complete all your assignments.

Because Dad caught the chicken pox, we canceled our vacation.

After the wedding, the guests attended the reception.

Use a comma to separate elements in a series. Although there is no set rule that requires a comma before the last item in a series, it seems to be a general academic convention to include it. The examples below demonstrate this trend.

On her vacation, Lisa visited Greece, Spain, and Italy.

In their speeches, many of the candidates promised to help protect the environment, bring about world peace, and end world hunger.

Use a comma to separate nonessential elements from a sentence. More specifically, when a sentence includes information that is not crucial to the message or intent of the sentence, enclose it in or separate it by commas.

John's truck, a red Chevrolet, needs new tires.

When he realized he had overslept, Matt rushed to his car and hurried to work.

Use a comma between coordinate adjectives (adjectives that are equal and reversible).

The irritable, fidgety crowd waited impatiently for the rally speeches to begin.

The sturdy, compact suitcase made a perfect gift.

Use a comma after a transitional element (*however, therefore, nonetheless, also, otherwise, finally, instead, thus, of course, above all, for example, in other words, as a result, on the other hand, in conclusion, in addition*)

For example, the Red Sox, Yankees, and Indians are popular baseball teams.

If you really want to get a good grade this semester, however, you must complete all assignments, attend class, and study your notes.

Use a comma with quoted words.

"Yes," she promised. Todd replied, saying, "I will be back this afternoon."

Use a comma in a date.

October 25, 1999
Monday, October 25, 1999
25 October 1999

Use a comma in a number.

15,000,000
1614 High Street

Use a comma in a personal title.

Pam Smith, MD
Mike Rose, Chief Financial Officer for Operations, reported the quarter's earnings.

Use a comma to separate a city name from the state.

West Lafayette, Indiana
Dallas, Texas

Avoid comma splices (two independent clauses joined only by a comma). Instead, separate the clauses with a period, with a comma followed by a coordinating conjunction, or with a semicolon.

Semicolon

Use a semicolon to join two independent clauses when the second clause restates the first or when the two clauses are of equal emphasis.

Road construction in Dallas has hindered travel around town; streets have become covered with bulldozers, trucks, and cones.

Use a semicolon to join two independent clauses when the second clause begins with a conjunctive adverb (*however, therefore, moreover, furthermore, thus, meanwhile, nonetheless, otherwise*) or a transition (*in fact, for example, that is, for instance, in addition, in other words, on the other hand, even so*).

Terrorism in the United States has become a recent concern; in fact, the concern for America's safety has led to an awareness of global terrorism.

Use a semicolon to join elements of a series when individual items of the series already include commas.

Recent sites of the Olympic Games include Athens, Greece; Salt Lake City, Utah; Sydney, Australia; Nagano, Japan.

Colon

Use a colon to join two independent clauses when you wish to emphasize the second clause.

> Road construction in Dallas has hindered travel around town: parts of Main, Fifth, and West Street are closed during the construction.

Use a colon after an independent clause when it is followed by a list, a quotation, an appositive, or other idea directly related to the independent clause.

> Julie went to the store for some groceries: milk, bread, coffee, and cheese.

> In his Gettysburg Address, Abraham Lincoln urges Americans to rededicate themselves to the unfinished work of the deceased soldiers: "It is for us the living rather to be dedicated here to the unfinished work which they who fought here have thus far so nobly advanced. It is rather for us to be here dedicated to the great task remaining before us — that from these honored dead we take increased devotion to that cause for which they gave the last full measure of devotion — that we here highly resolve that these dead shall not have died in vain, that this nation under God shall have a new birth of freedom, and that government of the people, by the people, for the people shall not perish from the earth."

> I know the perfect job for her: a politician.

Use a colon at the end of a business letter greeting.

> To Whom It May Concern:

Use a colon to separate the hour and minute(s) in a time notation.

> 12:00 p.m.

Use a colon to separate the chapter and verse in a Biblical reference.

> Matthew 1:6

Parentheses

Parentheses are used to emphasize content. They place more emphasis on the enclosed content than commas. Use parentheses to set off nonessential material, such as dates, clarifying information, or sources, from a sentence.

> Muhammed Ali (1942-present), arguably the greatest athlete of all time, claimed he would "float like a butterfly, sting like a bee."

Use parentheses to enclose numbered items in a sentence.

> He asked everyone to bring (1) a folding tent, (2) food and water for two days, and (3) a sleeping bag.

Also use parentheses for literary citations embedded in text or to give the explanation of an acronym.

> Research by Wegener and Petty (1994) supports...
> The AMA (American Medical Association) recommends regular exercise.

Dash

Dashes are used to set off or emphasize the content enclosed within dashes or the content that follows a dash. Dashes place more emphasis on this content than parentheses.

> Perhaps one reason why the term has been so problematic—so resistant to definition, and yet so transitory in those definitions—is because of its multitude of applications.

> In terms of public legitimacy—that is, in terms of garnering support from state legislators, parents, donors, and university administrators—English departments are primarily places where advanced literacy is taught.

The U.S.S. *Constitution* became known as "Old Ironsides" during the War of 1812—during which the cannonballs fired from the British H.M.S. *Guerriere* merely bounced off the sides of the *Constitution*.

To some of you, my proposals may seem radical—even revolutionary.

Use a dash to set off an appositive phrase that already includes commas. An appositive is a word that adds explanatory or clarifying information to the noun that precedes it.

The cousins—Tina, Todd, and Sam—arrived at the party together.

Quotation Marks

Use quotation marks to enclose direct quotations. Note that commas and periods are placed inside the closing quotation mark, and colons and semicolons are placed outside. The placement of question and exclamation marks depends on the situation.

He asked, "When will you be arriving?" I answered, "Sometime after 6:30."

Use quotation marks to indicate the novel, ironic, or reserved use of a word.

History is stained with blood spilled in the name of "justice."

Use quotation marks around the titles of short poems, song titles, short stories, magazine or newspaper articles, essays, speeches, chapter titles, short films, and episodes of television or radio shows.

"Self-Reliance," by Ralph Waldo Emerson
"Just Like a Woman," by Bob Dylan
"The Smelly Car," an episode of Seinfeld

Do not use quotation marks in indirect or block quotations. Indirect quotations are not exact wordings but rather rephrasings or summaries of another person's words. In this case, it is not necessary to use quotation marks. However, indirect quotations still require proper citations, and you will be committing plagiarism if you fail to do so.

Mr. Johnson, a local farmer, reported last night that he saw an alien spaceship on his own property.

Italics

Underlining and Italics are often used interchangeably. Before word-processing programs were widely available, writers would underline certain words to indicate to publishers to italicize whatever was underlined. Although the general trend has been moving toward italicizing instead of underlining, you should remain consistent with your choice throughout your paper. To be safe, you could check with your teacher to find out which he/she prefers. Italicize the titles of magazines, books, newspapers, academic journals, films, television shows, long poems, plays of three or more acts, operas, musical albums, works of art, websites, and individual trains, planes, or ships.

Time
Romeo and Juliet by William Shakespeare
The Metamorphosis of Narcissus by Salvador Dali
Amazon.com
Titanic

Italicize foreign words.

Semper fi, the motto of the U.S. Marine Corps, means "always faithful."

Italicize a word or phrase to add emphasis.

The *truth* is of utmost concern!

Italicize a word when referring to that word.

The word *justice* is often misunderstood and therefore misused.

Hyphen

Two words brought together as a compound may be written separately, written as one word, or connected by hyphens. For example, three modern dictionaries all have the same listings for the following compounds:

hair stylist
hairsplitter
hair-raiser

Another modern dictionary, however, lists *hairstylist*, not *hair stylist*. Compounding is obviously in a state of flux, and authorities do not always agree in all cases, but the uses of the hyphen offered here are generally agreed upon.

1. Use a hyphen to join two or more words serving as a single adjective before a noun:

    a one-way street
    chocolate-covered peanuts
    well-known author

    However, when compound modifiers come after a noun, they are not hyphenated:

    The peanuts were chocolate covered.
    The author was well known.

2. Use a hyphen with compound numbers:

    forty-six
    sixty-three
    Our much-loved teacher was sixty-three years old.

3. Use a hyphen to avoid confusion or an awkward combination of letters:

    re-sign a petition (vs. resign from a job)
    semi-independent (but semiconscious)
    shell-like (but childlike)

4. Use a hyphen with the prefixes *ex-* (meaning former), *self-*, *all-*; with the suffix *-elect*; between a prefix and a capitalized word; and with figures or letters:

    ex-husband
    self-assured
    mid-September
    all-inclusive
    mayor-elect
    anti-American
    T-shirt
    pre-Civil War
    mid-1980s

5. Use a hyphen to divide words at the end of a line if necessary, and make the break only between syllables:

    pref-er-ence
    sell-ing
    in-di-vid-u-al-ist

6. For line breaks, divide already hyphenated words only at the hyphen:

    mass-
    produced

Apostrophe

The apostrophe has three uses:

- to form possessives of nouns
- to show the omission of letters
- to indicate certain plurals of lowercase letters

Forming Possessives of Nouns

To see if you need to make a possessive, turn the phrase around and make it an "of the..." phrase. For example:

the boy's hat = the hat of the boy
three days' journey = journey of three days

If the noun after "of" is a building, an object, or a piece of furniture, then **no** apostrophe is needed!

room of the hotel = hotel room
door of the car = car door
leg of the table = table leg

Once you've determined whether you need to make a possessive, follow these rules to create one.

- **add 's to the singular form of the word (even if it ends in *-s*):**

  the owner's car
  James's hat (James' hat is also acceptable. For plural, proper nouns that are possessive, use an apostrophe after the 's': "The Eggles' presentation was good." The Eggles are a husband and wife consultant team.)

- **add 's to the plural forms that do not end in *-s*:**

  the children's game
  the geese's honking

- **add ' to the end of plural nouns that end in *-s*:**

  houses' roofs
  three friends' letters

- **add 's to the end of compound words:**

  my brother-in-law's money

- **add 's to the last noun to show joint possession of an object:**

  Todd and Anne's apartment

Showing omission of letters

Apostrophes are used in contractions. A contraction is a word (or set of numbers) in which one or more letters (or numbers) have been omitted. The apostrophe shows this omission. Contractions are common in speaking and in informal writing. To use an apostrophe to create a contraction, place an apostrophe where the omitted letter(s) would go. Here are some examples:

don't = do not
I'm = I am
he'll = he will
who's = who is
could've= could have (NOT "could of"!)
'60 = 1960

Don't use apostrophes for possessive pronouns or for noun plurals.

Apostrophes should not be used with possessive pronouns because possessive pronouns already

© 2011 College Board. All rights reserved.

show possession — they don't need an apostrophe. *His, her, its, my, yours, ours* are all possessive pronouns. Here are some examples:

wrong: his' book
correct: his book

wrong: The group made it's decision.
correct: The group made its decision.

(Note: *Its* and *it' s* are not the same thing. *It' s* is a contraction for "it is" and *its* is a possessive pronoun meaning "belonging to it." It's raining out= it is raining out. A simple way to remember this rule is the fact that you don't use an apostrophe for the possessive *his* or *hers*, so don't do it with *its*!)

wrong: a friend of yours'
correct: a friend of yours

Proofreading for apostrophes

A good time to proofread is when you have finished writing the paper. Try the following strategies to proofread for apostrophes:

- If you tend to leave out apostrophes, check every word that ends in *-s* or *-es* to see if it needs an apostrophe.
- If you put in too many apostrophes, check every apostrophe to see if you can justify it with a rule for using apostrophes.

Ellipsis

An ellipsis (a row of three dots: ...) must be used whenever anything is omitted from within a quoted passage—word, phrase, line, or paragraph-- regardless of its source or use. It would, therefore, apply to all usage, including technical, non-technical, medical, journalistic, fiction, etc. The usual form is a "bare" ellipsis (just the three dots, preceded and followed by a space), although the MLA Handbook for Writers of Research Papers recommends that the writer enclose an ellipsis in brackets [...] when omitting part of an original quotation, to differentiate instances of deleted text from ellipses included in the original text. In all cases, the entire quoted passage, including ellipses, is preceded and followed by quotation marks and the source properly cited.

Two things to consider: 1) using ellipses is a form of "editing" the source material, so be certain that the final outcome does not change the original meaning or intent of the quoted passage; and 2) if quoted text ends up with more ellipses than words, consider paraphrasing rather than using direct quotes.

Brackets

Brackets are most often used to clarify the meaning of quoted material. If the context of your quote might be unclear, you may add a few words to provide clarity. Enclose the added material in brackets.

Added Material: The quarterback told the reporter, "It's quite simple. They [the other team] played a better game, scored more points, and that's why we lost."

Resources

SpringBoard Learning Strategies

READING STRATEGIES

STRATEGY	DEFINITION	PURPOSE
Close Reading	Accessing small chunks of text to read, reread, mark, and annotate key passages, word-for-word, sentence-by-sentence, and line-by-line	To develop comprehensive understanding by engaging in one or more focused readings of a text
Diffusing	Reading a passage, noting unfamiliar words, discovering meaning of unfamiliar words using context clues, dictionaries, and/or thesauruses, and replacing unfamiliar words with familiar ones	To facilitate a close reading of text, the use of resources, an understanding of synonyms, and increased comprehension of text
Double-Entry Journal	Creating a two-column journal (also called Dialectical Journal) with a student-selected passage in one column and the student's response in the second column (e.g., asking questions of the text, forming personal responses, interpreting the text, reflecting on the process of making meaning of the text)	To respond to a specific passage with comments, questions, or insights to foster active involvement with a text and to facilitate increased comprehension
Graphic Organizer	Using a visual representation for the organization of information	To facilitate increased comprehension and discussion
KWHL Chart	Setting up discussion with use of a graphic organizer. Allows students to activate prior knowledge by answering "What do I *know*?" sets a purpose by answering "What do I *want* to know?" helps preview a task by answering "*How* will I learn it?" and reflects on new knowledge by answering "What have I *learned*?"	To organize thinking, access prior knowledge, and reflect on learning to increase comprehension and engagement
Marking the Text	Selecting text by highlighting, underlining, and/or annotating for specific components, such as main idea, imagery, literary devices, and so on	To focus reading for specific purposes, such as author's craft, and to organize information from selections; to facilitate reexamination of a text
Metacognitive Markers	Responding to text with a system of cueing marks where students use a **?** for questions about the text; a **!** for reactions related to the text; and an ***** for comments about the text and underline to signal key ideas	To track responses to texts and use those responses as a point of departure for talking or writing about texts
Predicting	Making guesses about the text by using the title and pictures and/or thinking ahead about events which may occur based on evidence in the text	To help students become actively involved, interested, and mentally prepared to understand ideas
Previewing	Examining a text's structure, features, layout, and so on, prior to reading	To gain familiarity with the text, make connections to the text, and extend prior knowledge to set a purpose for reading
QHT	Expanding prior knowledge of vocabulary words by marking words with a Q, H, or T (Q signals words students do not know; H signals words students have heard and might be able to identify; T signals words students know well enough to teach to their peers.)	To allow students to build on their prior knowledge of words, to provide a forum for peer teaching and learning of new words, and to serve as a pre-reading exercise to aid in comprehension

STRATEGY	DEFINITION	PURPOSE
Questioning the Text*	Developing literal, interpretive, and universal questions about the text while reading a text	To engage more actively with texts, read with greater purpose and focus, and ultimately answer questions to gain greater insight into the text
Quickwrite	Responding to a text by writing for a short, specific amount of time about a designated topic or idea related to a text	To activate background knowledge, clarify issues, facilitate making connections, and allow for reflection
RAFT	Responding to and analyzing text by brainstorming various roles (e.g., self, characters from other texts), audiences (e.g., a different character, a real person), formats (e.g., letter, brochure, essay, travel guide), and topics; readers may choose one particular role, audience, format, and topic to create a new text	To initiate reader response; to facilitate an analysis of a text to gain focus prior to creating a new text
Rereading	Encountering the same text with more than one reading	To identify additional details; to clarify meaning and/or reinforce comprehension of texts
SIFT*	Analyzing a fictional text by examining stylistic elements, especially symbol, images, and figures of speech, in order to show how all work together to reveal tone and theme.	To focus and facilitate an analysis of a fictional text by examining the title and text for symbolism, identifying images and sensory details, analyzing figurative language and identifying how all these elements reveal tone and theme
Skimming/Scanning	Skimming by rapid or superficial reading of a text to form an overall impression or to obtain a general understanding of the material; scanning by focusing on key words, phrases, or specific details to provide speedy recognition of information	To quickly form an overall impression prior to an in-depth study of a text; to answer specific questions or quickly locate targeted information or detail in a text

*AP strategy

READING STRATEGIES (Continued)

STRATEGY	DEFINITION	PURPOSE
SMELL*	Analyzing a persuasive speech or essay by asking five essential questions: • **S**ender-receiver relationship—What is the sender-receiver relationship? Who are the images and language meant to attract? Describe the speaker of the text. • **M**essage—What is the message? Summarize the statement made in the text. • **E**motional Strategies—What is the desired effect? • **L**ogical Strategies—What logic is operating? How does it (or its absence) affect the message? Consider the logic of the images as well as the words. • **L**anguage—What does the language of the text describe? How does it affect the meaning and effectiveness of the writing? Consider the language of the images as well as the words.	To analyze a persuasive speech or essay by focusing on five essential questions
SOAPSTone*	Analyzing text by discussing and identifying *Speaker, Occasion, Audience, Purpose, Subject,* and *Tone*	To use an analytical process to understand the author's craft
Summarizing/ Paraphrasing	Restating in one's own words the main idea or essential information expressed in a text, whether it be narration, dialogue, or informational text	To facilitate comprehension and recall of a text
Think Aloud	Talking through a difficult passage or task by using a form of metacognition whereby the reader expresses how he/she has made sense of the text	To reflect on how readers make meaning of challenging texts
TP-CASTT*	Analyzing a poetic text by identifying and discussing *Title, Paraphrase, Connotation, Attitude, Shift, Theme,* and *Title* again	To use an analytical process to understand the author's craft
Visualizing	Forming a picture (mentally and/or literally) while reading a text	To increase reading comprehension and promote active engagement with text
Word Maps	Using a clearly defined graphic organizer such as concept circles or word webs to identify and reinforce word meanings	To provide a visual tool for identifying and remembering multiple aspects of words and word meanings

*AP strategy

WRITING STRATEGIES

STRATEGY	DEFINITION	PURPOSE
Adding	Making conscious choices to enhance a text by adding additional words, phrases, sentences, or ideas	To refine and clarify the writer's thoughts during revision and/or drafting
Brainstorming	Using a flexible but deliberate process of listing multiple ideas in a short period of time without excluding any idea from the preliminary list	To generate ideas, concepts, or key words that provide a focus and/or establish organization as part of the prewriting or revision process
Deleting	Providing clarity and cohesiveness for a text by eliminating words, phrases, sentences, or ideas	To refine and clarify the writer's thoughts during revision and/or drafting
Double-Entry Journal	Creating a two-column journal (also called Dialectical Journal) with a student-selected passage in one column and the student's response in the second column (e.g., asking questions of the text, forming personal responses, interpreting the text, reflecting on the process of making meaning of the text)	To assist in organizing key textual elements and responses noted during reading in order to generate textual support that can be incorporated into a piece of writing at a later time
Drafting	Composing a text in its initial form	To incorporate brainstormed or initial ideas into a written format
Free writing	Using a fluid brainstorming process to write without constraints in order to solidify and convey the writer's purpose	To refine and clarify the writer's thoughts, spark new ideas, and/or generate content during revision and/or drafting
Generating Questions	Clarifying and developing ideas by asking questions of the draft. May be part of self-editing or peer editing	To clarify and develop ideas in a draft. Used during drafting and as part of writer response
Graphic Organizer	Representing ideas and information visually (e.g., Venn diagrams, flowcharts, cluster maps)	To provide a visual system for organizing multiple ideas, details, and/or textual support to be included in a piece of writing
Looping	Focusing on one section of a text and using that section to generate new ideas and then repeating the process with the newly generated segments	To refine and clarify the writer's thoughts, spark new ideas, and/or generate new content during revision and/or drafting
Mapping	Focusing on one section of a text and generating new ideas from that section and then repeating the process with the newly generated segments	To generate ideas, concepts, or key words that provide a focus and/or establish organization during the prewriting, drafting, or revision process

STRATEGY	DEFINITION	PURPOSE
Marking the Draft	Interacting with the draft version of a piece of writing by highlighting, underlining, color-coding, and annotating to indicate revision ideas.	To encourage focused, reflective thinking about revising drafts
Outlining	Using a system of numerals and letters in order to identify topics and supporting details and ensure an appropriate balance of ideas	To generate ideas, concepts, or key words that provide a focus and/or establish organization prior to writing an initial draft and/or during the revision process
Quickwrite	Writing for a short, specific amount of time about a designated topic related to a text	To generate multiple ideas in a quick fashion that could be turned into longer pieces of writing at a later time (May be considered as part of the drafting process)
RAFT	Generating and/or transforming a text by identifying and/or manipulating its component parts of *Role, Audience, Format,* and *Topic*	To consider the main elements of the writer's own work in order to generate a focus and purpose during the prewriting and drafting stages of the writing process
Rearranging	Selecting components of a text and moving them to another place within the text and/or modifying the order in which the author's ideas are presented	To refine and clarify the writer's thoughts during revision and/or drafting
Revisiting Prior Work	Looking through a collection of previously completed work to identify successes and challenges that may have been encountered with particular formats, conventions, style, word choice, and so on	To build on prior experience in preparation for a new piece of writing and/or to revise a previous piece of writing
Self-Editing/Peer Editing	Working with a partner to examine a text closely in order to identify areas that might need to be corrected for grammar, punctuation, spelling	To provide a systematic process for editing a written text to ensure correctness of identified components such as conventions of standard English
Sharing and Responding	Communicating with another person or a small group of peers who respond to a piece of writing as focused readers (not necessarily as evaluators)	To make suggestions for improvement to the work of others and/or to receive appropriate and relevant feedback on the writer's own work, used during the drafting and revision process
Sketching	Drawing or sketching ideas or ordering of ideas. Includes storyboarding, visualizing	To generate and/or clarify ideas by visualizing them; may be part of prewriting
Substituting	Replacing original words or phrases in a text with new words or phrases that achieve the desired effect	To refine and clarify the writer's thoughts during revision and/or drafting
Transformation of Text	Providing opportunities for students to create new text from a studied text by changing the genre, vernacular, time period, culture, point of view, and so on	To highlight the elements of a genre, point of view and so on; to illustrate how elements of style work together
TWIST*	Arriving at a thesis statement that incorporates the following literary elements: tone, word choice (diction), imagery, style and theme	To craft an interpretive thesis in response to a prompt about a passage
Webbing	Developing a graphic organizer that consists of a series of circles connected with lines to indicate relationships among ideas	To generate ideas, concepts, or key words that provide a focus and/or establish organization prior to writing an initial draft and/or during the revision process

*AP strategy

SPEAKING AND LISTENING STRATEGIES

STRATEGY	DEFINITION	PURPOSE
Notetaking	Creating a record of information while listening to a speaker	To facilitate active listening; to record and organize ideas that assist in processing information
Oral Interpretation	Reading a text orally while providing the necessary inflection and emphasis that demonstrate an understanding of the meaning of the text	To share with an audience the reader's personal insight into a text through voice, fluency, tone, and purpose
Oral Reading	Reading aloud one's own text or the texts of others (e.g., echo reading, choral reading, paired readings).	To share one's own work or the work of others; build fluency and increase confidence in presenting to a group
Role Playing	Assuming the role or persona of a character	To develop the voice, emotions, and mannerisms of a character to facilitate improved comprehension of a text
Rehearsal	Encouraging multiple practices of a piece of text prior to a performance	To provide students with an opportunity to clarify the meaning of a text prior to a performance as they refine the use of dramatic conventions (e.g., gestures, vocal interpretations, facial expressions)

COLLABORATIVE STRATEGIES

STRATEGY	DEFINITION	PURPOSE
Think-Pair-Share	Considering and thinking about a topic or question and then writing what has been learned; pairing with a peer or a small group to share ideas; sharing ideas and discussion with a larger group	To construct meaning about a topic or question; to test thinking in relation to the ideas of others; to prepare for a discussion with a larger group
Discussion Groups	Engaging in an interactive, small group discussion, often with an assigned role; to consider a topic, text, question, and so on	To gain new understanding or insight of a text from multiple perspectives

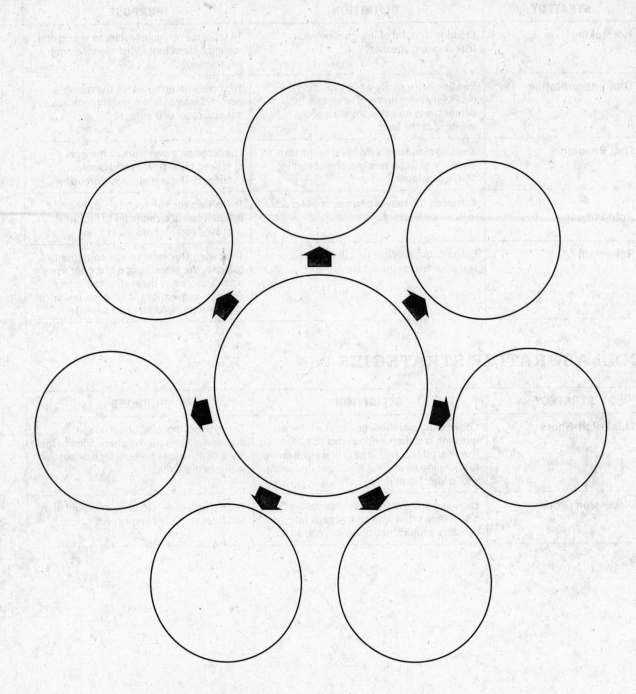

Word Map

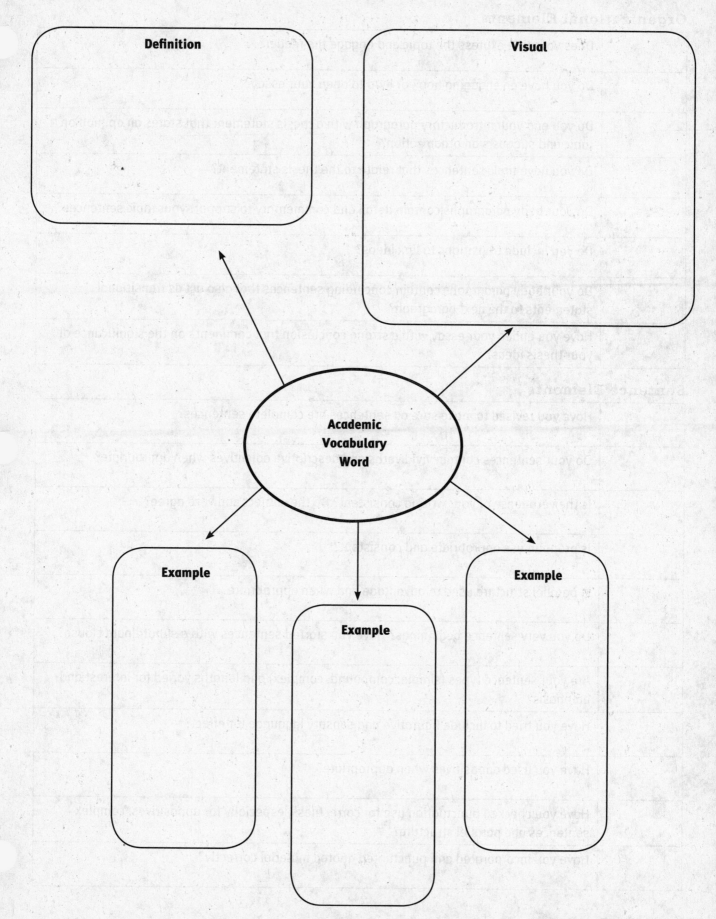

Definition

Visual

Academic Vocabulary Word

Example

Example

Example

Editor's / Writer's Checklist

Organizational Elements

	Does your title express the topic and engage the reader?
	Do you have an engaging hook or lead to open your essay?
	Do you end your introductory paragraph with a thesis statement that states an opinion on a topic and suggests an organization?
	Do you have topic sentences that relate to the thesis statement?
	Do your body paragraphs contain detail and commentary to support your topic sentences?
	Do you include transitions to link ideas?
	Do your body paragraphs contain concluding sentences that also act as transitional statements to the next paragraph?
	Have you ended your essay with a strong conclusion that comments on the significance of your thesis ideas?

Sentence Elements

	Have you revised to make sure all sentences are complete sentences?
	Do your sentences contain vivid verbs and descriptive adjectives when appropriate?
	Is the verb tense of your writing consistent? Do the subject and verb agree?
	Is pronoun use appropriate and consistent?
	Is parallel structure used to advantage and when appropriate?
	Do you vary sentence beginnings? Have you started sentences with a subordinate clause?
	Are your sentence types (simple, compound, complex) and lengths varied for interest and emphasis?
	Have you tried to include figurative and sensory language for effect?
	Have you used appositives when appropriate?
	Have you checked punctuation use for correctness, especially for appositives, complex sentences and parallel structure?
	Have you incorporated and punctuated quoted material correctly?

SOAPSTone:

SOAPSTone	Analysis	Textual Support
Speaker: What does the reader know about the writer?		
Occasion: What are the circumstances surrounding this text?		
Audience: Who is the target audience?		
Purpose: Why did the author write this text?		
Subject: What is the topic?		
Tone: What is the author's tone, or attitude?		

TP-CASTT Analysis

Poem Title:

Author:

Title: Make a prediction. What do you think the title means before you read the poem?

Paraphrase: Translate the poem in your own words. What is the poem about? Rephrase difficult sections word for word.

Connotation: Look beyond the literal meaning of key words and images to their associations.

Attitude: What is the speaker's attitude? What is the author's attitude? How does the author feel about the speaker, about other characters, about the subject?

Shifts: Where do the shifts in tone, setting, voice, etc., occur? Look for time and place, keywords, punctuation, stanza divisions, changes in length or rhyme, and sentence structure. What is the purpose of each shift? How do they contribute to effect and meaning?

Title: Reexamine the title. What do you think it means now in the context of the poem?

Theme: Think of the literal and metaphorical layers of the poem. Then determine the overall theme. The theme must be written in a complete sentence.

Glossary
Glosario

A

active-voice verbs: a verb form indicating that the subject performs the action

verbos en voz activa: forma verbal que indica que el sujeto realiza la acción

advertising techniques: specific methods used in print, graphics, or videos to persuade people to buy a product or use a service

técnicas publicitarias: métodos específicos usados en impresos, gráfica o videos para persuadir a las personas a comprar un producto o usar un servicio

alliteration: the repetition of initial consonant sounds in words that are close together

aliteración: repetición de sonidos consonánticos iniciales en palabras cercanas

allusion: a reference to a well-known person, event, or place from history, music, art, or another literary work

alusión: referencia a una persona, evento o lugar muy conocidos de la historia, música, arte u otra obra literaria

anaphora: the repetition of the same word or group of words at the beginnings of two or more clauses or lines

anáfora: repetición de la misma palabra o grupo de palabras al comienzo de una o más cláusulas o versos

anecdotal evidence: evidence based on personal accounts of incidents

evidencia anecdótica: evidencia basada en relatos personales de los hechos

annotated bibliography: a list of sources used in research along with comments about each source

bibliografía anotada: lista de fuentes utilizadas en la investigación, junto con comentarios acerca de cada fuente

antagonist: the character who opposes or struggles again the main character

antagonista: personaje que se opone o lucha contra el personaje principal

aphorism: a succinct statement expressing an opinion or general truth

aforismo: afirmación breve que expresa una opinión o verdad general

archetypes: universal symbols—images, characters, motifs, or patterns—that recur in myths, art and literature through the world

arquetipos: símbolos universales —imágenes, personajes, motivos o patrones— reiterativos en los mitos, el arte y la literatura alrededor del mundo

archival footage: film footage taken from another, previously recorded, source

cortometraje de archivo: fragmento de película tomada de otra fuente grabada previamente

argument: a form of writing that presents a particular opinion or idea and supports it with evidence

argumento: forma de redacción que presenta una opinión o idea particular y la apoya con evidencia

argumentation: the structure of an argument includes the *hook* (quotation, example, or idea that catches readers' attention), *claim* (the opinion or thesis statement), *support* (evidence in the form of facts, statistics, examples, anecdotes, or expert opinions), *concession* (the writer's admission that the other side of the argument has a valid point), *refutation* (a well-reasoned denial of an opponent's point, based on solid evidence), and *call to action* (an inspired request of readers)

argumentación: la estructura de una argumentación incluye el gancho (cita, ejemplo o idea que capta la atención del lector), afirmación (declaración de opinión o tesis), apoyo (evidencia en forma de hechos, estadísticas, ejemplos, anécdotas u opiniones de expertos), concesión (admisión por parte del escritor de que la otra parte del debate tiene un punto válido), refutación (negación bien razonada de una opinión del oponente, basada en evidencia sólida) y llamado a la acción (petición inspirada de lectores)

argument by analogy: a comparison of two similar situations, implying that the outcome of one will resemble the outcome of the other

argumento por analogía: comparación de dos situaciones semejantes, infiriendo que el resultado de será parecido al resultado de la otra

aside: a short speech spoken by an actor directly to the audience and unheard by other actors on stage

aparte: alocución breve dicha por un actor directamente al público y que no escuchan los demás actores que están en el escenario

assonance: the repetition of similar vowel sounds in accented syllables, followed by different consonant sounds, in words that are close together

asonancia: repetición de sonidos vocálicos similares en sílabas acentuadas, seguida de diferentes sonidos consonánticos, en palabras que están cercanas

audience: the intended readers, listeners, or viewers of specific types of written, spoken or visual texts

público: lectores objetivo, oyentes o espectadores de tipos específicos de textos escritos, hablados o visuales

audience analysis: determining the knowledge, beliefs, and needs of a target audience in order to reach them successfully

análisis del público: determinar los conocimientos, creencias y necesidades de una audiencia objetivo de modo de llegar a ella con éxito

author's purpose: the specific reason or reasons for the writing; what the author hopes to accomplish

propósito del autor: razón específica para escribir; lo que el autor espera lograr

B

balanced sentence: a sentence that presents ideas of equal weight in similar grammatical forms to emphasize the similarity or difference between the ideas

oración balanceada: oración que representa ideas de igual peso en formas gramaticales similares para enfatizar la semejanza o diferencia entre las ideas

bias: an inclination or mental leaning for or against something, which prevents impartial judgment

sesgo: inclinación o tendencia mental a favor o en contra de algo, lo que impide una opinión imparcial

blank verse: unrhymed verse

verso libre: verso que no tiene rima

blocking: in drama, how actors position themselves in relation to one another, the audience, and the objects on the stage

bloqueo: en drama, el modo en que los actores se sitúan entre sí, con el público y los objetos en el escenario

C

caricature: a visual or verbal representation in which characteristics or traits are exaggerated or distorted for emphasis

caricatura: representación visual o verbal en la que las características o rasgos se exageran o se distorsionan para dar énfasis

characterization: the methods a writer uses to develop characters

caracterización: métodos que usa un escritor para desarrollar personajes

characters: people, animals, or imaginary creatures that take part in the action of a story. A short story usually centers on a *main character*, but may also contain one or more *minor characters*, who are not as complex, but whose thoughts, words, or actions move the plot along. A character who is *dynamic* changes in response to the events of the narrative; a character who is *static* remains the same throughout the narrative. A *round* character is fully developed—he or she shows a variety of traits; a *flat* character is one-dimensional, usually showing only one trait.

personajes: personas, animales o criaturas imaginarias que participan en la acción de un cuento. Un cuento corto normalmente se centra en un *personaje principal*, pero puede también contener uno o más *personajes secundarios*, que no son tan complejos, pero cuyos pensamientos, palabras o acciones hacen avanzar la trama. Un personaje que es *dinámico* cambia según los eventos del relato; un personaje que es *estático* permanece igual a lo largo del relato. Un personaje *complejo* está completamente desarrollado: muestra una diversidad de rasgos; un personaje *simple* es unidimensional, mostrando normalmente sólo un rasgo.

chorus: in traditional or classic drama, a group of performers who speak as one and comment on the action of the play

coro: en el drama tradicional o clásico, grupo de actores que hablan al unísono y comentan la acción de la obra teatral

cinematic elements: the features of cinema—movies, film, video—that contribute to its form and structure: *angles* (the

view from which the image is shot); *framing* (how a scene is structured); *lighting* (the type of lighting used to light a scene); and *mise en scène* (the composition, setting, or staging of an image, or a scene in a film); *sound* (the sound effects and music accompanying each scene)

elementos cinematográficos: las características del cine— películas, filmaciones, video—que contribuyen a darle forma y estructura: *angulación* (vista desde la cual se toma la imagen); *encuadre* (cómo se estructura una escena); *iluminación* (tipo de iluminación que se usa para una escena); y *montaje* (composición, ambiente o escenificación de una imagen o escena en una película); *sonido* (efectos sonoros y música que acompañan cada escena)

claim: a position statement (or thesis) that asserts an idea or makes an argument

afirmación: declaración de opinión (o tesis) que asevera una idea o establece un debate

cliché: an overused expression or idea

cliché: expresión o idea que se usa en exceso

climax: the point at which the action reaches its peak; the point of greatest interest or suspense in a story; the turning point at which the outcome of the conflict is decided

clímax: punto en el que la acción alcanza su punto culminante; punto de mayor interés en un cuento; punto de inflexión en el que se decide el resultado del conflicto

coherence: the quality of unity or logical connection among ideas; the clear and orderly presentation of ideas in a paragraph or essay

coherencia: calidad de unidad o relación lógica entre las ideas; presentación clara y ordenada de las ideas en un párrafo o ensayo

commentary: in an expository essay or paragraph, the explanation of the importance or relevance of supporting detail and the way the details support the larger analysis

comentario: ensayo o párrafo expositivo, explicación de la importancia o relevancia de los detalles de apoyo, y la manera en que los detalles apoyan el análisis principal

complex sentence: a sentence containing one independent clause and one or more subordinate clauses

oración compleja: oración que contiene una cláusula independiente y una o más cláusulas subordinadas

complications: the events in a plot that develop the conflict; the complications move the plot forward in its rising action

complicaciones: sucesos de una trama que desarrollan el conflicto; las complicaciones hacen avanzar la trama en su acción ascendente

compound sentence: a sentence containing two independent clauses

oración compuesta: oración que contiene dos cláusulas independientes

concession: an admission in an argument that the opposing side has valid points

concesión: admitir en un debate que el lado opositor tiene opiniones válidas

conflict: a struggle or problem in a story. An *internal conflict* occurs when a character struggles between opposing needs or desires or emotions within his or her own mind. An *external conflict* occurs when a character struggles against an outside force. This force may be another character, a societal expectation, or something in the physical world.

conflicto: lucha o problema en un cuento. Un *conflicto interno* ocurre cuando un personaje lucha entre necesidades o deseos o emociones que se contraponen dentro de su mente. Un *conflicto externo* ocurre cuando un personaje lucha contra una fuerza externa. Esta fuerza puede ser otro personaje, una expectativa social o algo del mundo físico.

connotation: the associations and emotional overtones attached to a word beyond its literal definition or denotation. A connotation may be positive, negative, or neutral.

connotación: asociaciones y alusiones emocionales unidas a una palabra más allá de su definición literal o denotación. Una connotación puede ser positiva, negativa o neutra.

consonance: the repetition of final consonant sounds in stressed syllables with different vowel sounds

consonancia: repetición de sonidos consonánticos finales en sílabas acentuadas con diferentes sonidos vocálicos

context: the circumstances or conditions in which something takes place

contexto: circunstancias o condiciones en las que algo ocurre

conventions: standard practices and forms

convenciones: prácticas y formas usuales

couplet: two consecutive lines of verse with end rhyme; a couplet usually expresses a complete unit of thought

copla: dos líneas de versos consecutivos con rima final; una copla normalmente expresa una unidad de pensamiento completa

credibility: the quality of being trusted or believed

credibilidad: calidad de ser confiable o creíble

critical lens: a particular identifiable perspective as in Reader Response Criticism, Cultural Criticism, etc., through which a text can be analyzed and interpreted

ojo crítico: punto de vista particular identificable como por ejemplo Teoría de la recepción, Crítica sociocultural, etc., por medio del que se puede analizar e interpretar un texto

cultural conflict: a struggle that occurs when people with different cultural expectations or attitudes interact

conflicto cultural: lucha que ocurre cuando interactúan personas con diferentes expectativas o actitudes culturales

culture: the shared set of arts, ideas, skills, institutions, customs, attitude, values and achievements that characterize a group of people, and that are passed on or taught to succeeding generations

cultura: conjunto de artes, ideas, destrezas, instituciones, costumbres, actitud, valores y logros compartidos que caracterizan a un grupo de personas, y que se transfieren o enseñan a las generaciones siguientes

cumulative (or loose) sentence: a sentence in which the main clause comes first, followed by subordinate structures or clauses

oración acumulativa (o frases sueltas): oración cuya cláusula principal viene primero, seguida de estructuras o cláusulas subordinadas

D

deductive reasoning: a process of using general information from which to draw a specific conclusion

razonamiento deductivo: proceso en que se usa información general para sacar una conclusión específica

denotation: the exact literal meaning of a word

denotación: significado literal exacto de una palabra

detail: a specific fact, observation, or incident; any of the small pieces or parts that make up something else

detalle: hecho, observación o incidente específico; cualquiera de las pequeñas piezas o partes que constituyen otra cosa

dialect: the distinctive language, including the sounds, spelling, grammar, and diction, of a specific group or class of people

dialecto: lenguaje distintivo, incluyendo sonidos, ortografía, gramática y dicción, de un grupo o clase específico de personas

dialogue: the words spoken by characters in a narrative or film

diálogo: palabras que dicen los personajes en un relato o película

diction: the writer's choice of words; a stylistic element that helps convey voice and tone

dicción: selección de palabras por parte del escritor; elemento estilístico que ayuda a transmitir voz y tono

diegetic sound: actual noises associated with the shooting of a scene, such as voices and background sounds

sonido diegético: sonidos reales asociados con la filmación de una escena, como por ejemplo voces y sonidos de fondo

discourse: the language or speech used in a particular context or subject

discurso: lenguaje o habla usada en un contexto o tema en particular

documentary or nonfiction film: a genre of filmmaking that provides a visual record of factual events, using photographs, video footage, and interviews

documental o película de no-ficción: género cinematográfico que realiza un registro visual de sucesos basados en hechos por medio del uso de fotografías, registro en videos y entrevistas

drama: a play written for stage, radio, film, or television, usually about a serious topic or situation

drama: obra teatral escrita para representar en un escenario, radio, cine o televisión, normalmente sobre un tema o situación seria

E

editorial: an article in a newspaper or magazine expressing the opinion of its editor or publisher

editorial: artículo de periódico o revista, que expresa la opinión de su editor

effect: the result or influence of using a specific literary or cinematic device

efecto: resultado o influencia de usar un recurso literario o cinematográfico específico

empirical evidence: evidence based on experiences and direct observation through research
evidencia empírica: evidencia basada en experiencias y en la observación directa por medio de la investigación

epigram: a short witty saying
epigrama: dicho corto e ingenioso

ethos: (ethical appeal) a rhetorical appeal that focuses on ethics, or the character or qualifications of the speaker
ethos: (recurso ético) recurso retórico centrado en la ética o en el carácter o capacidades del orador

evidence: the information that supports or proves an idea or claim; forms of evidence include facts, statistics (numerical facts), expert opinions, examples, and anecdotes; *see also*, anecdotal, empirical, and logical evidence
evidencia: información que apoya o prueba una idea o afirmación; formas de evidencia incluyen hechos, estadística (datos numéricos), opiniones de expertos, ejemplos y anécdotas; *ver también* evidencia anecdótica, empírica y lógica

exaggeration: representing something as larger, better, or worse than it really is
exageración: representar algo como más grande, mejor o peor que lo que realmente es

explicit theme: a theme that is clearly stated by the writer
tema explícito: tema que está claramente establecido por el escritor

exposition: events that give a reader background information needed to understand a story. During exposition, characters are introduced, the setting is described, and the conflict begins to unfold.
exposición: sucesos que dan al lector los antecedentes necesarios para comprender un cuento. Durante la exposición, se presentan los personajes, se describe el ambiente y se comienza a revelar el conflicto.

extended metaphor: a metaphor extended over several lines or throughout an entire poem
metáfora extendida: metáfora que se extiende por varios versos o a través de un poema completo

F

falling action: the events in a play, story, or novel that follow the climax, or moment of greatest suspense, and lead to the resolution
acción descendente: sucesos de una obra teatral, cuento o novela posteriores al clímax, o momento de mayor suspenso, y que conllevan a la resolución

fallacy: a false or misleading argument
falacia: argumento falso o engañoso

figurative language: imaginative language not meant to be taken literally; figurative language uses figures of speech
lenguaje figurativo: lenguaje imaginativo que no pretende ser tomado literalmente; el lenguaje figurativo usa figuras literarias

flashback: an interruption in the sequence of events to relate events that occurred in the past
flashback: interrupción en la secuencia de los sucesos para relatar sucesos ocurridos en el pasado

fixed form: a form of poetry in which the length and pattern are determined by established usage of tradition, such as a sonnet
forma fija: forma de poesía en la que la longitud y el patrón están determinados por el uso de la tradición, como un soneto

foil: a character whose actions or thoughts are juxtaposed against those of a major character in order to highlight key attributes of the major character
antagonista: personaje cuyas acciones o pensamientos se yuxtaponen a los de un personaje principal con el fin de destacar atributos clave del personaje principal

folk tale: a story without a known author that has been preserved through oral retellings
cuento folclórico: cuento sin autor conocido que se ha conservado por medio de relatos orales

footage: literally, a length of film; the expression is still used to refer to digital video clips
metraje: literalmente, la longitud de una película; la expresión aún se usa para referirse a video clips digitales

foreshadowing: the use of hints or clues in a narrative to suggest future action
presagio: uso de claves o pistas en un relato para sugerir una acción futura

free verse: poetry without a fixed pattern of meter and rhyme
verso libre: poesía que no sigue ningún patrón, ritmo o rima regular

G

genre: a kind or style of literature or art, each with its own specific characteristics. For example, poetry, short story, and novel are literary genres. Painting and sculpture are artistic genres.
género: tipo o estilo de literatura o arte, cada uno con sus propias características específicas. Por ejemplo, la poesía, el cuento corto y la novela son géneros literarios. La pintura y la escultura son géneros artísticos.

genre conventions: the essential features and format that characterize a specific genre
convenciones genéricas: características básicas y el formato que caracterizan un género específico

graphics: images or text used to provide information on screen
gráfica: imágenes o texto que se usa para dar información en pantalla

graphic novel: a book-length narrative, or story, in the form of a comic strip rather than words
novela gráfica: narrativa o cuento del largo de un libro, en forma de tira cómica más que palabras

H

hamartia: a tragic hero's fatal flaw; an ingrained character trait that causes a hero to make decisions that ultimately lead to his or her death or downfall
hamartia: error fatal de un héroe trágico; característica propia de un personaje que causa que un héroe tome decisiones que finalmente llevan a su muerte o caída

hero: the main character or protagonist of a play, with whom audiences become emotionally invested

héroe: personaje principal o protagonista de una obra teatral, con el que el público se involucra emocionalmente

hook: an interesting quotation, anecdote, or example at the beginning of a piece of writing that grabs readers' attention

gancho: cita, anécdota o ejemplo interesante al comienzo de un escrito, que capta la atención del lector

humor: the quality of being amusing

humor: calidad de ser divertido

hyperbole: exaggeration used to suggest strong emotion or create a comic effect

hipérbole: exageración que se usa para sugerir una emoción fuerte o crear un efecto cómico

I

iamb: a metrical foot that consists of an unstressed syllable followed by a stressed syllable

yambo: pie métrico que consta de una sílaba átona seguida de una sílaba acentuada

iambic pentameter: a rhythmic pattern of five feet (or units) of one unstressed syllable followed by a stressed syllable

pentámetro yámbico: patrón rítmico de cinco pies (o unidades) de una sílaba átona seguida de una sílaba acentuada

image: a word or phrase that appeals to one of more of the five senses and creates a picture

imagen: palabra o frase que apela a uno o más de los cinco sentido y crea un cuadro

imagery: the verbal expression of sensory experience; descriptive or figurative language used to create word pictures; imagery is created by details that appeal to one or more of the five senses

imaginería: lenguaje descriptivo o figurativo utilizado para crear imágenes verbales; la imaginería es creada por detalles que apelan a uno o más de los cinco sentidos

implied theme: a theme that is understood through the writer's diction, language construction, and use of literary devices

tema implícito: tema que se entiende a través de la dicción del escritor, construcción lingüística y uso de recursos literarios

inductive reasoning: a process of looking at individual facts to draw a general conclusion

razonamiento inductivo: proceso de observación de hechos individuales para sacar una conclusión general

interior monologue: a literary device in which a character's internal emotions and thoughts are presented

monólogo interior: recurso literario en el que se presentan las emociones internas y pensamientos de un personaje

irony: a literary device that exploits readers' expectations; irony occurs when what is expected turns out to be quite different from what actually happens. *Dramatic irony* is a form of irony in which the reader or audience knows more about the circumstances or future events in a story than the characters within it; *verbal irony* occurs when a speaker or narrator says one thing while meaning the opposite; *situational irony* occurs

when an event contradicts the expectations of the characters or the reader.

ironía: recurso literario que explota las expectativas de los lectores; la ironía ocurre cuando lo que se espera resulta ser bastante diferente de lo que realmente ocurre. La *ironía dramática* es una forma de ironía en la que el lector o la audiencia saben más acerca de las circunstancias o sucesos futuros de un cuento que los personajes del mismo; la *ironía verbal* ocurre cuando un orador o narrador dice una cosa queriendo decir lo contrario; la *ironía situacional* ocurre cuando un suceso contradice las expectativas de los personajes o del lector.

J

justice: the quality of being reasonable and fair in the administration of the law; the ideal of rightness or fairness

justicia: calidad de ser razonable e imparcial en la administración de la ley; ideal de rectitud o equidad

juxtaposition: the arrangement of two or more things for the purpose of comparison

yuxtaposición: ordenamiento de dos o más cosas con el objeto de compararlas

L

literary theory: attempts to establish principles for interpreting and evaluating literary texts

teoría literaria: intento de establecer principios para interpretar y evaluar textos literarios

logical evidence: evidence based on facts and a clear rationale

evidencia lógica: evidencia basada en hechos y una clara fundamentación

logos: (logical appeal) a rhetorical appeal that uses logic to appeal to the sense of reason

logos: (apelación lógica) apelación retórica que usa la lógica para apelar al sentido de la razón

M

metacognition: the ability to know and be aware of one's own thought processes; self-reflection

metacognición: capacidad de conocer y estar consciente de los propios procesos del pensamiento; introspección

metaphor: a comparison between two unlike things in which one thing is spoken of as if it were another; for example, the moon was a crisp white cracker

metáfora: comparación entre dos cosas diferentes en la que se habla de una cosa como si fuera otra; por ejemplo, la luna era una galletita blanca crujiente

meter: a pattern of stressed and unstressed syllables in poetry

métrica: patrón de sílabas acentuadas y átonas en poesía

monologue: a dramatic speech delivered by a single character in a play

monólogo: discurso dramático que hace un solo personaje en una obra teatral

montage: a composite picture that is created by bringing together a number of images and arranging them to create a connected whole

montaje: cuadro compuesto que se crea al reunir un número de imágenes y que al organizarlas se crea un todo relacionado

mood: the atmosphere or general feeling in a literary work
carácter: atmósfera o sentimiento general en una obra literaria

motif: a recurrent image, symbol, theme, character type, subject, or narrative detail that becomes a unifying element in an artistic work.
motivo: imagen, símbolo, tema, tipo de personaje, tema o detalle narrativo recurrente que se convierte en un elemento unificador en una obra artística.

myth: a traditional story that explains the actions of gods or heroes or the origins of the elements of nature
mito: cuento tradicional que explica las acciones de dioses o héroes, o los orígenes de los elementos de la naturaleza

N

narration: the act of telling a story
narración: acto de contar un cuento

non-diegetic sound: voice-overs and commentary, sounds that do not come from the action on screen.
sonido no diegético: voces y comentarios superpuestos, sonidos que no provienen de la acción en pantalla.

O

objective: based on factual information
objetivo: basado en información de hechos

objectivity: the representation of facts or ideas without injecting personal feelings or biases
objetividad: representación de los hechos o ideas sin agregar sentimientos o prejuicios personales

ode: a lyric poem expressing feelings or thoughts of a speaker, often celebrating a person, event, or a thing
oda: poema lírico que expresa sentimientos o pensamientos de un orador, que frecuentemente celebra a una persona, suceso o cosa

onomatopoeia: words whose sound suggest their meaning
onomatopeya: palabras cuyo sonido sugiere su significado

oral tradition: the passing down of stories, tales, proverbs, and other culturally important stories and ideas through oral retellings
tradición oral: traspaso de historias, cuentos, proverbios y otras historias de importancia cultural por medio de relatos orales

oxymoron: words that appear to contradict each other; e.g., cold fire
oxímoron: palabras que parecen contradecirse mutuamente; por ejemplo, fuego frío

P

parallel structure (parallelism): refers to a grammatical or structural similarity between sentences or parts of a sentence, so that elements of equal importance are equally developed and similarly phrased for emphasis
estructura paralela (paralelismo): se refiere a una similitud gramatical o estructural entre oraciones o partes de una

oración, de modo que los elementos de igual importancia se desarrollen por igual y se expresen de manera similar para dar énfasis

paraphrase: to briefly restate ideas from another source in one's own words
parafrasear: volver a presentar las ideas de otra fuente en nuestras propias palabras

parody: a literary or artistic work that imitates the characteristic style of an author or a work for comic effect or ridicule
parodia: obra literaria o artística que imita el estilo característico de un autor o una obra para dar un efecto cómico o ridículo

passive-voice verbs: verb form in which the subject receives the action; the passive voice consists of a form of the verb be plus a past participle of the verb
verbos en voz pasiva: forma verbal en la que el sujeto recibe la acción; la voz pasiva se forma con el verbo ser más el participio pasado de un verbo

pathos: (emotional appeal) a rhetorical appeal to readers' or listeners' senses or emotions
pathos: (apelación emocional) apelación retórica a los sentidos o emociones de los lectores u oyentes

periodic sentence: a sentence that makes sense only when the end of the sentence is reached; that is, when the main clause comes last
oración periódica: oración que tiene sentido sólo cuando se llega al final de la oración; es decir, cuando la cláusula principal viene al final

persona: the voice assumed by a writer to express ideas or beliefs that may not be his or her own
personaje: voz que asume un escritor para expresar ideas o creencias que pueden no ser las propias

personification: a figure of speech that gives human qualities to an animal, object, or idea
personificación: figura literaria que da características humanas a un animal, objeto o idea

persuasive argument: an argument that convinces readers to accept or believe a writer's perspective on a topic
argumento persuasivo: argumento que convence a los lectores a aceptar o creer en la perspectiva de un escritor acerca de un tema

perspective: a way of looking at the world or a mental concept about things or events, one that judges relationships within or among things or events
perspectiva: manera de visualizar el mundo o concepto mental de las cosas o sucesos, que juzga las relaciones dentro o entre cosas o sucesos

photo essay: a collection of photographic images that reveal the author's perspective on the subject
ensayo fotográfico: recolección de imágenes fotográficas que revelan la perspectiva del autor acerca del tema

plagiarism: the unattributed use of another writer's words or ideas
plagio: usar como propias las palabras o ideas de otro escritor

plot: the sequence of related events that make up a story or novel
trama: secuencia de sucesos relacionados que conforman un cuento o novela

poetic structure: the organization of words, lines, and images as well as ideas
estructura poética: organización de las palabras, versos e imágenes, así como también de las ideas

point of view: the perspective from which a narrative is told; i.e., first person, third person limited, third person omniscient
punto de vista: perspectiva desde la cual se cuenta un relato; es decir, primera persona, tercera persona limitada, tercera persona omnisciente

precept: a rule, instruction, or principle that guides somebody's actions and/or moral behavior
precepto: regla, instrucción o principio que guía las acciones y/o conducta moral de alguien

primary footage: film footage shot by the filmmaker for the text at hand
metraje principal: filmación hecha por el cineasta para el texto que tiene a mano

primary source: an original document containing firsthand information about a subject
fuente primaria: documento original que contiene información de primera mano acerca de un tema

prologue: the introduction or preface to a literary work
prólogo: introducción o prefacio de una obra literaria

prose: ordinary written or spoken language using sentences and paragraphs, without deliberate or regular meter or rhyme; not poetry or song
prosa: forma común del lenguaje escrito o hablado, usando oraciones y párrafos, sin métrica o rima deliberada o regular; ni poesía ni canción

protagonist: the central character in a work of literature, the one who is involved in the main conflict in the plot
protagonista: personaje central de una obra literaria, el que participa en el conflicto principal de la trama

Q

quatrain: a four-line stanza in a poem
cuarteta: en un poema, estrofa de cuatro versos

R

reasoning: the thinking or logic used to make a claim in an argument
razonamiento: pensamiento o lógica que se usa para hacer una afirmación en un argumento

refrain: a regularly repeated line or group of lines in a poem or song, usually at the end of a stanza
estribillo: verso o grupo de versos que se repiten con regularidad en un poema o canción, normalmente al final de una estrofa

refutation: the reasoning used to disprove an opposing point
refutación: razonamiento que se usa para rechazar una opinión contraria

reliability: the extent to which a source provides good quality and trustworthy information
confiabilidad: grado en el que una fuente da información confiable y de buena calidad

repetition: the use of any element of language—a sound, a word, a phrase, a line, or a stanza—more than once
repetición: uso de cualquier elemento del lenguaje—un sonido, una palabra, una frase, un verso o una estrofa—más de una vez

resolution (denouement): the end of a play, story, or novel in which the main conflict is finally resolved
resolución (desenlace): final de una obra teatral, cuento o novela, en el que el conflicto principal finalmente se resuelve

résumé: a document that outlines a person's skills, education, and work history
currículum vitae: documento que resume las destrezas, educación y experiencia laboral de una persona

rhetoric: the art of using words to persuade in writing or speaking
retórica: arte de usar las palabras para persuadir por escrito o de manera hablada

rhetorical appeals: the use of emotional, ethical, and logical arguments to persuade in writing or speaking
recursos retóricos: uso de argumentos emocionales, éticos y lógicos para persuadir por escrito o de manera hablada

rhetorical context: the subject, purpose, audience, occasion, or situation in which writing occurs
contexto retórico: sujeto, propósito, audiencia, ocasión o situación en que ocurre el escrito

rhetorical devices: specific techniques used in writing or speaking to create a literary effect or enhance effectiveness
dispositivos retóricos: técnicas específicas que se usan al escribir o al hablar para crear un efecto literario o mejorar la efectividad

rhetorical question: a question that is asked for effect or one for which the answer is obvious
pregunta retórica: pregunta hecha para producir un efecto o cuya respuesta es obvia

rhyme: the repetition of sounds at the ends of words
rima: repetición de sonidos al final de las palabras

rhyme scheme: a consistent pattern of rhyme throughout a poem
esquema de la rima: patrón consistente de una rima a lo largo de un poema

rhythm: the pattern of stressed and unstressed syllables in spoken or written language, especially in poetry
ritmo: patrón de sílabas acentuadas y no acentuadas en lenguaje hablado o escrito, especialmente en poesía

rising action: the movement of a plot toward a climax or moment of greatest excitement; the rising action is fueled by the characters' responses to the conflict
acción ascendente: movimiento de una trama hacia el clímax o momento de mayor emoción; la acción ascendente es impulsada por las reacciones de los personajes ante el conflicto

S

satire: a manner of writing that mixes a critical attitude with wit and humor in an effort to improve mankind and human institutions
sátira: manera de escribir que mezcla una actitud crítica con ingenio y humor en un esfuerzo por mejorar a la humanidad y las instituciones humanas

scenario: an outline, a brief account, a script, or a synopsis of a proposed series of events
escenario: bosquejo, relato breve, libreto o sinopsis de una serie de sucesos propuestos

secondary source: discussion about or commentary on a primary source; the key feature of a secondary source is that it offers an interpretation of information gathered from primary sources
fuente secundaria: discusión o comentario acerca de una fuente primaria; la característica clave de una fuente secundaria es que ofrece una interpretación de la información recopilada en las fuentes primarias

sensory details: details that appeal to or evoke one or more of the five senses--sight, sound, smell, taste, touch
detalles sensoriales: detalles que apelan o evocan uno o más de los cinco sentidos: vista, oído, gusto, olfato, tacto

sensory images: images that appeal to the reader's senses— sight, sound, smell, taste, touch
imágenes sensoriales: imágenes que apelan a los sentidos del lector: vista, oído, olfato, gusto, tacto

setting: the time and place in which a story happens
ambiente: tiempo y lugar en el que ocurre un relato

simile: a comparison of two or more unlike things using the words *like or as*; for example, the moon was as white as milk
símil: comparación entre dos o más cosas diferentes usando las palabras *como o tan*; por ejemplo, la luna estaba tan blanca como la leche

slanters: rhetorical devices used to present the subject in a biased way.
soslayo: recursos retóricos para presentar el tema de modo sesgado.

slogan: a short, catchy phrase used for advertising by a business, club, or political party
eslogan: frase corta y tendenciosa que usa como publicidad para un negocio, club o partido político

social commentary: an expression of an opinion with the goal of promoting change by appealing to a sense of justice
comentario social: expresión de una opinión con el objeto de promover el cambio al apelar a un sentido de justicia

soliloquy: a long speech delivered by an actor alone on the stage
soliloquio: discurso largo realizado por un actor sobre el escenario

sonnet: a fourteen-line lyric poem, usually written in iambic pentameter and following a strict pattern of rhyme
soneto: poema lírico de catorce versos, normalmente escrito en un pentámetro yámbico y que sigue un patrón de rima estricto

speaker: the imaginary voice or persona of the writer or author
orador: voz o persona imaginaria del escritor o autor

stakeholder: a person motivated or affected by a course of action
participante: persona motivada o afectada por el curso de una acción

stanza: a group of lines, usually similar in length and pattern, that form a unit within a poem
estrofa: grupo de versos, normalmente similares en longitud y patrón, que forman una unidad dentro de un poema

stereotype: an oversimplified, generalized conception, opinion, and/or image about particular groups of people.
estereotipo: concepto generalizado, opinión y/o imagen demasiado simplificada acerca de grupos específicos de personas.

structure: the way a literary work is organized; the arrangement of the parts in a literary work
estructura: manera en que la obra literaria está organizada; disposición de las partes en una obra literaria

style: the distinctive way a writer uses language, characterized by elements of diction, syntax, imagery, etc.
estilo: manera distintiva en que un escritor usa el lenguaje, caracterizada por elementos de dicción, sintaxis, lenguaje figurado, etc.

subculture: a smaller subsection of a culture; for example, within the culture of a high school may be many subcultures
subcultura: subsección más pequeña de una cultura; por ejemplo, dentro de la cultura de una escuela secundaria puede haber muchas subculturas

subjectivity: based on one's personal point of view, opinion, or values
subjetividad: en base en nuestro punto de vista, opinión o valores personales

subtext: the underlying or implicit meaning in dialogue or the implied relationship between characters in a book, movie, play or film. The subtext of a work is not explicitly stated.
subtexto: significado subyacente o implícito en el diálogo o la relación implícita entre los personajes de un libro, película, u obra teatral. El subtexto de una obra no se establece de manera explícita.

survey: a method of collecting data from a group of people; it can be written, such as a print or online questionnaire, or oral, such as an in-person interview
encuesta: método para recolectar datos de un grupo de personas; puede ser escrita, como un impreso o cuestionario en línea, u oral, como en una entrevista personal

symbol: anything (object, animal, event, person, or place) that represents itself but also stands for something else on a figurative level
símbolo: cualquier cosa (objeto, animal, evento, persona o lugar) que se representa a sí misma, pero también representa otra cosa a nivel figurativo

symbolic: serving as a symbol; involving the use of symbols or symbolism

simbólico: que sirve como símbolo; que implica el uso de símbolos o simbolismo

syntax: the arrangement of words and the order of grammatical elements in a sentence; the way in which words are put together to make meaningful elements, such as phrases, clauses, and sentences

sintaxis: disposición de las palabras y orden de los elementos gramaticales en una oración; manera en que las palabras se juntan para formar elementos significativos, como frases, cláusulas y oraciones

synthesis: the act of combining ideas from different sources to create, express, or support a new idea

síntesis: acto de combinar ideas de diferentes fuentes para crear, expresar o apoyar una nueva idea

T

target audience: the intended group for which a work is designed to appeal or reach

público objetivo: grupo al que se pretende apelar o llegar con una obra

thematic statement: an interpretive statement articulating the central meaning or message of a text

oración temática: afirmación interpretativa que articula el significado o mensaje central de un texto

theatrical elements: elements employed by dramatists and directors to tell a story on stage. Elements include *costumes* (the clothing worn by actors to express their characters), *makeup* (cosmetics used to change actors' appearances and express their characters), *props* (objects used to help set the scene, advance a plot and make a story realistic), *set* (the place where the action takes place, as suggested by objects, such as furniture, placed on a stage), *acting choices* (gestures, movements, staging, and vocal techniques actors use to convey their characters and tell a story).

elementos teatrales: elementos que utilizan los dramaturgos y directores para contar una historia en el escenario. Los elementos incluyen *vestuario* (ropa que usan los actores para expresar sus personajes), *maquillaje* (cosméticos que se usan para cambiar la apariencia de los actores y expresar sus personajes), *elementos* (objetos que se usan para ayudar a montar la escena, avanzar la trama y crear una historia realista), *plató* (lugar donde tiene lugar la acción, según lo sugieren los objetos, como muebles, colocados sobre un escenario), *opciones de actuación* (gestos, movimientos, representación y técnicas vocales que se usan para transmitir sus personajes y narrar una historia).

theme: a writer's central idea or main message about life; *see also*, explicit theme, implied theme

tema: idea central o mensaje principal acerca de la vida de un escritor; *véase también*, tema explícito, tema implícito

thesis: the main idea or point of an essay or article; in an argumentative essay the thesis is the writer's position on an issue

tesis: idea o punto principal de un ensayo o artículo; en un ensayo argumentativo, la tesis es la opinión del autor acerca de un tema

topic sentence: a sentence that states the main idea of a paragraph; in an essay, it also makes a point that supports the thesis statement

oración principal: oración que establece la idea principal de un párrafo; en un ensayo, también establece una proposición que apoya el enunciado de la tesis

tone: a writer's or speaker's attitude toward a subject

tono: actitud de un escritor u orador acerca de un tema

tragedy: a dramatic play that tells the story of a character, usually of a noble birth, who meets an untimely and unhappy death or downfall, often because of a specific character flaw or twist of fate

tragedia: obra teatral dramática que cuenta la historia de un personaje, normalmente de origen noble, que encuentra una muerte o caída imprevista o infeliz, con frecuencia debido a un defecto específico del personaje o una vuelta del destino

tragic hero: an archetypal hero based on the Greek concept of tragedy; the tragic hero has a flaw that makes him vulnerable to downfall or death

héroe trágico: héroe arquetípico basado en el concepto griego de la tragedia; el héroe trágico tiene un defecto que lo hace vulnerable a la caída o a la muerte

U

understatement: the representation of something as smaller or less significant than it really is; the opposite of exaggeration or hyperbole

subestimación: representación de algo como más pequeño o menos importante de lo que realmente es; lo opuesto a la exageración o hipérbole

V

valid: believable or truthful

válido: creíble o verídico

validity: the quality of truth or accuracy in a source

validez: calidad de verdad o precisión en una fuente

vignette: a picture or visual or a brief descriptive literary piece

viñeta: ilustración o representación visual o pieza literaria descriptiva breve

vocal delivery: the way words are expressed on stage, through volume, pitch, rate or speed of speech, pauses, pronunciation, and articulation

presentación vocal: manera en que se expresan las palabras en el escenario, por medio del volumen, tono, rapidez o velocidad del discurso, pausas, pronunciación y articulación

voice: the way a writer or speaker uses words and tone to express ideas as well as his or her personas

voz: manera en que el escritor u orador usa las palabras y el tono para expresar ideas, así como también su personaje

Index of Skills

Literary Skills

Ad hominem appeal, 395
Allusion, 218, 280
Analogies, 31, 67, 258, 351
Argumentation, 317
Author's purpose, 164, 165, 172, 174
Autobiography, 147
Biography, 147
Character foil, 281
Characterizations, 47, 265, 281, 376
Characters, 47, 96–103, 258, 293, 295, 299, 303, 306, 366, 376, 387, 399
  main, 105, 378
  minor, 105, 378
  primary, 402
  protagonists, 17, 259, 281, 284
  secondary, 402
Comedy, 262
Conflict, 105, 390, 392, 399
  external, 122, 133
  internal, 122, 133
Couplet, 225
Details, narrative, 8, 12, 73, 104, 105, 114, 138, 153, 177, 306, 312, 343, 366, 372, 375, 378, 387, 389
Dialogue, 112, 168, 169, 280, 381
Diction, 4, 7, 8, 12, 17, 18, 34, 41, 60, 69, 75, 79, 142, 177, 213, 244, 369, 370, 371
  formal, 123, 267
Drama, 258
Dramaturges, 273, 274, 285, 287, 323
Effect, 165, 176, 178
Ethos, 73
Figurative language, 123, 217, 218, 222, 223, 226, 254, 265, 293
First-person narration, 27
Flashback, 166, 365
Foreshadowing, 88, 105, 386
Gloss, 27
Hyperbole, 18, 20, 208, 218, 219, 280
Idioms, 123
Imagery, 4, 7, 11, 12, 18, 21, 23, 24, 25, 30, 34, 41, 88, 108, 133, 162, 177, 213, 214, 215, 226, 280, 299, 369, 370

Interpretation, 268, 270, 289
Irony, 88, 105, 106, 107
  dramatic, 312
  verbal, 107
Logos, 73
Metaphors, 30, 123, 204, 217, 230, 265, 280
  extended, 216, 222
Monologue, 256
Mood, 153, 155, 162, 177, 291, 292
Motif, 88, 105, 106, 162, 378, 381
Odes, 222–223, 224
Onomatopoeia, 241
Organization, 177
Oxymoron, 293
Pathos, 73
Personification, 265, 280
Plot, 266
  climax, 105
  complications, 105
  exposition, 105
  falling action, 105
  resolution/denouement, 105
Poetic shift, 231
Poetry, 34
  free verse, 191
  Iambic pentameter, 225, 262
  pentameter, 225
  rhyme scheme, 225, 260, 262
  sonnets, 225, 261
  structure of, 211–212
Point of view, 41, 88, 105, 106, 113, 118, 119, 120, 177, 191, 365
  first person, 118, 119, 120, 376
  third-person limited, 118, 119, 120
  third-person omniscient, 118, 119, 120
Prologue, 260, 261, 262
Prose, 34, 267
Puns, 254, 281
Quatrain, 225
Repetition, 217
Rhetorical questions, 70
Setting, 19, 105, 303, 343, 387, 392
Short stories, 88, 90, 110, 121
Similes, 18, 19, 21, 30, 123, 222, 265
Stanzas, 230
Style, 24, 133, 142, 153, 158, 165,

176, 177, 218, 244
Subtext, 297
Symbolism, 122, 217
Synonyms, 261, 262
Syntax, 7, 9, 12, 18, 23, 25, 34, 41, 177
  inverted, 254
Tableau, 258, 259
Theatrical elements, 268, 270
Theme, 24, 92, 105, 115, 131, 133, 145, 313, 378, 399
Timeline chart, 293
Tone, 4, 8, 12, 24, 25, 92, 131, 133, 153, 155, 162, 177, 231
Tragedy, 259, 262
Visual prompt, 49, 217, 278, 291, 303
Voice, 4, 7, 19, 20, 213, 280
Word choice, 133

Reading Skills

Annotating text, 110, 112, 373
Close reading, 5, 63, 89, 107, 137, 154, 159, 161, 162, 164, 166, 168, 174, 175, 189, 190, 209, 229, 230, 255, 268, 299, 303, 305, 307, 311, 326, 341, 347, 361, 364, 368, 370, 373, 377, 379, 381, 390, 393, 401
Compare and contrast, 34, 64, 278, 390
Context clues, 28, 94, 97, 162, 299
Diffusing the text, 27, 94, 95, 225, 261, 264, 299, 361, 364, 365, 373
Venn diagram, 145, 269
Independent reading, 88, 188, 254, 340
Inferring, 161, 382
KWHL chart, 273, 345, 351
KWL chart, 5, 56, 57, 89, 189, 341
Marking the text, 5, 9, 12, 19, 22, 43, 50, 57, 63, 65, 86, 88, 89, 92, 96, 105, 110, 117, 121, 122, 142, 147, 188, 189, 191, 194, 206, 209, 210, 214, 217, 221, 229, 232, 245, 252, 254, 257, 259, 289, 297, 302, 326, 338, 340, 341, 346, 352, 353, 361, 365, 368, 373, 381, 382, 390, 393
Paired reading, 24

Writing Skills

Media Skills

colon, 426, 440

commas, 53, 147, 179, 219, 346, 381, 382, 438

comma splices, 424

dashes, 370, 441

ellipsis, 444

exclamation marks, 381

fused sentences, 424

hyphen, 442

parentheses, 440

periods, 381

question marks, 381

quotation marks, 40, 219, 370, 381, 441

semicolons, 179, 382, 439

Quotations, 90, 219

direct, 12, 40, 54, 57, 381

indirect, 12, 40, 54, 57

Relative pronouns, 426

Repetition, 70

Run-ons, 19

Sentences

balanced, 43, 46

complex, 10, 113, 430

compound, 10, 113, 179, 382, 430

compound-complex, 10, 113

cumulative, 43, 45, 46

declarative, 10

exclamatory, 10

fragments, 424

imperative, 10

interrogative, 10

inverted, 259

lengths of, 9

periodic, 43, 46

simple, 10, 429

types of, 9, 70, 429

Series, 368

Subject-verb agreement, 431

Synonyms, 261, 262, 365

Syntax, 18, 19, 20, 25, 34, 41, 147, 244, 264, 280

inverted, 254, 264

Transitions, 279, 317, 356

Verbals, 101, 416

gerunds, 416

infinitives, 419

participles, 417

Verbs, 101, 191, 259

action, 16

agreement, 244

commonly confused, 436

tenses, 432–434

Voice

active, 410, 433

passive, 410, 434

Vocabulary Skills

Academic Vocabulary, 2, 7, 70, 73, 86, 165, 167, 186, 211, 213, 217, 252, 258, 268, 272, 338, 343, 352, 355, 376, 389

Analogies, 143, 233, 258

cause-effect, 351

function, 31, 67

Connotation, 206, 230, 233, 234, 245

Denotation, 233, 234

Foreign words, 68, 95, 105, 281, 347, 395

Diffusing, 27, 94, 95, 225, 261, 264, 299, 361, 364, 365, 373

Prefixes, 382

Sorting words, 94

Synonyms, 261, 262, 365

Index of Authors and Titles

Text Credits:

"My Name" from *The House on Mango Street*. Copyright © 1984 by Sandra Cisneros. Published by Vintage Books, a division of Random House, Inc., and in hardcover by Alfred A. Knopf in 1994. By permission of Susan Bergholz Literary Services, New York, and Lamy, NM. All rights reserved.

"Why Couldn't I Have Been Named Ashley" by Immaculeta Achilike. Used by permission.

"Eleven" from *Woman Hollering Creek*. Copyright © 1991 by Sandra Cisneros. Published by Vintage Books, a division of Random House, Inc., New York and originally in hardcover by Random House, Inc. By permission of Susan Bergholz Literary Services, New York, and Lamy, NM. All rights reserved.

"Oranges" from *New and Selected Poems* by Gary Soto. Copyright © 1995 by Gary Soto. Used with permission of Chronicle Books LLC, San Francisco. Visit ChronicleBooks. com

"Spotlight" from *Speak* by Laurie Halse Anderson. Copyright © 1999 by Laurie Halse Anderson. Reprinted by permission of Farrar, Straus and Giroux, LLC.

"Cut" by Bob Green from *Cheeseburgers: The Best of Bob Greene* by Bob Greene, G. K. Hall, 2005. Copyright by Bob Greene. Reproduced by permission of SLL/Sterling Lord Literistic, Inc.

From *Always Running—La Vida Loca, Gang Days in L.A.* by Luis J. Rodriguez. (Curbstone Press, 1993) Reprinted with permission of Curbstone Press. Distributed by Consortium.

"'Race' Politics" from *Poems Across The Pavement* by Luis J. Rodriguez. Copyright © 1998 by Luis J. Rodriguez. Published by Tia Chucha Press. By permission of Susan Bergholz Literary Services, New York, NY and Lamy, NJ. All rights reserved.

From "The Looking Glass Shame" from *Silent Dancing* by Judith Ortiz Cofer. Copyright © 1990 Arte Público Press - University of Houston. Reprinted with permission from the publisher.

"Bethany only looking ahead" by Jan TenBruggencate from *The Honolulu Advertiser*, November 21, 2003. Copyright 2003 The Honolulu Advertiser. Used by permission.

"As If! Marketing to Older Teens" by Judith Rosen from *Publishers Weekly*, July 18, 2005. Used with permission of Publishers Weekly. Copyright © 2009. All rights reserved.

"The Stolen Party" by Liliana Heker, © 1982, which appeared in *Other Fires: Short Fiction* by Latin American Women, edited and translated by Alberto Manguel, © 1985. Reprinted by permission of Westwood Creative Artists Ltd.

"Marigolds" by Eugenia Collier. Originally published in *Negro Digest*, November 1969. Reappeared in *Breeder and Other Stories* by Eugenia Collier, Black Classic Press, 1994. Used by permission of the author.

"Hollywood Outsider Tim Burton," March 5, 2006, CBS News. Reproduced by permission of CBS News Archives.

From *Charlie and the Chocolate Factory* by Roald Dahl, copyright © 1964, renewed 1992 by Roald Dahl Nominee Limited. Used by permission of Alfred A. Knopf, an imprint of Random House Children's Books, a division of Random House, Inc.

"Poetry" from *Selected Poems by Pablo Neruda*, translated by Alastair Reid, edited by Nathaniel Tarn and published by Jonathan Cape. Reprinted by permission of The Random House Group Ltd.

From *Poemcrazy* by Susan G. Woodridge, copyright © 1996 Susan G. Woodridge. Used by permission of Crown Publishers, a division of Random House, Inc.

"Nikki Rosa" from *Black Feeling, Black Talk, Black Judgment* by Nikki Giovanni. Copyright © 1968, 1970 by Nikki Giovanni. Reproduced by permission of HarperCollins Publishers.

"We Real Cool" by Gwendolyn Brooks. Reprinted by consent of Brooks Permissions.

"Fast Break" from *Wild Gratitude* by Edward Hirsch, copyright © 1985 by Edward Hirsch. Used by permission of Alfred A. Knopf, a division of Random House, Inc.

"Identity" by Julio Noboa Polanco. Used by permission of the author.

"Ego Tripping" from *The Selected Poems of Nikki Giovanni* by Nikki Giovanni. Compilation copyright © 1996 by Nikki Giovanni. Reproduced by permission of HarperCollins Publishers.

"Hanging Fire" from *The Collected Poems of Audre Lorde* by Audre Lorde. Copyright © 1978 by Audre Lorde. Used by permission of W. W. Norton & Company, Inc.

"Ode to My Socks" from *Full Woman, Fleshly Apple, Hot Moon: Selected Poetry of Pablo Neruda* by Pablo Neruda, translated by Stephen Mitchell. Translation copyright © 1997 by Stephen Mitchell. Reproduced by permission of HarperCollins Publishers.

From *My Wicked Wicked Ways*. Copyright © 1987 by Sandra Cisneros. Published by Third Woman Press and in hardcover by Alfred A. Knopf. By permission of Susan Bergholz Literary Services, New York, and Lamy, NM. All rights reserved.

"In Response to Executive Order 9066" by Dwight Okita. Used by permission.

"Young" by Anne Sexton, from *All My Pretty Ones*. Copyright © 1962 by Anne Sexton. Reproduced by permission of SLL/Sterling Lord Literistic, Inc.

"Combing" by Gladys Cardiff, from *Puget Soundings*, March 1971. Used by permission of Gladys Cardiff.

"Harlem (2) ["What happens to a dream deferred..."]" from *The Collected Poems of Langston Hughes* by Langston Hughes, edited by Arnold Rampersad with David Roessel, Associate Editor, copyright © 1994 by the Estate of Langston Hughes. Used by permission of Alfred A. Knopf, a division of Random House, Inc.

"Scars" from *Selected Poems by Daniel Halpern*, copyright © 1994 by Daniel Halpern. Used by permission of Alfred A. Knopf, a division of Random House, Inc.

"American Hero," copyright © 1992 Essex Hemphill from *Ceremonies*, reprinted by permission of The Frances Goldin Literary Agency.

"The Beep Beep Poem" form *Cotton Candy on a Rainy Day* by Nikki Giovanni. Copyright © 1978 by Nikki Giovanni. Reproduced by permission of HarperCollins Publishers.

"kidnap poem" from *The Selected Poems of Nikki Giovanni* by Nikki Giovanni. Compilation copyright © 1996 by Nikki Giovanni. Reproduced by permission of HarperCollins Publishers.

"Jim Crow: Shorthand for Separation" by Rick Edmonds. Reproduced from Forum, the magazine of the Florida Humanities Council, an affiliate of the National Endowment for the Humanities.

From *To Kill a Mockingbird* by Harper Lee. Copyright © 1960 by Harper Lee. Foreword copyright © 1993 by Harper Lee. Reprinted by permission of HarperCollins Publishers.

From *In Defense of To Kill a Mockingbird* by Nicholas J. Karolides, Lee Burress, and John M. Keam, 1993, Scarecrow Press. Used by permission.

Photo credits:

21 BVT/BigStockPhoto.com; 23 abacusmage/BigStockPhoto.com; 27 andres/BigStockPhoto.com; 28 Mark Ross/BigStockPhoto.com; 31 llandrea/BigStockPhoto.com; 35 flippo/BigStockPhoto.com; 36 Truckershutterbug/BigStockPhoto.com; 38 mccale/BigStockPhoto.com; 42 sgame/BigStockPhoto.com; 53 sgame/BigStockPhoto.com; 54 phred/BigStockPhoto.com; 65 InvisibleViva/ BigStockPhoto.com; 66 Vivid Pixels/BigStockPhoto.com; 68 phodopus/BigStockPhoto.com. 92 Lightbearer/BigStockPhoto.com; 97 Daneel/BigStockPhoto.com; 98 sundikva/BigStockPhoto.com; 100 toddtaulman/BigStockPhoto.com; 103 nmonckton/BigStockPhoto.com; 111 Global Photographers/BigStockPhoto.com; 113 jgroup/BigStockPhoto.com; 114 DonG/BigStockPhoto.com; 115 Honjune/BigStockPhoto.com; 123 alle/BigStockPhoto.com; 126 victorburnside/BigStockPhoto.com; 129 Djapeman/BigStockPhoto.com; 149 rachelreveley/BigStockPhoto.com; 150 Onestepbeyond/BigStockPhoto.com; 154 Joss/BigStockPhoto.com; 156 argus456/BigStockPhoto.com; 157 digitalr/BigStockPhoto.com. 191 rhambley/BigStockPhoto.com; 192 llandrea/BigStockPhoto.com; 195 sil63/BigStockPhoto.com; 196 shh-photos/BigStockPhoto.com; 199 leine/BigStockPhoto.com; 201 HALIMA AHKDAR/BigStockPhoto.com; 202 zt/BigStockPhoto.com; 203 Max2/BigStockPhoto.com; 205 teekaygee/BigStockPhoto.com; 211 shippee/BigStockPhoto.com; 215 Albo/BigStockPhoto.com; 219 rbouwman/BigStockPhoto.com; 220 nitipong_b/BigStockPhoto.com, maximus/BigStockPhoto.com; 223 Catsmeow/BigStockPhoto.com; 224 digitalphotonut/BigStockPhoto.com; 230 felinda/BigStockPhoto.com; 232 milosluz/BigStockPhoto.com; 235 mjp/BigStockPhoto.com; 236 Olga Sweet/BigStockPhoto.com; 238 rainette/BigStockPhoto.com; 240 kjpargeter/BigStockPhoto.com; 242 marilynv/BigStockPhoto.com. 257 serge75/BigStockPhoto.com; 261 Sarah Nicholl/BigStockPhoto.com. 301 pzAxe/BigStockPhoto.com; 367 Oddphoto/BigStockPhoto.com; 411 phodopus/BigStockPhoto.com.